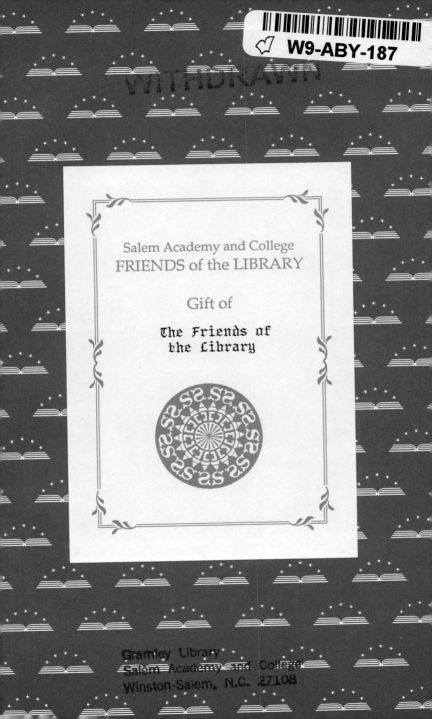

W9-ABY-187

W. S. MERWIN

W. S. MERWIN

COLLECTED POEMS 1952–1993

J. D. McClatchy, *editor*

THE LIBRARY OF AMERICA

The paper used in this publication meets the
minimum requirements of the American National Standard for
Information Sciences—Permanence of Paper for Printed
Library Materials, ANSI Z39.48—1984.

Distributed to the trade in the United States
by Penguin Group (USA) Inc.
and in Canada by Penguin Books Canada Ltd.

Library of Congress Control Number: 2012945848
ISBN 978-1-59853-208-1

———

First Printing
The Library of America—240

Contents

THE SECOND FOUR BOOKS OF POEMS

FLOWER & HAND

THE FIRST FOUR
BOOKS OF POEMS

A Mask for Janus
The Dancing Bears
Green with Beasts
The Drunk in the Furnace

A MASK FOR JANUS

(1952)

for Dorothy

Habit is evil,—all habit, even speech;
and promises prefigure their own breach.
JOHN WHEELWRIGHT

. . . pone cara de mia . . .
PEDRO SALINAS

Anabasis (I)

Then we poised, in time's fullness brought
As to a new country, the senses
In the mutations of a sallow light,
A season of signs and speechless;

Thought momently on nothing, knew
No oratory, no welcome:
Silence about our silence grew;
Beached by the convenient stream.

Night is familiar when it comes.
On dim gestures does the mind
Exorcise abandoned limbs,
Disbodied of that other land

Estranged almost beyond response,
A bleached and faintly relevant
Signature to stir the sense
In veteran usage and intent.

One dreams fixed beasts that drowse or wonder,
Not blinking; by the stream a few
Poplars and white beeches where
Exhausted leaves, suspended, through

The distant autumn do not fall,
Or, fallen, fired, are unconsumed,
The flame perduring, the still
Smoke eternal in the mind.

(Embarrassed, these scarred Penates
Smile, between raw stones supported,
Musing perhaps an anomalous
Speech no longer understood.)

We ponder, after damp sundown,
The slow boats, departing, heavy,
In another time; our direction
Moved in the cool rain away:

We with brief knowledge hazarded
Alien influence and tropic,
Entered and did diversely thread
What degradations, false music,

Straits whose rocks lean to the sound,
Monstrous, of their declivities,
As lovers on their private ground
See no distance, but face and face;

We have passed in a warm light
Islands whose charmed habitants
Doze on the shore to dissipate
The seasons of their indolence;

Even against those borders led
Lapped by the forgetful rivers
Have stood among the actual dead,
No breath moving the gray flowers.

The remnant of all passage lies
Cold or distorted in the brain
As tall fables of strangers, as
Lisped visions of other men.

(The neighbor waters flame and wave:
All that we could not bring away
Our hands, as though with courage, have
Burned, and the tired ships where they lay.)

The covenant we could but seize
Fractionally by the ear
And dreamed it substance, that the eyes
Might follow—and its motions were

Hands that toy about a door
In dreams and melt where they caress,
Not displacing the wind they wear—
Brought us to this final place.

We see the various brain enclosed
Never the promise, but its guise:
Terrain in private we supposed
That always in its Easter is.

Rather, in priestly winter bide
Our shadows where no prayers will work
That unison we faintly, toward
Our time and litany, invoke.

You, satisfied under no sky,
Even from this air your air is fled,
Your singular authority
Vain, no richness where you bled,

But you are dwindled and now die
To a vexed but promissory shape
For an old man stroked always by
The vague extremities of sleep:

So were he tangled to believe,
By euphory and the leaves' dictions.
His grave members did walk and weave,
Blessed, among the many mansions.

Anabasis (II)

After the first night and bare morning passed
We remembered the gray wings of a gull
That traced us seaward when our eyes had lost
The thread of last whiteness where the land fell.

After the first days, one when the world turned
Dark and the rain came, we remembered fires
In lost houses; we stared and lurched half-blind
Against new darkness, neither night's nor ours.

We survived the selves that we remembered;
We have dozed on gradual seas where slowly
The hours changed on the silence, and a word,
Falling, expired in the sufficient day.

Sometimes through a mirage or evening rose
Towers where the myths sleep and the lanterns;
We fled a saeculum what sick repose,
But woke at morning where the fever burned.

We have slid on a seizure of the wind
To spume-blindness where our fear became
A whirling without chronicle or end;
There we circled and bent the thought of time

Till, saved by violence from violence,
We, the gesture of rages not our own,
Forsook and followed, motion without sense,
Where we were drawn, from pool and tempest thrown.

In wake of storms we came where the gulls cry
Allusions to dim archipelagoes;
We coaxed our soils and sembled where we lay
The last exhaustion, as the buzzard knows.

We had seen strengths flee or degenerate:
Even the wind starved in our tracks and died,
Till, on the mirror, we, the image, thought,
After the petrel-, of the halcyon-dead.

Thus calmed we lay and hungered east or west
But drifted on what warm meridian,
Grazing the reefs of dying; yet we passed
Through that peripety and afternoon.

We saw the islands of a new season.
We were made young with watching, and our eyes
Believed a garden and reserve where swung
The fruits that from all hungers immunize.

There when we called, the startled land returned
A precipitate waking as of a child;
Our vision built on the approaching sand;
We entered channels where the coral smiled,

And but the countries of occasion found:
There at sundown, lodged where the tide lingers,
Among the driftwood and the casual drowned,
Slept on the lulled questions of those rivers.

We have half-waked to hear the minutes die
And heard our minds that, waiting toward the east,
Embraced the seed and thought of day, and we
Were by the pool of dark the crouchèd beast.

But not the watchers of unheard-of shores
Know to repeat our prayers when we became
The eyes of sleep that chased receding fires
Through the bodiless exile of a dream.

Between sleep and the vacant excellence
Of seas we suffered music that declares
The monstrous fixities of innocence;
We are children of a different curse.

In dream there was no answer or command,
Yet there did rumors beyond reason sway
Waters that slipped from an escaping land
All night, and we are tidal and obey.

We were already far when morning died.
We watched the colors sink, and all the light.
We turned from silence and fearfully made
Our small language in the place of night.

In fear of the swift bird that shouts and sees
In these tides and dark entrails the curled
Augurs of unreasonable seas
We seek a new dimension for the world.

But sentenced are the seasons that we know.
The serpent holds and the whirlwind harries
The last oceans where the drowned pursue
The daze and fall of fabulous voyages.

Still we are strange to orisons and knees
Fixed to bone only, foreign as we came,
We float leeward till mind and body lose
The uncertain continent of a name.

Rime of the Palmers

Where, and in the morning,
Palmers, do you pass?
The sudden birds sing
In the poplar trees.

Where, and away from morning,
Palmers, do you follow,
And where are you going
That you take no shadow,

And what carry, stranger,
That no shadow take?
—Hunger is sleeping where
Staff and shadow break.

Bone and vein are full
Where we sat at meat;
We seek the still
Wonder that we eat.

Our motion is our form
And our passage raiment;
Between stillness and time
We pass, improvident.

—Form is a thing goes slyly
And escapes our ears;
In another country
What did you love, palmers,

And what do you remember
This morning and light?
—We go (may wonder
Send and receive our feet)

Half-remembering
Where our bones were hid
And the wind at evening
There where hunger died,

And the evening wind
That everywhere and sorely
Turned and complained
As we came away.

—The wind is at morning
On the high meadow;
What are you singing,
Palmers, as you go,

And what do your lips say
When I hear no sounds?
—Speech is a thorny way
In a hard land,

And into absence,
Into quiet goes:
Before the silence,
After the voice,

We sing, and without words,
An air of promise,
As the waking birds
In the poplar trees.

—The last stars show
On the chill season;
You start betimes, you go,
Palmers, in night and dawn:

You move to what increase,
Neither night's nor day's?
—The winds disposing peace
There where our vision is;

But, moving, shall we say
We are fire or storm,
Or as one that, wholly
Name, or without a name,

Comes, or has appeared,
Or the voice thereafter?
Who knows the word
That we are carol for?

—A word is a little thing,
And the letter kills,
And you are far who sing
From the morning hills,

And what is the high road,
And the road where you go?
—We have been the dead
And what the dead know:

At the broken bridge
Where the cold rivers
Move in a rage,
Let the breath be prayers;

If music speak softly
Forget what it tells
Where you go blind and high
By the wild hills;

At the nighted gates
By the last mountain
There age forgets
And the child is slain:

If hope bring you there
Where night's self darkly burns,
Abandon hope to air
And to the wind's returns;

If a dim leaf tremble
And then the dawn come back,
Oh, begin carols
By that morning lake.

—But pleasure discovers
By what sense and lights,
Bridge and hills, palmers,
And the nighted gates?

But you leave us. Afterward
What shall we say, palmers?
Say: the birds suddenly
Sing in the poplar trees.

That the word was morning once
That is common day;
In mention of our bones,
Of our bodies say:

Rain is a perilous friend,
The sweet wind blows foreign;
These pictures made of mind
And these hungers gone

And these palmers that on
A field of summer went
Are perfect and lie down
Thus, lest the land repent.

Ballad of John Cable and Three Gentlemen

He that had come that morning,
One after the other,
Over seven hills,
Each of a new color,

Came now by the last tree,
By the red-colored valley,
To a gray river
Wide as the sea.

There at the shingle
A listing wherry
Awash with dark water;
What should it carry?

There on the shelving,
Three dark gentlemen.
Might they direct him?
Three gentlemen.

"Cable, friend John, John Cable,"
When they saw him they said,
"Come and be company
As far as the far side."

"Come follow the feet," they said,
"Of your family,
Of your old father
That came already this way."

But Cable said, "First I must go
Once to my sister again;
What will she do come spring
And no man on her garden?"

"She will say, 'Weeds are alive
From here to the Stream of Friday;
I grieve for my brother's plowing,'
Then break and cry."

"Lose no sleep," they said, "for that fallow:
She will say before summer,
'I can get me a daylong man,
Do better than a brother.'"

Cable said, "I think of my wife:
Dearly she needs consoling;
I must go back for a little
For fear she die of grieving."

"Cable," they said, "John Cable,
Ask no such wild favor;
Still, if you fear she die soon,
The boat might wait for her."

But Cable said, "I remember:
Out of charity let me
Go shore up my poorly mother,
Cries all afternoon."

They said, "She is old and far,
Far and rheumy with years,
And, if you like, we shall take
No note of her tears."

But Cable said, "I am neither
Your hired man nor maid,
Your dog nor shadow
Nor your ape to be led."

He said, "I must go back:
Once I heard someone say
That the hollow Stream of Friday
Is a rank place to lie;

"And this word, now I remember,
Makes me sorry: have you
Thought of my own body
I was always good to?

"The frame that was my devotion
And my blessing was,
The straight bole whose limbs
Were long as stories—

"Now, poor thing, left in the dirt
By the Stream of Friday
Might not remember me
Half tenderly."

They let him nurse no worry;
They said, "We give you our word:
Poor thing is made of patience;
Will not say a word."

"Cable, friend John, John Cable,"
After this they said,
"Come with no company
To the far side.

"To a populous place,
A dense city
That shall not be changed
Before much sorrow dry."

Over shaking water
Toward the feet of his father,
Leaving the hills' color
And his poorly mother

And his wife at grieving
And his sister's fallow
And his body lying
In the rank hollow,

Now Cable is carried
On the dark river;
Not even a shadow
Followed him over.

On the wide river
Gray as the sea
Flags of white water
Are his company.

Meng Tzu's Song

The sparrows gleaning gutters
Kick and shuffle the horsehair,
And the simple wind that stirs
Their feathers stirs my hair.

How can I know, now forty
Years have shuffled my shoulders,
Whether my mind is steady
Or quakes as the wind stirs?

Because one sparrow, running
On the old wind-ruts, can be
Turned by an unseen thing,
A small wind in the sky,

And changes, it sets me thinking;
Yet I know not if my mind
Is moved, or is but sinking
Alone to its own kind.

If my mind moves not in wind
Or other breaths, it is not
Strange; at forty the mind
Of Kao Tzu wavered not.

Lo, how is the kept wind let
Out to make trouble with me!
How can one remain not
Moving before his eye?

One cultivates bravery
That the skin's hair not flinch
Nor the frail eye flee
Nor the blood blanch.

One is as the trodden inch
Of horsehair on the bare ground
At the marketplace: wrench
Nor kick wrings from him sound.

Thinks he as though he were sand
Or horsehair, should the stiff sword
Shave the strength from his mind
And stab away his word.

Thinks of defeat and blood,
All hairs blown from control,
The hands like hair in mud
As though it mattered little.

How can the thin mind be able?
How put off quaking only,
Keeping all else simple,
Even in wind steady?

The wind is stiff and is high.
Simple the wind. The open
Coat of horsehair on three
Sides flaps without passion.

Blind William's Song

Stand from my shadow where it goes
Threaded upon a white dream,
From my clear eyes that take no light
And give no mercy.

I stood in clean Monday and heard
Seventy tongues of fire
Burn down from their talk.
I am the ash that walk.

Tuesday was dusty feet;
I shall not be the first
Who walked and did not know
The earth, the middle earth.

Wednesday, if it came,
I was a blown curse
And who are you not withered?
Tempt not my memory.

But though I was, on Thursday,
In that late morning,
Multiple as rain
And fell as rain falls

And have been on Friday,
Say, a white horse racing
—Since I see no motion
All speed is easy—

I have not been the sea
(My dry bone forbids me)
Whose blind repeated loss
Any loud tide will serve.

Lull the stones over me,
I that on Saturday
Closed about myself
And raged and was the grave.

Sunday I lie down
Within without my body;
All colored creation
Is tamed white by time.

For a Dissolving Music

What shall be seen?
Limbs of a man
old and alone,
his shadow with him,
going and gone.
What shall be heard?
A hollow rime:
the heart gone tame
knocking afraid.
What shall be known?
Briefly the name,
but its frame shaken,
house of time
blown and broken,
drafty room,
dwindled flame,
red coal come
out of the warm,
dry honeycomb,
ended dream.

What shall be said?
This word if any:
time and blood
are spent money,
rain in a sieve;
summer is dead
(whom fools believe)
in a far grave,
worms receive
her fire to wive,
fear walks alive,
prayers I would weave,
pains I have,
hopes not many;
wherefore grieve
O splintered stave,

withered glove,
dry groove,
shaken sleeve
empty of love.

What shall be sung?
This song uneven:
eleven, seven,
chance cloven,
joints spavin,
blood chill-driven,
flesh craven,
breath not often,
teeth riven,
all day shriven,
last coven,
all night raven,
all doom woven,
none forgiven,
no curse ungraven,
no peace at even,
remnant for leaven,
promise true-given,
field but shaven,
nor hope of heaven.

Half Roundel

I make no prayer
For the spoilt season,
The weed of Eden.
I make no prayer.
        Save us the green
        In the weed of time.

Now is November;
In night uneasy
Nothing I say.

I make no prayer.
>Save us from water
>That washes us away.

What do I ponder?
All smiled disguise,
Lights in cold places.
I make no prayer.
>Save us from air
>That wears us loosely.

The leaf of summer
To cold has come
In little time.
I make no prayer.
>From earth deliver
>And the dark therein.

Now is no whisper
Through all the living.
I speak to nothing.
I make no prayer.
>Save us from fire
>Consuming up and down.

A Dance of Death

KING

>I saw from a silk pillow
>All high stations and low
>Smile when I spoke, and bow,
>And obey and follow.
>All men do as I do.
>I went in gold and yellow,
>Ermine and gemmed shoe,
>And was human even so,
Et, ecce, nunc in pulvere dormio.

MONK

> I hoped that all sinners who
> Wore a saintly sorrow
> Into heaven should go.
> All this did I do:
> Walk with the eyes low,
> Keep lonely pillow,
> Many days go
> Fasting and hollow,
> All my bounty bestow,

Et, ecce, nunc in pulvere dormio.

SCHOLAR

> I sat like a shadow,
> The light sallow,
> Reasoning yes and no.
> One thing I came to know.
> I heard the mouse go,
> Heard whispers in the tallow,
> Wind disputing, "Although . . ."
> Night on the candle blow,

Et, ecce, nunc in pulvere dormio.

HUNTSMAN

> The wind blew
> In the cold furrow;
> The falcon flew;
> These did I follow:
> Deerhound, doe,
> Fox upon snow,
> And sent the arrow,
> And was chased, who did follow,
> And came to this burrow,

Et, ecce, nunc in pulvere dormio.

FARMER

> I walked with plow
> On the green fallow;
> All I did harrow
> Dirt does undo.

Out at elbow
I lie to mellow,
Set in a furrow,
The weeds' fellow,
Quod, ecce, nunc in pulvere dormio.

WOMAN

I was as green willow,
My hands white and slow,
Love and increase below.
Be reaped as you did sow.
I am bitter as rue.
Now am I also
Defaced and hollow,
Nursing no shadow,
Quod, ecce, nunc in pulvere dormio.

EPITAPH

Lords, I forget what I knew;
I saw false and true,
Sad and antic show,
Did profane and hallow,
Saw the worthies go
Into the still hollow
And wrote their words, even so,
Et, ecce, nunc in pulvere dormio.

Variation on a Line by Emerson

In May, when sea-winds pierced our solitudes,
In the May winds not yet warmed out of malice,
At a certain doorway once I stood, my face
Leaning westward, a little before evening—
Oh, though all breath be seasonal, who can tell
A story like new grass blown in sunlight?

In May when winds blow westward into the light,
As though both would depart our solitudes,
Though the door be different, what can I tell,
Feeling the sun thus fail from all life and malice?
But once the measure and sight of day, at evening,
Died in the shadows, so, of a cold face.

You that have forsaken the door, the face,
Burgeon, body, decrease, the turning light,
Who keep such single quiet both morning and evening
That approach but multiplies your solitudes,
Whether the bodily death is death to malice
Not the intrusions of sea-wind tell.

Let a kind diction out of the shadows tell,
Now toward my slumber, a legend unto my face
Of sleep as a quiet garden without malice
Where body moves, after the bitter light,
A staid dance among innocent solitudes;
So let me lie in a story, heavy with evening.

But I dream of distances where at evening
Ghost begins (as no migrant birds can tell)
A journey through outlandish solitudes,
Hair all ways lifted, leaves wild against face,
Feet trammeled among dune grass, with spent light,
And finds no roof at last against wind or malice.

Sir, who have locked your doors, but without malice,
Or Madam, who draw your shawl against evening,
By the adumbrations of your thin light
What but this poor contention can you tell:
Ceaseless intruders have demeaned your face
And contrived homesteads in your solitudes.

Tell me who keeps infrangible solitudes
But the evening's dead on whose decided face
Morning repeats the malice and the light.

Over the Bier of the Worldling

My friends, what can I say,
Having forgotten the feeling and the time
When it seemed that a dull body,
That even a dead man could dream
Those small belligerent birds, perhaps one gull,
Turning over the foul
Pond by the colliery,
These waters flicked by a regardless wind,
And the clouds, not of this country,
Sailing, as I had imagined;
Then these faces, even as I am, stilled,
Conforming to the world.
That which I kept, one body
And a few clothes, are brought to following
Processes as of poverty,
Suffering but not knowing,
Lying unimproved by the long season
And the falling rain.

Epitaph on Certain Schismatics

These were they whom the body could not please,
Shaded between the shaded lights who rose
Quavering and forsook the arrogant knees,
The bodies death had made incredulous.
They had known, that season, lights in the trees
Moving when none felt wind, whisper of candles,
Pursuit of strange hinds, signs in snarled spindles,
Omens from alien birds, and after these
They descended into Hell. "Suffering is
Measure of nothing, now measure is lost," one said.
They fell to stroking their shyest histories.
Even cool flesh (so gaunt they grew and loveless),
When they could best remember it, only made
A wry shadow between the quick and the dead.

Suspicor Speculum
to Sisyphus

Seeing, where the rock falls blind, this figure
At whispers swaying the drained countenance,
As might a shadow stand, I have stayed an hour
To no sound but his persistent sibilance,
Aghast, as should the populous dreaming head
See evils colder than the brain yet burn,
Or swift and tomorrow the enormous dead
Scatter their pose and, Sisyphus, return.
Patience betrays and the time speaks nothing. Come,
Pursed in the indigent small dark, confess:
Is mine this shade that to all hours the same
Lurches and fails, marine and garrulous—
A vain myth in the winter of his sense,
Capable neither of song nor silence?

Epitaph

Death is not information.
Stone that I am,
He came into my quiet
And I shall be still for him.

Ode: The Medusa Face

When did I pass the pole where I deprived
Three hags of their one eye, then, staring, seized
The total of their dark
And took their answer?
For that way I came though the eye forgets:
Now tall over the breathless shore this day
Lifts on one equal glare
The crass and curling face.

I cannot tell if stone is upon me
Healing me, clotting time until I stand
Dead. If the heart yet moves,
What shield were faithful found,
What weapon? I stand as in sloth of stone,
Amazed, for a maimed piece of one's own death,
Should that lithe hair stiffen,
Were the shape of her fall.

Festival

Laughter is not celebration
And may not coax with renewal
The closed heads bending
In their garden at heal of evening.

I that am king of no country—
Shall a mind of dry leaves
On the erstwhile meadow
Invoke for me a gray retinue?

I would have a weather
Of spells and reflections
Whether dawn or a moon hang
In the green lagoon where fish swim.

You have seen the afternoon
Turn among shadows under
A flutter of paper and laurel.
Was that a dance or hesitancy?

And a body that made
A specter his companion,
Fruitless and dark,
Lay down and embraced a lean shadow.

Dictum: For a Masque of Deluge
for Dido

There will be the cough before the silence, then
Expectation; and the hush of portent
Must be welcomed by a diffident music
Lisping and dividing its renewals;
Shadows will lengthen and sway, and, casually
As in a latitude of diversion
Where growth is topiary, and the relaxed horizons
Are accustomed to the trespass of surprise,
One with a mask of Ignorance will appear
Musing on the wind's strange pregnancy.

And to him the one must enter from the south
In a feigned haste, with disaster on his lips,
And tales of distended seas, continents
Submerged, worlds drowned, and of drownings
In mirrors; unto this foreboding
Let them add sidelong but increasing mention,
With darkening syllables, of shadows, as though
They stood and traded restlessness beneath
A gathering dark, until their figures seem
But a flutter of speech down an expense of wind.

So, with talk, like a blather of rain, begun,
Weather will break and the artful world will rush
Incontinent. There must be a vessel.
There must be rummage and shuffling for salvation
Till on that stage and violence, among
Curtains of tempest and shaking sea,
A covered basket, where a child might lie,
Timbered with osiers and floated on a shadow,
Glides adrift, as improbably sailing
As a lotus flower bearing a bull.

Hills are to be forgotten; the patter of speech
Must lilt upon flatness. The beasts will come;
And as they come, let one man, by the ark,
Drunken with desolation, his tongue

Rounding the full statement of the seasons,
Tremble and stare, his eyes seeming to chase
A final clatter of doomed crows, to seek
An affirmation, a mercy, an island,
Or hills crested with towns, and to find only
Cities of cloud already crumbling.

And these the beasts: the bull from the lotus flower
With wings at his shoulders; and a goat, winged;
A serpent undulating in the air;
A lion with wings like falling leaves;
These are to wheel on a winged wheel above
The sullen ark, while hare, swine, crocodile,
Camel, and mouse come; and the sole man, always,
Lurches on childish limbs above the basket—
To his mere humanity seas shall not attain
With tempest, nor the obscure sky with torches.

(Why is it rumored that these beasts come in pairs
When the anatomies of their existence
Are wrought for singularity? They walk
Beside their shadows; their best motions are
Figments on the drapery of the air.
Their propagation is a redoubling
Merely of dark against the wall, a planetary
Leaning in the night unto their shadows
And stiffening to the moment of eclipse;
Shadows will be their lean progeny.)

At last the sigh of recession: the land
Wells from the water; the beasts depart; the man
Whose shocked speech must conjure a landscape
As of some country where the dead years keep
A circle of silence, a drying vista of ruin,
Musters himself, rises, and stumbling after
The dwindling beasts, under the all-colored
Paper rainbow, whose arc he sees as promise,
Moves in an amazement of resurrection,
Solitary, impoverished, renewed.

A falling frond may seem all trees. If so
We know the tone of falling. We shall find
Dictions for rising, words for departure;
And time will be sufficient before that revel
To teach an order and rehearse the days
Till the days are accomplished: so now the dove
Makes assignations with the olive tree,
Slurs with her voice the gestures of the time:
The day foundering, the dropping sun
Heavy, the wind a low portent of rain.

The Bones of Palinurus Pray to the North Star

Console us. The wind chooses among us.
Our whiteness is a night wake disordered.
Lone candor, be constant over
Us desolate who gleam no direction.

Sestina

for Robert Graves

Where I came by torchlight there is dawn-song:
Leaves remembering, sudden as a name
Recalled from nowhere, remembering morning,
Fresh wind in high grass, cricket on plowshare,
Whisper of stream in the green-shadowed place,
Thrush and tanager keeping season.

Have I not also willed to be heard in season?
Have I not heard anger raised in a song
And watched when many went out to a wild place
And fought with the dark to make themselves a name?
I have seen of those champions how thin a share
After one night shook off their sleep at morning.

In a stony month a long cloud darkened morning.
Their feet gone white, shuffling the cold season,
The breath of some was worn too small to share.
Have I not heard how fragile then grew song?
Gray water lashed at the island of one's name.
And some stayed to flutter empty in that place.

What road is it one follows out of that place?
I remember no direction. I dreamed of morning,
Walking, warming the tongue over a name.
And a few of us came out of that season
As though from sleep, and stood too bleak for song,
And saw hills and heaven in the one dawn share.

Whom shall I praise before the gray knife share?
I have gone like seed into a dark place.
Whom shall I choose to make new with song?
For there will be sinking between night and morning,
Lisp of hushed voices, a dwindled season,
The small lights that flicker at a name.

Where again shall I walk with various name?
Merciless restlessness falls to my share.
Whose house shall I fill for more than a season?
I woke with new words, and in every place,
Under different lights, evening and morning,
Under many masters studied one song.

A breathed name I was with no resting-place,
A bough of sleep that had no share of morning,
Till I had made body and season from a song.

Herons

As I was dreaming between hills
That stones wake in a changing land,
There in the country of morning
I slept, and the hour and shadow slept.

I became the quiet stone
By a river where the winds
Favor honest thoughts. Three herons
Rose into a hemlock tree.

And I heard, "All day I stand
Dreaming that the night has come;
Beneath my wings, beneath my feet
The resignation and the death."

And, "When will darkness bury me
Who stand all day with open eye,
The small eye through which the years pass
From one place to another place."

And, "I have neither eye nor dream;
Dumb as with sleep or dignity
I stand, and others speak of me
In questions, but no prophecy."

But I knew neither dream nor eye
And held my question till a wind
Shook them in their hemlock tree
And I became the man who fell

After the lightning long ago
At his own window; there he stood
And leaned out on the afternoon
Till someone touched him, and he fell.

Daylong I dreamed as one who sets
His impudence in a falling house
And laughs and sleeps. The ruined hour
Moves and outmodes this comedy.

Who will see me if I fall?
I waked between the quiet hills;
I saw the dark and came away
And night where I had lain all day.

Song with the Eyes Closed

I am the shape in sleep
While the seasonal beasts
With petulant rough step
Forsake my random coasts.

I am the face recedes
Though the pool be constant
Whose double kingdom feeds
The sole vein's discontent.

I have seen desire, such
As a violent hand,
Murder my sleep—as much
Is suffered of the wind.

Canción y Glosa

Y yo, mientras, hijo
tuyo, con más secas
hojas en las venas.
JUAN RAMÓN JIMÉNEZ

Among the almond trees
whiteness more than winter's,
speech where no name is,
flowers broken from sleep;
and you their litany,
a breath upon this fervor,
you their reason, Lady,
seem as a name, meanwhile,
for an immortal season,
who stand in such whiteness
with those green leaves in your hands.

There is no breath of days
in that time where I was,
in that place, through the trees;

no winds nor satellites,
seasons nor bodies rise;
are no descent of rivers,
wavering of fishes,
indecision of tides,
languor before pause,
nor any dance to please,
nor prayers, pleasure of knees,
coupling, smile of increase,
swaying of fruit and seas,
genesis, exodus,
tremor of arteries,
decay by calendars,
hum of carrion flies;
and no shadow-plays,
trepidation of fingers,
ruse of limbs or faces,
ghosts nor histories
shift before the eyes,
but that vain country lies
in savorless repose.

      Among the names of these,
yet as the eyes remove
now from the polities
of these disstated things,
I their artifice,
a breath among such languor,
I their name, Lady,
seem as one nameless, leaning
through such stillness meanwhile
with these dry leaves in my hands.

Carol

On vague hills the prophet bird
Chants now the night is drained;
What was the stem this night stirred
And root from the winter ground?

Lord, Lord, and no night remained,
But heaven only, whence comes
Light such as no sun contained,
And the earth shook, and our limbs.

By song we were brought to stand
By that flower where frail our eyes
Strayed among beasts and found
Dim kings dreaming on their knees.

Lord, Lord, and earth's hours were torn
To dreams and we beheld there
On that silence newly born
Heaven's light in the still flower.

From such a quiet wakened,
After the vision has burned
On such birth, to what end
Have dew and hours returned?

Lord, Lord, and what remember
We of dreams when the day comes,
And the loud bird laughs on wonder
And white sheep lying like tombs?

We who are flesh have no word
And distraction is our music,
Who on the anxious night heard
Peace over our voices break.

Carol of the Three Kings

How long ago we dreamed
Evening and the human
Step in the quiet groves
And the prayer we said:
Walk upon the darkness,
Words of the Lord,
Contain the night, the dead,
And here comfort us.
We have been a shadow
Many nights moving,
Swaying many nights
Between yes and no.
We have been blindness
Between sun and moon
Coaxing the time
For a doubtful star.
Now we cease, we forget
Our reasons, our city,
The sun, the perplexed day,
Noon, the irksome labor,
The flushed dream, the way,
Even the dark beasts,
Even our shadows.
In this night and day
All gifts are nothing:
What is frankincense
Where all sweetness is?
We that were followers
In the night's confusion
Kneel and forget our feet
Who the cold way came.
Now in the darkness
After the deep song
Walk among the branches
Angels of the Lord,
Over earth and child
Quiet the boughs.
Now shall we sing or pray?

Where has the night gone?
Who remembers day?
We are breath and human
And awake have seen
All birth and burial
Merge and fall away,
Seen heaven that extends
To comfort all the night,
We have felt morning move
The grove of a few hands.

Carol

Lady, the dew of years
Makes sodden the world
And yet there is no morning.
Lady, we cannot think you
Indifferent or far,
And we lean and call after
You who in the night,
As a morning, among
This our heaviness came
And our eyes called you maiden.
We are in the darkness,
Our eyes turned to the door,
Waiting. Because you passed
Through the room where we are,
Your form not cumbered
With our weight and gesture;
Waiting, because you went
Uncontained by our shadows,
As a light, quietly;
Leaning, as though you might
Come again where our eyes
Are lost that follow after
You who as a light
Through the room where we are
With grace carried a flower.

A Poem for Dorothy

No shape in darkness single stands
And we in privacy and night,
Taking surprise of love for light,
Merged the dark fortunes of our hands.

Patience of fire insists and warms
Through dust, through dusty bone the breath;
The ear and intellect of death
Direct of love the heated forms.

Sitting on stones we kiss to please
Some stilled remembrance that shares our blood,
And warmth whose shape and name are dead
From ruin moving amends our peace.

Hermione on Simulacra
for Diana Wynyard

(Paulina draws back a curtain and discovers Hermione as a statue.)

For comfort I became a stone,
Silent where whispers stir,
I who had longed to be immune
To all tongues that infest the air.

I schooled the body where it dreamed,
I hushed all offices till I
Quiet and blind as Justice seemed,
And I reigned in a still kingdom.

I banished motion, but have found
No simplicity in stone,
For one comes who believes and bends
Before me and makes me many things.

As one who stares and seems a prey
To the darkness of premonitions,
So in a fantasy he comes
And finds it already night.

He is a vagrant in my shadow,
An alien darkness, how should he know
I have conspired to this deathly
Dancing to unmoving music?

Both cause and image I became;
I am his innocence who grieves,
And while he tells all he believes
I of us both the mirror am.

I am the patience of a pool
Where all the planets sway, and I
Am the moon's self, a watery star
Beheld at night in the blue river.

I am the night where he is blind
And I the orbit of his prayers;
Quiet above the suppliant hand,
I am the heaven of fixed stars.

I the elusive phoenix seem,
And a man is my age and fire,
For he has breathed me to this flame,
And I, seeming myself, seem fire.

Thus I who have not moved a limb,
Who feigned but changelessness and keep
Only the semblance that I was
Am all faces of time and sleep.

I had intended but to be
My picture in a stone, but I
Took shape of death and have become
Death, and all things come to me.

Death, in my varied majesty
I am astonished in flesh and stone
That you should be simplicity
Whose visage so resembles me.

Song

How have I dreamed you, Lady,
Stricken among flames dark auburn:
O Lady, does your chimney burn?
Winds are moving dangerously;
I may be slow to warn;
Give me tidings in my concern:
O Lady, Lady, does your chimney burn?

If it would please you, Lady,
I could make your defenses stubborn
Against odd wind and conflagration;
Or if flame owns you utterly
I might assure return
Better than ashes in your urn.
O Lady, Lady, does your chimney burn?

Or do you lack, Lady,
An intimate subaltern,
A tall sentry near your postern?
I shall fulfill as you employ me,
Turn as you bid me turn,
And be pleased if you so govern.
O Lady, Lady, does your chimney burn?

Or if I might be sea
To your green island laced with fern,
I should betide your coasts in turn
Learning your seasons, and so be
Fierce, as you pleased, or southern,
Wearing the air that you had worn.
O Lady, Lady, does your chimney burn?

Even, for your pleasure, Lady,
I could become your heat and learn
To rise for you when your mood is eastern,
And I should by such service, surely,
More than bare praises earn,
And all I received of you return;
O Lady, Lady, does your chimney burn?

Song

Mirrors we lay wherein desire
Traded, by dark, conceits of fire;
As gardened minds whose delicacy
Could neither close with flesh nor flee,

Who watched by fire a bush inflect
What flame a window could reflect
Where dark and distance were control
So the leaves burned yet rested whole;

But flesh, dark forest to the mind,
Took at our breaths repeated wind
And from our eyes an equal glare:
Our distance broke and burned us there.

In married dark these fevers learn
Alternate loss; the bodies, worn
Indefinite, attend together
Night's pleasure and the press of weather.

THE DANCING BEARS

(1954)

for Dido

—marveling

. . . la parole humaine est comme un chaudron fêlé où
nous battons des mélodies à faire danser les ours, quand
on voudrait attendrir les étoiles.

FLAUBERT

Tower

Now I have come again
To the common country
Where all faces are mirrors and tell me
I return white-faced as the dawn.

Have I outrun belief
And walk in a superstition?
Ignorant and alone,
Without haste I went only

Among the innocent
Noon-laden fields, then
Among thickets, the way growing
Black and white and thorny,

And at the cockshut hour
—The summer dusk among
Its hedges drowsing—came
Upon the odor of apples,

Upon the darkling tower
Hung with no flutter of birds,
Puff of smoke, or banner;
And when I called

No echo stirred nor answer,
Pin nor shutter, only
By the door a hanging wheel
In no wind was turning slowly.

Round and still as a finger
Laid upon lips, stone
Above stone, the tower. Its shadow
Fell as far as evening.

Dark spool wound within silence,
Ringed with stillness as with trees
—Birches stood hushed in the green air,
And moat-lapped apple trees.

Polished were the dark stones;
As ice they rose. Is it
That there the crevices
Run at neck-level, always,

That where the water stands
Almost as ice, the rippling
Tails of salmon cut
The throats of all reflection?

I saw my body
As a smooth alien
On stones and water walking
Headless, not noticing;

And my head, drifting
Bereft of body, gave me
Again from every stone
My astonishment.

A pebble might have rung
A crash of seven years' portent
On that water falling.
Or turn away the face.

But there was enough of portent
Folding that stony bobbin
If the failing light could limn
And limb such legerdemain.

And what if all motion
Were a web into that stance
And all shattering
But served that severance?

I cannot learn from mirrors
Or faces of this country
Which of me, head or body,
Still fronts itself there,

Still winds in unmoving dance
About itself while the shadows
Turn alike about flesh,
About stone, about trees,

Till dizzy would the wind be
If wind there were; and yet
No apple falls, nor the green
Light like leaves from the trees;

And from somewhere unseen
The deceitful magpie sings,
"Love, love, O lover,
O King live forever."

Runes for a Round Table

CAPRICORN

Where darkness is
Once a mirror was
And I therein was king.
Bearded, lecherous,
Still I stand recalling
The windy cities
Like reeds wailing.

AQUARIUS

This is faithbearing:
All seas turning
On one's shoulders, to stand
Patiently as though painted,
Though the fish be gone.

PISCES

Let the stars quaver
In night blue as a pool;
I rise, though the tide fall,

I turn, but I am still
And wiser than any water
In the eddying sky.

ARIES

I bear suspicion
Like a golden fleece,
And horns like auguries
Curling into nothing;
On these the world has wheeled.

TAURUS

White as a flower,
As a floating flower,
As a white child,
Eleven kings I wield;
Afloat in gentle water,
I trample on what is,
I am what is to be.

GEMINI

He sinks when I rise,
He laughs when I die;
We twain are single
As the same rain falling
On two sides of a tree.

CANCER

Multitudes bow to me
On shores where no wave bows,
To me who slip sideways
In the heat of day
With the blank stars for sand.

LEO

What greater ravage
Than this: to become
The multiple shield
Of the gilt marauder,
To hold a honeycomb,
Whose taste was for rage.

VIRGO

Not so much as a song
In my most silver dream
Has ravished my ear.
Damage by beast and man
And by the scandalous sun
Sing out, but I am not there.

LIBRA

One man confronting two,
Each side on twelve legs walking,
Yet is no balance between:
The one outweighs the two,
For all hands are uneven
But the wheel is equal.

SCORPIO

All unbidden
I offer an island;
Let the bidden man
Turn, flee like a season;
Mine is the turning end;
My bitterness, immortal,
Finds the mortal heel.

SAGITTARIUS

All quarry flees. The arrow
Drawn always to my ear I still
Have not let fly, and yet they fall.

The Lady with the Heron

I walk athirst
In a month of rain;
Drought I learned
At the feet of a heron.

Green trees, full rivers;
Athirst I went,
With a shrieking bird
In the drawn breath.

At the only spring
When I went for water
I met a lady
And thirst I had none.

I say, at the fountain
There I met a lady,
She led a blue heron
By the beck of her hand.

Moon-wise the owl is,
The wren not tame,
But I unlearned patience
At the feet of a heron.

So deep a water
As those her eyes
Kissed I never
At the lip of April.

Drink, sir, she said,
Of so sweet water.
The bird was blind
That she led by a shadow.

Lady, I said,
Thirst is no longer.
But she led my eyes
By the beck of her hand.

Of her eyes I drank
And no other water.
Hope I unlearned
At the feet of a bird,

And saw no face
When I bent there;
Such saw I never
In other water.

My lips not wet,
Yet was she gone
Leading a heron
By the shade of her hand.

And my eyes thirst
On the birdless air;
Blindness I learned
At the feet of a heron.

When I Came from Colchis

When I came from Colchis
Where the spring fields lay green,
A land famed for fine linen,
Bounded northerly
By the glistering Caucasus,
By the Euxine westerly,

Most I spoke of fine linen
But did, in truth, tell something
Of Jason who had come sailing
And poised upon that shore
His fabulous excursion.
All turned the incredulous ear.

From Troy, over the water
Returning, I recounted
The tale of wrecked walls, but said
That gray waves lap and surround
That shore as any other.
With a shrewd smile they listened.

Now if, amazed, I come
From the deep bourn of your hand,
A stranger up from the sunned
Sea of your eyes, lady,
What fable should I tell them,
That they should believe me?

You, Genoese Mariner

You, Genoese mariner,
Your face most perfectly
A mask about a vision,
Your eyes most clear when turned
On the bewildering west,
You, so your story goes,
Who believed that that direction
Toward which all breath and knowledge
Although their eyes cling elsewhere
Make ignorant declension,
Must by its own token,
Continuing, contain
A grammar of return,
A world's unknown dimension,
You, nevertheless, in search
Of gilt and spice, who fancied
Earth too circumscribed
To imagine and cradle,
Where no map had suspected,
The distances and marvels,
The unfingered world—
I whose face has become,
O mistaken sailor,
Suddenly a frame
For astonishment, stand
In the long light of wonder
Staring upon the shadows
That circle and return

From another's eyes,
I, after so long,
Who have been wrong as you.

Fable

I am a mad precarious man
Making a prayer for folly
At the midnight and heartless hour,
Moon-beset, and my best of prayer
Is incontinently to complain
Upon a foolish story.

Long ago in a laurel wood—
Pray for the love of folly—
Once a lover, and he heartless,
And his lady, heartless likewise,
Loving, but without heart, there stood,
And they wept grievously.

He said: As though with a heart I grieve—
Pray for the poor in folly—
That we in whom great love there is
Should love less well than loveless bodies
For scarcely do we dare to love
Lest we love heartlessly.

She said: Some stint there must be done—
Pray for the lips of folly—
For how should we this pain abide
As thorough as though hearts we had
Yet suffer and love as though alone,
However entwined we be.

So they one heart between them made—
Pray for the hands of folly—
Of all heat and belief they knew,

For the sustenance whereof they two
Made tributary their own blood
And rejoiced heartily.

Dark it was in the laurel wood—
Pray for the eyes of folly—
A noise as of a breathing beast
Swung between them; when they kissed,
All about them it raged and played,
But nothing could they see.

Reverence overcame them then—
Pray for the heart of folly—
That they out of mere need could make
From nothing and a bit of dark
What had failed them from their creation,
And they sank upon knee.

And most religiously they swore—
Pray for the word of folly—
That never would they look upon
The warm marvel that beat between,
Lest, should their eyes prove so familiar,
It take offense and die.

So they took heart, and the heart, grown wild—
Pray for the limbs of folly—
Would lunge on the hollow dark like pain,
And then, till love came round again,
Lie and be gentled like a child
And feed on intimacy.

Almost nine hours they lived at ease—
Pray for the life of folly—
Yet dawn, ubiquitous, could watch
How they grew curious till each,
Unknown to the other, raised his eyes
Out of their dark and pity

And saw within the other's eyes—
Pray for the bells of folly—
Where they all tenderness had set,
Burning upon the day, a great
Bull-shouldered beast with horns of brass
Who cried in fury,

Who lunged between them like all pain—
Pray for the death of folly—
In mortal rage, till brass and beast
Gored nothing but the ground at last,
And empty, where a heart had been,
Love's body lay.

Ghosts are heartless that tease the blood—
Pray for the soul of folly—
And ghostly as a coil of rain
Heartless they stood once again,
Day-stricken in the laurel wood,
And they wept grievously.

I am a sullen unseemly man—
Pray now no more for folly—
Who in the bleak and tolling hour
Walk like a chime without a tower,
Reading a story, and complain
Heartless and foolishly.

The Passion

In that garden at evening
We could not speak save in prayer
Unto each other saying,
"Each other's will be done";
Nor could we walk under
Bare thorn but the branches
Unnaturally would compose
Over our heads a crown.
Non enim sciunt quid faciunt

Truly, strong bulls of Bashan
Had beset us round;
Our doom, though falsely, had been
Foretold, and where we came
Hands were washed of our end;
And there was that fretful spouse
Had suffered, because of us,
Many things in a dream.
        Non enim sciunt quid faciunt

Each of us, we knew,
Must be unto the other
The singular cross; yet how
Could either of us hang painful
Upon the other, either
Upon the other weigh
As burden? Merrily
We went out to that hill.
        Non enim sciunt quid faciunt

We heard the nails scream
In the wood as they were drawn
Out from the last time,
And felt their pain; the cry
You swore was old affection
And smiled upon the sound
Not woodenly, but I turned
My wooden face away.
        Non enim sciunt quid faciunt

Three hours we hung as though
To veil the sun; thereafter
The earth shook; and, although
You said it was not real,
The dark was ours: no other
Voices, at last no thirst;
Doubt not, love, though the first
Death is original.
        Non enim sciunt quid faciunt

On the stroke of our absence,
They say, the sainted dead
Rose from their double patience
In jealousy, for we seemed
Our own heaven. Through the rifted
Temple veil we saw only
Darkness, and virgins darkly
Coming with their lamps untrimmed.
> *Non enim sciunt quid faciunt*

They led us away
To this place we were to harrow
And rise from, the third day,
And how so scripture be truthful,
Yet this pain we pass through,
Though shared, consumes us by
Dividing infinitely,
Is at all times eternal.
> *Non enim sciunt quid faciunt*

Margery's Song

I am a jill-whisper
And a cold sister
And a windy daughter
With hawthorn in my hair.

Five fingers of thin willow
Flicker my preferment;
I go feat but drafty
With a ghost of rag about me.

A nimble bird I saw;
Ruses were its children;
And friendly was the wind
But spoke me hungerly.

A little coin, a morsel,
Give me for my sleeking
For fear trespass should busy
Hands no better than bony.

Whose dish is cold and clever?
I saw a bone shiver.
In name of shadows bleating
Yet meatily the mouth feeds.

Soul is thin confusion.
I am vagary
Snared in a bony body
With hawthorn in my hair.

Song of the Mad Menagerie

I on whom the wild sun
Upon unvaried journey
Burned with jealousy
Because of my unreason,

Know I was legendary.
On straw I lie down.
Wise hand, be wary:
My rage is uneven.

In a cautious country
The wild shadows came down
As though athirst, came softly
And drank of the clear moon.

But the wind was tamed away,
But all the palms fell down.
The bright aviary
Sings, "O daughters of Zion."

Thirst is yet necessary:
The lean shade comes down
Of my own savagery
To sip my dry distraction.

Hands, befriend cautiously:
Now I pace alone
That mad menagerie,
The body behind bone.

Song of Marvels

The day is down.
All a shiver of gold,
Age talks in the trees.
All faces rise out of the sea.

Think, think of the marvel:
One time there was a beggar
Loved a great lady
For the sake of white hands.

I hear a whisper break
Cavernous upon coral;
The hours like fishes
Wheel in amber undersea.

Sing, sing of the marvel:
A beggar with his two hands
Killed a great lady
For the love of patience.

I see the speech of leaves
That lisp in the late garden
And eyes like fishes,
In deep amber waving.

Sing, sing of the marvel:
Our hands are fathomless,
Our eyes shake in the gold,
All for the love of patience.

Song of Three Smiles

Let me call a ghost,
Love, so it be little:
In December we took
No thought for the weather.

Whom now shall I thank
For this wealth of water?
Your heart loves harbors
Where I am a stranger.

Where was it we lay
Needing no other
Twelve days and twelve nights
In each other's eyes?

Or was it at Babel
And the days too small
We spoke our own tongue,
Needing no other?

If a seed grow green
Set a stone upon it
That it learn thereby
Holy charity.

If you must smile
Always on that other,
Cut me from ear to ear
And we all smile together.

Song of the New Fool

Let the sea and all her women
With their combs and white horses,
Their mirrors and shells, the green-flaming
Bushes, the bull-necked hills,

The uncombed crags, and the trees
Shading their leopards and thrushes,
The shadows and loud peacocks,
Rocks, and the laughing geese,

And the fires, and the fire that stood
Still over Jericho,
The stars and the wet moon,
And the day and the night

(But caution: for the west wind
Is secret, the west wind's hunger
All love and ghost
May not satisfy),

And laughter and the unicorn
Come in the morning
While the air is a blue girl
And eat from my hand.

For I filled my hands
With fists and cursed till the bone
Heart of the world broke;
And my hands are tender.

East of the Sun and West of the Moon

Say the year is the year of the phoenix.
Ordinary sun and common moon,
Turn as they may, are too mysterious
Unless such as are neither sun nor moon
Assume their masks and orbits and evolve
Neither a solar nor a lunar story
But a tale that might be human. What is a man
That a man may recognize, unless the inhuman
Sun and moon, wearing the masks of a man,
Weave before him such a tale as he
—Finding his own face in a strange story—
Mistakes by metaphor and calls his own,
Smiling, as on a familiar mystery?

The moon was thin as a poor man's daughter
At the end of autumn. A white bear came walking
On a Thursday evening at the end of autumn,
Knocked at a poor man's door in a deep wood,
And, "Charity," when the man came he said,
"And the thin hand of a girl have brought me here.
Winter will come, and the vixen wind," he said,
"And what have you but too many mouths to feed,
Oh, what have you but a coat like zither-strings
To ward that fury from your family?
But I though wintry shall be bountiful
Of furs and banquets, coins like summer days,
Grant me but the hand of your youngest daughter."

"By a swooning candle, in my porchless door,
While all I wedded or sired huddle behind me,
The night unceremonious with my hair,
I know I cut a poor figure," the man said,
"And I admit that your cajolery
(For opulence was once my setting-on)
Finds me not deaf; but I must ask my daughter.
And no, she says. But come again on Thursday:
She is more beautiful than the story goes,
And a girl who wants a week for her persuading

Merits that slow extravagance," he said.
Further in autumn by a week's persuading
The youngest girl on a white bear went riding.

The moon played in a painted elder tree;
He said, when they had gone a while, "We walk
In a night so white and black, how can you tell
My shoulder from a moon-struck hill, my shadow
From the towering darkness; are you not afraid?"
And, "You are thin and colorful who ride
Alone on a thin and monstrous thing; suppose
I rose up savage in a desolate place;
Are you not afraid?" And, "What if I were to wander
Down a black ladder, in a trope of death,
Through seven doors all of black ice, and come
On a land of hyperbole, stiff with extremes;
Would it not make the hair rise on your head?"

The wind with moonlit teeth rippled and sulked
In the paper trees, but three times "No" she said.
"Oh, then hold fast by the hair of my shoulders,"
He said, "hold fast my hair, my savage hair;
And let your shadow as we go hold fast
The hair of my shadow, and all will be well."
Later than owls, all night, a winter night,
They traveled then, until the screaming wind
Fell behind or dead, till no stars glittered
In the headlong dark; and each step dark and long
As falling in the valley of the blind;
Yet all the while she felt her yellow hair
Hang loose at her shoulders, as though she stood still.

They came before daylight to a stone hill
Steep as a pier glass, where no shrub grew,
Nor grass rustled, nor breeze stirred before dawn.
When the bear knocked, a door swung wide. Their eyes
Enormous with the dark, a hall they entered
That blazed between mirrors, between pilasters
Of yellow chrysolite; on walls of brass
Gold branches of dead genealogies

Clutched candles and wild torches whence the flames
Rose still as brilliants. Under a fiery
Garnet tree with leaves of glass, sunken
In a pool of sea-green beryl as in still water
A gold salmon hung. And no sound came.

The wall healed behind them. When she turned,
The wall steep as a pier glass, the door
Vanished like a face in ruffled water,
And they stood dumb in the echoing light
While no flame crackled, no water fell. They passed
Between the rows of burning, between the rings
Of extinct animals that stared from sockets
In the braziered walls; hour upon hour,
Hall upon blazing hall, and came at last
Through obsequious curtains to a closed room
Where she descended; at a beck of his head
A gold table leapt from the air; she dined
That night on lapwing and wine of pomegranates.

The bear had gone. She touched a silver bell.
She stood straightway in a white chamber
By a bed of lapis lazuli. Red agate
And yellow chrysolite the floors. A white
Carnelian window gave upon cut hills
Of amethyst and yellow serpentine
Pretending summer; when she stood naked there
Her nakedness from the lighted stones
Sprang a thousand times as girl or woman,
Child or staring hag. The lamps went black;
When she lay down to sleep, a young man came
Who stayed all night in the dark beside her
But was gone before dawn came to that country.

Nightly he came again. Once he said,
"I am the white bear, who once was a man;
In a Christian body, in a green kingdom
One time I had dominion. Now I keep
Not so much as the shadow that I had,
And my own shape only by dark; by day

Compelled I am to that pale beast. Let it be
Ensample to your forbearance: here love
Must wander blind or with mistaken eyes,
For dissolution walks among the light
And vision is the sire of vanishing."
What love soever in the dark there were,
Always at daylight she wakened alone.

By day she walked in the espaliered garden
Among pheasants and clear flowers; she said,
"What if these pheasants amble in white glass,
Ducks strut ridiculous in stone, the streams
Slither nowhere in beryl; why should I
Complain of such inflexible content,
Presume to shudder at such serenity,
Who walk in some ancestral fantasy,
Lunar extravagance, or lost pagoda
That dreams of no discipline but indolence?
What shall be rigid but gems and details
While all dimensions dance in the same air?
And what am I if the story be not real?

"But what it is," she said, "to wander in silence,
Though silence be a garden. What shall I say,
How chiseled the tongue soever, and how schooled
In sharp diphthongs and suasive rhetorics,
To the echoless air of this sufficiency?
Where should I find the sovereign aspirate
To rouse in this world a tinkle of syllables,
Or what shall I sing to crystal ears, and where
All songs drop in the air like stones; oh, what
Shall I do while the white-tongued flowers shout
Impossible silence on the impossible air
But wander with my hands over my ears?
And what am I if the story be not real?

"He says the place is innocent; and yet
I may not see his face; claims he is held
Equivocating between prince and beast
By the ministrations of an evil stepdame,

But such might be mere glittering deviltry.
Here is no nightly moon or tidal water
But mornings miming at mutability
Where all stands new at noon and nothing fades
Down the perfect amber of the afternoons;
All, simultaneous and unwearied, comes
Guesting again at evening. But a day
Must dwindle before dawn be real again;
And what am I if the story be not real?"

She said at night when he lay beside her,
"Why should I raise the singular dissent
Who delight in an undiminished country
Where all that was or shall be transitory
Stands whole again already? Yet I sigh
For snipes to whir and fall, for hawks to fall,
For one more mortal crimson that will fade,
For one glimpse of the twisted holly tree
Before my mother's door, and the short-lived
Wren by my mother's window, and the tame crane
Walking in shallow water. I would learn
Whether I dreamed then or walk now in a dream,
For what am I if the story be not real?"

Suddenly where no sound had been she heard
A distant lisp and crumble, like a wave,
Like the whisper of tidal water, emulous
Of its own whispers: his echoing heart. "Shall I
Pace an eternity of corridors,
Alone among sad topaz, the reflections
Flickering only on your emptiness,
And the soundlessness be like a sound of mourning,
That seemed a sound of joy? Nevertheless,
Go you shall if you wish; but promise,
Lest a malicious word undo us both,
Never to walk or talk alone," he said,
"With your mother, who is as wise as you."

It was a Sunday. Gold on the glass leaves.
She sat in the garden on the white bear's shoulders.

She touched a silver bell, and instantly
Saw the swaying of incorrigible meadows
Ripening, a green wind playful in barley,
The holly, contorted at her mother's door,
The fluttering wren—the brief feathers
Provisional about mortality—
At her mother's window, the tame crane walking
As though not real where the real shallows ran.
She had descended; the bear was gone;
She heard the whistling grass, and the holly leaves
Saying, "Your mother, who is wise as you."

She was greeted like a lost season.
Daylong she walked again in affluent summer,
But one day walked at last aside, and talked
Alone with her mother, who was wise as she.
"Equivocation between prince and beast,
The ministrations of an evil stepdame,
Might be a devilish tale; how could you tell,"
Her mother said, "should it be the devil's self
Or some marvel of ugliness you lay beside?
Take, better than advice, this end of candle
To light when he sleeps next you in the dark;
Only be careful that no drops fall."
The grass might whistle under the holly leaves.

On a day of no clouds he came to fetch her.
It was a Sunday. A soft wind stroking
The fields already white almost to harvest.
"Shall we not ride a while in the mortal air
Before we go," he asked, "for the love of fading?
But wish, when you are weary, for the sound
Of the silver bell, and we shall instantly
Be home again. Did all happen as I said?"
"Yes," she said, "how might it be otherwise?"
"Did you, then, walk aside with your mother?" he asked;
"Did you listen to your mother's advice?"
"Oh no," she said. "Then all may yet be well."
But she wished for the sound of the silver bell.

That night when she was sure he slept
She rose in the dark and struck light
To the end of candle, and held it above his face.
What blaze was this, what prince shaming with beauty
The sun peerless at noon? The dazzled stones
Seemed each a blond particular summer wringing
In the one thirst the lion and the nightingale.
The shadows bowed; they fell down amazed.
"And I with my foolish arm upraised . . .
But love so beggars me of continence,
Either I must kiss him or die," she said,
And bent, therewith, and kissed his head. Three times
The tallow folly from the candle fell.

"Oh, why must all hope resolve to vanity?"
Waking, he cried; "Why could you not entertain
A curious patience but for one whole year,
For then had we been saved, and my spell broken.
Now this kingdom must shatter and I depart
For the wheeling castle of my stepmother
And marry a princess with a nose three ells long,
When I might have married you." "O love," she cried,
"May I not learn the way and follow you?"
"There is no way there that a body might follow;
Farther than dreams that palace lies,
East of the sun and west of the moon, girt
With rage of stars for sea. There no one comes."

She seemed to sleep, for she woke again
On a usual morning in a different world,
Bright grass blowing, birds loud in the trees;
That precious kingdom, that charmed lover
Gone. She was kneeling under a willow
In her salt tears. When she had called
And cried till she was weary she walked on
Slowly, walked the length of a day, and seemed
None the more weary for all her walking
But traveled, it seemed, in a landscape of exceptions
Where no evening came but a shadowy

Skeptical bird who settled in a tree
And sang, "All magic is but metaphor."

Under a crag, when it should have been evening,
Where there should have been shadows, by an apple tree,
She saw a hag who laughed to herself and tossed
A golden apple. "Good day, hag," she said;
"Can you tell me how I might find the castle
That lies east of the sun and west of the moon?"
"Whoever comes and calls me hag, haggard
May she sit also, unless it be the lady
Who should marry the prince there. Are you she?
'Yes,' she says. Yet the way I cannot tell.
Take, rather, this gold apple, mount this horse
To ride to ask my sister, and once there,
Tap him behind the left ear; he will come home."

Long she rode as the patience of stones
And saw again, when it should have been evening,
A hag who played with a golden carding comb.
"If withering were a signature of wisdom,
I were a miracle of sagacity,"
She said, "my brow invisible with laurel,
But I am bare parchment where a word might be,
And any road that might lead to that castle
Is a thing I never knew. All I can offer
By way of blessing is this gold carding comb,
But you might ask my sister; take my own horse.
When he has brought you where she sits, tap him
Behind the left ear; he will come home again."

The third hag said, "I have been young as you,
And shall be so again, unless the stars
Tell lies in the shifty dark, but whether
More pleasure is to be young and pass for fair
Or to be haggard and seem knowledgeable,
I am too wise to choose, and yet the way
That castle lies is a thing I never knew;
But there you will come, late or never. I give you,

Beside that wisdom, this golden spinning wheel,
And if you wish, you may ride my own horse
To ask the East Wind. When you are there,
Tap the beast once behind the left ear,
And he will be off and come to me again."

Oh, then she rode such waste of calendars
She should have found the end of weariness
But came instead to the house of the East Wind.
"O Wind," she called, "which way would you blow,
Which way might I follow to come to the castle
That lies east of the sun and west of the moon?"
"I, bold of wing beyond the glimpse of morning,
Have found the dark where no birds sleep,
Have shivered and returned, have many times
Heard of that castle, but never blown so far
Nor learned the way. But I have a brother," he said,
"An infinite voyager: be pleased to sit
Between my shoulders and I shall take you there."

Though faster then than summoned ghosts they flew,
Long was that journey as the wisdom of owls
Before they came to the roof of the West Wind.
"For all I am prodigious of voyages,
Whistle heyday and holiday, make light
Of the poor limbs of summer and have sailed
Beyond the hueless sighing of drowned days
Into the dark where no shades sigh,
Have shuddered and come home a different way,
Unholy be the whisper of my name
If ever I were a wind about that tower
Or knew the way; but come with me," he said:
"I have a brother who has blown farther than I."

"I might shriek till the world was small
As a turtle's egg; I have whipped my savagery
A pride of days beyond where the world ends
In burning, into the dark where no flames twitch,
Have blessed myself and hastily blown elsewhere,
But never glimpsed wrack nor wisp of that castle,

And whether there be any such place at all
I gravely doubt; but I have a brother
Wields the gale that flaps the chittering dead
Beyond where the world ends in ice; be sure
Unless his storm can shiver your conundrum
It is a thing unknown." The South Wind's wings
Howled, till they came to the door of the North Wind.

"Oh, once," he roared, "I blew an aspen leaf
Beyond the glimmering world, over
The glass eaves of time, into that dark
Where no ice gleams; there, bristling, found that other
Wind of fear, but a rage stayed me until
The star-lashed sea, until I found the castle
That lies east of the sun and west of the moon.
But never I told a soul, for there I lay
Three weeks, frail as the aspen leaf, on the wild
Shore before I dared blow home again.
But if you be the lady that you claim,
Stay while I rest tonight and I shall try
Tomorrow if I can fly so far again."

Who has outflown the nightmare? Yet fast
Almost as she they flew in the morning
Beyond all boreal flickerings, headlong
Over the glass caves of time and found
The breathless dark where no souls stir,
But hair in another wind; broke, almost blind,
At last over a mad famished sea;
Then long as unspoken love they whirled.
But he wearied. The waves snapped at his knees,
The dogtoothed waves, till he whispered, "My wings fail,"
Sinking. But she cried, "I see a white shore,
A shadowy pinnacle that may be the castle
That lies east of the sun and west of the moon."

What if the breakers gulped and craved his thighs?
Where he had set her on the white shore
He fell forward and slept. Already
A foot beyond the frustrate sea there drowsed

Silence of forests, indolent, rimmed
With flutter of birches like birds in the tender
Sun, with thirsty osiers, pale hawthorn,
Perpetual apple trees, the capricious-limbed.
She saw in that light how the castle vanished
Above fancy among faithful clouds,
Saw the door, but nowhere near the door she went,
But sat under a guelder rose and sang
"Ah, well-a-day," and played with the gold apple.

Till from an upper window of the castle
A princess with a nose three ells long
Called, "Who are you, singing 'well-a-day'
Under my window, and, oh, what will you take
And give me that golden apple?" "I am a lady
Of foreign ways singing to my own hair
A dirge for diminishing under a pale tree,
Am a hazard waif blown from the scapegrace sea,
Am an aspen leaf; but nothing you own
Will I exchange for this gold apple,
Unless it should be that I might sleep tonight
Alone all night in his room with the prince
Who lives in this castle." And that could be arranged.

But she was returned, for earnest of gold,
Only a sleeping body and a sleep:
When she was led at evening into his room
Already he lay sleeping; for all she cried
His name aloud, for all she cried and kissed
His face and forehead, all night he lay sleeping.
What might she be but chorus to a dream,
But one who strokes a dream of chrysolite,
Glass pheasants, ducks ridiculous in stone,
A gold salmon in a beryl pool,
As reliquary, as meager communicance
Till daylight, then departs and sits again
By the tower and plays with the gold carding comb?

"Nothing whatever will I take," she said
When the princess called, "for my gold carding comb,

But to sleep tonight by the same prince."
But where was the unrecking fantasy,
The concord of distraught belief
She had named for love and understood by love,
If when she lay, and the second time, beside him
Nothing would answer to her kiss but sleep?
Must she before she wake still find a dream
Wherein she lay beside him, and he, waking,
Dreamed still of her? Although beside him, dream
Of yet more fortunate wakenings, till daylight,
Then sing by a gold spinning wheel, dreaming?

"I am a thirsty lady wishing I walked
Beside no water but a pool of beryl;
I sing to drown the silence of far flowers
And though I am deaf to all sounds other
Than a deafening heart in a distant room, I dream
I wander with my hands over my ears."
She argued with the princess as yesterday,
Parted with the gold spinning wheel. Oh, must
Love's many mansions, the patient honeycomb
Of hope unlearn their heavens and at a sleep
Triply be consigned to cerements,
Or must salvation shrink to the unlikely
Monstrance of another's wakening?

Suppose the requisite vigil. Say one lay
Two nights awake beside the prince's room,
Heard crying there, as toward a vanishing specter,
Told the prince, and he, thus wise against potions
The third night, sleepless, with wide arms received her,
Calling, "O love, is blessedness a risk
So delicate in time, that it should be
Tonight you find me? Tomorrow, always tomorrow
It is that my stepmother was to prevail,
It is that I was to marry that other princess.
But we are the sense of dawn beneath pretense
Of an order of darkness. Now lie in wisdom, mindful
Only of love, and leave to me tomorrow."

In the morning, to proud stepdame and coy princess,
"Call me a wry intransigent, a glass
Of fickle weathers, but what care I," he said,
"For decorum, though it be my wedding day?
Shall I be yoked to an unproven woman?
But who she may be can wash this shirt of mine,
Stained with three drops of tallow, white again
As once it was, she and no other lady
Will I marry. All wet the hands who wish;
All beat the board; all wring the linen; all wash
In the one water." Howsoever the princess
Dipped and wrung, the stains ran gray; or stepdame
Scrubbed, the shirt grew black as knavery.

"There is a girl outside the castle door,"
One said who loitered there and watched; "Perhaps
She if she tried might wash it white again."
But vexed stepdame and angry princess
Raged then and screamed, "No, no! Shall we have a tattered
Waif with outlandish ways for rival, and we
With our royal hands in water?" Yet the prince
Answered, "Let her come in, whoever she be."
She dipped the linen and once drew it forth
White as a leper; drew it forth again
White as blown snow; a third time raised it
Spotless, white as the violent moon; she said,
"How should I not, since all pallor is mine?"

The moon was musing in her high chamber
Among nine thousand mirrors. "Oh, what am I,"
She cried, "but a trick of light, and tropically?
I walk in a wild charactery of night,
In a game of darkness figurative with tapers,
Toying with apples, and come upon myself
More often than is meet for sanity,
Oh, who would be shown, save in analogy,
—What for gold handsels and marvelous equerry—
As three hags sitting under an apple tree?
But I walk multifarious among
My baubles and horses; unless I go in a mask
How shall I know myself among my faces?"

"All metaphor," she said, "is magic. Let
Me be diverted in a turning lantern,
Let me in that variety be real.
But let the story be an improvisation
Continually, and through all repetition
Differ a little from itself, as though
Mistaken; and I a lady with foreign ways
To sing therein to my own hair." To the sun,
"You who tomorrow are my Pentecost,
Come dance with me—oh, but be white, be wintry;
Oh, lest I fall an utter prey to mirrors,
Be a white bear," she said, "and come a-walking,
And ask my hand. I am a peasant's daughter."

It is for nothing that a troupe of days
Makes repeated and perpetual rummage
In the lavish vestry; or should sun and moon,
Finding mortality too mysterious,
Naked and with no guise but its own
—Unless one of immortal gesture come
And by a mask should show it probable—
Believe a man, but not believe his story?
Say the year is the year of the phoenix.
Now, even now, over the rock hill
The tropical, the lucid moon, turning
Her mortal guises in the eye of a man,
Creates the image in which the world is.

On the Subject of Poetry

I do not understand the world, Father.
By the millpond at the end of the garden
There is a man who slouches listening
To the wheel revolving in the stream, only
There is no wheel there to revolve.

He sits in the end of March, but he sits also
In the end of the garden; his hands are in
His pockets. It is not expectation

On which he is intent, nor yesterday
To which he listens. It is a wheel turning.

When I speak, Father, it is the world
That I must mention. He does not move
His feet nor so much as raise his head
For fear he should disturb the sound he hears
Like a pain without a cry, where he listens.

I do not think I am fond, Father,
Of the way in which always before he listens
He prepares himself by listening. It is
Unequal, Father, like the reason
For which the wheel turns, though there is no wheel.

I speak of him, Father, because he is
There with his hands in his pockets, in the end
Of the garden listening to the turning
Wheel that is not there, but it is the world,
Father, that I do not understand.

Proteus

By the splashed cave I found him. Not
(As I had expected) patently delusive
In a shape sea-monstrous, terrible though sleeping,
To scare all comers, nor as that bronze-thewed
Old king of Pharos with staring locks,
But under a gray rock, resting his eyes
From futurity, from the blinding crystal
Of that morning sea, his face flicked with a wisp
Of senile beard, a frail somnolent old man.

Who would harness the sea-beast
To the extravagant burden of his question
Must find him thus dreaming of his daughters,
Of porpoises and horses; then pitiless
Of an old man's complaints, unawed

At what fierce beasts are roused under his grasp,
Between the brutal ignorance of his hands
Must seize and hold him till the beast stands again
Manlike but docile, the neck bowed to answer.

I had heard in seven wise cities
Of the last shape of his wisdom: when he,
Giver of winds, father as some said
Of the triple nightmare, from the mouth of a man
Would loose the much-whistled wind of prophecy.
The nothing into which a man leans forward
Is mother of all restiveness, drawing
The body prone to falling into no
Repose at last but the repose of falling.

Wherefore I had brought foot to his island
In the dead of dawn, had picked my way
Among the creaking cypresses, the anonymous
Granite sepulchres; wherefore, beyond these,
I seized him now by sleeping throat and heel.
What were my life, unless I might be stone
To grasp him like the grave, though wisdom change
From supposition to savage supposition;
Unless the rigor of mortal hands seemed deathly?

I was a sepulchre to his pleadings,
Stone to his arguments, to his threats;
When he leapt in a bull's rage
By horn and tail I held him; I became
A mad bull's shadow, and would not leave him;
As a battling ram he rose in my hands;
My arms were locked horns that would not leave his horns;
I was the cleft stick and the claws of birds
When he was a serpent between my fingers.

Wild as heaven erupting into a child
He burst under my fists into a lion;
By mane and foot I grappled him;
Closer to him than his own strength I strained
And held him longer. The sun had fought

Almost to noon when I felt the beast's sinews
Fail, the beast's bristles fall smooth
Again to the skin of a man. I loosed him then.
The head he turned toward me wore a face of mine.

Here was no wisdom but my own silence
Echoed as from a mirror; no marine
Oracular stare but my own eyes
Blinded and drowned in their reflections;
No voice came but a voice we shared, saying,
"You prevail always, but deathly, I am with you
Always." I am he, by grace of no wisdom,
Who to no end battles the foolish shapes
Of his own death by the insatiate sea.

Colloquy at Peniel

Countenance like lightning, why do you stand
In ebony raiment after no invocation
Suddenly where I knew no face, as though
You had stood so forever?

                              —Say that the light
That is today, after so long becomes me,
Or that love's pleading incense that rose once
For mercy pleads now no longer, whereupon
The air conceives new clarity, and there
Suddenly I am visible. But know
I was the urgency that framed that love
And made it cry for mercy, the question
And the voice of the woman whispering, "Be content,
Be content."
                    I am that which you lost
Behind you which you seek before you, for I
Am certain: sullen under your gaiety
And still its root and entrepreneur; footloose,
Not musical, but moving in all your music,

Assumed in all apostrophes.
                              Think of me
As of a dusk through which no herds go home,
Quiet, perhaps, yet inexcusably
Disquieting, with a voice of infinite patience,
Gentle until resisted, like sheep bells
In the next valley.
                    And I am he
With whom on a desperate hill, because I was
The closest combatant, always last night
You wrestled, as with the angel of your dark,
And overcame, yet in defeat who found
Such re-creation, always I rose with dawn
Enlarged by falling, as though I were the angel,
Equally, of your day. Yet one day
—Heaven and hills having endured—your arm,
Hopeless long since of conquest, will strike upon
Fatal surprise and end me there; and through
The evening slanting always at hand among
Unstartled trees, under a world of birds
Settling like dust despite the clang of triumph,
It will be your body that will fall.

December: Of Aphrodite

Whatever the books may say, or the plausible
Chroniclers intimate: that I was mad,
That an unsettling wind that season
Fretted my sign and fetched up violence
From the vagaries of dream, or even that pride
Is a broad road with few turnings, do not
Believe them. In her name I acted.

(Vidal once, the extravagant of heart,
For the love of a woman went mad, mad as a dog,
And the wolves ate him; Hercules, crazed
By that jealous goddess, murdered his children;

Samson, from a woman's lap, woke blinded,
Turning a mill in Gaza; Adam, our father,
Eating from his wife's hand, fell from the garden.)

Not that from heaven she twisted my tenderness
Into a hand of rage, nor because she delighted
In burnt offering, I in my five senses
Cut throats of friends, burned the white harvest, waged
Seven months' havoc even among
Her temples; but because she waited always
There in the elegant shell, asking for sweetness.

And though it was in her name the land was ravaged,
Spilled and dishonored, let it not be said
That by her wiles it was done, nor that she gave
That carnage her blessing. All arrogant demons
Pretending changelessness, who came first when she called,
Have faded and are spent, till out of the strong,
Without death, she conjured the honeycomb.

She sits at evening under a gray arch
Where many marvels fell, where all has fallen:
The blue over her dolphins, the poplar leaves,
The cold rain, all but the grave myrtle
And the rings of her ringdoves. The doge of one calendar
Would give her a name of winter, but where I stand
In the hazed gold of her eyes, the world is green.

Canso

Was there truly in that afternoon
No sorcery, when the leaves between us
In the October garden fell like words
Through the long sun before the gathering winter;
Was there no enchantment but your imputation?
I was a name inconstant; I had come,
Unlooked for, from the shifting sea, my face

A field for doubting, my tales untrustworthy;
You believed, and therewith I was credible.

And that stern evening, speaking of snares
Where the hunter had fallen, where even the wise might fall,
Or speaking, in November, of primroses,
When doubt possessed me, and my eyes fell
To stones, half trusting in stones, and my mind fell
To a merciless winter of bleak words, yet you
Beyond words believed me to be a gentle
Season, and I, as from sleep returning,
Was thence the sign and green wind of spring.

You are the tender hazel and diviner
Whose faith is delicacy; yet had you
Believed me anything but what I was
I should have come—still without violence
But gently as that legendary beast
The unicorn, who did not exist
Until conceived in the mind of a virgin—
Through the woods of change, and laid down my head
To fill the lap and hand of your supposition.

For you, by all the faiths in which we figure,
Are undeceivable: we are not ourselves
And I but a shadow in your superstition
Unless love be an imagination
Framing the single metaphor of coherence
In the dying riot of random generation,
Unless it be the passion of an order
Informs you so to this innocent
Authority, this peculiar knowledge.

And have you not become, by much believing,
Yourself the prime breath, the infusion of the real
Upon this dust? I walked incredible
As death, a gaunt preposterous ghost, until
Your creed included me among the living:
But not until I had, as from despair,

Abandoned claim to all the probable senses
And had become your trope and tenet merely,
Could I inherit the familiar body.

I am renewed as you imagine me,
For all the orders which love believes
Are the one order. There, listening, the child
In love with wonder, ascribing contradictions
To the different gesture of a heroic world,
Attributing the bruited failure
To an alien but more excellent mode
Of triumph, creates a possible
World for the impossible legionary.

There forlorn clown and painted masquer
Do not move in a demonstration merely,
Cynical, of the necessity of error,
But perform in ordered rage of jubilation,
And the eye in love with compassion believes
The figures of compassion: the mad girl
Mourning her father, the fretted prince delaying
Particular confusion till the confusion
Of death be absolute and general.

The idiom of order is celebration,
An elegance to redeem the graceless years;
So those the nine-years-enraged for a filched doxy
Who contend forever in the fanciful song
Are the real, and those who with tangible
Bronze fought are now the unbelievable dead,
Their speech inconceivable, their voyages in vain,
Their deeds inaccurate, save as they coincide
With the final tale, the saving celebration.

But you, believing, name a new paradigm
That existed, nonetheless, before
The hour of your believing: for the order
Is, although the place where it exist
Be nowhere but a possibility;

And your believing spins continually
Its own newness: as time continues
Out of the possibility of itself.
Time is a creature like the unicorn.

It is by your faith that I believe, I am.
Therein is genesis, as though a man,
In love with existence, should bring to belief
A divinity, an imagination
That might move upon the idea of nothing
And imagine a man; as though a man could make
A mirror out of his own divinity,
Wherein he might believe himself, and be.
So, in your articles, we love, you are.

And our hands are a shape of confidence,
A gesture of releasing, where joy is always
Young as its own beginning. Thus the falling
Water is confident and falls, thus summer
Confidently fails, and both are new
As often as they fall. Believing is
Conception, is without artifice the making
Perpetually new, is that first holy
Aura and ordinance of creation.

I have pronounced you the single luminary,
And we are housed in an embrace of whiteness,
But shadows would threaten and the dark descend
In all the rooms where we believe. O love,
Believe this candor indivisible,
That I, perfected in your love, may be,
Against all dissolution sovereign,
Endlessly your litany and mirror,
About your neck the amulet and song.

Canso

Must there be in the continuum and whorl
Of love always this whisper, on the tender
Horizon this supposition always,
A boreal shudder of feared light, a voice
That in my own voice cries to you, "Love, love,
Must you, in time more compromised than I,
In time be spoken from me, and I be left
To sit alone as it were forever,
Telling over the scandal that is time
In this dark room where the pictures hang
On the silence as though it were a wall?"

Or why should it be that we walk always
Slowly as though to lag long after time
And be alone there, that we perform
All of affection with a ceremony
Of more than patience, as though there were to be
Presently an end, or that I see you
Always, my eyes clear as on that day
When in fear of winter we watched the high ridge,
The tilted plain complacent in such summer,
Knowing we saw them for the last time, and love
Became itself a sense of leave-taking?

If you, if you my word and so my life
And so the mode and vessel of my death,
Should die before me, I would not go
—Although turned phantom by your truancy—
Calling the earth of you; neither, impelled
By what pain soever, with a zeal
As of an antiquarian, cull, compose
At last a vacancy of you and there become
An impresario of emptiness
Swaying before defection. What are the patterned
Potsherds to him who knows what wine there was?

It is not the comforts of a chiliast,
Nor of a mind mnemonic and apart
As an old man rocking in the doorway at

Irrelevant evening that I would wish to hear
Mumbling, "There was a world, there was, as it were,
A world wherein she walked once and was loved.
Is this, among worlds, not similar? And if
A tree wherein a throstle sang should lose
Not leaves but the bird only, would it not
Be, though without that singing, yet as green
As ever?" It would be the tree had died.

And what profit would there be to me then
In the lure of song, the twanged incantation,
Which on a time so played on savagery
With order, that the beasts came: phoenix and sow,
Cat, unicorn, chimera came, swimming
Through the incredibility of themselves
As through the air, to sit in a round,
To hear, to hear a wish? Unless they might
By virtue of the same order, as by love,
But changelessly, stand listening so forever
And there be real in the ultimate song.

Unless you also in that animal
Constraint of death having become
Incredible, might nevertheless by such
Enchantment, as once by love, but changelessly,
Be tamed out of that emptiness, and come
To stand again, as in flesh, in a place
Of possibility. Unless there be
Within the figure of mortality
This mind of heaven whereby I may
Fashion the lips and be as breath again
In the mouth in which you were a word.

Or may the mind of heaven be a mind
Of questions? As: Is there not a country
Or the negation of a country, where
The mortal tree where the bird sang, the season
Where you walked living, once existed only
In their own deaths before their tides and branches
Were from negation made? It is that world
That I would have wherein you might be loved,

And I would seek it in its own death, and shape
Its life out of your death, for it must be
Created out of the nothing that you are.

There must be found, then, the imagination
Before the names of things, the dicta for
The only poem, and among all dictions
That ceremony whereby you may be named
Perpetual out of the anonymity
Of death. I will make out of my grief
A river, and my rage shall be the coin
To catch its ferryman; out of my fear
A dog shall spring; I will fling my bitterness
To stop his throats. I will myself become
A Hades into which I can descend.

It will be a domain of déjà-vus,
The final most outlandish fastness of
Familiarity without memory,
Whose set dimensions, whose mode of privacy
And mode of pain I with my living breath
Shall enter, saying, "Like an Icarus
I have fallen into my shadow." There shall be seen
The death of the body walking in shapes of bodies,
Departure's self hid in a guise of sojourn,
As it seems among the living. But on those hills
The shadows of sheep are folded, not the sheep.

But on those lakes or the mirages of
Those lakes not birds are reflected but the flight
Of birds across no sky. It is nevertheless
A place of recognition, though it be
Of recognition of nothing; a place of knowledge
Though it be knowledge of nothing; in this land
No landscape but a demeanor of distance
Where interchangeably the poles are death
And death, as in an opposition of mirrors
Where no beginning is, no end, I have lived
Not recognizing, for as long as knowledge.

Say it is the idea of a place
That has no imagination of its own;
Yet in these nothing-fertile notions of
Valleys, this static nature in a mind
Of motion were all motion and all mind
And the actual lake moving its metaphor
Under real birds conceived, although conceived
Only for uses elsewhere. It is between
These twin antinomies that I must walk
Casting, it seems, no image; between these poles
Of vanity that I must make you real.

And say that even here, this place that I
Make in a shadow, though I cast no image,
Make even as I walk here, there must be
In a kingdom of mirrors a king among
Mirrors, although he be no more
Than that image I do not cast: as it were
An ear upon the infinite silence, a something
Sovereign, before whom in some manner
I can stand to dispute his sovereignty
As before a mirror, saying, "Master of these
Echoing revels whose silence I violate . . ."

Or better, to a genius more alien there,
A deeper shadow more sorrowfully reposed,
Folded almost in memory, but sconced
In the necessity of that kingdom
As in an ancient throne, Persephone,
To say, "O Moon among such sanity,
O Other among the simulacra, Virgin
Madonna of the lap of sleep, conceiving
All flesh and holiness, I come to you calling,
Making you in a prayer, that your name
May know my voice and conceive a mercy."

Take it for answer when the hair lifts
There in no wind as in an insolence
Of wind: it is the self of highness in
That hollow, counterpart and partisan

Born of the argument, who listens. "Mistress,
I speak what you know: where the shadows were real
I loved a lady. Be not surprised
Now if I stand beyond lamentations, fictive
In places prepared for loss: save where she is
I am anomaly. O Name, what is her name
In anonymity, that I may call

"And she be with me? For what is your Lord
Of Anonymity, Lord of Nothing
And Nowhere, if I know his name?
Unless he be also furtively somewhere
A lord of names? Mistress, what is your
Arrogant Chief Jack of Death but a hollow
Tale, my figment, nothing at all, unless
He be somewhere alive, alive? Tell him
That I who cast no shadow taunt him there
With the bogey of his name. How would he be
Death if I should imagine him otherwise?

"Or rather, let me not be told her name
In death, for with such appellation
If I should call it would be in the attributes
Of death that she would come, and I am not used
To such reserves between us. But now, should I
Pronounce her as though she were alive,
Say it is a new word I make: not new
Merely for what the old words would not cover,
But an affirmation of what heretofore
Had not been so; let what has never been,
Suddenly, in terms of what is, be.

"For I am instructed of this silence, Lady,
That what is not is of a nature
With what has never been; and Mention, though
It be the scholiast of memory,
Makes yet its presences from emptiness,
Speaks for the first time always, an improvisation,
Though in an ancient mode, a paradigm
For the unmentionable. Yet may the word

Be celebration of a permanence,
Make, so, a presence and a permanence,
The articulate dance, the turning festival."

"Creation," she says, "is your idea, then?"
"Lady, you know. Creation waits upon
The word; but you in silence are the conception
And the consent of speech, the metaphor
In the midst of chaos, whose word is love.
And though I would in her name shatter, drown
The clamorous dialectic of this silence
With irrefutable song, and though I had
Imagination to remove mountains
Out of their shadows, and did not have this love,
I were a vain instrument; I were nothing."

There in her shadow, voice in a gown of silence,
She says, "I, though I be the predicate
Of love, the image in the blather of death
To make that monotone intelligible
To itself, am yet this image in the blather
And terms of death, whose parlance will not be
By its own intelligibility gainsaid.
Creation," she says, "is perforce and always
The creation of a world, the world; it is
An infinite nature making infinite nature,
But death exacts therefor an infinite price.

"What if, by uttering the terms of living
Upon this mortuary air, your head
Should become anomalous on your body
And neither be satisfied, but both walk, strange,
Fictive, among real familiars, or
Real but immortal among the figurative
But dying; or, undelighted by what fades,
Alien, unbelieving, unbelieved,
Live in a heart of celebration only?"
"If the terms stand, so be it. There in her
Living intimacy I am not foreign."

"There must be, before creation is,
A concept of beginnings, a notion
As of a rocking cradle not yet rocking
Where yet no cradle is: therein may time
The prodigy impossibly conceived
Upon itself, born of itself and still
Unborn, be laid, the sage, the quiet child
Conceiving timelessness." "I imagine
A song not temporal wherein may walk
The animals of time; I conceive a moment
In which time and that timelessness begin."

Creation is not raw, is not refined.
In a landscape of raw antecedent
Before belief, or a country refined
Beyond belief, without motion, without
Farewells, to which one does not say good-bye,
I, conceiving of creation, have
Conceived the novelty of farewell. I said,
"Let it be a time the sand whereof
May run somewhere besides away, may run
Nowhere perhaps at all. A time that lies
Immutable under eternal leaves."

And I therewith am already elsewhere
In a littoral not time's, though time has been
Godfather there and blessing, an ambit
As though of memory, but not memory's,
Where with a word I divide the literal
From the dead. Why should I notice the waters
Sundering from the waters, or suddenly
The first tree waving ancient fronds, or how
From novel shadows the new beasts come, the savage
Modulations of holiness, in love's name
Where other names are profanation?

For it is you that are the world thereof,
You whom, possessing, I have still desired,
And touching, have still dreamed of; you the sense,
The echo there waiting upon this word,

The circle making all within it real,
The sole order; for I have painfully
Wrought you from vacancy to this full air
And sung you to the tender instrument
Of my ten fingers till you have become
The poem in whose arbor we may kiss,
The summer into which we can ascend.

You know the story, its denouement. You know
Death is by definition a terrain
Of no return save to itself, where all
Appearances are voices calling, "Look
Now, oh, look if now only"; is a face whereon
To look is to know loss; and what if I
Should turn but once, and you vanish? The song is nothing
If not a resurrection. Therein I sing you,
Love, always more real, though in the fraying
Edges of patience the teased harpies
Hone the incredible silence against their tongues.

Canso

I believe at dark solstice in the white moon sailing new;
And in my love, and in her hand, though the green shoot
      withered,
And in the twice-joining sea between us, and I believe
I lay long with the cold dead, although the word was summer,
The violent dead, and now
When the sun hangs in the low branches
Bleeding, and phoenix-like the white-feathered
Childish sibyl sings in the leaves of the dead year,
And northerly on another island
She smiles into the swirling mist, her trees
Half-sleeved in white, I believe
Resurrection stirs like the robin
Through the waters of the dead, and the buried blood,
Through the rain of two islands
To float like a lotus into the waking year

And stand wide-eyed like a lamb; I believe the dead
Mirrors of the sea shine soft with her new image always.

She is clear amber and the heaven's face
Seen under simple waters: there below
The lights, the vessels, the shore, the drift-shells stroking
The whipped weeds of the tide-race,
Under the fish flying and the laughter of her dolphins,
First cold, final echoes, and the salt dead, she is marine
And always the child among horses
At autumn by the dove-keep,
And the woman in tears in the green
Drowned wood in no time by the lost house on the slow
River, and always she is ancient as the sea's daughters,
As the green beginning; always the rites of her tides keen
Tender in my ears, her birds call me fair, her twining hands
Run gentle to my hands for honey, her lips bid me love
Her limbs in coral and the bursts of her dolphins
Always, the softness of her sea-changes
And the pride of her horses.

And there where the spume flies and the mews echoed and
    beckoned
The bowing drowned, because in her hands love and the one
    song
Leap and the long faith is born gladly, there through the waters
Of the dead, like the robin, singing, like the floating year,
The deep world in one island,
Streaming white from every dark-folded
Valley, till the green burgeons, and the long
Ghosts dripping leave the washed gold and the mounding joy,
The fruit swaying yellow, the shimmering birches
And the wise beaches lapped with the serpents and dead
Of the forgiving waters,
There, across green the gold light hanging,
The bees in the rosemary, the flashing pigeons,
Bud and harvest together,
The world in one island, because her hands are joy,
To no trumpet, all tongues singing the full silence,
Rises now and forever to gleam new as the white sea.

(Who sings now of the desperate seas, the bleak
Voyages by darkness, when the wind fell,
When the shadow waxed between us, and hails faded
And oar-sounds, when the last streak
Of the other lantern dwindled, and groped wakes, one by one
Ended in nothing, when separately we sailed seeking
By the four points and the foreign stars
Falling that may guide no man,
The treasure, the landfall, the morning,
Gray ease after night-fear, after shoal and cold swell
The harbor of one hand? Who sings, after the black
    whale-beds,
Tideless, and nautilus-marches, of the poles, the towers
Where we came each alone, of the widdershins wheels turning
By blue flames, where we lay dead in the grave's waters,
    though all
The world was summer? For the seven seas are one,
The four winds, and all journeys and treasures
And islands, and the sung stars.)

Here is the gate of psalms, swordless, and the angel's country
For which we became as children; known earth and known
    heaven
Washed new in the ancient wonder; here in the high pastures,
Its roots in another story, offering innocence
Like apples, is the same tree;
Under the leaves and holy shadows
The same brightness springs where the stones begin
Laughter and green singing in the ancient rivers
And the new hours like the first shallows run;
There beyond pools and sheep bells where the dark browses
Already the gold pastures,
Are hushed grass and the bell of silence,
The silk-gray dusk, the mackerel sky for the moonrise,
Then the same moon riding new
Over the fields, the lulled falling of four rivers
And the praising hills and white leaves of paradise,
And swimming silver across the eyes and in the same sea.

Nightingales will sleep in the sycamores
Till there is no night; here will not the dark
Worm come with his sliding season, though the leaves fall,
Nor the snake in the small hours
Molest the young doves and thrushes with the snare of his
　　hands
Nor sicken the drowsing fruit with the shadow of his tongue,
Nor chains nor temptations, till the end
Of time, nor any serpent,
Save the long tides, till the sea return.
She is clear amber, and the dawn found in the dark
By faith at last, by following sea-sounds, by the lost
Shells' singing, and like the sea she walks always beside me
Telling, and the warm deeps of her waters are never sung
Where, amid fathomless musics subtle beneath voices,
Softly she draws me down with her whispers and hands,
Her floods and eyes, face-to-face, telling me
Her white love, world without end.

Now, now I enter the first garden and the promised moon,
The silver of her thighs and shoulders; oh, here where the
　　sheaves
And shadows sway to her breath, in the caroling darkness
We embrace at last, and are night and morning together
And the gray-gold afternoon
Of marvels sinking over the hill
And the first and last tree; and all the leaves
Of our deaths are chanting, "Holy, holy, holy
Always were taper-light and ember-light,
Moonlight, the bowing stars, and that first glory still
Singing day from the darkness;
And never, save unto our amen,
Shall the white sea surrender its dead, oh never,
Oh never. Amen. Amen."
We listen, and shall here, love, with the sea's holy
Song in the shells of our ears, lie down forever
To sleep in the turning garden for as long as the sea.

GREEN WITH BEASTS

(1956)

To Dido

With dumb belongings there can be
The gesture that bestows, for its own reasons;
Its mumbled inadequacy reminds us always
In this world how little can be communicated.
And for these, they too are only tokens
Of what there is no word for: their worth
Is a breath or nothing, and the spirit who can convey?
I have doubts whether such things can be dedicated.
They themselves determine whose they are,
Announcing unbidden their conception
In a still place of perpetual surprise.
Can one offer things that know their own way
And will not be denied? These were bodied forth
In the country of your love: what other
Landscapes they may name, from that place
Is their language. In the cadences of that tongue
They learned what they are. How more can I make them yours?

PART ONE

Physiologus: Chapters for a Bestiary

Leviathan

This is the black sea-brute bulling through wave-wrack,
Ancient as ocean's shifting hills, who in sea-toils
Traveling, who furrowing the salt acres
Heavily, his wake hoary behind him,
Shoulders spouting, the fist of his forehead
Over wastes gray-green crashing, among horses unbroken
From bellowing fields, past bone-wreck of vessels,
Tide-ruin, wash of lost bodies bobbing
No longer sought for, and islands of ice gleaming,
Who ravening the rank flood, wave-marshaling,
Overmastering the dark sea-marches, finds home
And harvest. Frightening to foolhardiest
Mariners, his size were difficult to describe:
The hulk of him is like hills heaving,
Dark, yet as crags of drift-ice, crowns cracking in thunder,
Like land's self by night black-looming, surf churning and
     trailing
Along his shores' rushing, shoal-water boding
About the dark of his jaws; and who should moor at his edge
And fare on afoot would find gates of no gardens,
But the hill of dark underfoot diving,
Closing overhead, the cold deep, and drowning.
He is called Leviathan, and named for rolling,
First created he was of all creatures,
He has held Jonah three days and nights,
He is that curling serpent that in ocean is,
Sea-fright he is, and the shadow under the earth.
Days there are, nonetheless, when he lies
Like an angel, although a lost angel
On the waste's unease, no eye of man moving,
Bird hovering, fish flashing, creature whatever
Who after him came to herit earth's emptiness.
Froth at flanks seething soothes to stillness,
Waits; with one eye he watches
Dark of night sinking last, with one eye dayrise
As at first over foaming pastures. He makes no cry
Though that light is a breath. The sea curling,

Star-climbed, wind-combed, cumbered with itself still
As at first it was, is the hand not yet contented
Of the Creator. And he waits for the world to begin.

Blue Cockerel

Morning was never here, nor more dark ever
Than now there is; but in the fixed green
And high branch of afternoon, this bird balances,
His blue feet splayed, folding nothing, as though
The too-small green limb were ground; and his shout
Frames all the silence. Not Montezuma nor all
The gold hills of the sun were ever so plumed
As the blue of his neck, his breast's orange, his wings'
Blazing, and the black-green sickles of his tail.
It seems to be summer. But save for his blue hackles
And the light haze of his back, there is no sky,
Only the one tree spreading its green flame
Like a new habit for heaven. It seems to be summer;
But on the single tree the fruits of all seasons
Hang in the hues of ripeness; but on the ground
The green is of spring, and the flowers
Of April are there. And he suspended, brilliant and foreign,
His wings as though beating the air of elsewhere,
Yet if he is not there, the rest is not either.
A cry must be painted silent: the spread red hand
Of his comb thrown back, beak wide, and the one eye
Glaring like the sun's self (for there is no other),
Like the sun seen small, seen rimmed in red secret,
May be the shape of jubilation crowing,
Or the stare and shriek of terror. And whose body
Is this in the foreground lying twisted sideways,
Eyes glazed, whose stiff posture would become
The contorted dead? Though its face gleams white
It might be the self of shadow we have not seen,
Night who was never here, or the hour itself
There to be sung unmoved. Surely it is
The eye's other center, and upon this,

This only, the bird stares, and for this cause
Cries, cries, and his cry crashes
Among the branches, the blades of great leaves
Looming like towers, the fruits and petals, green
Thickets of light deeper than shadows, the moon-white
Ears of that body lying, and makes
And lends echo and moment to all that green
Watery silence. But does he scream
In joy unfading that now no dark is,
Or what wakening does he herald with all terror?

Two Horses

Oh, in whose grove have we wakened, the bees
Still droning under the carved wall, the fountain playing
Softly to itself, and the gold light, muted,
Moving long over the olives; and whose,
Stamping the shadowy grass at the end of the garden,
Are these two wild horses tethered improbably
To the withes of a young quince? No rider
Is to be seen; they bear neither saddle nor bridle;
Their brute hooves splash the knee-high green
Without sound, and their flexed tails like flags float,
Whipping, their brows down like bulls. Yet the small tree
Is not shaken; and the broken arches
Of their necks in the dim air are silent
As the doorways of ruins. Birds flit in the garden:
Jay and oriole, blades in the hanging shadows,
Small cries confused. And dawn would be eastward
Over the dark neck, a red mane tossed high
Like flame, and the dust brightening along the wall.
These have come up from Egypt, from the dawn countries,
Syria, and the land between the rivers,
Have ridden at the beaks of vessels, by Troy neighed,
And along the valley of the Danube, and to Etruria;
And all dust was of their making; and passion
Under their hooves puffed into flight like a sparrow
And died down when they departed. The haze of summer

Blows south over the garden terraces,
Vague through the afternoon, remembering rain;
But in the night green with beasts as April with grass
Orion would hunt high from southward, over the hill,
And the blood of beasts herald morning. Where these have
   passed,
Tramping white roads, their ears drinking the sword-crash,
The chariots are broken, bright battle-cars
Shambles under earth; whether by sharp bronze
Or the years' ebbing, all blood has flowed into the ground;
There was wailing at sundown, mourning for kings,
Weeping of widows, but these went faint, were forgotten,
And the columns have fallen like shadows. Crickets
Sing under the stones; and beyond the carved wall
Westward, fires drifting in darkness like the tails
Of jackals flaring, no hounds heard at their hunting,
Float outward into the dark. And these horses stamp
Before us now in this garden; and northward
Beyond the terraces the misted sea
Swirls endless, hooves of the gray wind forever
Thundering, churning the ragged spume-dusk
High that there be no horizons nor stars, and there
Are white islands riding, ghost-guarded, twisted waves flashing,
Porpoises plunging like the necks of horses.

Dog

He does not look fierce at all, propped scarcely erect
On skinny forelegs in the dust in the glare
In the dog-day heat, the small brown pariah at the edge
Of the shimmering vista of emptiness
Unbroken by any shade and seeming too permanent
To be of any day the afternoon.
Under the sky no color or rather
The natural beige, dust-color, merely
A brighter glare than the ground, beginning
Where the dust does not leave off, and rising
Through the shining distance that weighs and waves

Like water he does not have the air at all
Of vigilance: hindquarters collapsed
Under him like a rag lying shapeless
In the shrunk puddle of his shadow, coat
Caked and staring, hangdog head
That his shoulders can hardly hold up from the dust
And from it dangling the faded tongue, the one
Color to be seen. *Cave canem*; beware
The dog. But he squats harmless,
At his wildest, it might be, wishing that the feeble
Green cast the glare gives to his shadow
Could be green in truth, or be at least a wider
Shadow of some true green; and though he is
Free not tethered (but what in this place
Could one be free of if not the place) surely
He would never attack, nor move except perhaps,
Startled, to flee; surely those dirty tufts
Of coarse hair at his shoulders could never rise
Hostile in hackles, and he has forgotten
Long since the wish to growl; or if he should bare
His teeth it would not be with a lifting
Of lips but with a letting-fall, as it is
With the grins of the dead. And indeed what is there here
That he might keep watch over? The dust? The empty
Distance, the insufferable light losing itself
In its own glare? Whatever he was to guard
Is gone. Besides, his glazed eyes
Fixed heavily ahead stare beyond you
Noticing nothing; he does not see you. But wrong:
Look again: it is through you
That he looks, and the danger of his eyes
Is that in them you are not there. He guards indeed
What is gone, what is gone, what has left not so much
As a bone before him, which vigilance needs
No fierceness, and his weariness is not
From the length of his watch, which is endless,
But because nothing, not the weight of days
Not hope, the canicular heat, the dust, nor the mortal
Sky, is to be borne. Approach
If you dare, but doing so you take

In your hands what life is yours, which is less
Than you suppose, for he guards all that is gone,
And even the shimmer of the heated present,
Of the moment before him in which you stand
Is a ghost's shimmer, its past gone out of it, biding
But momently his vigil. Walk past him
If you please, unmolested, but behind his eyes
You will be seen not to be there, in the glaring
Uncharactered reaches of oblivion, and guarded
With the rest of vacancy. Better turn from him
Now when you can and pray that the dust you stand in
And your other darlings be delivered
From the vain distance he is the power of.

White Goat, White Ram

The gaiety of three winds is a game of green
Shining, of gray-and-gold play in the holly bush
Among the rocks on the hillside, and if ever
The earth was shaken, say a moment ago
Or whenever it came to be, only the leaves and the spread
Sea still betray it, trembling; and their tale betides
The faintest of small voices, almost still.
A road winds among the gray rocks, over the hill,
Arrives from out of sight, from nowhere we know,
Of an uncertain color; and she stands at the side
Nearer the sea, not far from the brink, legs straddled wide
Over the swinging udder, her back and belly
Slung like a camp of hammocks, her head raised,
The narrow jaw grinding sideways, ears flapping sideways,
Eyes wide apart like the two moons of Mars
At their opposing. So broadly is she blind
Who has no names to see with: over her shoulder
She sees not summer, not the idea of summer,
But green meanings, shadows, the gold light of now, familiar,
The sense of long day-warmth, of sparse grass in the open
Game of the winds; an air that is plenitude,
Describing itself in no name; all known before,

Perceived many times before, yet not
Remembered, or at most felt as usual. Even the kids,
Grown now and gone, are forgotten,
As though by habit. And he on the other side
Of the road, hooves braced among spurge and asphodel,
Tears the gray grass at its roots, his massive horns
Tossing delicately, as by long habit, as by
Habit learned, or without other knowledge
And without question inherited, or found
As first he found the air, the first daylight, first milk at the tetter,
The paths, the pen, the seasons. They are white, these two,
As we should say those are white who remember nothing,
And we for our uses call that innocence,
So that our gracelessness may have the back of a goat
To ride away upon; so that when our supreme gesture
Of propitiation has obediently been raised
It may be the thicket-snared ram that dies instead of the son;
So even that we may frame the sense that is now
Into a starred figure of last things, of our own
End, and there by these beasts know ourselves
One from another: some to stay in the safety
Of the rock, but many on the other hand
To be dashed over the perilous brink. There is no need
Even that they should be gentle, for us to use them
To signify gentleness, for us to lift them as a sign
Invoking gentleness, conjuring by their shapes
The shape of our desire, which without them would remain
Without a form and nameless. For our uses
Also are a dumbness, a mystery,
Which like a habit stretches ahead of us
And was here before us; so, again, we use these
To designate what was before us, since we cannot
See it in itself, for who can recognize
And call by true names, familiarly, the place
Where before this he was, though for nine months
Or the world's full age he housed there? Yet it seems
That by such a road, arriving from out of sight,
From nowhere we know, we may have come, and these
Figure as shapes we may have been. Only, to them
The road is less than a road, though it divides them,

A bit of flat space merely, perhaps not even
A thing that leads elsewhere, except when they
Are driven along it, for direction is to them
The paths their own preference and kinds have made
And follow: routes through no convenience
And world of ours, but through their own sense
And mystery. Mark this; for though they assume
Now the awkward postures of illustrations
For all our parables, yet the mystery they stand in
Is still as far from what they signify
As from the mystery we stand in. It is the sign
We make of them, not they, that speaks from their dumbness
That our dumbness may speak. There in the thin grass
A few feet away they browse beyond words; for a mystery
Is that for which we have not yet received
Or made the name, the terms, that may enclose
And call it. And by virtue of such we stand beyond
Earthquake and wind and burning, and all the uncovenanted
Terror of becoming, and beyond the small voice; and on
Another hand, as it were, a little above us
There are the angels. We are dumb before them, and move
In a different mystery; but there may be
Another road we do not see as a road; straight, narrow,
Or broad or the sector of a circle, or perhaps
All these, where without knowing it we stand
On one side or another? I have known such a way
But at moments only, and when it seemed I was driven
Along it, and along no other that my preference
Or kind had made. And of these others above us
We know only the whisper of an elusive sense,
Infrequent meanings and shadows, analogies
With light and the beating of wings. Yet now, perhaps only
A few feet away in the shaking leaves they wait
Beyond our words, beyond earthquake, whirlwind, fire,
And all the uncovenanted terror of becoming,
And beyond the small voice. Oh, we cannot know and we are
    not
What we signify, but in what sign
May we be innocent, for out of our dumbness
We would speak for them, give speech to the mute tongues

Of angels. Listen: more than the sea's thunder
Foregathers in the gray cliffs; the roots of our hair
Stir like the leaves of the holly bush where now
Not games the wind ponders but impatient
Glories, fire: and we go stricken suddenly
Humble, and the covering of our feet
Offends, for the ground where we find we stand is holy.

PART TWO

The Bathers

They make in the twining tide the motions of birds.
Such are the cries, also, they exchange
In their nakedness that is soft as a bird's
Held in the hand, and as fragile and strange.

And the blue mirror entertains them till they take
The sea for another bird: the crumbling
Hush-hush where the gentlest of waves break
About their voices would be his bright feathers blowing.

Only the dull shore refrains. But from this patient
Bird each, in the plumage of his choice,
Might learn the deep shapes and secret of flight

And the shore be merely a perch to which they might
Return. And the mirror turns serpent
And their only sun is swallowed up like a voice.

The Wilderness

Remoteness is its own secret. Not holiness,
Though, nor the huge spirit miraculously avoiding
The way's dissemblings, and undue distraction or drowning
At the watercourse, has found us this place,

But merely surviving all that is not here,
Till the moment that looks up, almost by chance, and sees
Perhaps hand, feet, but not ourselves; a few stunted juniper trees
And the horizon's virginity. We are where we always were.

The secret becomes no less itself for our presence
In the midst of it; as the lizard's gold-eyed
Mystery is no more lucid for being near.

And famine is all about us, but not here;
For from the very hunger to look, we feed
Unawares, as at the beaks of ravens.

The Wakening

Looking up at last from the first sleep
Of necessity rather than of pure delight
While his dreams still rode and lapped like the morning light
That everywhere in the world shimmered and lay deep

So that his sight was half-dimmed with its dazzling, he could
    see
Her standing naked in the day-shallows there,
Face turned away, hands lost in her bright hair;
And he saw then that her shadow was the tree:

For in a place where he could never come
Only its darkness underlay the day's splendor,
So that even as she stood there it must reach down

Through not roots but branches with dark birdsong, into a
    stream
Of silence like a sky but deeper
Than this light or than any remembered heaven.

The Prodigal Son

for Leueen MacGrath Kaufman

I

Except for the flies, except that there is not water
Enough for miles to make a mirror, the face
Of the afternoon might seem an empty lake,
Still, shining, burnished beyond the semblance
Of water until the semblance of afternoon
Was all the surface that shimmered there, even
The dust shining and hanging still, the dusty
Carob trees and olives gleaming, all hung
Untouchable and perfect, as in its own
Mirage. Or else the afternoon, the shapes
So still in the heat, and burnished, in such intensity
Of shining stillness, seem other than themselves,

Seem fragments and faces half-seen through their own
Glare, shaping another life, another
Lifelessness that mirrors this as might
Its own mirage. Except for the flies. There
Where the far hills seem the sheen of a dusty hanging
Hovering like a breath just out of reach
The slack tents of the herders lean, and the flocks
Lie motionless under the trees, the men
Not moving, lying among them. And between
There and the ruled shade of this white wall
There is nothing: distance is dead, unless
It is in distance that the flies hum.

II

And the silence off on the hills might be an echo
Of the silence here in the shadow of the white wall
Where the old man sits brooding upon distance,
Upon emptiness. His house behind him,
The white roofs flat and domed, hushed with the heat
And the hour, and making what it can of shadow
While no one stirs, is it in fact the same
In which lifelong he has believed and filled
With life, almost as a larger body, or is it,
Now suddenly in this moment between mirage
And afternoon, another, and farther off
Than the herdsmen, oh, much farther, its walls glaring
White out of a different distance, deceiving
By seeming familiar, but an image merely
By which he may know the face of emptiness,
A name with which to say emptiness? Yet it is the same
Where he performs as ever the day's labor,
The gestures of pleasure, as is necessary,
Speaks in the name of order, and is obeyed
Among his sons, except one, except the one
Who took his portion and went. There is no distance
Between himself now and emptiness; he has followed
The departing image of a son beyond
Distance into emptiness. The flies crawl
Unnoticed over his face, through his drooping
Beard, along his hands lying loose as his beard,

Lying in his lap like drying leaves; and before him
The smeared stalls of the beasts, the hens in the shade,
The water-crane still at the wellhead, the parched
Fields that are his as far as the herdsmen
Are emptiness in his vacant eyes.

III

                               But distance,
He remembers, was not born at a son's departure
Nor died with his disappearance; and he recognizes
That emptiness had lodged with him before,
Lived with him in fact always, but humbly,
In corners, under different names, showing
Its face but seldom, and then had been for the most part
Ignored. And now at the loss of one son
Only when all else remains, not fearful
For the sake of what remains, but for the love, simply,
Of what is lost (unto this has been likened
The kingdom of heaven) he sits in the afternoon
Of vacancy, by license of vacancy,
For emptiness is lord of his hollow house,
Sits at his side at table, devouring,
Shows him from room to room, for all faces
Of loss, the known and the foreboded, all
Figments of fear and grieving, the new
And the remembered, are swollen and grown
To insolent possession there, feed
At home on all the limbs of his life, fix and focus
Their image there on the dying in distance
Of distance, on dying by distances,
On that one departure, as on the empty frame
Of the door the son went out by.

IV

                              He went out by that door
Eagerly, not lingering to look back,
Bearing with him all that could be carried
Of his inheritance, since he was of an age
To take what was his and leave, and his father
Gave him his portion, who would not willingly

Have had him lack for anything, not even
For the distance beyond his doors. He went out
Looking for something his father had not given,
Delights abroad, some foreign ease, something
Vague because distant, which he must give
Himself, something indeed which he carried,
Unknowing, already with him; or, say, an ampler
Body, an assured content, something
Which, unknowing, he was leaving behind, yet
Which he had to leave to be able to find. And wasted
His substance in wild experiment and found
Emptiness only, found nothing in distance,
Sits finally in a sty and broods
Upon emptiness, upon distance.
                                        Except
For the flies hovering and crawling before
His eyes, insisting that the afternoon
He sees is there, the dusty grass, the unholy
Swine, the shared husks, the shared hut shining
Like brass in the oddest places might be a mirage
Merely in which he had no part, a strange
Vista made of familiar pieces caught
In an odd light in a mirror, an image
Of emptiness out of a restive daydream
Gone wrong at home; unreal, if he could turn
The mirror, open his eyes. And all between
This hour and corner where he sits and his father's
Door that day when he walked away, surely
Is unreal, a picture in which he has no part,
Leading to this—the loud junketings, the women,
The silks, columns, the intricate pleasure
Of generosity; his mind turns among
Those vacancies as a mirror hung by a string
In a ruin. Distance might be dead
Except for the flies, and instead of the emptiness
On which he stares, the backs of the sleeping swine
Might be the far hills beyond the hens,
Beyond the hushed water-crane and the fields
By his father's house; the shade where he sits
Be the ruled shadow of the white wall, or at least

He might be lying just out of reach under
A tree among the herders; oh, except
For the flies' insistence, the sty must be
A heap of ashes, and the swineherd's fouled garment
Sackcloth.

V

            So in the empty frame of an old man's
Mind the figments of afternoon
Wait between a substance that is not theirs
And an illusion that is another's: the herders
Wait on the hills, the dusty olives, the fields,
Well-crane and white walls are a held
Breath waiting; and the dozing calf
Fattens and waits, the other sons asleep
With their wives in complacent dreams
Wait in emptiness and do not know
That it is emptiness, that they are waiting,
That the flies are wrong and hover in nothing,
That distance is dead, that in the same mirage
Nearer than the flies or the herders, the lost son,
Hesitant, stumbling among the swine (unto this
Has been likened the kingdom of heaven), hoping
For little, takes the first step toward home.

The Annunciation

It was not night, not even when the darkness came
That came blacker than any night, and more fearful,
Like a bell beating and I under its darkness dying
To the stun of the sound. Before that
It was not dark nor loud nor any way strange,
Just the empty kitchen, with the smell of the bean-flowers,
In their late blossom, coming in at the window,
And the stillness, just that empty hour of the afternoon
            When it is hard indeed to believe in time.

When the young grass sleeps white in the sun, and the tree's
    shadow
Lies so still on the small stone by the doorway
You would think the stone was only a shadow
Rounded, and nothing beneath, and the air
Forgets to move, forgets, and you can hear a humming,
It is like a humming, but it is not a sound
But the edges of the silence whirring
To tell you how deep the silence is. When, even
Though it is spring, and the coldness of winter
And the coldness of morning still under the air,
If you do not think, you can feel already
The turned summer, the daze, the dryness,
                    The light heavy in the air.

So that time is hard to believe, but it is with you
More than ever, for you can feel the stillness
Rushing more sudden than ever, in the open day
More secret than ever, and farther and harder
To understand, and all so still. And I was thinking,
Can it be true, like the stone under the shadow;
Can it be true? And thinking how they tell
That a woman is for a man, and that from a man
She learns many things and can make names for them
That, before, she was empty of. And of this man
That will take me as a woman, and he is a good man.
And yet thinking how men and women, even
Together in their understanding, are lost
In that secret, and the names they made. And sometimes
You can stand in that emptiness till you are thinking
Of nothing, and it sounds as though a kind
Of joy began whirring at the edge of that sadness,
Like a sudden peace that was there, but it is not whirring
It is so still, but you are drawn out on it
Till you are empty as the hushed hour,
                    And there is no word for it all.

That was the way it was, and in the fragrant light
That came in at the window, I was standing
Still, that way, seeing nothing but the light,

As though I were gliding out on the peaceful light
Like water; and what I was, in myself
I was nothing. And had even forgotten whatever
I should have been doing; only in my two hands
I was holding a cup, I remember, the kind
You would measure flour or drink water in,
But wherever I was going with it, and why,
I had stopped and forgotten, because of the secret
Way of the stillness, and myself, and the light,
So that now, the reason why I was holding
That cup in my hands is one of the things I cannot
                    Remember nor understand.

Then the darkness began: it brushed
Just lightly first, as though it might be the wing
Of a bird, a soft bird, that flutters,
As it comes down. It brushed the hem of the light
And in my eyes, where I was nothing. But grew
Clouding between my eyes and the light
And rushing upon me, the way the shadow
Of a cloud will rush over the sunned fields
In a time of wind; and the black coming down
In its greatness, between my eyes and the light,
Was like wings growing, and the blackness
Of their shadow growing as they came down
Whirring and beating, cold and like thunder, until
All the light was gone, and only that noise
And terrible darkness, making everything shake
As though the end of it was come, and there was
No word for it, And I thought, Lord, Lord, and thought
How if I had not gone out on the light
And been hidden away on the vanished light
So that myself I was empty and nothing
I would surely have died, because the thing
That the darkness was, and the wings and the shaking,
That there was no word for it, was a thing that in myself
I could not have borne and lived. And still came
Nearer and darker, beating, and there was
A whisper in the feathers there, in the wings'
Great wind, like a whirring of words, but I could not

Say the shape of them, and it came to me
They were like a man, but none has yet come to me,
And I could not say how. Only, in the place
Where, myself, I was nothing, there was suddenly
A great burning under the darkness, a fire
Like fighting up into the wings' lash and the beating
Blackness, and flames like the tearing of teeth,
With noise like rocks rending, such that no word
Can call it as it was there, and for fire only,
Without the darkness beating and the wind, had I
Been there, had I not been far on the hiding light
I could not have borne it and lived. And then the stillness:
The wings giving way all at once, and the fire quiet
Leaving neither day nor darkness, but only the silence
That closed like a last clap of the thunder
And was perfect. And the light lying beyond, like a ring,
And the things in it lying, and everything still
With no moving at all, and no pulse, nor any breath,
And no rushing in that stillness, for time was not there,
Nor the emptiness, the way time falls into emptiness,
But only fullness, as though it were forever,
As though it were everything from the beginning and always,
In itself and still, and not even waiting,
Because it was there. And in the silence
And in the fullness it came, it was there
As though it had not come but was there, whatever it was
          That above all I cannot name.

Though in itself it was like a word, and it was
Like no man and no word that ever was known,
Come where I was; and because I was nothing
It could be there. It was a word for
The way the light and the things in the light
Were looking into the darkness, and the darkness
And the things of the darkness were looking into the light
In the fullness, and the way the silence
Was hearing, as though it was hearing a great song
And the song was hearing the silence forever
And forever and ever. And I knew the name for it;
There in the place where I was nothing in

The fullness, I knew it, and held it and knew
The way of it, and the word for how it was one,
I held it, and the word for why. Or almost,
Or believed I knew it, believed, like an echo
That when it comes you believe you know
The word, while it rings, but when it is gone
You had not learned it, and cannot find it, even
Though the sound still breathes in your ear. Because
Then the light looked away from the darkness
Again, and the song slid into the silence
And was lost again, and the fullness rose, going,
And the sound of its going was the sound of wings
Rushing away in darkness, and the sound
That came after them was the stillness rushing
Again, and time sudden and hard to believe,
And forever was emptiness again, where time fell,
And I was standing there in myself, in the light,
With only the shape of the word that is wonder,
                    And that same cup still in my hands.

And I could not say how long it had been
That I had stood there forever, while the end
Looked into the beginning, and they were one
And the word for one. Because the shadow
Had not changed on the stone, and nothing had moved
In all that time, if it was in time at all,
Because nothing had changed. But I did not doubt
For the wonder that was in me, quickening,
As in your ear the shape of a sound
When the sound is gone. And because when
At last I moved my hand, slowly, slowly,
As though it could not believe, to touch myself, to see
If it could be true, if I had truly come back
From the light, and touched myself like something
Hard to believe, I knew I was not the same
And could not say how. Then a long time I stood there
Pondering the way of it in my heart, and how
                    The coming of it was a blessing.

Afterward, though, there was the emptiness
And not as it was before: not drifting
About the place where I stood, like the afternoon
Light and the smell of the bean-flowers, but as though
There was emptiness only, and the great falling
And nothing besides, and it was all inside me
In the place where I had been nothing: the stillness
Rushing, and time not hard to believe then
But undeniable in the pain of its falling,
And the darkness where time fell and men and women
Together in their understanding, and the names
That they made and everything from the beginning
As though they were falling inside me, in the emptiness
That I was, and because of me they were falling,
Because I had been nothing. So that I thought then
That that was the change I had known, the only change,
But yet I would not believe that, but I cannot
Say why. And so that I would have prayed
That it be removed from me, the grief of it,
The keen that was in me at all their falling
In the emptiness that I was be removed from me,
But then how should I have named it, and what am I
That He should be mindful of? But I prayed,
But for that I did not pray, but yet I
Cannot say why, but in my heart that also
I pondered. And it went when its time was,
Because in the place where we are, the shadow
Moves and there is the stone again, and the day
Going and things to be done, the same
As always, the way they have to be; and because
Such emptiness as that was, you could not
Bear it for long and live, or I could not.
So I moved away about something
That all that time I should have been doing, with
That cup in my hands; whatever it was
                         I have forgotten again.

And I moved away because you must live
Forward, which is away from whatever
It was that you had, though you think when you have it

That it will stay with you forever. Like that word
I thought I had known and held surely and that it
Was with me always. In the evening
Between the shadows the light lifts and slides
Out and out, and the cold that was under the air
Is the darkness you remember, and how it was
There all the time and you had forgotten.
It carries its own fragrance. And there is this man
Will take me as a woman, and he is a good man,
And I will learn what I am, and the new names. Only
If I could remember, if I could only remember
The way that word was, and the sound of it. Because
There is that in me still that draws all that I am
Backward, as weeds are drawn down when the water
Flows away; and if I could only shape
And hear again that word and the way of it—
But you must grow forward, and I know
That I cannot. And yet it is there in me:
If I could only remember
The word, if I could make it with my breath
It would be with me forever as it was
Then in the beginning, when it was
The end and the beginning, and the way
They were one; and time and the things of falling
Would not fall into emptiness but into
The light, and the word tell the way of their falling
Into the light forever, if I could remember
                    And make the word with my breath.

The Mountain

Only on the rarest occasions, when the blue air,
Though clear, is not too blinding (as, say,
For a particular moment just at dusk in autumn)
Or if the clouds should part suddenly
Between freshets in spring, can one trace the rising
Slopes high enough to call them contours; and even
More rarely see above the tree line. Then

It is with almost a shock that one recognizes
What supposedly one had known always:
That it is, in fact, a mountain; not merely
This restrictive sense of nothing level, of never
Being able to go anywhere
But up or down, until it seems probable
Sometimes that the slope, to be so elusive
And yet so inescapable, must be nothing
But ourselves; that we have grown with one
Foot shorter than the other, and would deform
The levelest habitat to our misshapen
Condition, as is said of certain hill creatures.

Standing between two other peaks, but not
As they: or so we have seen in a picture
Whose naive audacity, founded, as far as can be
Determined, on nothing but the needs
Of its own composition, presents all three
As shaped oddly, of different colors, rising
From a plain whose flatness appears incredible
To such as we. Of course to each of us
Privately, its chief difference from its peers
Rests not even in its centrality, but its
Strangeness composed of our own intimacy
With a part of it, our necessary
Ignorance of its limits, and diurnal pretense
That what we see of it is all. Learned opinions differ
As to whether it was ever actively
Volcanic. It is believed that if one could see it
Whole, its shape might make this clearer, but that
Is impossible, for at the distance at which in theory
One could see it all, it would be out of sight.

Of course in all the senses in which any
Place or thing can be said not to exist
Until someone, at least, is known to have been there,
It would help immeasurably if anyone
Should ever manage to climb it. No one,
From whatever distance, has ever so much as seen
The summit, or even anywhere near it; not, that is,

As far as we know. At one time the attempt
Was a kind of holy maelstrom, Mecca
For fanatics and madmen, and a mode of ritual
And profane suicide (since among us there is nowhere
From which one could throw oneself down). But there have
    been
Expeditions even quite recently, and with the benefit
Of the most expensive equipment. Very few
Who set out at all seriously have
Come back. At a relatively slight distance
Above us, apparently the whole aspect and condition
Of the mountain changes completely; there is ceaseless wind
With a noise like thunder and the beating of wings.

Indeed, if one considers the proximity
Of the point at which so much violence
Is known to begin, it is not our failure
That strikes one as surprising, but our impunity:
The summer camps on near gradients, ski lifts in winter,
And even our presence where we are. For of those
Who attained any distance and returned, most
Were deafened, some permanently; some were blind,
And these also often incurably; all
Without exception were dazzled, as by a great light. And those
Who perhaps went farthest and came back, seemed
To have completely lost the use of our language,
Or if they spoke, babbled incoherently
Of silence bursting beyond that clamor, of time
Passed there not passing here, which we could not understand,
Of time no time at all. These characteristic
Effects of the upper slopes—especially the derangement
Of time-sense, and the dazzling—seem from earliest
Antiquity to have excited speculation.

Our legend has it that a remote king-priest figure
Once gained the summit, spent some—to him nonsequent
But to them significant—time there, and returned
"Shining," bearing ciphers of the arcane (which,
Translated into the common parlance, proved
To be a list of tribal taboos) like clastic

Specimens, and behaved with a glacial violence
Later construed as wisdom. This, though
Charming, does not, in the light of current endeavor,
Seem possible, even though so long ago. Yet
To corroborate this story, in the torrent
Gold has been found which even at this
Late date appears to have been powdered by hand,
And (further to confuse inquiry) several
Pediments besides, each with four sockets shaped
As though to receive the hoof of a giant statue
Of some two-toed ungulate. Legend being
What it is, there are those who still insist
He will come down again some day from the mountain.

As there are those who say it will fall on us. It
Will fall. And those who say it has already
Fallen. It has already fallen. Have we not
Seen it fall in shadow, evening after evening,
Across everything we can touch; do we not build
Our houses out of the great hard monoliths
That have crashed down from far above us? Shadows
Are not without substance, remind and predict;
And we know we live between greater commotions
Than any we can describe. But more important:
Since this, though we know so little of it, is
All we know, is it not whatever it makes us
Believe of it—even the old woman
Who laughs, pointing, and says that the clouds across
Its face are wings of seraphim? Even the young
Man who, standing on it, declares it is not
There at all? He stands with one leg habitually
Bent, to keep from falling, as though he had grown
That way, as is said of certain hill creatures.

Saint Sebastian

So many times I have felt them come, Lord,
The arrows (a coward dies often), so many times,
And worse, oh worse often than this. Neither breeze nor bird
Stirring the hazed peace through which the day climbs.

And slower even than the arrows, the few sounds that come
Falling, as across water, from where farther off than the hills
The archers move in a different world in the same
Kingdom. Oh, can the noise of angels,

The beat and whirring between Thy kingdoms
Be even by such cropped feathers raised? Not though
With the wings of the morning may I fly from Thee; for it is

Thy kingdom where (and the wind so still now)
I stand in pain; and, entered with pain as always,
Thy kingdom that on these erring shafts comes.

The Isaiah of Souillac

Why the prophet is dancing the sculptor knew. If
The prophet is dancing. Or even if it is only
Wind, a wind risen there in the doorway
Suddenly as a fish leaps, lifting his garments,
His feet, like music, a whirling breath carved
There in the narrow place that is enough for a man.
You see a wind in its signs but in itself not.
You hear a spirit in its motion, in its words, even
In its stillness, but in itself not. Know it here in the stance
Of a prophet, and his beard blown in a doorway.
His words stream in the stony wind; woe
Unto the dust that is deaf, for even stones
Can rise as with feet when the spirit passes
Upon the place where they are. But they are all gone away
Backward; from the soles of their feet to their heedless heads
There is no measure nor soundness in them. His fingers,

Frail as reeds making the music they move to,
Embody a lightness like fire. They shall be moved
With burning whom this breath moves not, who have refused
The waters of Shiloh that go softly shall the river
Rise over, out in the sunlight, roaring
Like the sea, like lions, spreading its wings like a wind.
And yet will the wind of heaven wear the shape of a man,
Be mortal as breath, before men, for a sign, and stand
Between good and evil, the thieves of the left and right hand.
And the sign of a wind is dancing, the motion
Of a sign is dancing and ushered with words beating
And with dancing. So there is terrible gentleness
Unleashed in the stone of his eyes, so
The words dance as a fire, as a clapping
Of hands, as the stars dance, as the mountains
Leap swelling, as the feet of the prophet, faithful
Upon them, dance, dance, and still to the same song.

The Station

Two boards with a token roof, backed
Against the shelving hill, and a curtain
Of frayed sacking which the wind absently
Toyed with on the side toward the sea:
From that point already so remote that we
Continually caught ourselves talking in whispers
No path went on but only the still country
Unfolding as far as we could see
In the luminous dusk its land that had not been lived on
Ever, or not within living memory.

This less than shelter, then, was the last
Human contrivance for our encouragement:
Improvised so hastily, it might have been
Thrown together only the moment
Before we arrived, yet so weathered,
Warped, and parched, it must have stood there
Longer than we knew. And the ground before it

Was not scarred with the rawness of construction
Nor even beaten down by feet, but simply barren
As one felt it always had been: something between
Sand and red shale with only the spiky dune-grass
Growing, and a few trees stunted by wind.

Some as they arrived appeared to be carrying
Whole households strapped onto their shoulders,
Often with their tired children asleep
Among the upper baskets, and even
A sore dog limping behind them. Some
Were traveling light for the journey:
A knife and matches, and would sleep
In the clothes they stood up in. And there were
The barefoot ones, some from conviction
With staves, some from poverty with nothing.

Burdens and garments bore no relation
To the ages of the travelers; nor, as they sat
In spite of fatigue talking late
Into the night, to the scope and firmness
Of their intentions. It was, for example,
A patriarch herding six grandchildren
In his family, and who had carried
More than his own weight of gear all day
Who insisted that three days' journey inland
Would bring them to a sheltered valley
Along a slow river, where even the clumsiest farmer
Would grow fat on the land's three crops a year.

And a youth with expensive hiking shoes
And one blanket to carry, who declaimed
Most loudly on the effort of the trip,
The stingy prospects, the risks involved
In venturing beyond that point. Several
Who had intended to go farthest mused
That the land thereabouts was better
Than what they had left and that tramping
Behind his own plow should be far enough afield

For any grown man, while another to all
Dissuasions repeated that it had been
The same ten years ago at—naming a place
Where we had slept two nights before.
Until one who looked most energetic
Changed the subject with his theory
That a certain block of stone there
Before the doorway had been shaped
By hand, and at one time had stood
As the pedestal of a wayside shrine.

Yet in spite of the circling arguments
Which grew desperate several times before morning
Everyone knew that it was all decided:
That some, even who spoke with most eloquence
Of the glories of exodus and the country
Waiting to be taken, would be found
Scrabbling next day for the patch of ground
Nearest the shelter, or sneaking back
The way they had come, or hiring themselves out
As guides to this point, and no one would be able
To explain what had stopped them there; any more
Than one would be able afterward to say
Why some who perhaps sat there saying least,
And not, to appearances, the bravest
Or best suited for such a journey,
At first light would get up and go on.

The Master

Not entirely enviable, however envied;
And early outgrew the enjoyment of their envy,
For other preoccupations, some quite as absurd.
Not always edifying in his action: touchy
And dull by turns, prejudiced, often not strictly
Truthful, with a weakness for petty meddling,
For black sheep, churlish rancors and out-of-hand damning.

The messes he got himself into were of his own devising.
He had all the faults he saw through in the rest of us;
As we have taken pains, and a certain delight, in proving
Not denying his strength, but still not quite sure where it was;
But luck was with him too, whatever that is,
For his rightful deserts, far from destroying him,
Turned out to be just what he'd needed, and he used them.

Opportunist, shrewd waster, half calculation,
Half difficult child; a phony, it would seem
Even to his despairs, were it not for the work, and that certain
Sporadic but frightening honesty allowed him
By those who loathed him most. Not nice in the home,
But a few loved him. And he loved. Who? What? Some still
Think they know, as some thought they knew then, which is
    just as well.

In this lifetime what most astonished those
Acquainted with him, was the amount of common
Detail he could muster, and with what intimate ease,
As though he knew it all from inside. For when
Had he seen it? They recalled him as one who most often
Seemed slow, even stupid, not above such things surely,
But absent, with that air maybe part fake, and part shifty.

Yet famously cursed in his disciples:
So many, emulous, but without his unique powers,
Could only ape and exaggerate his foibles.
And he bewildered them as he did no others,
Though they tried to conceal it: for, like mirrors
In a fun-house, they were static, could never keep up with him,
Let alone predict. But stranded on strange shores following
    him.

So the relief, then the wide despair, when he was gone;
For not only his imitators did he leave feeling
Naked, without voice or manner of their own:
For over a generation his ghost would come bullying
Every hand: all modes seemed exhausted, and he had left
    nothing

Of any importance for them to do,
While what had escaped him eluded them also.

For only with his eyes could they see, with his ears hear
The world. He had made it. And hard, now, to believe
In the invention: all seems so styleless, as though it had come
  there
By itself, since the errors and effort are in their grave.
But real: here we are walking in it. Oh, what we can never
  forgive
Is the way every leaf calls up to our helpless remembrance
Our reality and its insupportable innocence.

Tobacco

"Nothing in the world like it; you can tell Aristotle."
And a filthy habit too; yet the ghost of this burning,
Imbibed with practice, is balm undeniable,
So rejoicing the senses, so pleasant to the tongue,
That once they know it, they crave it still. Which, faking
With pencil shavings, in a pipe where the soap still bubbled,
I would pretend I was addicted to, as a child.

Grows faster than you would believe, once it gets going.
The devil green in it. And lovely
The big leaves, in the least air wagging and slatting
Like hands strung up loose at the wrists, or heads vacantly
Disapproving; but if we are made that way
It is lunacy, surely, to carp at nature
Especially when there is so much to enjoy in her.

To avoid the tax on it (we will soon
Be assessed for breathing), if you have even one green finger
The weed will flourish in your own garden
—Hoe often: the roots like access to God's sweet air—
Though the result may prove rather more rank than you prefer
If the cure of it is dependent on just your own
Crude devices: the drying, the disguising of the poison.

Oh yes, a vice. You knew it beforehand. And you
Would give it up, normally, but it's a help when you're working.
You can keep it within reason. Just the same, it will kill you
In the end: you can feel it now tarring
Your lungs to a shameful squeak, feel your heart constricting;
But as you bemoan it in horrified amaze
At how much it costs, think too what fun it is.

Burning the Cat

In the spring, by the big shuck-pile
Between the bramble-choked brook where the copperheads
Curled in the first sun, and the mud road,
All at once it could no longer be ignored.
The season steamed with an odor for which
There has never been a name, but it shouted above all.
When I went near, the wood-lice were in its eyes
And a nest of beetles in the white fur of its armpit.
I built a fire there by the shuck-pile
But it did no more than pop the beetles
And singe the damp fur, raising a stench
Of burning hair that bit through the sweet day-smell.
Then thinking how time leches after indecency,
Since both grief is indecent and the lack of it,
I went away and fetched newspaper,
And wrapped it in dead events, days and days,
Soaked it in kerosene and put it in
With the garbage on a heaped nest of sticks:
It was harder to burn than the peels of oranges,
Bubbling and spitting, and the reek was like
Rank cooking that drifted with the smoke out
Through the budding woods and clouded the shining
    dogwood.
But I became stubborn: I would consume it
Though the pyre should take me a day to build
And the flames rise over the house. And hours I fed
That burning, till I was black and streaked with sweat;

And poked it out then, with charred meat still clustering
Thick around the bones. And buried it so
As I should have done in the first place, for
The earth is slow, but deep, and good for hiding;
I would have used it if I had understood
How nine lives can vanish in one flash of a dog's jaws,
A car, or a copperhead, and yet how one small
Death, however reckoned, is hard to dispose of.

Dog Dreaming

The paws twitch in a place of chasing
Where the whimper of this seeming-gentle creature
Rings out terrible, chasing tigers. The fields
Are licking like torches, full of running,
Laced odors, bones stalking, tushed leaps.
So little that is tamed, yet so much
That you would find deeply familiar there.
You are there often, your very eyes,
The unfathomable knowledge behind your face,
The mystery of your will, appraising
Such carnage and triumph; standing there
Strange even to yourself, and loved, and only
A sleeping beast knows who you are.

Backwater Pond: The Canoeists

Not for the fishermen's sake
Do they drop their voices as they glide in from the lake,
And take to moving stealthily on that still water,
Not to disturb its stillness, hour on hour.
So that when at last a turtle, scuttling
Surprised from a stump, dives with a sudden splashing,
It startles them like a door slamming;
And then there is a faint breeze and echo of laughter

Dying as quickly, and they float still as before
Like shadows sliding over a mirror
Or clouds across some forgotten sky,
All afternoon, they cannot say why.

River Sound Remembered

That day the huge water drowned all voices until
It seemed a kind of silence unbroken
By anything: a time unto itself and still;

So that when I turned away from its roaring, down
The path over the gully, and there were
Dogs barking as always at the edge of town,

Car horns and the cries of children coming
As though for the first time through the fading light
Of the winter dusk, my ears still sang

Like shells with the swingeing current, and
Its flood echoing in me held for long
About me the same silence, by whose sound

I could hear only the quiet under the day
With the land noises floating there far-off and still;
So that even in my mind now turning away

From having listened absently but for so long
It will be the seethe and drag of the river
That I will hear longer than any mortal song.

After the Flood

The morning it was over, I walked
To the Jersey side, where there is a park,
And where even in summer the river

Is at least two feet higher than it is on our side,
Because of the way it bends. It had not been
A bad rise, such as many remember.
A line of flotsam, full of
Exotic-looking dark foliage stretched
Crosswise through the park, just meeting
The river wall at the end corner. Things
I felt I must surely remember, they looked so
Familiar, had fished up there with sudden
Histories to them that would never get told.
I remembered how I had climbed the dike
Two days before, when the lower bridge
Was in danger. Coming in sight of the river then
The amazing thing was how much
More quiet the swollen water seemed
Than I had expected, how slowly
It seemed to move, like some beast sneaking.
Now it seemed noisy again, but I could hear
Other sounds coming over it. A seagull creaking,
Not tempted by the miserable leavings.
Almost disappointed myself, I made myself
Think of how much we had been spared,
How much that was cherished had, other times,
Been swept down the river. I noticed
Near the bottom of the park, just below
The high-water line, an old coat hanging
Snagged on a tree branch, and caught myself wondering
What sort of drunken creature had passed there.

In the Heart of Europe

Farmers hereabouts, for generations now
Have owned their own places; their names
Covered the country before the families
Of the former kings were heard of, and having
Survived masters and serfdom, describe still the same spot.
They partake of their land's very features: it is
Theirs as it can be no others'. What keeps and has

Kept them? Can you call it love
That is a habit so ancient that a man's span
Is brief in its practice; whose beginnings
Are no more remembered than the hills' genesis? A thing
Inexplicable, but so casual, and for which
They have no names but their own? Why, even,
They build their houses that way, they could never tell you.
It is as though, in a thing so established
They knew themselves tenants, merely, till the country
Turns from them to their children. You feel they would never
Say the place belonged to them: a reticence
Like love's delicacy or its quiet assurance.

A Sparrow Sheltering Under a Column
of the British Museum

Conceived first by whom? By the Greeks perfected,
By the Romans, the Renaissance, and the Victorians copied.

Almost from the first more massive than our uses
And so indicating something more, the stone rises

Into the clear sunlight rare for a London January.
Why about columns does it seem always windy?

Still, he restores this one to bare use, convenient
For huddling between its base and pediment

Where though the wind still ruffles him it is somewhat broken.
Porches are places of passage; and again

To us they indicate something beyond; to him
Its shape and position in the wind are the column.

And whereas to him the feet of children and scholars
Who pass all day through the merely useful doors

To inquire of the rich uncertainty of their farthing
Are not shaped like danger unless too near, may even bring

Crumbs to offer to a necessity
Which they both conciliate so differently

(He, alive not to limits but presences,
They hungering less for shapes than significances),

Skelton's bird or Catullus's, or even
That pair whose fall figured our need of heaven

Would mean nothing to him, for he would never
Recognize them as now they are

Beyond doors there, where the wind is unknown,
But knows simply that this stone

Shelters, rising into the native air,
And that, though perhaps cold, he is at home there.

Learning a Dead Language

There is nothing for you to say. You must
Learn first to listen. Because it is dead
It will not come to you of itself, nor would you
Of yourself master it. You must therefore
Learn to be still when it is imparted,
And, though you may not yet understand, to remember.

What you remember is saved. To understand
That least thing fully you would have to perceive
The whole grammar in all its accidence
And all its system, in the perfect singleness
Of intention it has because it is dead.
You can learn only a part at a time.

What you are given to remember
Has been saved before you from death's dullness by
Remembering. The unique intention
Of a language whose speech has died is order
Incomplete only where someone has forgotten.
You will find that that order helps you to remember.

What you come to remember becomes yourself.
Learning will be to cultivate the awareness
Of that governing order, now pure of the passions
It composed; till, seeking it in itself,
You may find at last the passion that composed it,
Hear it both in its speech and in yourself.

What you remember saves you. To remember
Is not to rehearse, but to hear what never
Has fallen silent. So your learning is,
From the dead, order, and what sense of yourself
Is memorable, what passion may be heard
When there is nothing for you to say.

Three Faces

In half profile, one behind the other,
As in a Greek frieze the edges of horses
One behind the other; between them
A family resemblance, no more:
Not the multiplied identity
Which in the drunkard's vision spreads and shifts,
Nor the unity of the Trinity.

All three, looming long as the heads of horses,
Are shaped as tears falling upward in a wind
Whose darkness fashions them, defining
In each the pallid half-light, vast eyes,
Distorting them singly and together to those
Irregularities which are their features.
Chins in their hands, elbows on solid darkness.

So their differences are of darkness,
Whose reflection three times varied in
Their eyes, shows not itself but them
Changing on one hand and on the other
Through gradations which must be infinite;
And yet their shape it is, and common nature,
And to their partial spectrum the white light.

Her Wisdom

So is she with love's tenderness
Made tender—and touched tenderness is pain;
Pain in fit subjects distorts or burns into wisdom—

That she both by usual things and presences
Too delicate for usual ears and eyes
At all hands is touched and made wise,

Being instructed by stones of their rough childhoods,
In the migratory tides of birds seeing the cold
Hand of the moon and the shape of their shore;

She suffers too the noise of night's shadow flexing
Invisible in the unrustling air of noon,
With a sound between parchment stretched and a bat's squeak;

Is aware at all hours of the scream and sigh
Of shadows, of each moment: things forever violated,
Forever virgin; hears sleep falling wherever it falls.

Such understanding, uncommunicable
To other senses, and seeming so simple,
Is more a mystery than things not known at all;

For pain is common, but learned of not often,
Taught never; and who, could she speak it,
Would have ears to hear? She would not if she could,

Because of her tenderness. But should
Love's wisdom so wound her that she die
Would the knowledge then to which she succumbed

Most resemble the fear which we hear in the leaves' falling,
Hope as it falters in our failing questions,
Or joy as it overtakes us even in pain?

The Sapphire

After a dream in which your love's fullness
Was heaven and earth, I stood on nothing in darkness,
Neither finding nor falling, without hope nor dread,
Not knowing pleasure nor discontented.
In time, like the first beam arriving from
The first star, a ray from a seed of light came,
Whose source, coming nearer (I could not say whether
It rose or descended, for there was no higher or lower),
To a trumpet's thin sweet highest note
Which grew to the pitch of pain, showed how its white
Light proceeded all from a blue crystal stone
Large as a child's skull, shaped so, lucent as when
Daylight strikes sideways through a cat's eyes;
Blue not blinding, its light did not shine but was;
And came, as the trumpet pierced through into silence,
To hover so close before my hands
That I might have held it, but that one does not handle
What one accepts as a miracle.
A great sapphire it was whose light and cradle
Held all things: there were the delights of skies, though
Its cloudless blue was different; of sea and meadow,
But their shapes not seen. The stone unheld was mine,
But yours the sense by which, without further sign
I recognized its visionary presence
By its clarity, its changeless patience,
And the unuttered joy that it was,
As the world's love before the world was.

Thorn Leaves in March

Walking out in the late March midnight
With the old blind bitch on her bedtime errand
Of ease stumbling beside me, I saw

At the hill's edge, by the blue flooding
Of the arc lamps, and the moon's suffused presence,
The first leaves budding pale on the thorn trees,

Uncurling with that crass light coming through them,
Like the translucent wings of insects
Dilating in the dampness of birth;

And their green seemed already more ghostly
Than the hour drowned beneath bells, and the city sleeping,
Or even than the month with its round moon sinking.

As a white lamb the month's entrance had been:
The day warm, and at night unexpectedly
An hour of soft snow falling silently,

Soon ceasing, leaving transfigured all traceries,
These shrubs and trees, in white and white shadows; silk screens
Where were fences. And all restored again in an hour.

And as a lamb, I could see now, it would go,
Breathless, into its own ghostliness,
Taking with it more than its tepid moon.

And here there would be no lion at all that is
The beast of gold, and sought as an answer,
Whose pure sign in no solution is,

But between its two lambs the month would have run
As its varying moon, all silver,
That is the color of questions.

Oh, there as it went was such a silence
Before the water of April should be heard singing
Strangely as ever under the knowing ground

As fostered in me the motion of asking
In hope of no answer that fated leaves,
Sleep, or the sinking moon might proffer,

And in no words, but as it seemed in love only
For all breath, whose departing nature is
The spirit of question, whatever least I knew,

Whatever most I wondered. In which devotion
I stayed until the bell struck and the silver
Ebbed before April, and might have stood unseizing

Among answers less ghostly than the first leaves
On the thorn trees, since to seize had been
Neither to love nor to possess;

While the old bitch nosed and winded, conjuring
A congenial spot, and the constellations
Sank nearer already, listing toward summer.

Low Fields and Light

I think it is in Virginia, that place
That lies across the eye of my mind now
Like a gray blade set to the moon's roundness,
Like a plain of glass touching all there is.

The flat fields run out to the sea there.
There is no sand, no line. It is autumn.
The bare fields, dark between fences, run
Out to the idle gleam of the flat water.

And the fences go on out, sinking slowly,
With a cowbird halfway, on a stunted post, watching

How the light slides through them easy as weeds
Or wind, slides over them away out near the sky

Because even a bird can remember
The fields that were there before the slow
Spread and wash of the edging light crawled
There and covered them, a little more each year.

My father never plowed there, nor my mother
Waited, and never knowingly I stood there
Hearing the seepage slow as growth, nor knew
When the taste of salt took over the ground.

But you would think the fields were something
To me, so long I stare out, looking
For their shapes or shadows through the matted gleam, seeing
Neither what is nor what was, but the flat light rising.

Birds Waking

I went out at daybreak and stood on Primrose Hill.
It was April: a white haze over the hills of Surrey
Over the green haze of the hills above the dark green
Of the park trees, and over it all the light came up clear,
The sky like deep porcelain paling and paling,
With everywhere under it the faces of the buildings
Where the city slept, gleaming white and quiet,
St. Paul's and the water tower taking the gentle gold.
And from the hill chestnuts and the park trees
There was such a clamor rose as the birds woke,
Such uncontainable tempest of whirled
Singing flung upward and upward into the new light,
Increasing still as the birds themselves rose
From the black trees and whirled in a rising cloud,
Flakes and waterspouts and hurled seas and continents of
    them
Rising, dissolving, streamering out, always
Louder and louder singing, shrieking, laughing.

Sometimes one would break from the cloud but from the
    song never,
And would beat past my ear dinning his deafening note.
I thought I had never known the wind
Of joy to be so shrill, so unanswerable,
With such clouds of winged song at its disposal, and I thought:
O Voice that my demand is the newest name for,
There are many ways we may end, and one we must,
Whether burning, or the utter cold descending in darkness,
Explosion of our own devising, collision of planets, all
Violent, however silent they at last may seem;
Oh, let it be by this violence, then, let it be now,
Now when in their sleep, unhearing, unknowing,
Most faces must be closest to innocence,
When the light moves unhesitating to fill the sky with clearness
And no dissent could be heard above the din of its welcome,
Let the great globe well up and dissolve like its last birds
With the bursting roar and uprush of song!

PART THREE

Evening with Lee Shore and Cliffs

Sea-shimmer, faint haze, and far out a bird
Dipping for flies or fish. Then, when over
That wide silk suddenly the shadow
Spread skating, who turned with a shiver
High in the rocks? And knew, then only, the waves'
Layering patience: how they would follow after,
After, dogged as sleep, to his inland
Dreams, oh beyond the one lamb that cried
In the olives, past the pines' derision. And heard
Behind him not the sea's gaiety but its laughter.

The Fishermen

When you think how big their feet are in black rubber
And it slippery underfoot always, it is clever
How they thread and manage among the sprawled nets, lines,
Hooks, spidery cages with small entrances.
But they are used to it. We do not know their names.
They know our needs, and live by them, lending them wiles
And beguilements we could never have fashioned for them;
They carry the ends of our hungers out to drop them
To wait swaying in a dark place we could never have chosen.
By motions we have never learned they feed us.
We lay wreaths on the sea when it has drowned them.

Two Paintings by Alfred Wallis

I. VOYAGE TO LABRADOR

Tonight when the sea runs like a sore,
Swollen as hay and with the same sound,
Where under the hat-dark the iron
Ship slides seething, hull crammed
With clamors the fluttering hues of a fever,

Clang-battened in, the stunned bells done
From the rung-down quartans, and only
The dotty lights still trimmed
Abroad like teeth, there dog-hunched will the high
Street of hugging bergs have come
To lean huge and hidden as women,
Untouched as smoke and, at our passing, pleased
Down to the private sinks of their cold.
Then we will be white, all white, as cloths sheening,
Stiff as teeth, white as the sticks
And eyes of the blind. But morning, mindless
And uncaring as Jesus, will find nothing
In that same place but an empty sea
Colorless, see, as a glass of water.

II. SCHOONER UNDER THE MOON

Waits where we would almost be. Part
Pink as a tongue; floats high on the olive
Rumpled night-flood, foresails and clouds hiding
Such threat and beauty as we may never see.

Senility Cay

Like a nail-paring cast from the moon's leprosy
The beach sheens white to the moon's tooth;
All the birds are dying along the sand, you would say
A camp croaking feeble with a fever;
Gray grass twitching like cheeks, and the scurf
Crawling dry on the palsied sea.
Not a sail there. Not a face in sight. But here
Thin as a fishbone, left open so it stares
Is the gaunt gap where what was a man will be.

Fog

You see, shore-hugging is neither surety
Nor earns salt pride braving the long sea-sweeps.
This came up in the dark while some of us
Bore on in our sleep. Was there
In the dogwatch already, hiding the Dog Star.
We woke into it, rising from dreams
Of sea-farms slanting on cliffs in clear light
And white houses winking there—sweet landmarks
But no help to us at the helm. Hours now
We have been drifting. It would be near noon.
Feeling the tides fight under our feet
Like a crawling of carpets. Turning our heads
To pick up the cape-bell, the hoots of the shoal-horn
That seem to come from all over. Distrusting
Every direction that is simple, to shoreward. This
Landfall is not vouchsafed us for
We have abused landfalls, loving them wrong
And too timorously. What coastline
Will not cloud over if looked at long enough?
Not through the rings running with us of enough
Horizons, not wide enough risking,
Not hard enough have we wrought our homing.
Drifting itself now is danger. Where are we?
Well, the needle swings still to north, and we know
Even in this blindness which way deep water lies.
Ships were not shaped for haven but if we were
There will be time for it yet. Let us turn head,
Out oars, and pull for the open. Make we
For midsea, where the winds are and stars too.
There will be wrung weathers, sea-shakings, calms,
Weariness, the giant water that rolls over our fathers,
And hungers hard to endure. But whether we float long
Or founder soon, we cannot be saved here.

The Shipwreck

The tale is different if even a single breath
Escapes to tell it. The return itself
Says survival is possible. And words made to carry
In quiet the burden, the isolation
Of dust, and that fail even so,
Though they shudder still, must shrink the great head
Of elemental violence, the vast eyes
Called blind looking into the ends of darkness,
The mouth deafening understanding with its one
All-wise syllable, into a shriveled
History that the dry-shod may hold
In the palms of their hands. They had her
Under jib and reefed mizzen, and in the dark
Were fairly sure where they were, and with sea-room,
And it seemed to be slacking a little, until
Just before three they struck. Heard
It come home, hollow in the hearts of them,
And only then heard the bell ringing, telling them
It had been ringing there always telling them
That there it would strike home, hollow, in
The hearts of them. Only then heard it
Over the sunlight, the dozing creak
Of the moorings, the bleaching quay, the heat,
The coiled ropes on the quay the day they would sail
And the day before, and across the water blue
As a sky through the heat beyond
The coils, the coils, with their shadows coiled
Inside them. And it sprang upon them dark,
Bitter, and heavy with sound. They began to go
To pieces at once under the waves' hammer.
Sick at heart since that first stroke, they moved
Nevertheless as they had learned always to move
When it should come, not weighing hope against
The weight of the water, yet knowing that no breath
Would escape to betray what they underwent then.
Dazed too, incredulous, that it had come,
That they could recognize it. It was too familiar,
And they in the press of it, therefore, as though

In a drifting dream. But it bore in upon them
Bursting slowly inside them where they had
Coiled it down, coiled it down: this sea, it was
Blind, yes, as they had said, and treacherous—
They had used their own traits to character it—but without
Accident in its wildness, in its rage,
Utterly and from the beginning without
Error. And to some it seemed that the waves
Grew gentle, spared them, while they died of that knowledge.

The Eyes of the Drowned Watch Keels Going Over

Where the light has no horizons we lie.
It dims into depth not distance. It sways
Like hair, then we shift and turn over slightly.
As once on the long swing under the trees
In the drowse of summer we slid to and fro
Slowly in the soft wash of the air, looking
Upward through the leaves that turned over and back
Like hands, through the birds, the fathomless light,
Upward. They go over us swinging
Jaggedly, laboring between our eyes
And the light. Churning their wrought courses
Between the sailing birds and the awed eyes
Of the fish, with the grace of neither, nor with
The stars' serenity that they follow.
Yet the light shakes around them as they go.
Why? And why should we, rocking on shoal-pillow,
With our eyes cling to them, and their wakes follow,
Who follow nothing? If we could remember
The stars in their clarity, we might understand now
Why we pursued stars, to what end our eyes
Fastened upon stars, how it was that we traced
In their remote courses not their own fates but ours.

Mariners' Carol

So still the night swinging,
Wind of our faring,
Only the bows' seethe to lap us,
Stays and wake whispering,
The thin bell striking,
And our hearts in their blindness.
O star, shine before us!

The serpent's deep sliding,
Wind of our faring,
Is everywhere around us,
Heaves under us, gliding;
We know its toothed curling
The whole world encircles.
O star, shine before us!

Crushed in its drag and keeping,
Wind of our faring,
The darkened dead have no peace,
World-without-end shifting;
All, all are there, and no resting.
It exults above their faces.
O star, shine before us!

The horizon's perfect ring,
Wind of our faring,
None enters nor ever has.
And we, like a cradle, rocking:
For the first glimpse of our homing
We roll and are restless.
O star, shine before us!

Till, heaven and earth joining,
Wind of our faring,
It is born to us
Like the first line of dawn breaking;
For that word and sight yearning
We keep the long watches.
O star, shine before us!

THE DRUNK IN THE FURNACE

(1960)

for my mother and father

Odysseus

for George Kirstein

Always the setting forth was the same,
Same sea, same dangers waiting for him
As though he had got nowhere but older.
Behind him on the receding shore
The identical reproaches, and somewhere
Out before him, the unraveling patience
He was wedded to. There were the islands
Each with its woman and twining welcome
To be navigated, and one to call "home."
The knowledge of all that he betrayed
Grew till it was the same whether he stayed
Or went. Therefore he went. And what wonder
If sometimes he could not remember
Which was the one who wished on his departure
Perils that he could never sail through,
And which, improbable, remote, and true,
Was the one he kept sailing home to?

The Iceberg

It is not its air but our own awe
That freezes us. Hardest of all to believe
That so fearsome a destroyer can be
Dead, with those lights moving in it,
With the sea all around it charged
With its influence. It seems that only now
We realize the depth of the waters, the
Abyss over which we float among such
Clouds. And still not understanding
The coldness of most elegance, even
With so vast and heartless a splendor
Before us, stare, caught in the magnetism
Of great silence, thinking: this is the terror
That cannot be charted, this is only
A little of it. And recall how many

Mariners, watching the sun set, have seen
These peaks on the horizon and made sail
Through the darkness for islands that no map
Had promised, floating blessèd in
The west. These must dissolve
Before they can again grow apple trees.

Foghorn

Surely that moan is not the thing
That men thought they were making, when they
Put it there, for their own necessities.
That throat does not call to anything human
But to something men had forgotten,
That stirs under fog. Who wounded that beast
Incurably, or from whose pasture
Was it, full grown, and time closed round it
With no way back? Who tethered its tongue
So that its voice could never come
To speak out in the light of clear day,
But only when the shifting blindness
Descends and is acknowledged among us,
As though from under a floor it is heard,
Or as though from behind a wall, always
Nearer than we had remembered? If it
Was we who gave tongue to this cry
What does it bespeak in us, repeating
And repeating, insisting on something
That we never meant? We only put it there
To give warning of something we dare not
Ignore, lest we should come upon it
Too suddenly, recognize it too late,
As our cries were swallowed up and all hands lost.

Deception Island

for Arthur Mizener

You can go farther. The south itself
Goes much farther, hundreds of miles, first
By sea, then over the white continent,
Mountainous, unmapped, all the way to the pole.

But sometimes imagination
Is content to rest here, at harbor
In the smooth bay in the dead mountain,
Like a vessel at anchor in its own reflection.

The glassy roadstead sleeps in a wide ring
Of ice and igneous shingle, whose gradual
Slopes rise, under streaks of white and black all
The swept shapes of wind, to the volcano's ridges.

It is like being suspended in the open
Vast wreck of a stony skull dead for ages.
You cannot believe the crater was ever
Fiery, before it filled with silence, and sea.

It is not a place you would fancy
You would like to go to. The slopes are barren
Of all the vegetation of desire.
But a place to imagine lying at anchor,

Watching the sea outside the broken
Temple of the cold fire-head, and wondering
Less at the wastes of silence and distance
Than at what all that lonely fire was for.

Sea Wife

There must be so many souls washing
Up and down out there just out of sight,
You would think the sea would be full; one day
It will surely be full and no more sea.
We will not live to see it. You can see
That the eyes of fish, used to staring at souls,
Can never believe us: standing up and breathing air.
So much the sea changes things. Husbands
Maybe you never know, but sons, fathers,
Above all brothers—they are fished from us
And gone in the holds of boats, and only
Strangers come in to us from the sea, even
If sometimes they be the same strangers.
Or else their names, sounding like strangers, on
The church wall. Us too it changes; just
With hating it our eyes take on its distance
And our hair its blowing whiteness. But we
Are the same, here with God and the bells. And the boats,
Maybe they are the same when we see them.
But we were never close to them, they were always
Untouchable as though in bottles. Do not learn it
From us; the bells are old and impartial
And upright and will tell you: beyond
The last channel nun and the cape horn
God is not righteous, doom calls like women,
The fish wait for friends. God is our rock here
In His goodness. The bells tell where He is,
They tell of His righteousness, and they moan seaward
Mourning for the souls, the souls, that are lost there.

The Frozen Sea

We walked on it, in the very flesh
No different only colder, as was
The sea itself. It was simple as that.
Only, the wind would not have it, would not

Have it: the whiteness at last
Bearing us up where we would go. Screamed
With lungs we would never have guessed at,
Shrieked round us, whipping up the cold crust,
Lashing the rigid swell into dust. It would
Find the waves for us, or freeze out
The mortal flaw in us: then we might stay.
And it was right: it was not any light
From heaven that hurt our eyes, but
The whiteness that we could not bear. It
Turned bloody in our carnal eyes. Virtues
That had borne us thus far turned on us, peopling
The lashed plains of our minds with hollow voices
Out of the snouted masks of beasts. Their
Guts would feed on God, they said. But danger
Had given shape, stiffening shape, to our
Pride, and that sustained us in silence
As we went over that screaming silence.
Yet how small we were around whom the howling
World turned. We could not see half a mile.
And only a soulless needle to tell us where
In the round world we were. We had come so far
To whiteness, and it was cruel in our eyes,
To the pure south, and whichever way we turned
Was north, the sides of the north, everywhere.

Sailor Ashore

What unsteady ways the solid earth has
After all. The lamps are dead on their feet
Blinking and swaying above the wet cobbles;
The darkness yaws out and back, sprawling
And slithering on the walls; the sleeping houses
Reel and almost fall but never wake;
And the echo of feet goes round and round
Like a buffeted gull, and can find no place
To alight. Somebody said it would be
Like this: the sea is everywhere.

But worst here where it is secret and pretends
To keep its mountains in one place. If you
Put your foot down the spot moves: the waters are
Under the earth. Nowhere to run from them.
It is their tides you feel heaving under you,
Sucking you down, when you close your eyes with women.
They wink in bottles, and you are washed off
And under. Gull shriek, boozy guffaw, woman
Laughing—turn your back on each in turn
And you hear the waters' laughter. Which is
What they gave you a back for. Better to stay
In one place, and sleep like the lamps, standing;
Then get back to the bare-faced original
Bitch-sea. Which is what they gave you legs for.

The Portland *Going Out*

Early that afternoon, as we keep
Remembering, the water of the harbor
Was so smooth you wanted to walk on it,
It looked that trustworthy: glassy and black
Like one of those pools they have in the lobbies
Of grand hotels. And, thinking back, we say
That the same bells we had heard telling
Their shoals and hours since we were children,
Sounded different, as though they were
Moving about the business of strangers. By
Five it was kicking up quite a bit,
And the greasiest evening you ever saw,
We had just come in, and were making fast,
A few minutes to seven, when she went
Down the harbor behind us, going out,
Passing so close over our stern that we
Caught the red glow of her port light for
A moment on our faces. Only
When she was gone did we notice
That it was starting to snow. No, we were
Not the last, nor even nearly the last

To see her. A schooner that lived through it
Glimpsed her, at the height of the storm,
In a clear patch, apparently riding it;
That must have been no more than minutes
Before she went down. We had known storms
Before, almost as brutal, and wrecks before
Almost as unexplained, almost
As disastrous. Yet we keep asking
How it happened, how, and why Blanchard sailed,
Miscalculating the storm's course. But what
We cannot even find questions for
Is how near we were: brushed by the same snow,
Lifted by her wake as she passed. We could
Have spoken, we swear, with anyone on her deck,
And not had to raise our voices, if we
Had known anything to say. And now
In no time at all, she has put
All of disaster between us: a gulf
Beyond reckoning. It begins where we are.

Sea Monster

We were not even out of sight of land
That afternoon when we saw it. A good day
With the sea making but still light. Not
One of us would have hesitated
As to where we were, or mistaken the brown
Cliffs or the town on top. Just after
The noon watch, it was, that it slid
Into our sight: a darkness under
The surface, between us and the land, twisting
Like a snake swimming or a line of birds
In the air. Then breached, big as a church,
Right there beside us. None of us will
Agree what it was we saw then, but
None of us showed the least surprise, and truly
I felt none. I would say its eyes
Were like the sea when the thick snow falls

Onto it with a whisper and slides heaving
On the gray water. And looked at us
For a long time, as though it knew us, but
Did not harm us that time, sinking at last,
The waters closing like a rush of breath. Then
We were all ashamed at what we had seen,
Said it was only a sea-trick or
A dream we had all had together. As it
May have been, for since then we have forgotten
How it was that, on sea or land, once
We proved to ourselves that we were awake.

Cape Dread

For those who come after, that is how we named it;
You may find that some other suits it better. Only
We pray you, for no saint christen it. The toll of us
That it took, we do not yet know the unhallowed
End of it, any more than we can assess
Our own ends beforehand. All summer
We had coursed a strange ocean, the winds driving
From quarters that seem unnatural, and the set
Of the currents sorted not with our learning.
But in autumn sometimes all waters seem familiar,
With leaves, quite far out, littering the groundswell
On smooth days when the wind is light. And in
The haze then you can believe you are anywhere:
Standing off a home shore, and can even smell
The sweet dankness of smoke from known hearths. So we
Bore on, feeling courage more fresh in us
Than on the day of our sailing, musing
How far we might fetch before winter. Then
Through the mist we raised it, the abrupt cape
Looming dark and too near to leeward;
And recognized, like a home-thought too, in that landfall
The other side of autumn: that the year
Would bear us no farther, that we would not

Get beyond this. Perhaps it was named
At that moment in our minds, when we sighted
The shape of what we knew we would not pass.
You cannot mistake it: the dun headland
Like a dreaming Dutchman, dough-faced, staring
Seaward to the side we did not penetrate.
You almost think he will turn as you
Grope your way in with the lead line. Hope suddenly
Was as far behind us as home, and maybe
That made us clumsy, dull of heart going in.
But the waters are treacherous off that point,
With a fierce knot of currents twisting, even
At slack tide, snatching you from your seaway,
Sucking over a jagged shelving, and there is
Rough shoal beyond that. Three ships we lost
And many of their men there, and only we
Because we were driven far to port, almost
To the drag at the cliff's foot, and made in
Through the very spray, found the channel. There is
Nine fathoms all the way in there, to the broad pool
Of quiet water behind the tide-race;
You can anchor in five fathoms at
The lowest tide, with good holding, and sheltered.
You will use the harbor; in other years you will
Set out from there, in the spring, and think
Of that headland as home, calling it Cape
Delight, or Dutchman's Point. But what we found
You will find for yourselves, somewhere, for
Yourselves. We have not gone there again,
Nor ventured ever so far again. In
The south corner of the cove there is
An inlet flowing with sweet water,
And there are fruits in abundance, small
But delectable, at least at that season.

Bell Buoy

So we set signs over the world to say
To ourselves, returning, that we know the place,
Marking the sea too with shaped tokens
Of our usage, which even while they serve us
Make one with the unmeasured mist, sea-slap,
Green rock awash with the gray heave just
Out of sight, wet air saturated with sounds
But no breath—and in no time they are seen
To be in league with the world's remoteness
Whose features we grope for through fog and can never
Seize to our satisfaction. First the sound
Comes, and again, from the caged bell lost in the gray
Out ahead. Then into the glasses,
And gone, and again sighted, staying:
A black shape like nothing, rounded, rocking like
A chair, with a gull on top. Clearer
The dreaming bronze clangs over the lifting
Swell, through the fog-drift, clangs, not
On the sea-stroke but on the fifth second clangs,
Recalling something, out of some absence
We cannot fathom, with itself communing.
Was it we who made this, or the sea's necessity?
You can hear the wash on its rolling plates
Over your own wake, as you come near
And confirm: black can, odd number crusted
Already with gull crap over the new paint,
Green beard and rust speckling its undersides
As you see when it rolls. Nothing you can
Say as you pass, though there are only you two
And you come so close and seem to share
So much. And it will twist and stare after you
Through the closing fog, clanging. It is
A dead thing but we have agreed upon it: kept
To port, entering, starboard departing, as
May your fortune be, it can assure you
Of where you are, though it knows nothing
Of where you are going or may have been.

The Bones

It takes a long time to hear what the sands
Seem to be saying, with the wind nudging them,
And then you cannot put it in words nor tell
Why these things should have a voice. All kinds
Of objects come in over the tide-wastes
In the course of a year, with a throaty
Rattle: weeds, driftwood, the bodies of birds
And of fish, shells. For years I had hardly
Considered shells as being bones, maybe
Because of the sound they could still make, though
I knew a man once who could raise a kind
Of wailing tune out of a flute he had,
Made from a fibula; it was much the same
Register as the shells'; the tune did not
Go on when his breath stopped, though you thought it would.
Then that morning, coming on the wreck,
I saw the kinship. No recent disaster
But an old ghost from under a green buoy,
Brought in by the last storm, or one from which
The big wind had peeled back the sand grave
To show what was still left: the bleached, chewed-off
Timbers like the ribs of a man or the jawbone
Of some extinct beast. Far down the sands its
Broken cage leaned out, casting no shadow
In the veiled light. There was a man sitting beside it
Eating out of a paper, littering the beach
With the bones of a few more fish, while the hulk
Cupped its empty hand high over him. Only he
And I had come to those sands knowing
That they were there. The rest was bones, whatever
Tunes they made. The bones of things; and of men too
And of man's endeavors whose ribs he had set
Between himself and the shapeless tides. Then
I saw how the sand was shifting like water,
That once could walk. Shells were to shut out the sea,
The bones of birds were built for floating
On air and water, and those of fish were devised

For their feeding depths, while a man's bones were framed
For what? For knowing the sands are here,
And coming to hear them a long time; for giving
Shapes to the sprawled sea, weight to its winds,
And wrecks to plead for its sands. These things are not
Limitless: we know there is somewhere
An end to them, though every way you look
They extend farther than a man can see.

The Highway

It seems too enormous just for a man to be
Walking on. As if it and the empty day
Were all there is. And a little dog
Trotting in time with the heat waves, off
Near the horizon, seeming never to get
Any farther. The sun and everything
Are stuck in the same places, and the ditch
Is the same all the time, full of every kind
Of bone, while the empty air keeps humming
That sound it has memorized of things going
Past. And the signs with huge heads and starved
Bodies, doing dances in the heat,
And the others big as houses, all promise
But with nothing inside and only one wall,
Tell of other places where you can eat,
Drink, get a bath, lie on a bed
Listening to music, and be safe. If you
Look around you see it is just the same
The other way, going back; and farther
Now to where you came from, probably,
Than to places you can reach by going on.

Fable

However the man had got himself there,
There he clung, kicking in midair,
Hanging from the top branch of a high tree
With his grip weakening gradually.
A passerby who noticed him
Moved a safe distance from under the limb,
And then stood with his arms akimbo, calling,
"Let go, or you'll be killed; the tree is falling."
The man up on the branch, blindly clinging,
With his face toward heaven, and his knees heaving,
Heard this, through his depending to and fro,
And with his last ounce of good faith, let go.
No creature could have survived that fall,
And the stranger was not surprised at all
To find him dead, but told his body, "You
Only let go because you wanted to;
All you lacked was a good reason.
I let you hope you might save your skin
By taking the most comfortable way."
Then added, smiling, as he walked away,
"Besides, you'd have fallen anyway."

Luther

That old slider, the Prince of Falsehood,
I could recognize him in my cradle.
Though masked as the preacher, he took the pulpit,
Though he appeared as a swine, as a burning
Wisp of straw, or would be dandled in
The shape of an infant, always I could
Name him out. And yet there he stood
Mocking me with a scholar's prim tone,
Insisting that I could not say
What he was, with any authority;
Smiling to remind me that Holy
Church alone could pronounce him other

Than my own image, gnarled in my mind's mirror,
But that Holy Church might, for pay,
Countenance even that aspect of me
And indulge it with kindlier names
Than Evil. Then I flung the inkwell.
And every man may know the devil
From this day forth, who can tell
Black from white, for the devil
Is black. He is black. I have made him so.

Bucolic

Having enough plowshares,
The best will in the world, and fat pastures,
They beat the rest of their swords into shears.

The rewards of peace
They reap! With each haired, maned, shag beast,
As each tamed field, fattened for its fleece.

If, as of old,
But with stuffed bellies, the shorn wolves seek the fold,
It is only in winter, from the cold:

Whole days, when the snow is deep,
They lie, pink and harmless, among the sheep,
Nodding, whether in agreement or sleep.

Under the Old One

Helpless improver,
Grown numerous and clever
Rather than wise or loving,
Nothing is newer than ever
Under the sun:

Still specious, wanton, venal,
Your noises as dull
And smiles self-flattering
As was usual
Under any heaven.

How often, before this,
You went on knees
To moons of your own making,
Abject, with no peace
Under the old one.

No One

Who would it surprise
If (after the flash, hush, rush,
Thump, and crumpling) when the wind of prophecy
Lifts its pitch, and over the drifting ash
At last the trump splits the sky,
No One should arise

(No one just as before:
No limbs, eyes, presence;
Mindless and incorruptible) to inherit
Without question the opening heavens,
To be alone, to be complete,
And so forever?

Who had kept our secrets,
Whose wisdom we had heeded,
Who had stood near us (we proved it) again
And again in the dark, to whom we had prayed
Naturally and most often,
Who had escaped our malice—

No more than equitable
By No One to be succeeded,

Who had known our merits, had believed
Our lies, before ourselves whom we had considered
And (after ourselves) had loved
Constantly and well.

In a Cloud of Hands

Shadows shaped like rabbits and the mottlings
Of cats shake loose into a frenzy
Of gesticulation, with a sound
Of washing, and, as you were aware,
The whole night is alive with hands,

Is aflame with palms and offerings
And racked with a soft yammer for alms
Disclosing always the same craving
Through the three seasons of leaves
And in midwinter when the trees
Are hung with empty gloves all over:
The coin called out for is ourselves.

As you knew, you knew, born into hands,
To be handed away, in time.

Meantime these soft gordians
The fists of infants, these hands,
Padded crabs raining their prints
As on charts the contours of islands,
Vulnerable as eyes, these fans
Without feathers, knuckled sticks over
Breasts flowing like shawls or seawater,
That can learn flights exact as swallows,
Make music, pain, prayer, these
Rags dangling like moss from ancient wrists,

Loose, are sometimes generous,
Closed, can hold fast for a time;
Uncurled, as in supplication, empty

As crystals and shallow as dry lagoons
Scrawled over by water bugs, what have they
To offer but love in ignorance,
Uncertain even of its own questions,
As of the maps on its hands, whether
They lead anywhere at all.

In Stony Country

Somewhere else than these bare uplands dig wells,
Expect flowers, listen to sheep bells.
Wind; no welcome; and nowhere else
Pillows like these stones for dreaming of angels.

Catullus XI

Furius and Aurelius, bound to Catullus
Though he penetrate to the ends of the Indies
Where the eastern ocean crashing in echoes
      Pours up the shore,

Or into Hyrcania, soft Arabia,
Among Tartars or the archers of Parthia,
Or where the Nile current, seven times the same,
      Colors the waters,

Or through the beetling Alps, by steep passes, should come
To look on the monuments of great Caesar,
Gaul, the Rhine, and at the world's bitter end
      The gruesome Britons,

Friends, both prepared to share with me all these
Or what else the will of heaven may send,
To my mistress take these few sentiments,
      Put none too nicely:

Let her spread for her lechers and get her pleasure,
Lying wide to three hundred in one heat,
Loving none truly, but leaving them every one
      Wrung out and dropping;

But as for my love, let her not count on it
As once she could: by her own fault it died
As a flower at the edge of a field, which the plow
      Roots out in passing.

Summer

    Be of this brightness dyed
    Whose unrecking fever
    Flings gold before it goes
    Into voids finally
    That have no measure.

    Bird-sleep, moonset,
    Island after island,
    Be of their hush
    On this tide that balance
    A time, for a time.

    Islands are not forever,
    Nor this light again,
    Tide-set, brief summer,
    Be of their secret
    That fears no other.

Some Winter Sparrows

I

I hear you already, choir of small wheels,
                    Through frayed trees I see your
          Shaken flight like a shiver
          Of thin light on a river.

II

On a bitter day I juggle feathers,
                    My hands hatch, I am better
          Answered than puppet masters,
          With small winds at my fingers.

III

You pursue seeds, wings open on the snow,
                    Coming up then with white
          Beak, speaking; in my deep footprints
          You vanish, then you flower.

IV

Like no other: one white feather in either
                    Wing, every turn of yours
          Surprises me; you are quicker,
          Girl, than the catch in my breath.

V

Vanity: alone with many crumbs, teasing
                    Each briefly. When the rest
          Get here, the crumb nearest you
          Will be worth scrapping over.

VI

Caught in flight by harbor winds, you stumble
                    In air, your strung-out flock
          Shudders sideways, sinking, like
          A net when heavy fish strike.

VII

More snow: under a green fir-bush bowed low
            With flakes broad as cats' paws
        You hunch, puffed: if you do not
        Move maybe it will go away.

VIII

I find you too late, shriveled lid half-drawn,
            Grimy eye, your wings' rigor,
        Disheveled breast feathers worse
        Than ice inside my closed hand.

IX

And more than one. Who would save bits of string
            Kinked as stubbornly, as short,
        As dirty, knotted together
        Into fours, as your feet are?

X

You shriek like nails on a slate, one of you
            Falls dead at my feet, skull
        Split; and it is still winter,
        Not yet the season for love.

XI

Those blue pigeons: there is snow still to fall,
            But in the brief sun they
        Bob, gobble, begin their dance.
        You doze then, row of old men.

XII

Whether the gray cat is at the corner,
            The hawk hunting over
        The graves, or the light too late
        To trust, you will not come down.

Plea for a Captive

Woman with the caught fox
By the scruff, you can drop your hopes:
It will not tame though you prove kind,
Though you entice it with fat ducks
Patiently to your fingertips
And in dulcet love enclose it
Do not suppose it will turn friend,
Dog your heels, sleep at your feet,
Be happy in the house,
                              No,

It will only trot to and fro,
To and fro, with vacant eye,
Neither will its pelt improve
Nor its disposition, twisting
The raw song of its debasement
Through the long nights, and in your love,
In your delicate meats tasting
Nothing but its own decay
(As at firsthand I have learned),
                              Oh,

Kill it at once or let it go.

Choice of Prides
for Dido

To tell the truth, it would have its points
(Since fall we must) to do it proud:
To ride for your fall on a good mount
Hung with honors and looped garlands,
Moved by the crowd's flattering sounds,
Or to advance with brash din, banners,
Flights of arrows leaping like hounds.

But from a choice of prides I would pick
(Or so I hope) the bare cheek
To amble out, innocent of arms
And alone, under the cocked guns
Or what missiles might be in season,
And this in the pure brass of the act
Attired, and in no other armor.

Considering that, of every species
(I should reason) mine is most naked,
For all its draperies enacting
As a pink beast its honest nature,
I will take in this raw condition
What pride I can, not have my boast
In glad rags, my bravery plated.

And I should think myself twice lucky
(Stuck with my choice) if I could be sure
That I had been egged on by nothing
But neat pride, and not (as is common)
Brought to it by the veiled promptings
Of vanity, or by poverty
Or the fecklessness of despair.

The Climb

Where, like a whip, at the foot of the stairs
The banister rail licks round at them,
In a hushed flock they find they are huddled:
The night defunct, in their upturned faces
The party gone out like a light,
And more than one of them openmouthed
As horses reined up suddenly,

                              Hearing
Above the blood drumming in their ears
And the crepitant bulb in the dumb house,
Strained banisters creaking like rockers
Where the lurching cripple, drunk as a kite,

Scrapes, thuds, and snuffling half the time
On all fours, hauls himself upward
On the stairs over their heads,
                                        Like
Some weakness of their own: not to be helped
(Rather turn offensive) and at no time
To be denied—inviting himself
Along with them on the wrong occasion
That way, and soon goatish in his liquor,
Stumbling in boats by the moonlit lake,
Clawing and hugging not to fall—
                                        Ground out
From under his scuffling and skew stumps,
The racketing music of his ascent
Rains down on their faces, like stones dropped
Into a well, and it will echo,
Discordant, among them long after
They have heard him reach his room finally
And heard the door shut on their shame.

Blind Girl

     Silent, with her eyes
Climbing above her like a pair of hands drowning,
Up the tower stairs she runs headlong, turning
In a spiral of voices that grow no fainter, though
At each turn, through the tiny window,
The blood-shrieking starlings, flaking into the trees,
     Sound farther below.

     Still, as she runs
Turn above turn round the hollow flights, so
Ringing higher, the towering voices follow,
Out of each room renewed as she passes,
To echo, hopeless: their shrieked entreaties
Singing their love, and their gross resonance
     Her beauty's praises,

With no name too tender,
High, or childish to din their desperate
Invocations; confessing; swearing to dedicate
Their split hearts on salvers if only she
Will pause. Each raw plea raucous less to delay,
At last, than to claim her: "Though you turn for no other,
        Dear soul, this is me, me!"

But buffeted and stunned
By their spun cries as in clambering water,
Now if she tried she could not remember
Which door among those, nor what care, crime,
Possession, name, she had bolted from,
Nor how, the way opening to her blind hand,
        She had slipped past them,

Nor how many centuries
Ago. Only tells herself over and over
That their winding calls cannot forever
Build, but at their shrill peak stairs, tower, all
Into the loose air sprung suddenly, will fall,
Breathless, to nothing, and instantly her repose
        Be silent and final.

One-Eye

"In the country of the blind the one-eyed man is king."

On that vacant day
After kicking and moseying here and there
For some time, he lifted that carpet-corner
        His one eyelid, and the dyed light
Leapt at him from all sides like dogs. Also hues
That he had never heard of, in that place
        Were bleeding and playing.

Even so, it was
Only at the grazing of light fingers
Over his face, unannounced, and then his

Sight of many mat eyes, paired white
Irises like dried peas looking, that it dawned
On him: his sidelong idling had found
        The country of the blind.

        Whose swarming digits
Knew him at once: their king, come to them
Out of a saying. And chanting an anthem
        Unto his one eye, to the dry
Accompaniment that their leaping fingers made
Flicking round him like locusts in a cloud,
        They took him home with them.

        Their shapely city
Shines like a suit. On a plain chair he was set
In a cloak of hands, and crowned, to intricate
        Music. They sent him their softest
Daughters, clad only in scent and their own
Vast ears, meantime making different noises
        In each antechamber.

        They can be wakened
Sometimes by a feather falling on the next
Floor, and they keep time by the water-clocks'
        Dropping even when they sleep. Once
He would expound to them all, from his only
Light, day breaking, the sky spiked and the
        Earth amuck with color,

        And they would listen,
Amazed at his royalty, gaping like
Sockets, and would agree, agree, blank
        As pearls. At the beginning.
Alone in brightness, soon he spoke of it
In sleep only; "Look, look," he would call out
        In the dark only.

        Now in summer gaudy
With birds he says nothing; of their thefts, often
Beheld, and their beauties, now for a long time

Nothing. Nothing, day after day,
To see the black thumb big as a valley
Over their heads descending silently
Out of a quiet sky.

Small Woman on Swallow Street

Four feet up, under the bruise-blue
Fingered hat-felt, the eyes begin. The sly brim
Slips over the sky, street after street, and nobody
Knows, to stop it. It will cover
The whole world, if there is time. Fifty years'
Start in gray the eyes have; you will never
Catch up to where they are, too clever
And always walking, the legs not long but
The boots big with wide smiles of darkness
Going round and round at their tops, climbing.
They are almost to the knees already, where
There should have been ankles to stop them.
So must keep walking all the time, hurry, for
The black sea is down where the toes are
And swallows and swallows all. A big coat
Can help save you. But eyes push you down; never
Meet eyes. There are hands in hands, and love
Follows its furs into shut doors; who
Shall be killed first? Do not look up there:
The wind is blowing the building-tops, and a hand
Is sneaking the whole sky another way, but
It will not escape. Do not look up. God is
On High. He can see you. You will die.

The Gleaners

They always gather on summer nights there
On the corner under the buggy streetbulb,
Chewing their dead stubs outside the peeling
      Bar, those foreign old men,

Till the last streetcar has squealed and gone
An hour since into the growing silence,
Leaving only the bugs' sounds, and their own breathing;
      Sometime then they hobble off.

Some were already where they stay, last night,
In rooms, fumbling absently with laces,
Straps, trusses, one hand was nearly to a glass
      With a faceful of teeth

At the time the siren went shrieking for
The fire in the cigar factory there,
Half the town by then stinking like a crooked
      Stogie. Well there they are

Where all day they have been, beetling over
The charred pile, teetering like snails and careful
Under sooty hats, in ankle shoes, vests,
      Shirts grimed at collars and wrists,

Bending, babying peck baskets as they
Revolve on painful feet over the rubble,
Raking with crooked knuckles the amber pools
      For limp cheroots.

After dark there will still be a few turning
Slowly with flashlights. Except for coughs they are quiet;
Sober; they always knew something would happen,
      Something would provide.

Pool Room in the Lions Club

I'm sure it must be still the same,
Year after year, the faded room
Upstairs out of the afternoon,
The spidery hands, stalking and cautious
Round and round the airless light,
The few words like the dust settling
Across the quiet, the shadows waiting
Intent and still around the table
For the ivory click, the sleeves stirring,
Swirling the smoke, the hats circling
Remote and hazy above the light,
The board creaking, then hushed again.
Trains from the seaboard rattle past,
And from St. Louis and points west,
But nothing changes their concern,
Hurries or calls them. They must think
The whole world is nothing more
Than their gainless harmless pastime
Of utter patience protectively
Absorbed around one smooth table
Safe in its ring of dusty light
Where the real dark can never come.

John Otto

John Otto of Brunswick, ancestor
On my mother's side, Latin scholar,
Settler of the Cumberland Valley,
Schoolmaster, sire of a family,
Why, one day in your white age,
Did you heave up onto your old man's legs
In the house near Blaine, in Perry County,
And shut the gate and shuffle away
From the home of eighty years or so
And what cronies were left, and follow
The road out of the valley, up the hill,

Over the south mountain, to Carlisle,
The whole way on foot, in the wagon tracks,
To die of fatigue there, at ninety-six?
I can see Carlisle Valley spread below
And you, John, coming over the hill's brow,
Stopping for breath and a long look;
I can hear your breath come sharp and quick,
But why it was that you climbed up there
None of us remembers any more.
To see your son and his family?
Was the house too quiet in Perry County?
To ask some question, tell some secret,
Or beg some pardon before too late?
Or was it to look once again
On another valley green in the sun
Almost as in the beginning, to remind
Your eyes of a promise in the land?

Uncle Hess

Wryest of uncles, and most remote, Sam Hess,
Who named your tall daughter for the goddess
Minerva, whom all agreed she resembled
Till her car smashed with her and Olympus crumbled,
You had had enough of deities by then—
With neither of you as young as you had been,
And she some years a widow—for gods had proved
As mortal as anything that could be loved,
And lovable only as they seemed human.
Folks said they'd know that walk of yours in Japan,
But not what you would do next, who provided
A thermometer for the chicken shed
So the hens, if they chose, could read how hot
In the tin shade the latter day had got
And comfort themselves with knowledge. Whereas you
   deigned
To recognize your family, in the end,
Only on certain days when the air was right,

You were always, while not approachable, polite,
And wore your panama till the hour you died,
For the mad world must be kept mystified
Or it would bite. Canny and neat, whatever
You were was unmistakable, but never
Could be explained. And I wonder whether
Even now you would tell me anything more
Of every kinship than its madness,
If I could ask you, here, under your trees,
By your big house that watches the river still
Turning the cranky wheels of your mill
Before it twists toward Ohio around the bend
As though there were no questions and no end.

Grandfather in the Old Men's Home

Gentle at last, and as clean as ever,
He did not even need drink any more,
And his good sons unbent and brought him
Tobacco to chew, both times when they came
To be satisfied he was well cared for.
And he smiled all the time to remember
Grandmother, his wife, wearing the true faith
Like an iron nightgown, yet brought to birth
Seven times and raising the family
Through her needle's eye while he got away
Down the green river, finding directions
For boats. And himself coming home sometimes
Well-heeled but blind drunk, to hide all the bread
And shoot holes in the bucket while he made
His daughters pump. Still smiled as kindly in
His sleep beside the other clean old men
To see Grandmother, every night the same,
Huge in her age, with her thumbed-down mouth, come
Hating the river, filling with her stare
His gliding dream, while he turned to water,
While the children they both had begotten,

With old faces now, but themselves shrunken
To child-size again, stood ranged at her side,
Beating their little Bibles till he died.

Grandmother Watching at Her Window

There was always the river or the train
Right past the door, and someone might be gone
Come morning. When I was a child I mind
Being held up at a gate to wave
Good-bye, good-bye to I didn't know who,
Gone to the War, and how I cried after.
When I married I did what was right
But I knew even that first night
That he would go. And so shut my soul tight
Behind my mouth, so he could not steal it
When he went. I brought the children up clean
With my needle, taught them that stealing
Is the worst sin; knew if I loved them
They would be taken away, and did my best
But must have loved them anyway
For they slipped through my fingers like stitches.
Because God loves us always, whatever
We do. You can sit all your life in churches
And teach your hands to clutch when you pray
And never weaken, but God loves you so dearly
Just as you are, that nothing you are can stay,
But all the time you keep going away, away.

Grandmother Dying

Not ridden in her Christian bed, either,
But her wrenched back bent double, hunched over
The plank tied to the arms of her rocker
With a pillow on it to keep her head

Sideways up from her knees, and three others
Behind her in the high chair to hold her
Down so the crooked might be straight, as if
There was any hope. Who for ninety-three years,
Keeping the faith, believed you could get
Through the strait gate and the needle's eye if
You made up your mind straight and narrow, kept
The thread tight and, deaf both to left and to right
To the sly music beyond the ditches, beat
Time on the Book as you went. And then she fell.
She should have did what she was told, she should
Have called for what she needed, she did look
Sleeping on the pillows and to be trusted
Just for a bit, and Bid was not downstairs
A minute before hearing the hall creak
And the door crash back in the bathroom as
She fell. What was it, eighteen months, they took
Care of her crooked that way, feeding from
The side, hunching down to hear her, all
Knowing full well what the crooked come to
When their rockers stop. Still could hear what she
Thought good to hear, still croak: You keep my
Candy hid in that sweater drawer, Bid,
Only for company one piece, then you put it
Back again, hear? One after the other
A family of fevers visited her,
And last a daughter-in-law with a nasty
Cough combed her hair out pretty on the plank,
With a flower in it, and held a mirror
For her to see till it made her smile, But
Bid, she whispered, you keep wide of that new
Nurse's cough, she has TB. And where
Were the wars that still worried her, when
Most were dead a long time ago, and one
Son had come back and was there hanging
In sunlight, in a medal of glory, on
The wall in her room smelling of coal-gas
And petunias. One daughter lived and dusted
A nice brick house a block away, already
Rehearsing how she'd say, "Well, we was always

Good to our mumma anyway." Outside
The crooked river flowed easy, knowing
All along; the tracks smiled and rang away;
Help would come from the hills. One knotted hand
Of hers would hang up in the air above
Her head for hours, propped on its elbow, waving
In that direction. And when she heaved up
Her last breath, to shake it like a fist,
As out of a habit so old as to be
Nearly absent, at the dirty river
Sliding always there the same as ever,
Bid says you could not hear her because there
Came a black engine that had been waiting
Up the tracks there for ninety-four years, and
Snatched it out from her lips, and roared off
With it hooting downriver, making the tracks
Straighten out in front of it like a whip,
While the windows rattled loud to break, the things
On the shelves shook, the folds of her face jarred
And shivered; and when it was gone, for a long
Time the goosed laundry still leaped and jiggled
In the smutty wind outside, and her chair went on
Rocking all by itself with nothing alive
Inside it to explain it, nothing, nothing.

The Native

for Agatha and Stephen Fassett

He and his, unwashed all winter,
In that abandoned land in the punished
North, in a gnashing house sunk as a cheek,
Nest together, a bunting bundle crumpled
Like a handkerchief on the croaking
Back-broken bed jacked up in the kitchen; the clock
Soon stops, they just keep the cooker going; all
Kin to begin with when they crawl in under,
Who covers who they don't care.

He and his, in the settled cozy,
Steam like a kettle, rock-a-bye, the best
Went west long ago, got out from under,
Waved bye-bye to the steep scratched fields and scabby
Pastures: their chapped plaster of newspapers
Still chafes from the walls, and snags of string tattling
Of their rugs trail yet from stair-nails. The rest,
Never the loftiest, left to themselves,
                Descended, descended.

      Most that's his, at the best of times,
Looks about to fall: the propped porch lurches
Through a herd of licked machines crutched in their last
Seizures, each as ominously leaning
As the framed ancestors, trapped in their collars,
Beetling out of oval clouds from the black
Tops of the rooms, their unappeasable jowls
By nothing but frayed, faded cords leashed
              To the leaking walls.

      But they no more crash
Onto him and his than the cobwebs, or
The gritting rafters, though on the summer-people's
Solid houses the new-nailed shingles open
All over like doors, flap, decamp, the locked
Shutters peel wide to wag like clappers
At the clattering windows, and the cold chimneys
Scatter bricks downwind, like the smoking heads
              Of dandelions.

      In his threadbare barn, through
The roof like a snagtoothed graveyard the snow
Cradles and dives onto the pitched backs
Of his cow and plowhorse each thin as hanging
Laundry, and it drifts deep on their spines
So that one beast or other, almost every winter
Lets its knees stiffly down and freezes hard
To the barn floor; but his summer employers
              Always buy him others.

For there is no one else
Handy in summer, there in winter,
And he and his can dream at pleasure,
It is said, of houses burning, and do so
All through the cold, till the spooled snakes sleeping under
The stone dairy-floor stir with the turned year,
Waken, and sliding loose in their winter skins
Like air rising through thin ice, feed themselves forth
                    To inherit the earth.

Burning Mountain

No blacker than others in winter, but
The hushed snow never arrives on that slope.
An emanation of steam on damp days,
With a faint hiss, if you listen some places,
Yes, and if you pause to notice, an odor,
Even so near the chimneyed city, these
Betray what the mountain has at heart. And all night,
Here and there, popping in and out of their holes
Like groundhogs gone nocturnal, the shy flames.

Unnatural, but no mystery.
Many are still alive to testify
Of the miner who left his lamp hanging
Lit in the shaft and took the lift, and never
Missed a thing till, halfway home to supper
The bells' clangor caught him. He was the last
You'd have expected such a thing from;
The worrying kind, whose old-womanish
Precautions had been a joke for years.

Smothered and silent, for some miles the fire
Still riddles the fissured hill, deviously
Wasting and inextinguishable. They
Have sealed off all the veins they could find,
Thus at least setting limits to it, we trust.
It consumes itself, but so slowly it will outlast

Our time and our grandchildren's, curious
But not unique: there was always one of these
Nearby, wherever we moved, when I was a child.

Under it, not far, the molten core
Of the earth recedes from its thin crust
Which all the fires we light cannot prevent
From cooling. Not a good day's walk above it
The meteors burn out in the air to fall
Harmless in empty fields, if at all.
Before long it practically seemed normal,
With its farms on it, and wells of good water,
Still cold, that should last us, and our grandchildren.

Grandmother and Grandson

As I hear it, now when there is company
Always the spindly grandam, stuck standing
In her corner like a lady clock long
Silent, out of some hole in the talk
Is apt to clack cup, clatter teeth, and with
Saucer gesturing to no one special,
Shake out her paper voice concerning
That pimply boy her last grandson: "Now who,
Who does he remind you of?"

                              (Who stuffs there
With cake his puffed face complected half
Of yellow crumbs, his tongue loving over
His damp hands to lick the sticky
From bitten fingers; chinless; all boneless but
His neck and knees; and who now rolls his knowing
Eyes to their attention.)

                    In vain, in vain,
One after the other, their lusterless
Suggestions of faint likenesses; she
Nods at none, her gaze absent and more

Absent, as though watching for someone through
A frosted window, until they are aware
She has forgotten her own question.

When he is alone, though, with only her
And her hazy eyes in the whole house
To mind him, his way is to take himself
Just out of her small sight and there stay
Till she starts calling; let her call till she
Sounds in pain; and as though in pain, at last,
His answers, each farther, leading her
Down passages, up stairs, with her worry
Hard to swallow as a scarf-end, her pace
A spun child's in a blindfold, to the piled
Dust-coop, trunk- and junk-room at the top
Of all the stairs, where he hides till she sways
Clutching her breath in the very room, then
Behind her slips out, locking the door. His
Laughter down stair after stair she hears
Being forgotten. In the unwashed light,
Lost, she turns among the sheeted mounds
Fingering hems and murmuring, "Where, where
Does it remind me of?" Till someone comes.

The Hotel-Keepers

All that would meet
The eyes of the hawks who slid southward
        Like paired hands, year after year,
Over the ridge bloody with autumn
        Would be the two iron roofs,
House and barn, high in the gap huddled,
        Smoke leaking from the stone stack,
A hotel sign from one hook dangling,
        And the vacant wagon-track
Trailing across the hogbacked mountain
        With no other shack in sight
For miles. So an ignorant stranger

Might rein up there as night fell
(Though warned by his tired horse's rearing
    At nothing near the barn door)
And stopping, never be seen after;
    Thus peddlers' wares would turn up
Here and there minus their lost peddlers;
    Hounds nosing over the slope
Far downwind would give tongue suddenly
    High and frantic, closing in
On the back door; and in the valley
    Children raucous as starlings
Would start behaving at the mention
    Of the Hotel-Man.

Who was not tall,
Who stumped slowly, brawny in gum boots,
    And who spoke little, they said
(Quarrymen, farmers, all the local
    Know-it-alls). Who was seen once,
When a nosy passerby followed
    Low noises he thought were moans,
Standing with raised ax in the hayloft,
    And whose threats that time, although
Not loud, pursued the rash intruder
    For months. But who, even so,
Holed up in his squat house, five decades
    Outwintered the righteous wrath
And brute schemes they nursed in the valley,
    Accidents, as they well knew,
Siding with him, and no evidence
    With them. And survived to sit,
Crumpled with age, and be visited
    Blabbing in his swivel-chair
With eyes adrift and wits dismantled,
    From sagging lip letting fall
Allusions of so little judgment
    That his hotel doors at last
Were chained up and all callers fielded
    By his anxious wife.

A pleasant soul
Herself, they agreed: her plump features
          Vacant of malice, her eyes
Hard to abhor. And once he was crated
          And to his patient grave shrugged
(Where a weedy honor over him
          Seeded itself in no time)
They were soon fetching out their soft hearts
          To compare, calling to mind
Sickness, ruffians, the mountain winter,
          Her solitude, her sore feet,
Haling her down with all but music,
          Finally, to the valley,
To stand with bared gums, to be embraced,
          To be fussed over, dressed up
In their presents, and with kind people
          Be settled in a good house,
To turn chatty, to be astonished
          At nothing, to sit for hours
At her window facing the mountain,
          Troubled by recollections
No more than its own loosening stream
          Cracking like church pews, in spring,
Or the hawks, in fall, sailing over
          To their own rewards.

The Drunk in the Furnace

          For a good decade
The furnace stood in the naked gully, fireless
And vacant as any hat. Then when it was
No more to them than a hulking black fossil
To erode unnoticed with the rest of the junk-hill
By the poisonous creek, and rapidly to be added
          To their ignorance,

They were afterwards astonished
To confirm, one morning, a twist of smoke like a pale
Resurrection, staggering out of its chewed hole,
And to remark then other tokens that someone,
Cosily bolted behind the eyeholed iron
Door of the drafty burner, had there established
   His bad castle.

   Where he gets his spirits
It's a mystery. But the stuff keeps him musical:
Hammer-and-anviling with poker and bottle
To his jugged bellowings, till the last groaning clang
As he collapses onto the rioting
Springs of a litter of car seats ranged on the grates,
   To sleep like an iron pig.

   In their tar-paper church
On a text about stoke holes that are sated never
Their Reverend lingers. They nod and hate trespassers.
When the furnace wakes, though, all afternoon
Their witless offspring flock like piped rats to its siren
Crescendo, and agape on the crumbling ridge
   Stand in a row and learn.

THE SECOND FOUR
BOOKS OF POEMS

The Moving Target
The Lice
The Carrier of Ladders
Writings to an Unfinished Accompaniment

Preface

The title, with its numerological hopscotch, is of course intended to indicate that this book is the sequel to *The First Four Books of Poems*, originally published in 1975, which assembled the volumes of poems that I had written between 1947 and 1958.

The four volumes that make up the present collection span the sixties and the early years of the seventies. In several respects that have been noted since the first of them, *The Moving Target*, was published in 1963, they embody pronounced changes from the poems in the four books that preceded them. From the beginning they are less obviously formal—it might be more to the point to say that whatever may provide their form is less apparent. By the end of the poems in *The Moving Target* I had relinquished punctuation along with several other structural conventions, a move that evolved from my growing sense that punctuation alluded to and assumed an allegiance to the rational protocol of written language, and of prose in particular. I had come to feel that it stapled the poems to the page. Whereas I wanted the poems to evoke the spoken language, and wanted the hearing of them to be essential to taking them in.

By the time *The Lice* appeared in 1967 these formal changes and even some of the changes in tone and content that went with them, seemed less surprising to those who remarked on them in print, and it was possible for the new book to be considered as a reflection of its historic context, the world of the sixties.

It was an era, indeed an age, that has now receded a quarter of a century into the past and has become a time of legend. For many of us who lived through that period it remains in our minds as a moment of remarkable contradictions. There were the creeds of the flower children and the proliferation of nuclear weapons, the up-welling civil rights passions and the assassinations of King and the Kennedys, a nascent ecological consciousness and the development of events that became the undeclared war in Vietnam. Wild aspiration and vertiginous despair existed not alternately but at once, and at times we may have clung to visionary hopes not so much because they were really credible as because we felt it would be not only mean-spirited but fatal to abandon them. We knew a kind of willful desperation.

As we remember that time, some of us notice another contradiction, one that I suppose is familiar to many people in recalling moments of exceptional intensity. We know that age to be utterly beyond reach now, irretrievably past, a period whose distance we already feel as though it had stretched into centuries, and yet it appears to us to be not only recent but present, still with us not as a memory but as a part of our unfinished days, a ground or backdrop before which we live. It could be said that we are haunted by it, which would suggest that that time was not done with in us, that what we saw and felt then is still part of our incompleteness and our choices.

Of course I hope that is not the only reason why these books may still be read, and I hope that readers will continue to come to the poems and want to keep them long after the circumstances of the sixties and of the present century have gone. If they do so it will be because such readers continue to share with us something of history that is not strictly historic, something because of which we continue to write and read but which our words can never finally name.

Poems are written in moments of history, and their circumstances bear upon their language and tone and subject and feeling whether the authors are conscious of that happening or not, but it is hard to conceive of a poem being written only out of historic occasion. Somebody who was not a product of history alone had to be there and feel the need for words, hear them, summon them together.

My own life in the sixties also seemed to be made of contradictions: City life and rural life; Europe and America; Love of the old and a craving for change; Public issues and a disposition to live quietly. What has come to be called the cost of living was more moderate then. My own tastes were simple and I managed to live on little. Independence was something I treasured. In the early sixties I had an apartment in New York on the lower East Side, east of Tompkins Square, on the top floor of a building on East 6th Street that has since been torn down. The rent was very low. The front rooms looked out over a school and the old roofscapes of lower Manhattan to the Brooklyn Bridge. A political club, source of sinister rumors, occupied the ground floor of the building next door. Scaffolding came and went along the sidewalk, rising from the tide-lines of broken glass. Sometimes taxi drivers asked guests whether they really wanted to come to that neighborhood, and occasionally they even refused to drive there, but I loved living there and I walked endlessly through that section of the city and along the river to the end of the island. Much of the latter part of *The Moving Target* and the first part of *The Lice* was written there.

I had been born in New York, in a building that later became part of Columbia University and then was torn down, but I had grown up in other places. I felt bound to that city and time by ties that I was trying to fathom, and the poems reflected something of that and perhaps some of its excitement. They also testified to the deep foreboding that shadowed those years and which has not gone away since.

It was still possible then to take a boat to Europe, and if you applied early enough, even have a cabin to yourself for a couple of hundred dollars. In the early sixties my heaviest expense was traveling back and forth across the Atlantic to spend part of the spring, all summer, and the early fall, in the remote farmhouse in southwest France that I had acquired as a ruin some years before. I could live in that beautiful country for even less money than on the lower East Side. My life there was different in almost every respect from the life I knew in New York, but I had rapidly come to love that region and my neighbors, and to feel deeply attached to what I found there.

I had participated in the movement for nuclear disarmament since the late fifties and the Aldermaston marches in England, and after the Cuban missile crisis I found myself with new and urgent questions. It seemed clearer to me than ever that the menace of military destruction and the accelerating devastation of what remained of the natural world were effects of the same impulse. But one morning, looking south over the roofs of the city that I thought of as my own, I realized that if I were to be asked at that moment what I thought would be a good life I would not have a clear answer or one that would convince me. It occurred to me that I knew next to nothing about things that I took for granted every day: the roof over my head, the things I wore, the food I ate. I was over thirty and I thought it was time to know more about them than I did. Even so, such considerations might have led to nothing more than restless doubt if it had not been for the image of that old farmhouse and the perspectives it suggested. In the spring of 1963 I left New York and spent the next years in France, in the country, and the later poems in *The Lice*, with few exceptions, were written there, as were many of the poems in the two books that followed.

It was not a time or a life exempt from history. Papers, magazines, letters, brought the news. The Vietnam War phase by phase, and the disclosures of cruelty, ruin, arrogance and compounded dishonesty that it produced. The insistent awareness of the human wastage of the rest of life was set against a daily existence, and friendships, sights, sounds, the associations of a place that I regarded as a scarcely credible good fortune. I was convinced that the momentum of human projects was on a very unpromising course, and neither the quiet of the uplands nor the tenor of the news encouraged me to feel that the mere addition of a few more pages to the swelling flow of printed paper was a matter of great importance, but I continued to earn part of my income by translating. I felt at once a profound attraction to the ancient rural world in which I was living and a disquieting recognition of the fragility and uncertainty of my relation to it. For a while I wrote little unless words overtook me in the middle of doing something else such as repairing walls or working in the garden. Some of the latter poems in *The Lice* I wrote at a time when I thought I was not writing at all.

It is scarcely surprising that *The Lice* in particular has been described as dark and pessimistic. The general characterization ignores certain poems but it is true that the book is not predominantly sunny. Subsequent volumes, according to some readers, are less imbued with the imminence of menace and loss, more given to representation of the benison of Life. And so I have been asked whether my notion of our moment and its outlook has become more sanguine. The question, and perhaps these afterthoughts themselves, suggest that these poems were the more or less deliberate outcome of a kind of world-view or private ideology. I began with a resolution never to be guilty of anything of the kind, but poetry like speech itself is made out of paradox, contradiction, irresolvables. It employs words that are general and belong to everybody to convey something, whatever it is, that is specific and unique. It uses comparison to speak of what cannot be compared. It cannot be conscripted even into the service of good intentions. Its sources, as we know, are in sensibilities and the senses, not in reasons and opinions.

Yet reasons, thought, opinion, knowledge, contribute to the formation of a sensibility and to the life of the senses. Poets have been known to be smug about their fine uselessness, but the Vietnam War led many poets of my generation to try to use poetry to make something stop happening. We will never know whether all that we wrote shortened that nightmare by one hour, saved a single life or the leaves on one tree, but it seemed unthinkable to many of us not to make the attempt and not to use whatever talent we had in order to do it. In the process we produced a great many bad poems, but our opposition to that horror and degradation was more than an intellectual formulation, and sometimes it tapped depths of bewilderment, grief, rage, admiration, that took us by surprise. Occasionally it called forth writings that may be poems after all.

In the autumn of 1970 I traveled to southern Mexico, to Chiapas, to San Cristóbal de Las Casas, and I spent the winters there until 1973. Many of the poems in *Writings to an Unfinished Accompaniment* were written in an old adobe house on a back street in San Cristóbal—a place and time that added immeasurably to my sense of what has come to be called the Americas.

The current of the news since the most recent of these books was published has done nothing to brighten my view of history and where it is leading. Quite the contrary, perhaps, as cruelty, polymorphous nihilism, and organized obliteration have accelerated, and with them the racing disintegration of the entire evolutionary structure in which we are privileged still to exist. I think it is essential to recognize the probable result of what we have done and are doing, but when we have seen that and its roots in human motives, the menaced world may seem more to be treasured than ever. Certainly the anguish and anger we feel at the threat to it and the sleepless despoiling of it can lose their tragic complexity and become mere bitterness when we forget that their origin is a passion for the momentary countenance of the unrepeatable world.

W.S.M.

THE MOVING TARGET

(1963)

Home for Thanksgiving

I bring myself back from the streets that open like long
Silent laughs, and the others
Spilled into in the way of rivers breaking up, littered with
words,
Crossed by cats and that sort of thing,
From the knowing wires and the aimed windows,
Well this is nice, on the third floor, in back of the billboard
Which says Now Improved and I know what they mean,
I thread my way in and I sew myself in like money.

Well this is nice with my shoes moored by the bed
And the lights around the billboard ticking on and off like a
beacon,
I have brought myself back like many another crusty
Unbarbered vessel launched with a bottle,
From the bare regions of pure hope where
For a great part of the year it scarcely sets at all,
And from the night skies regularly filled with old movies of
my fingers,
Weightless as shadows, groping in the sluices,
And from the visions of veins like arteries, and
From the months of plying
Between can and can, vacant as a pint in the morning,
While my sex grew into the only tree, a joyless evergreen,
And the winds played hell with it at night, coming as they did
Over at least one thousand miles of emptiness,
Thumping as though there were nothing but doors, insisting
"Come out," and of course I would have frozen.

Sunday, a fine day, with my ears wiped and my collar buttoned
I went for a jaunt all the way out and back on
A streetcar and under my hat with the dent settled
In the right place I was thinking maybe—a thought
Which I have noticed many times like a bold rat—
I should have stayed making some of those good women
Happy, for a while at least, Vera with
The eau-de-cologne and the small fat dog named Joy,

Gladys with her earrings, cooking and watery arms, the one
With the limp and the fancy sheets, some of them
Are still there I suppose, oh no,

I bring myself back avoiding in silence
Like a ship in a bottle.
I bring my bottle.
Or there was thin Pearl with the invisible hair nets, the wind
     would not
Have been right for them, they would have had
Their times, rugs, troubles,
They would have wanted curtains, cleanings, answers, they
     would have
Produced families their own and our own, hen friends and
Other considerations, my fingers sifting
The dark would have turned up other
Poverties, I bring myself
Back like a mother cat transferring her only kitten,
Telling myself secrets through my moustache,
They would have wanted to drink ship, sea, and all or
To break the bottle, well this is nice,
Oh misery, misery, misery,
You fit me from head to foot like a good grade suit of longies
Which I have worn for years and never want to take off.
I did the right thing after all.

A Letter from Gussie

If our father were alive
The stains would not be defiling
The walls, nor the splintery porch
Be supported mostly by ants,
The garden, gone to the bad,
(Though that was purely Mother's)
Would not have poked through the broken
Window like an arm,
And you would never have dared
Behave toward me in this manner,

Like no gentleman and no brother,
Not even a card at Christmas
Last Christmas, and once again
Where are my dividends?

This is my reward
For remaining with our mother
Who always took your part,
You and your investments
With what she made me give you.
Don't you think I'd have liked
To get away also?
I had the brochures ready
And some nice things that fitted.
After all it isn't as though
You'd ever married. Oh
And the plumbing if I may say so
Would not have just lain down,
And the school children
Would not keep drilling the teeth
Which I no longer have
With their voices, and each time
I go out with a mouthful of clothespins
The pits of the hoodlums would not be
Dug nearer to the back steps.
Maybe you think my patience
Endures forever, maybe
You think I will die. The goat
If you recall I mentioned
I had for a while, died.
And Mother's canary, I
Won't pretend I was sorry.
Maybe you want me to think
You've died yourself, but I have
My information. I've told
Some people of consequence,
So anything can happen.
Don't say I didn't warn you.
I've looked long enough on the bright side,
And now I'm telling you

I won't stir from Mother's chair
Until I get an answer.
Morning noon and night
Can come and go as they please,
And the man from the funeral parlor
To change the calendars,
But I won't go to bed at all
Unless they come and make me,
And they'll have to bend me flat
Before they can put me away.

Lemuel's Blessing

> Let Lemuel bless with the wolf, which is a
> dog without a master, but the Lord hears his
> cries and feeds him in the desert.
> CHRISTOPHER SMART: *Jubilate Agno*

You that know the way,
Spirit,
I bless your ears which are like cypresses on a mountain
With their roots in wisdom. Let me approach.
I bless your paws and their twenty nails which tell their own
    prayer
And are like dice in command of their own combinations.
Let me not be lost.
I bless your eyes for which I know no comparison.
Run with me like the horizon, for without you
I am nothing but a dog lost and hungry,
Ill-natured, untrustworthy, useless.

My bones together bless you like an orchestra of flutes.
Divert the weapons of the settlements and lead their dogs a
    dance.
Where a dog is shameless and wears servility
In his tail like a banner,
Let me wear the opprobrium of possessed and possessors
As a thick tail properly used
To warm my worst and my best parts. My tail and my laugh
    bless you.

Lead me past the error at the fork of hesitation.
Deliver me

From the ruth of the lair, which clings to me in the morning,
Painful when I move, like a trap;
Even debris has its favorite positions but they are not yours;
From the ruth of kindness, with its licked hands;
I have sniffed baited fingers and followed
Toward necessities which were not my own: it would make me
An habitué of back steps, faithful custodian of fat sheep;

From the ruth of prepared comforts, with its
Habitual dishes sporting my name and its collars and leashes
    of vanity;

From the ruth of approval, with its nets, kennels, and
    taxidermists;
It would use my guts for its own rackets and instruments, to
    play its own games and music;
Teach me to recognize its platforms, which are constructed
    like scaffolds;

From the ruth of known paths, which would use my feet, tail,
    and ears as curios,
My head as a nest for tame ants,
My fate as a warning.

I have hidden at wrong times for wrong reasons.
I have been brought to bay. More than once.
Another time, if I need it,
Create a little wind like a cold finger between my shoulders,
    then
Let my nails pour out a torrent of aces like grain from a
    threshing machine;
Let fatigue, weather, habitation, the old bones, finally,
Be nothing to me,
Let all lights but yours be nothing to me.
Let the memory of tongues not unnerve me so that I stumble
    or quake.

But lead me at times beside the still waters;
There when I crouch to drink let me catch a glimpse of your
    image
Before it is obscured with my own.

Preserve my eyes, which are irreplaceable.
Preserve my heart, veins, bones,
Against the slow death building in them like hornets until the
    place is entirely theirs.
Preserve my tongue and I will bless you again and again.

Let my ignorance and my failings
Remain far behind me like tracks made in a wet season,
At the end of which I have vanished,
So that those who track me for their own twisted ends
May be rewarded only with ignorance and failings.
But let me leave my cry stretched out behind me like a road
On which I have followed you.
And sustain me for my time in the desert
On what is essential to me.

By Day and By Night

Shadow, index of the sun,
Who knows him as you know him,
Who have never turned to look at him since the beginning?

In the court of his brilliance
You set up his absence like a camp.
And his fire only confirms you. And his death is your freedom.

In the Gorge

Lord of the bow,
Our jagged hands
Like the ends of a broken bridge
Grope for each other in silence
Over the loose water.
Have you left us nothing but your blindness?

Separation

Your absence has gone through me
Like thread through a needle.
Everything I do is stitched with its color.

The Defeated

Beyond surprise, my ribs start up from the ground.
After I had sunk, the waters went down.
The horizon I was making for runs through my eyes.
It has woven its simple nest among my bones.

Noah's Raven

Why should I have returned?
My knowledge would not fit into theirs.
I found untouched the desert of the unknown,
Big enough for my feet. It is my home.
It is always beyond them. The future
Splits the present with the echo of my voice.
Hoarse with fulfilment, I never made promises.

As By Water

Oh
Together
Embracing departure
We hoisted our love like a sail

And like a sail and its reflection
However
We move and wherever
We shall be divided as by water
Forever forever
Though
Both sails shudder as they go
And both prows lengthen the same sorrow

Till the other elements
Extend between us also.

Things

Possessor
At the approach of winter we are there.
Better than friends, in your sorrows we take no pleasure,
We have none of our own and no memory but yours.
We are the anchor of your future.
Patient as a border of beggars, each hand holding out its whole
    treasure,

We will be all the points on your compass.
We will give you interest on yourself as you deposit yourself
    with us.
Be a gentleman: you acquired us when you needed us,
We do what we can to please, we have some beauty, we are
    helpless,
Depend on us.

Savonarola

Unable to endure my world and calling the failure God, I will
destroy yours.

Inscription for a Burned Bridge

Not your defeats, no.
I have gone in with the river.
I will serve you no longer but you may follow me.

Economy

No need to break the mirror.
Here is the face shattered,
Good for seven years of sorrow.

Lost Month

The light of the eyes in the house of the crow. Here the gods'
voices break and some will never sing again, but some come
closer and whisper. Never their names.

There are no hinges. One side of a door is simply forgotten
in the other.

In the windows the permissions appear, already lit, unasked,
but the wind is the wind of parsimony, and the shadows, which
are numerous and large, strain at their slender leashes. One fine
day the first knives come through the mirrors, like fins of sharks.
The images heal, but imperfectly.

We discover parts of ourselves which came to exist under this
influential sign.

Dead Hand

Temptations still nest in it like basilisks.
Hang it up till the rings fall.

Acclimatization

I entered at the top of my voice. I forget the song.
It came over me that they were deaf. They gave me
Their praise and left me mute.

I proceeded among them
Like a tourist liner among coin-divers.
I flung them what I had with me. Only then
I saw that their smiles were made of gold, and their
Hands and their wives. They gave me
Their thanks and left me penniless.

It was my fault, I
Got hungry, they fed me. I gave them
My solemn word in payment. And all
The bells in the city rang in triumph
Like cash registers. They gave me their credit
And left me with little hope.
When I woke I discovered
That they had taken my legs leaving me the shoes.

(Oh priceless city, the buildings
Rising at dawn to grip the first light
Like bars, and the mornings shattered
With trees into all the shapes of heartbreak!)

I sit among them
Smiling, but they
Demand, they demand, they demand.
There is no putting them off.
Theirs is the empire, and beyond the empire
There is only ignorance, where I could not survive
Without feet.

To deceive them is to perish. What
Do I have that is my own? I offer my
Degradation as a blind beggar offers his palm.
And I am given
This glass eye to set in the place of tears.

The Saint of the Uplands
for Margot Pitt-Rivers

Their prayers still swarm on me like lost bees.
I have no sweetness. I am dust
Twice over.
         In the high barrens
The light loved us.
Their faces were hard crusts like their farms
And the eyes empty, where vision
Might not come otherwise
Than as water.

They were born to stones; I gave them
Nothing but what was theirs.
I taught them to gather the dew of their nights
Into mirrors. I hung them
Between heavens.

I took a single twig from the tree of my ignorance
And divined the living streams under
Their very houses. I showed them
The same tree growing in their dooryards.
You have ignorance of your own, I said.
They have ignorance of their own.

Over my feet they waste their few tears.

I taught them nothing.
Everywhere
The eyes are returning under the stones. And over
My dry bones they build their churches, like wells.

The Nails

I gave you sorrow to hang on your wall
Like a calendar in one color.
I wear a torn place on my sleeve.
It isn't as simple as that.

Between no place of mine and no place of yours
You'd have thought I'd know the way by now
Just from thinking it over.
Oh I know
I've no excuse to be stuck here turning
Like a mirror on a string,
Except it's hardly credible how
It all keeps changing.
Loss has a wider choice of directions
Than the other thing.

As if I had a system
I shuffle among the lies
Turning them over, if only
I could be sure what I'd lost.
I uncover my footprints, I
Poke them till the eyes open.
They don't recall what it looked like.
When was I using it last?
Was it like a ring or a light
Or the autumn pond
Which chokes and glitters but
Grows colder?
It could be all in the mind. Anyway
Nothing seems to bring it back to me.

And I've been to see
Your hands as trees borne away on a flood,
The same film over and over,
And an old one at that, shattering its account
To the last of the digits, and nothing
And the blank end.

The lightning has shown me the scars of the future.

I've had a long look at someone
Alone like a key in a lock
Without what it takes to turn.

It isn't as simple as that.

Winter will think back to your lit harvest
For which there is no help, and the seed
Of eloquence will open its wings
When you are gone.
But at this moment
When the nails are kissing the fingers good-bye
And my only
Chance is bleeding from me,
When my one chance is bleeding,
For speaking either truth or comfort
I have no more tongue than a wound.

Sire

Here comes the shadow not looking where it is going,
And the whole night will fall; it is time.
Here comes the little wind which the hour
Drags with it everywhere like an empty wagon through leaves.
Here comes my ignorance shuffling after them
Asking them what they are doing.

Standing still, I can hear my footsteps
Come up behind me and go on
Ahead of me and come up behind me and
With different keys clinking in the pockets,
And still I do not move. Here comes
The white-haired thistle seed stumbling past through the
    branches
Like a paper lantern carried by a blind man.
I believe it is the lost wisdom of my grandfather
Whose ways were his own and who died before I could ask.

Forerunner, I would like to say, silent pilot,
Little dry death, future,
Your indirections are as strange to me
As my own. I know so little that anything
You might tell me would be a revelation.

Sir, I would like to say,
It is hard to think of the good woman
Presenting you with children, like cakes,
Granting you the eye of her needle,
Standing in doorways, flinging after you
Little endearments, like rocks, or her silence
Like a whole Sunday of bells. Instead, tell me:
Which of my many incomprehensions
Did you bequeath me, and where did they take you? Standing
In the shoes of indecision, I hear them
Come up behind me and go on ahead of me
Wearing boots, on crutches, barefoot, they could never
Get together on any door-sill or destination—
The one with the assortment of smiles, the one
Jailed in himself like a forest, the one who comes
Back at evening drunk with despair and turns
Into the wrong night as though he owned it—oh small
Deaf disappearance in the dusk, in which of their shoes
Will I find myself tomorrow?

Finally

My dread, my ignorance, my
Self, it is time. Your imminence
Prowls the palms of my hands like sweat.
Do not now, if I rise to welcome you,
Make off like roads into the deep night.
The dogs are dead at last, the locks toothless,
The habits out of reach.
I will not be false to you tonight.

Come, no longer unthinkable. Let us share
Understanding like a family name. Bring
Integrity as a gift, something
Which I had lost, which you found on the way.
I will lay it beside us, the old knife,
While we reach our conclusions.

Come. As a man who hears a sound at the gate
Opens the window and puts out the light
The better to see out into the dark,
Look, I put it out.

The Ships Are Made Ready in Silence

Moored to the same ring:
The hour, the darkness and I,
Our compasses hooded like falcons.

Now the memory of you comes aching in
With a wash of broken bits which never left port,
In which once we planned voyages.
They come knocking like hearts asking:
What departures on this tide?

Breath of land, warm breath,
You tighten the cold around the navel,
Though all shores but the first have been foreign,
And the first was not home until left behind.

Our choice is ours but we have not made it,
Containing as it does, our destination
Circled with loss as with coral, and
A destination only until attained.

I have left you my hope to remember me by,
Though now there is little resemblance.
At this moment I could believe in no change,
The mast perpetually
Vacillating between the same constellations,

The night never withdrawing its dark virtue
From the harbor shaped as a heart,
The sea pulsing as a heart,
The sky vaulted as a heart,
Where I know the light will shatter like a cry
Above a discovery:
"Emptiness.
Emptiness! Look!"
Look. This is the morning.

Route with No Number

If you want to come after me for any reason
I have left money in the bread-box,
Heart in the ice-box,
And in the mail-box, around the key,
A handkerchief for good-byes.
When you come to the end of the avenue of promises
And the dead bird falls from the limb
Turn away. It is the far fork. When you
Reach the street of the burying beetles
Follow their music as far as it will take you, skirting
The park where the famous
Sleep on their secrets.
And where the shout of the statue has filled
The square with long-dead silence,
Left.
At the turnstile of the hesitants I have left
A ticket for you in a little bee hole at eye level.
The toll keeper is not honest but he is
Cowardly and he has no legs.
Then in the empty boulevard with its view
Of the revolving hills you will see no car-tracks
But you will hear the sound of a streetcar and discover
That the road is moving under your feet, it is
Not bad: rows of portraits on either side
Like cell windows along a corridor, and
Your shadow ducking its head as it passes.

Oh it's passable, and besides I contrive
As I always did, to keep thinking
Of improvements, for instance
The other day ducks went over on their creaking wings
So I thought, "In the future there will be
No more migration, only travel,
No more exile, only distances."
Also it's hard to convey how indifferent
I had become to the jabber of bells
And the senseless applause of clocks.
And then today, without warning, at a place
Where they speak no language, the collectors come through
For my back taxes my present taxes
And my future taxes whether I arrive or not.
I fooled them of course in the old way.
And they fooled me in the old way
And took everything but a few false decisions in the old way,
And I pray for them in the old way:
May the tracks be laid over them
And their fingers be picked off like daisy petals:
"She loathes me, she loathes me not."

Either way, I must tell you, in my present place
I can't hold out hope or any other flags.
There's not even a little privacy: you can see
Eyes lined up to ripen on all the sills.
And once here you're better than I am
If you can find your way back again.
However, I have visited the Day of the Dog,
But it was not yet open and I passed on.
Tell Mrs. H. just the same,
Who said I'd never get anywhere.
What a juncture.
I have gone faithfully into all the churches
And passed on, disappointed.
I have seen streets where the hands of the beggars
Are left out at night like shoes in a hotel corridor.
Several I thought had once been mine and might be again.
I have found many lost things and I have left them that way,
I have created enough disturbance.

I have come on many wasted things.
I have not yet come to my youth.

Now I am sitting
Behind filthy nightscapes, in the echoing room provided,
Among a few retired ornaments.
All the words have been emptied from the books.
The heating is hopeless at any hour. I am
Eating one of my last apples and waiting
For my departure to overtake me
With its empty windows coming up
Like cards, the game
Always turns out the same,
Mother, Father, Luke and John,
My line, my sign, my love,
Think of the cards that were held out to me
And I had to choose this one!

To My Brother Hanson
B. Jan. 28, 1926 / D. Jan. 28, 1926

My elder,
Born into death like a message into a bottle,
The tide
Keeps coming in empty on the only shore.
Maybe it has lovers but it has few friends.
It is never still but it keeps its counsel, and

If I address you whose curious stars
Climbed to the tops of their houses and froze,
It is in hope of no
Answer, but as so often, merely
For want of another, for
I have seen catastrophe taking root in the mirror,
And why waste my words there?

Yes, now the roads themselves are shattered
As though they had fallen from a height, and the sky

Is cracked like varnish. Hard to believe,
Our family tree
Seems to be making its mark everywhere.
I carry my head high
On a pike that shall be nameless.

Even so, we had to give up honor entirely,
But I do what I can. I am patient
With the woes of the cupboards, and God knows—
I keep the good word close to hand like a ticket.
I feed the wounded lights in their cages.
I wake up at night on the penultimate stroke, and with
My eyes still shut I remember to turn the thorn
In the breast of the bird of darkness.
I listen to the painful song
Dropping away into sleep.

Blood
Is supposed to be thicker. You were supposed to be there
When the habits closed in pushing
Their smiles in front of them, when I was filled
With something else, like a thermometer,
When the moment of departure, standing
On one leg, like a sleeping stork, by the doorway,
Put down the other foot and opened its eye.
I
Got away this time for a while. I've come
Again to the whetted edge of myself where I
Can hear the hollow waves breaking like
Bottles in the dark. What about it? Listen, I've

Had enough of this. Is there nobody
Else in the family
To take care of the tree, to nurse the mirror,
To fix up a bite for hope when the old thing
Comes to the door,
To say to the pans of the balance
Rise up and walk?

In the Night Fields

I heard the sparrow shouting "Eat, eat,"
And then the day dragged its carcass in back of the hill.
Slowly the tracks darkened.

The smoke rose steadily from no fires.
The old hunger, left in the old darkness,
Turned like a hanged knife.
I would have preferred a quiet life.
The bugs of regret began their services
Using my spine as a rosary. I left the maps
For the spiders.
Let's go, I said.

     Light of the heart,
The wheat had started lighting its lanterns,
And in every house in heaven there were lights waving
Hello good-bye. But that's
Another life.
Snug on the crumbling earth
The old bottles lay dreaming of new wine.
I picked up my breast, which had gone out.
By other lights I go looking for yours

Through the standing harvest of my lost arrows.
Under the moon the shadow
Practices mowing. Not for me, I say,
Please not for my
Benefit. A man cannot live by bread
Alone.

Now and Again

Now that summer is lying with a stone for a lantern
You would think we could keep our thoughts
On the eyes of the living,

Those refugees,

Webs without spiders, needs without choice,
Lakes behind grids but without maps
Into which nothing keeps dropping like a stone.

Even our own.

Even the heart, that closed eye,
Has had its glimpses,
So that the marbled lid winced and fluttered.

You would think we would know the present when it came,
And would remember what we knew,

And would recognize its fish-eyed children, able
To stare through tears forever
Not knowing them for sorrow and their own.

When you consider how learning happens
You would think once might be enough.
You would suppose such pain would become knowledge
And such knowledge would be wisdom
And such wisdom would stay with us.

Each time
The leaves hesitate but finally they fall.

The stars that came with us this far have gone back.
The wings of the migrants wake into autumn, and through
The hammered leaves the walnuts
Drop to the road and open:
Here is the small brain of our extinct summer.
Already it remembers nothing.

Another Year Come

I have nothing new to ask of you,
Future, heaven of the poor.
I am still wearing the same things.

I am still begging the same question
By the same light,
Eating the same stone,

And the hands of the clock still knock without entering.

October

I remember how I would say, "I will gather
These pieces together,
Any minute now I will make
A knife out of a cloud."
Even then the days
Went leaving their wounds behind them,
But, "Monument," I kept saying to the grave,
"I am still your legend."

There was another time
When our hands met and the clocks struck
And we lived on the point of a needle, like angels.

I have seen the spider's triumph
In the palm of my hand. Above
My grave, that thoroughfare,
There are words now that can bring
My eyes to my feet, tamed.
Beyond the trees wearing names that are not their own
The paths are growing like smoke.

The promises have gone,
Gone, gone, and they were here just now.
There is the sky where they laid their fish.
Soon it will be evening.

Departure's Girl-Friend

Loneliness leapt in the mirrors, but all week
I kept them covered like cages. Then I thought
Of a better thing.

And though it was late night in the city
There I was on my way
To my boat, feeling good to be going, hugging
This big wreath with the words like real
Silver: *Bon Voyage.*

                    The night
Was mine but everyone's, like a birthday.
Its fur touched my face in passing. I was going
Down to my boat, my boat,
To see it off, and glad at the thought.
Some leaves of the wreath were holding my hands
And the rest waved good-bye as I walked, as though
They were still alive.

And all went well till I came to the wharf, and no one.

I say no one, but I mean
There was this young man, maybe
Out of the merchant marine,
In some uniform, and I knew who he was; just the same
When he said to me where do you think you're going,
I was happy to tell him.

But he said to me, it isn't your boat,
You don't have one. I said, it's mine, I can prove it:
Look at this wreath I'm carrying to it,
Bon Voyage. He said, this is the stone wharf, lady,
You don't own anything here.
                    And as I
Was turning away, the injustice of it
Lit up the buildings, and there I was
In the other and hated city
Where I was born, where nothing is moored, where
The lights crawl over the stone like flies, spelling now,

Now, and the same fat chances roll
Their many eyes; and I step once more
Through a hoop of tears and walk on, holding this
Buoy of flowers in front of my beauty,
Wishing myself the good voyage.

One Way

Oh hell, there once again hunger
Gets up in the middle of a meal and without
A word departs. I go after: what
Would I be without her?

                    It is

Night, I am
As old as pain and I have
No other story.
We do not keep to the telegraph lines.
"Is there a map for this?" I call
After. "Is there even
A name for this? I spend my
Life asking, is there even a name
For you?"

          And what a starved path,
Licking stones; often
I am sure one side has eaten the other.
And with what bitterness I remember
I had not yet had my fill
Of dissatisfaction. My mouth
Works like a heart. More and more
I get like shadows; I find out
How they hate.
                    And then she is gone.

No astonishment anywhere. The owls
Are digesting in silence.
I will not look up again to learn again

That despair has no star.
Don't ask me why, I
Lift my feet in their dice-boxes.
I believe I continue
As she would have done, I believe.

                                        Don't ask me
Why: this time it is not I
Waking the birds. Somewhere
The light begins to come to itself.
As I walk, the horizon
Climbs down from its tree and moves toward me
With offerings. There
At the table which she has set with
The old plates, she is waiting, and to us
The day returns like a friend
Bringing others.

Recognition

The bird of ash has appeared at windows
And the roads will turn away, mourning.
What distances we survived, the fire
With its one wing
And I with my blackened heart.

I came home as a web to its spider,
To teach the flies of my household
Their songs. I walked
In on the mirrors scarred as match-boxes,
The gaze of the frames and the ticking
In the beams. The shadows
Had grown a lot and they clung
To the skirts of the lamps.
Nothing
Remembered who I was.

The dead turn in their locks and
I wake like a hand on a handle. Tomorrow
Marches on the old walls, and there
Is my coat full of darkness in its place
On the door.
Welcome home,
Memory.

Invocation

The day hanging by its feet with a hole
In its voice
And the light running into the sand

Here I am once again with my dry mouth
At the fountain of thistles
Preparing to sing.

The Poem

Coming late, as always,
I try to remember what I almost heard.
The light avoids my eye.

How many times have I heard the locks close
And the lark take the keys
And hang them in heaven.

Second Sight

Turning the corner I
Realize that I have read this before.
It is summer. The sun
Sits on the fire-escape while its children

Tear their voices into little shreds.
I wish I could remember how it ended.

This is the passage where the mirrors
Are embarking at the ends of the streets.
The drawn shades are waving
From empty rooms, and the old days
Are fanning themselves here and there on the steps.
The fact is, I have come back
Again and again, as a wish on a postcard, only
This time the jewels are turning
In the faces, and it seems I should know
The motive for the laundry, and the name
Of the man with the teeth, at intervals saying
You want to buy your time.

I feel this is a bit that I know how it goes;
I should be able to call
Most of the windows
By their Christian names, they have whole
Chapters to themselves
Before the pigeons give up, and the brightest
Are reflections of darkness. But no,
They've got it wrong, they've got it wrong,
Like anywhere else.

It's the old story,
Every morning something different is real.
This place is no more than the nephew of itself,
With these cats, this traffic, these
Departures
To which I have kept returning,
Having tasted the apple of my eye,
Saying perennially
Here it is, the one and only,
The beginning and the end.
This time the dials have come with the hands and
Suddenly I was never here before.
Oh dust, oh dust, progress
Is being made.

Witnesses

Evening has brought its
Mouse and let it out on the floor,
On the wall, on the curtain, on
The clock. You with the gloves, in the doorway,
Who asked you to come and watch?

As the bats flower in the crevices
You and your brothers
Raise your knives to see by.
Surely the moon can find her way to the wells
Without you. And the streams
To their altars.

As for us, we enter your country
With our eyes closed.

The Indigestion of the Vampire

Look at this red pear
Hanging from a good family

Where the butcher hung the rag on the tree.

The bat's bloated again,
Hooked on his dark nimbus
Getting over it.
Here is the cure of pity
Upside down.

Elsewhere the laundry
Is buried,
The deer tracks left by his teeth
Look for the crossroads,
The veins that are still good
Hold out their hands.
                    Here's his story.

His bridges are not burned only folded.
In a while the swollen life
He calls his own
Will shrink back till it fits the mirrors,
No worse for no wear;
The eyes will come
To conceal movement again;
He will find his voice to fly by.

That's how he does it: rock-a-bye,
Hanging there with his silence all wool
And others at heart,
Two pounds in his pound bag,

Shaped like a tear but
Not falling for anyone.

The Singer

The song dripping from the eaves,
I know that throat

With no tongue,
Ignoring sun and moon,

That glance, that creature
Returning to its heart

By whose light the streams
Find each other.

Untameable,
Incorruptible,

In its own country
It has a gate to guard.

There arrived without choice
Take up water

And lay it on your eyes saying
Hail clarity

From now on nothing
Will appear the same

And pass through
Leaving your salt behind.

The Continuo

What can you do with this
Wind, you can't
Reason with it, entertain it, send
It back, live on it or with it, fold it
Away and forget it, coming at you

All the time perfectly
Empty no face no background,
Before you know it, needing
No doors,
Lighting out of trees, flags, windows of
Fallen buildings, with a noise that could
Run its own trains, what
Can you learn from it
Leaving its shoes all over the place
Turning day and night into
Back yards
Where it knows the way.

Vocations

I

Simplicity, if you
Have any time
Where do you spend it?
I tempt you with clear water.
All day I hang out a blue eye. All night
I long for the sound of your small bell
Of an unknown metal.

II

Seeing how it goes
I see how it will be:
The color leaves but the light stays,
The light stays but we cannot grasp it.
We leave the tree rocking its
Head in its hands and we
Go indoors.

III

The locked doors of the night were still sitting in their circle.
I recalled the promises of the bridges.
I got up and made my way
To wash my shadow in the river.
In a direction that was lost
The hands of the water have found tomorrow.

Air

Naturally it is night.
Under the overturned lute with its
One string I am going my way
Which has a strange sound.

This way the dust, that way the dust.
I listen to both sides
But I keep right on.

I remember the leaves sitting in judgment
And then winter.

I remember the rain with its bundle of roads.
The rain taking all its roads.
Nowhere.

Young as I am, old as I am,

I forget tomorrow, the blind man.
I forget the life among the buried windows.
The eyes in the curtains.
The wall
Growing through the immortelles.
I forget silence
The owner of the smile.

This must be what I wanted to be doing,
Walking at night between the two deserts,
Singing.

The Present

The walls join hands and
It is tomorrow:
The birds clucking to the horses, the horses
Doing the numbers for the hell of it,
The numbers playing the calendars,
The saints marching in,
It seems only yesterday,
                         when what
I keep saying to myself is
Take a leaf from the fire, open
Your hand, see
Where you are going,
When what I am trying to find is
The beginning,
In the ashes,

A wing, when what we are looking for
In each other
Is each other,

The stars at noon,

While the light worships its blind god.

Standards

Nothing will do but
I must get a new flag,
I've buried enough under this one,

And then there are my
Followers, mad for a bit of color,
Damn them,

And the end I suppose is not yet,
The way the trees come beating
Their horses, and the wheat is camped
Under its dead crow,
The rivers under themselves. And I'm not ready
To just sit down and let the horizon
Ride over me.

Maybe I thought
I could go on and on flying the same rag,
Like the fire,
But it's faded white and I'm
Not the fire, I'll have to find
Something bright and simple to signify
Me, what an order.

What an order but I'll have to do something.
Up until now the pulse
Of a stone was my flag
And the stone's in pieces.

From a Series

Division, mother of pain,
Look at you bringing
Your children up just as formerly
And look at me back again
In this former life,
You've all grown but I haven't.

You might as well ask me why
I come back to a month
All right
Why do I and when I think
There used to be eleven others
At one time as they say and those
Other days in the week
I see the posters have changed
But the day's the same and even
When it was here hope would wait
Out in the garden rocking the grave
Now she's dead too and that's a blessing.

Just the same it was nice the way
You had them trained
And as for me it was nice
The way I used to be able
To forget between
The last time I learned and the next time;
The way I loved
The east and the west my horses;
It had its points, surely, if only
I could have been one at a time.
How long

Can the hands of the clock go on drowning
Without my helping
One way or the other
How long
Before freedom looms in front of me
And the door falls in on my tongue?

Bread and Butter

I keep finding this letter
To the gods of abandon,
Tearing it up: Sirs,
Having lived in your shrines
I know what I owe you—

I don't, did I ever? With both hands
I've forgotten, I keep
Having forgotten. I'll have no such shrines here.
I will not bow in the middle of the room
To the statue of nothing
With the flies turning around it.
On these four walls I am the writing.

Why would I start such a letter?
Think of today, think of tomorrow.
Today on the tip of my tongue,
Today with my eyes,
Tomorrow the vision,
Tomorrow

In the broken window
The broken boats will come in,
The life boats
Waving their severed hands,

And I will love as I ought to
Since the beginning.

We Continue

for Galway Kinnell

The rust, a little pile of western color, lies
At the end of its travels,
Our instrument no longer.

Those who believe
In death have their worship cut out for them.
As for myself, we
Continue,
An old
Scar of light our trumpet,

Pilgrims with thorns
To the eye of the cold
Under flags made by the blind,
In one fist

This letter that vanishes
If the hand opens:

Charity, come home,
Begin.

Marica Lart

Now
We do not even know
What to wish for you

Oh sleep rocked
In an empty hand.

Reunion

At the foot of your dry well,
Old friend in ambush,
What did we expect?

Have we really changed?
You could never forgive me for
Pleasures divulged or defeats kept secret.

You have flowered in your little heat
Like an untrimmed wick.
It is plain what you are thinking

While I am thinking
How you have grown into your ugliness
Which at one time did not fit you.

Console your distaste for departures:
I find I brought only the one.
Hand me my coat.

Friend Reductio,
Would you have known delight
If it had knocked you down?

Walk-Up

The inspector of stairs is on the stairs
Oh my God and I thought it was Sunday,
His advance like a broom and those stairs going
Down to meet him, all right
What that's mine will he show me
To be ashamed of this time

The spiders in my face, the whistles
In the cupboards,
The darkness in my shoes, going out
To deep water

No

The sky's at home in these windows, and the maps
Of themselves on these walls,
And your letter is enough improvement
For anywhere, lying open
On my table, my
Love

I won't close a thing

Let him arrive fanning himself
With his calendar, let him become
At the door the inspector of doors and find
Mine open,
Inspector of hands—

            His name
Would mean nothing to me, his questions are not
His own, but let my answers
Be mine.

To Where We Are

With open arms the water runs in to the wheel.

I come back to where I have never been.
You arrive to join me.
We have the date in our hands.

We come on to where we are, laughing to think
Of the Simplicities in their shapeless hats
With a door so they can sit outside it

I hope I may say
Our neighbors
Natives of now, creatures of
One song,
Their first, their last,

Listen.

The Crossroads of the World Etc.

I would never have thought I would be born here

So late in the stone so long before morning
Between the rivers learning of salt

Memory my city

Hope my city Ignorance my city
With my teeth on your chessboard black and white
What is your name

With my dead on your
Calendar with my eyes
In your paint
Opening
With my grief on your bridges with my voice
In your stones what is your name
Typed in rain while I slept

The books just give
The names of locks
The old books names of old locks
Some have stopped beating

Photos of
Dead doors left to right still hide
The beginning
Which do you
Open if
Any
My shadow crosses them trying to strike a light

Today is in another street

I'm coming to that
Before me

The bird of the end with its
Colorless feet
Has walked on windows

I lose the track but I find it
Again again
Memory

In the mirrors the star called Nothing

Cuts us off

Wait for me

Ruin
My city
Oh wreck of the future out of which
The future rises
What is your name as we fall

As the mortar
Falls between the faces
As the one-legged man watching the chess game

Falls
As the moon withers in the blueprint
And from our graves these curtains blow

These clouds on which I have written
Hope

As I
Have done
Hearing the light flowing over a knife
And autumn on the posters

Hearing a shadow beating a bell
Ice cream in ambulances, a chain full of fingers
The trains on the
Trestles faster than their lights

The new scars around the bend
Arriving

Hearing the day pass talking to itself
Again
Another life

Once a key in another country
Now ignorance
Ignorance

I keep to your streets until they vanish
There is singing beyond
The addresses can I
Let it go home alone

A playing on veins a lark in a lantern

It conducts me to a raw Sabbath

On all sides bread
Has been begged, here are monuments
At their feet this
Section
The tubes tied off the cry gone

The cry
I would never have thought
The lightning rises and sets

Rust, my brothers, stone, my brothers
Hung your spirits on the high hooks
Can't reach them now

You've swallowed night I swallow night
I will swallow night
And lie among the games of papers
And the gills of nibbling
Fires

Will I

While the sky waits in the station like a man
With no place to go

Will I

I hear my feet in a tunnel but I move
Like a tear on a doorsill
It's now in my wrist

Ahead of me under
False teeth hanging from a cloud, his
Sign that digs for his house, Tomorrow,
The oldest man
Is throwing food into empty cages

Is it to me
He turns his cobweb
I go toward him extending
My shadow taking it to him
Is it to me he says no

Is it to me
He says no no I haven't time

Keep the lost garment, where would I find the owner?

Resolution

Back of the door the child is playing that
Piano drawn on a piece of paper
He keeps to the black notes it
Gets dark
He moves to the white notes it gets
Too dark I can't hear him any more

As I was

The customs men multiply between
He takes with him
Memory leaking feathers
If he knew what I
Know now in the same X-ray

The pictures turn to the walls here is
Death the same taste in
A different color
Thinks I will say it

The scars
Grow leaves the feeling
Runs ahead and hides in bushes with its
Knives painted out
I know

Thinks I will say
It say it
As the hole climbs the sky

> *Oh let it be yesterday surely*
> *It's time*

Never

Never

A usage I'm learning a beak at my ear
I hear

The hearts in bottles
The dice lying awake

The clock dropping its shoes and
No floor

Before That

It was never there and already it's vanishing

City unhealthy pale with pictures of
        Cemeteries sifting on its windows
        Its planets with wind in their eyes searching among
        The crosses again
        At night
        In dark clothes

        It was never there

        Papers news from the desert
        Moving on or
        Lying in cages
        Wrapping for their
        Voices

The river flowing past its other shore
Past the No Names the windows washed at night
And who is my
Name for

In my pocket
Slowly the photographs becoming saints
Never there

I put out my hand and the dark falls through it
Following a flag

Gutters made in my time rounded with
The wounded in mind
The streets roped off for the affectionate
Will do for the
Mutilated

If I
Lie down in the street and that smoke comes out of me

Who
Was it

It was a night like this that the ashes were made

Before that
Was always the fire

For the Grave of Posterity

This stone that is
not here and bears no writing commemorates
the emptiness at the end of
history listen you without vision you can still

hear it there is
nothing it is the voice with the praises
that never changed that called to the unsatisfied
as long as there was
time
whatever it could have said of you is already forgotten

This Day of This Month of This Year of This

How can I persuade today that it's

Here how can I

Say   My
Love

Outlined in knives

I'm tracing you with an
Opened finger the eye
Of my thumb is away
Is not
This your home where are you

Is not this
Your home

Drunks on the compass feathers on the floor yes here

Where the river flows around our suitcases
Where the light shakes the buildings
Where they teach silence in both schools on this block
    but
The streets give
                    Cry give cry all the time

Where Easter the phantom hounds the Holy Rollers
Where the months are shot at midnight by
A cop in civvies in a dark car on a side street
Where my birth came upon me comes upon me where

            My hand that found the hand
            Of day finds the hand of
            Absence

            Where my arm is smoke

Before the two cripples pass on their one crutch
Before the spittle rises from the sidewalk
Before the darkness comes out of the
Trumpet
Tunnel to itself subway with
No platform

                            I want
To declare myself

I want to declare Now

Her name is now wherever she is
            There is none beside her

            For whom my hands were split
I want

To make time with her under the same flag
Running water with running water I want
To point out the sights ahead of us would
There be sights ahead of us

With my story

With the child I left to die
                         Dying
With the love I wrapped in a map
                         There

With the uniform I wore
                         Black
                         As they all are

With my teeth graveyard for the nameless
With extinction my ancestor
With a fresh sparrow caught in the headlines
With the funerals in the bridges
                         From which the music
                         With
My lungs full of ashes
With what I empty from my shoes

With the other calendar other
        Facade in which I have a darkness
        Marked X to which my key marked X

        X in my hand in both hands
        X waiting

Oh with
        Death testing itself in my ocean cream in my coffee
        Death my window at which the birds come to
           drink at night

Oh with your face her face your
Face invisible

With death my hands

With my hands nothing oh with death my words

With my words nothing
One at a time

Oh with death my
Heart
With my heart

Lantern of ice

Oh with her shoes
                    Hanging
                    In the clock

The Way to the River

The way to the river leads past the names of
Ash the sleeves the wreaths of hinges
Through the song of the bandage vendor

I lay your name by my voice
As I go

The way to the river leads past the late
Doors and the games of the children born looking backwards
They play that they are broken glass
The numbers wait in the halls and the clouds
Call
From windows
They play that they are old they are putting the horizon
Into baskets they are escaping they are
Hiding

I step over the sleepers the fires the calendars
My voice turns to you

I go past the juggler's condemned building the hollow
Windows gallery
Of invisible presidents the same motion in them all
In a parked cab by the sealed wall the hats are playing
Sort of poker with somebody's
Old snapshots game I don't understand they lose
The rivers one
After the other I begin to know where I am
I am home

Be here the flies from the house of the mapmaker
Walk on our letters I can tell
And the days hang medals between us
I have lit our room with a glove of yours be
Here I turn
To your name and the hour remembers
Its one word
Now

Be here what can we
Do for the dead the footsteps full of money
I offer you what I have my
Poverty

To the city of wires I have brought home a handful
Of water I walk slowly
In front of me they are building the empty
Ages I see them reflected not for long
Be here I am no longer ashamed of time it is too brief its hands
Have no names
I have passed it I know

> *Oh Necessity you with the face you with*
> *All the faces*

This is written on the back of everything

But we
Will read it together

She Who Was Gone

Passage of lights without hands
Passage of hands without lights
This water between

I take in my arms

My love whose names I cannot say
Not knowing them and having a tongue
Of dust

My love with light flowing on her like tears

She on whom the bruise went sailing
She who was a shoe on a pillow
She who was gone

Under empty socks hanging mouth downward from the
    bridges
Under the color of no one
While feathers went on falling in the doorways

She who with a blank ticket waited
Under a flag made of flies while the sun brought
Blood in eyecups

I take in my arms

My love from the valley of dice my love in the valley of dice
Among the flowers smelling of lightning
My love on whom the light has forgotten nothing

We say good-bye distance we are here
We can say it quietly who else is there
We can say it with silence our native tongue

My Friends

My friends without shields walk on the target

It is late the windows are breaking

My friends without shoes leave
What they love
Grief moves among them as a fire among
Its bells
My friends without clocks turn
On the dial they turn
They part

My friends with names like gloves set out
Bare handed as they have lived
And nobody knows them
It is they that lay the wreaths at the milestones it is their
Cups that are found at the wells
And are then chained up

My friends without feet sit by the wall
Nodding to the lame orchestra
Brotherhood it says on the decorations
My friend without eyes sits in the rain smiling
With a nest of salt in his hand

My friends without fathers or houses hear
Doors opening in the darkness
Whose halls announce
Behold the smoke has come home

My friends and I have in common
The present a wax bell in a wax belfry
This message telling of
Metals this
Hunger for the sake of hunger this owl in the heart
And these hands one
For asking one for applause

My friends with nothing leave it behind
In a box
My friends without keys go out from the jails it is night
They take the same road they miss
Each other they invent the same banner in the dark
They ask their way only of sentries too proud to breathe

At dawn the stars on their flag will vanish

The water will turn up their footprints and the day will rise
Like a monument to my
Friends the forgotten

The Man Who Writes Ants

Their eggs named for his eyes I suppose
Their eggs his tears
His memory
                Into
The ground into the walls over the sills

At each crossroad
He has gone

With his days he has gone ahead
            Called by what trumpet

His words on the signs
His tears at their feet
            Growing wings

I know him from tunnels by side roads
I know him

Not his face if he has one

I know him by his writings I am
Tempted to draw him

As I see him
Sandals stride flag on his shoulder ship on it signaling
Mask on the back of his head
Blind

Called

By what trumpet

He leaves my eyes he climbs my graves
I pass the names

He is not followed I am not following him no

Today the day of the water
With ink for my remote purpose with my pockets full of black
With no one in sight
I am walking in silence I am walking in silence I am walking
In single file listening for a trumpet

The Next

The funeral procession swinging empty belts
Walks on the road on the black rain
Though the one who is dead was not ready

In the casket lid the nails are still turning
Behind it come the bearers
Of tires and wet pillows and the charred ladder
And the unrollers of torn music and a picture of smoke
And last the boy trailing the long
String cut off clean
Whom a voice follows calling Why a white one
When a red one would have done just as well

Under the casket the number
Is scratched out with signs of haste

We let it go we gather with other persuaders
In the parlor of the house of The Next
And I in my wax shoes my mind goes back
To the last dead Who was it I say

Could it have been my friend the old man
With the wet dog and the shed where he
Slept on a ladder till the whole place burned
Here just now was his other
Friend the carpenter
Who was besides a crusher of shells for cement
No they say he was months ago this was no one we knew
But he was one of us

We let it go we are
Gathered with other persuaders in the parlor
The Next is upstairs he is
Ten feet tall hale and solid his bed is no deathbed
He is surrounded by friends they enjoy the secret of safety
They are flush they are candle-lit they move to laughter
Downstairs it is not yet known
Who will go instead of him this time
Like the others one after the other because they were scared

The laughter keeps time on the stairs
These words start rising out of my wax shoes I
Say we must tell him
We must go up there we must go up there and You
Are The Next we must tell him
The persuaders say he would deafen us
When we say No no one hears us

My shoes are softening but at the same time I am saying
Someone would help us and it would be us
Even the carpenter would
Help us when he went out he said
He would not be gone long
Removing a knocker from a door
And the caskets are clearly numbered not ours we

Must rise under the turning nails
I say to the persuaders downstairs in the house of The Next

And when they say Yes no one hears them

The Students of Justice

All night I hear the hammers
Of the blind men in the next building
Repairing their broken doors

When it is silent it is
That they are gone
Before the sun lights the way for
The young thieves

All day the blind neighbors are at their lesson
Coloring a rough book
Oh a long story
And under their white hair they keep forgetting

It tells of gorges hung with high caves and
Little rotting flags
And through the passes caravans of bugs
Bearing away our blood in pieces

What can be done what can be done

They take their hammers to the lesson

The last words so they promise me
Will be thank you and they will know why

And that night they will be allowed to move

Every day
They leave me their keys which they never use

An Island in the Harbor

My own country my countrymen the exchanges
Yes this is the place

The flag of the blank wall the birds of money

Prisoners in the watch towers
And the motto
                    The hopes of others our
                    Guardians

Even here
Spring passes looking for the cradles

The beating on the bars of the cages
Is caught and parceled out to the bells

It is twelve the prisoners' own hour

The mouse bones in the plaster
Prepare for the resurrection

Mountain Town

My memory the invisible buffalo
Lumbers through the vacant street
Considering the fences their

Sorrows

And the lightning died in its
Mine oh it must be
Some time back its name
Is written everywhere in faded
Dust

One of its
Gloves wheels on the sky over
The blind movie
And the station where the white train still
Attends

A bell that I hung onto as long as I could
Is about to arrive and start ringing

For Now

The year a bird flies against the drum

I come to myself miles away with
Tickets dying in my hand

You are not here will the earth last till you come
I must say now what cannot
Be said later Goodbye
The name of the statues but who needs them
As for myself I

Look back at the rain
I grew up in the rooms of the rain
So that was home so let the grass grow
Goodbye faces in stains churches
In echoes dusters at windows
Schools without floors envelopes full of smoke
Goodbye hands of those days I keep the fossils
Goodbye iron Bible containing my name in rust
Cock Robin and
The date
Goodbye Cock Robin I never saw you

On plates upside down in token of mourning
I eat to your vanishing

I bearing messages
With all my words my silence being one

From childhood to childhood the
Message Goodbye from the shoulders of victory
To the followers
From the sea to the nearest of kin

From the roller skates to the death in the basement
From the lightning to
Its nest from myself to my name
Goodbye

I begin with what was always gone

Ancestors in graves of broken glass
In empty cameras

Mistakes in the mail Goodbye to the same name

Goodbye what you learned for me I have to learn anyway

You that forgot your rivers they are gone
Myself I would not know you

Goodbye as
The eyes of a whale say goodbye having never seen
Each other

And to you that vanished as I watched goodbye
Walter the First
Jacques the Clown
Marica the Good

Goodbye pain of the past that
Will never be made better goodbye
Pain of the innocent that will never
Not have existed
Goodbye you that are
Buried with the name of the florist in your hands

And a box from our
Box society your finger holding the place
Your jaws tied with a ribbon marked Justice
To help us

The dead say Look
The living in their distress sink upward weeping
But who could reach them in such a sea

Goodbye kites painted with open mouths over the
Scarlet road of the animals

Goodbye prophets sometimes we are
Here sometimes we remember it
Sometimes we walk in your
Eyes which sometimes you lost
Sometimes we walk in your old brains and are forgotten

Or this character gets on the bus with an open razor
Bends down to my face at once thinking he
Knows me goodbye
Yard where I was supposed
To be safe behind the fences of sand
Watched over by an empty parasol and the sound of
Pulleys I who
Had built the ark

Goodbye cement street address of cement tears
Grief of the wallpaper the witness
Cold banisters worn thin with fright
Photo of me wondering what it would be like
The girls at last the hips full of dice the names
In smoke for the lamps the
Calling Goodbye among the wishes
Among the horses

If I had known what to say there would be the same hands
Holding white crosses in front of the windows

Goodbye to the dew my master

And you masters with feathers on your key rings
Wardens of empty scales
When I find where I am goodbye

Goodbye sound of a voice spelling its name to a uniform
Spelling it
Again goodbye white
Truck that backs up to drugstores after dark
Arriving at
Apartment houses in the afternoon
And the neighbors calling can you come up for a minute

Goodbye anniversaries I pass without knowing
Days for which the chairs are wired
The law on the throne of ice above the salting floor
Its eyes full of falling snow
Friend Instead and the rest of the
Brothers Meaningless
Those who will drown next bow to their straws

Goodbye to the water a happy person
The longer its story the
Less it tells
Goodbye to the numbers starting with God

To the avenues
No one asked their permission so they had none

Goodbye hands wrapped in newspaper

And when the towers are finished the frameworks are
Thrown from the tops and descend slowly
Waving as they
Dissolve

Tell me what you see vanishing and I
Will tell you who you are
To whom I say Goodbye

You my neighbors in the windows in the registers you
The sizes of your clothes
You born with the faces of presidents on your eyelids

Tell me how your hands fall and I will tell you
What you will wave to next
Guests of yourselves expecting hosts
You in the cold of whose
Voices I can hear
The hanged man in the chimney turning
You with mouths full of pebbles
In the rising elevator in the falling building you
With your destinations written in your shoelaces
And your lies elected

They return in the same
Skins to the same seats by the flags of money
Goodbye to the Bibles hollowed for swearing on
A hole knocks on the panes but is not heard

Around them the crashes occur in silence
The darkness that flows from the sirens passes the windows
The blackness spreads from the headlines
Over their spectacles they light the ceilings

Goodbye what we may never see
Age would have kissed false teeth if any
Its caresses making a bed slowly
Even as a child I hoped it would spare me
I made tears for it I sang

As the cards are laid out they turn to ashes
I kiss
The light to those who love it it is brief

Goodbye before it is taken away
I have been with it the season could sign for me
The message sang in its bottle it would find me
I knew the king of the moths I knew the watchman's country

I knew where the phoebe lost herself I knew the story
I stepped in the lock I
Turned
My thumb was carved with the one map of a lost mountain
My scars will answer to no one but me
I know the planet that lights up the rings in the hems
I know the stars in the door

I know the martyrs sleeping in almonds
I know the gloves of the hours I know Pilate the fly
I know the enemy's brother

But it will happen just the same goodbye

Heart my elder

My habits of sand
My bones whose count is lost every night every day
The milestones of salt the rain my feet
Memory in its rivers
Goodbye my house my cat my spiders

Goodbye distance from whom I
Borrow my eyes goodbye my voice
In the monument of strangers goodbye to the sun
Among the wings nailed to the window goodbye
My love

You that return to me through the mountain of flags
With my raven on your wrist
You with the same breath

Between death's republic and his kingdom

Spring

On the water the first wind
Breaks it all up into arrows

The dead bowmen buried these many years

Are setting out again

And I
I take down from the door
My story with the holes
For the arms the face and the vitals
I take down the sights from the mantle
I'm going to my uncle the honest one
Who stole me the horse in the good cause

There's light in my shoes
I carry my bones on a drum
I'm going to my uncle the dog
The croupier the old horror
The one who takes me as I am

Like the rest of the devils he was born in heaven

Oh withered rain

Tears of the candles veins full of feathers
Knees in salt
I the bell's only son

Having spent one day in his house
Will have your answer

Daybreak

Again this procession of the speechless
Bringing me their words
The future woke me with its silence
I join the procession
An open doorway
Speaks for me
Again

THE LICE

(1967)

All men are deceived by the appearances of things, even
Homer himself, who was the wisest man in Greece; for he
was deceived by boys catching lice: they said to him, "What
we have caught and what we have killed we have left behind,
but what has escaped us we bring with us."

HERACLITUS

The Animals

All these years behind windows
With blind crosses sweeping the tables

And myself tracking over empty ground
Animals I never saw

I with no voice

Remembering names to invent for them
Will any come back will one

Saying yes

Saying look carefully yes
We will meet again

Is That What You Are

New ghost is that what you are
Standing on the stairs of water

No longer surprised

Hope and grief are still our wings
Why we cannot fly

What failure still keeps you
Among us the unfinished

The wheels go on praying

We are not hearing something different
We beat our wings
Why are you there

I did not think I had anything else to give

267

The wheels say it after me

There are feathers in the ice
We lay the cold across our knees

Today the sun is farther than we think

And at the windows in the knives
You are watching

The Hydra

No no the dead have no brothers

The Hydra calls me but I am used to it
It calls me Everybody
But I know my name and do not answer

And you the dead
You know your names as I do not
But at moments you have just finished speaking

The snow stirs in its wrappings
Every season comes from a new place

Like your voice with its resemblances

A long time ago the lightning was practising
Something I thought was easy

I was young and the dead were in other
Ages
As the grass had its own language

Now I forget where the difference falls

One thing about the living sometimes a piece of us
Can stop dying for a moment
But you the dead

Once you go into those names you go on you never
Hesitate
You go on

Some Last Questions

What is the head
          A. Ash
What are the eyes
          A. The wells have fallen in and have
              Inhabitants
What are the feet
          A. Thumbs left after the auction
No what are the feet
          A. Under them the impossible road is moving
              Down which the broken necked mice push
              Balls of blood with their noses
What is the tongue
          A. The black coat that fell off the wall
              With sleeves trying to say something
What are the hands
          A. Paid
No what are the hands
          A. Climbing back down the museum wall
              To their ancestors the extinct shrews that will
              Have left a message
What is the silence
          A. As though it had a right to more
Who are the compatriots
          A. They make the stars of bone

An End in Spring

It is carried beyond itself a little way
And covered with a sky of old bedding

The compatriots stupid as their tables
Go on eating their packages
Selling gloves to the clocks
Doing all right

Ceasing to exist it becomes a deity

It is with the others that are not there
The centuries are named for them the names
Do not come down to us

On the way to them the words
Die

I Live Up Here

I live up here
And a little bit to the left
And I go down only

For the accidents and then
Never a moment too soon

Just the same it's a life it's plenty

The stairs the petals she loves me
Every time
Nothing has changed

Oh down there down there
Every time
The glass knights lie by their gloves of blood

In the pans of the scales the helmets
Brim over with water
It's perfectly fair

The pavements are dealt out the dice
Every moment arrive somewhere

You can hear the hearses getting lost in lungs
Their bells stalling
And then silence comes with the plate and I
Give what I can

Feeling *It's worth it*

For I see
What my votes the mice are accomplishing
And I know I'm free

This is how I live
Up here and simply

Others do otherwise
Maybe

The Last One

Well they'd made up their minds to be everywhere because
    why not.
Everywhere was theirs because they thought so.
They with two leaves they whom the birds despise.
In the middle of stones they made up their minds.
They started to cut.

Well they cut everything because why not.
Everything was theirs because they thought so.
It fell into its shadows and they took both away.
Some to have some for burning.

Well cutting everything they came to the water.
They came to the end of the day there was one left standing.
They would cut it tomorrow they went away.
The night gathered in the last branches.
The shadow of the night gathered in the shadow on the water.
The night and the shadow put on the same head.
And it said Now.

Well in the morning they cut the last one.
Like the others the last one fell into its shadow.
It fell into its shadow on the water.
They took it away its shadow stayed on the water.
Well they shrugged they started trying to get the shadow away.
They cut right to the ground the shadow stayed whole.
They laid boards on it the shadow came out on top.

They shone lights on it the shadow got blacker and clearer.
They exploded the water the shadow rocked.
They built a huge fire on the roots.
They sent up black smoke between the shadow and the sun.
The new shadow flowed without changing the old one.
They shrugged they went away to get stones.

They came back the shadow was growing.
They started setting up stones it was growing.
They looked the other way it went on growing.
They decided they would make a stone out of it.
They took stones to the water they poured them into the
    shadow.
They poured them in they poured them in the stones vanished.
The shadow was not filled it went on growing.
That was one day.

The next day was just the same it went on growing.
They did all the same things it was just the same.
They decided to take its water from under it.
They took away water they took it away the water went down.
The shadow stayed where it was before.
It went on growing it grew onto the land.

They started to scrape the shadow with machines.
When it touched the machines it stayed on them.
They started to beat the shadow with sticks.
Where it touched the sticks it stayed on them.
They started to beat the shadow with hands.
Where it touched the hands it stayed on them.
That was another day.

Well the next day started about the same it went on growing.
They pushed lights into the shadow.
Where the shadow got onto them they went out.
They began to stomp on the edge it got their feet.
And when it got their feet they fell down.
It got into eyes the eyes went blind.

The ones that fell down it grew over and they vanished.
The ones that went blind and walked into it vanished.
The ones that could see and stood still
It swallowed their shadows.
Then it swallowed them too and they vanished.
Well the others ran.

The ones that were left went away to live if it would let them.
They went as far as they could.
The lucky ones with their shadows.

Unfinished Book of Kings

ALPHA

I In all the teeth Death turned over

II And the new whistles called for the first time in the streets
before daybreak

III Silence the last of the liberty ships had come up the river
during the night and tied up to wait until the wharf rotted
away

IV At that time the civil war between the dynasties of absence had been going on for many years

V But during that winter the lips of the last prophets had fallen from the last trees

VI They had fallen without a sound they had not stayed in spite of the assurances proceeding from the mouths of the presidents in the money pinned thick as tobacco fish over the eyes of the saints

VII And in spite of the little votes burning at the altars in front of the empty walls

VIII And the jailers' eagle headed keys renewed in the name of freedom

IX It had been many years since the final prophet had felt the hand of the future how it had no weight and had realized that he the prophet was a ghost and had climbed the cracks in the light to take his place with the others

X The fingers of the prophets fell but were not visible because they wore no rings

XI The feet of the prophets fell but were not visible since their goal had ceased to exist

XII The hearts of the prophets fell out of the old nests

XIII The eyes of the prophets fell and broke like rain and a people blind as hammers hurried through them in their thin shoes

XIV The ears of the prophets fell and after that there had been no one to hear Death saying But I keep trying to remember when I was young

BETA

I Before daybreak in the museums the skeletons of extinct horses held up the skeletons of extinct leaves to listen

II The light was that of the insides of quills and through it the legends of Accident the hero were marching away down roads that had not been there since the last free election

III Out of the morning stars the blood began to run down the white sky and the crowd in tears remembered who they were and raised their hands shouting Tomorrow our flag

IV The lips of the extinct prophets still lay on the ground here and there murmuring So much for the hair of the moon

V But all that really remained of the prophets was their hunger which continued to fall among the people like invisible fish lines without hooks

VI And morning the carpet bagger arrived with news of victories

VII The lovers of flutes embraced the lovers of drums again as though they trusted them

VIII The balloon went up that said The day is ours

GAMMA

I It had been discovered that the bread was photographs of unidentified seas and not for everyone but it was all taken care of it was put in the banks with the dead

II It had been discovered that the bitterness of certain rivers had no source but was caused by their looking for something through the darkness and finding

III Something lower

IV But it was taken care of the discovery was allowed to die of its own accord

V And Distance with his gaunt singers sat among the citizens unnoticed and never distinctly heard

VI He stood under the posters advertising the endless newsreels of the deposition and nobody recognized him

VII He went into the museums and sat in the undusted replicas of what was said to have been his crown and nobody saw him

VIII He conducted a chorus of forgiveness for his poor relations the rulers

IX Whose blessing was as the folding and unfolding of papers

DELTA

I Came the heralds with brushes

II Came the rats dragging their leashes some time before the soldiers

III Came the cripples walking on separate seas bearing on a long scroll the bill of suffering the signatures the crosses

IV Came the bearers of doors of wood and of glass came the eyes with dead wicks came the mourners with their inventories

V Cheers cheers but it was only a rehearsal

VI Yet the spirit was there and in full daylight voices of dogs were lit on the hills nibbled coins were flung from balconies and the matches tipped with blood were brought out and kept handy

VII The pictures of dead forbears were propped up at windows to be proud

VIII The darkness began to dance in the gloves and the cry caught on We have waited enough war or no war

IX Calling for the coronation of Their Own the last of the absences

It Is March

It is March and black dust falls out of the books
Soon I will be gone
The tall spirit who lodged here has
Left already
On the avenues the colorless thread lies under
Old prices

When you look back there is always the past
Even when it has vanished
But when you look forward
With your dirty knuckles and the wingless
Bird on your shoulder
What can you write

The bitterness is still rising in the old mines
The fist is coming out of the egg
The thermometers out of the mouths of the corpses

At a certain height
The tails of the kites for a moment are
Covered with footsteps

Whatever I have to do has not yet begun

Bread at Midnight

The judges have chains in their sleeves
To get where they are they have
Studied many flies
They drag their voices up a long hill
Announcing It is over

Well now that it is over
I remember my homeland the mountains of chaff

And hands hands deaf as starfish fetching
The bread still frozen
To the tables

Caesar

My shoes are almost dead
And as I wait at the doors of ice
I hear the cry go up for him Caesar Caesar

But when I look out the window I see only the flatlands
And the slow vanishing of the windmills
The centuries draining the deep fields

Yet this is still my country
The thug on duty says What would you change
He looks at his watch he lifts
Emptiness out of the vases
And holds it up to examine

So it is evening
With the rain starting to fall forever
One by one he calls night out of the teeth
And at last I take up
My duty

Wheeling the president past banks of flowers
Past the feet of empty stairs
Hoping he's dead

Pieces for Other Lives

I

Encouragement meant nothing

Inside it
The miners would continue to
Crawl out of their dark bodies
Extending the darkness making
It hollow
And how could they be rightly paid

Darkness gathered on the money
It lived in the dies the miners pursued it what
Was their reward

Some might bring flowers saying Nothing can last
Some anyway
Held out their whole lives in their glass hands

Sweeter than men till past the time
Some with a pure light burned but over
Their heads even theirs
Soot wrote on the ceiling
An unknown word

Shutting your eyes from the spectacle you
Saw not darkness but
Nothing

On which doors were opening

II

All that time with nothing to do
In that granite shed
The clinic by the rainy sea

While the doctor snake turned himself on at doors
In other rooms to study
Your life a small animal dying in a bottle

Out of what could be stolen and hidden you contrived
This model of the blood
A map in lost tubing and dead joints and you
Pointed out its comical story

It begins here it swells it goes along
It comes to the man sitting talking to a stick
Which he thinks is his dog or his wife
It comes to the river unwinding the stones
It takes up a thread it comes to the tailor saying
Thank you to his needle

Over and over here is the needle

It passes through his
One seam it comes to the door which is not shown

But which anyway is standing open
And beyond it there is

Salt water in unknown quantities

III

At one stroke out of the ruin
All the watches went out and
The eyes disappeared like martins into their nests

I woke to the slamming of doors and got up naked
The old wind vanished and vanished but was still there
Everyone but the cold was gone for good

And the carol of the miners had just ended

The Moths

It is cold here
In the steel grass
At the foot of the invisible statue

Made by the incurables and called
Justice

At a great distance
An audience of rubber tombstones is watching
The skulls of
The leaders
Strung on the same worm

Darkness moves up the nail

And I am returning to a night long since past
In which the rain is falling and
A crying comes from the stations
And near at hand a voice a woman's
In a jug under the wind
Is trying to sing

No one has shown her
Any statue and
The music keeps rising through her
Almost beginning and
The moths
Lie in the black grass waiting

Whenever I Go There

Whenever I go there everything is changed

The stamps on the bandages the titles
Of the professors of water

The portrait of Glare the reasons for
The white mourning

In new rocks new insects are sitting
With the lights off
And once more I remember that the beginning

Is broken

No wonder the addresses are torn

To which I make my way eating the silence of animals
Offering snow to the darkness

Today belongs to few and tomorrow to no one

Wish

The star in my
Hand is falling

All the uniforms know what's no use

May I bow to Necessity not
To her hirelings

The Wave

I inhabited the wake of a long wave

As we sank it continued to rush past me
I knew where it had been
The light was full of salt and the air
Was heavy with crying for where the wave had come from
And why

It had brought them
From faces that soon were nothing but rain

Over the photographs they carried with them
The white forests
Grew impenetrable but as for themselves
They felt the sand slide from
Their roots of water

The harbors with outstretched arms retreated along
Glass corridors then
Were gone then their shadows were gone then the
Corridors were gone
Envelopes came each enfolding a little chalk
I inhabited the place where they opened them

I inhabited the sound of hope walking on water
Losing its way in the
Crowd so many footfalls of snow

I inhabit the sound of their pens on boxes
Writing to the dead in
Languages
I inhabit their wrappings sending back darkness
And the sinking of their voices entering
Nowhere as the wave passes

And asking where next as it breaks

News of the Assassin

The clock strikes one one one
Through the window in a line pass
The bees whose flower is death

Why the morning smelled of honey

Already how long it is since the harvest
The dead animal fallen all the same way

On the stroke the wheels recall
That they are water
An empty window has overtaken me

After the bees comes the smell of cigars
In the lobby of darkness

April

When we have gone the stone will stop singing

April April
Sinks through the sand of names

Days to come
With no stars hidden in them

You that can wait being there

You that lose nothing
Know nothing

The Gods

If I have complained I hope I have done with it

I take no pride in circumstances but there are
Occupations
My blind neighbor has required of me
A description of darkness
And I begin I begin but

All day I keep hearing the fighting in the valley
The blows falling as rice and
With what cause
After these centuries gone and they had
Each their mourning for each of them grief
In hueless ribbons hung on walls
That fell
Their moment
Here in the future continues to find me
Till night wells up through the earth

I
Am all that became of them
Clearly all is lost

The gods are what has failed to become of us
Now it is over we do not speak

Now the moment has gone it is dark
What is man that he should be infinite
The music of a deaf planet
The one note
Continues clearly this is

The other world
These strewn rocks belong to the wind
If it could use them

The River of Bees

In a dream I returned to the river of bees
Five orange trees by the bridge and
Beside two mills my house
Into whose courtyard a blind man followed
The goats and stood singing
Of what was older

Soon it will be fifteen years

He was old he will have fallen into his eyes

I took my eyes
A long way to the calendars
Room after room asking how shall I live

One of the ends is made of streets
One man processions carry through it
Empty bottles their
Image of hope
It was offered to me by name

Once once and once
In the same city I was born
Asking what shall I say

He will have fallen into his mouth
Men think they are better than grass

I return to his voice rising like a forkful of hay

He was old he is not real nothing is real
Nor the noise of death drawing water

We are the echo of the future

On the door it says what to do to survive
But we were not born to survive
Only to live

The Widow

How easily the ripe grain
Leaves the husk
At the simple turning of the planet

There is no season
That requires us

Masters of forgetting
Threading the eyeless rocks with
A narrow light

In which ciphers wake and evil
Gets itself the face of the norm
And contrives cities

The Widow rises under our fingernails
In this sky we were born we are born

And you weep wishing you were numbers
You multiply you cannot be found
You grieve
Not that heaven does not exist but
That it exists without us

You confide
In images in things that can be
Represented which is their dimension you
Require them you say This
Is real and you do not fall down and moan

Not seeing the irony in the air

Everything that does not need you is real

The Widow does not
Hear you and your cry is numberless

This is the waking landscape
Dream after dream after dream walking away through it
Invisible invisible invisible

Looking East at Night

Death
White hand
The moths fly at in the darkness

I took you for the moon rising

Whose light then
Do you reflect

As though it came out of the roots of things
This harvest pallor in which

I have no shadow but myself

The Child

Sometimes it is inconceivable that I should be the age I am
Almost always it is at a dry point in the afternoon
I cannot remember what
I am waiting for and in my astonishment I
Can hear the blood crawling over the plains
Hurrying on to arrive before dark
I try to remember my faults to make sure
One after the other but it is never
Satisfactory the list is never complete

At times night occurs to me so that I think I have been
Struck from behind I remain perfectly
Still feigning death listening for the
Assailant perhaps at last
I even sleep a little for later I have moved
I open my eyes the lanternfish have gone home in darkness
On all sides the silence is unharmed
I remember but I feel no bruise

Then there are the stories and after a while I think something
Else must connect them besides just this me
I regard myself starting the search turning
Corners in remembered metropoli
I pass skins withering in gardens that I see now
Are not familiar
And I have lost even the thread I thought I had

If I could be consistent even in destitution
The world would be revealed
While I can I try to repeat what I believe
Creatures spirits not this posture
I do not believe in knowledge as we know it
But I forget

This silence coming at intervals out of the shell of names
It must be all one person really coming at
Different hours for the same thing
If I could learn the word for yes it could teach me questions

I would see that it was itself every time and I would
Remember to say take it up like a hand
And go with it this is at last
Yourself

The child that will lead you

A Debt

I come on the debt again this day in November

It is raining into the yellow trees
The night kept raising white birds
The fowls of darkness entering winter
But I think of you seldom
You lost nothing you need entering death

I tell you the basket has woven itself over you
If there was grief it was in pencil on a wall
At no time had I asked you for anything

What did you take from me that I still owe you

Each time it is
A blind man opening his eyes

It is a true debt it can never be paid
How have you helped me
Is it with speech you that combed out your voice till the ends
    bled
Is it with hearing with waking of any kind
You in the wet veil that you chose it is not with memory
Not with sight of any kind not
Yet

It is a true debt it is mine alone
It is nameless
It rises from poverty

It goes out from me into the trees
Night falls

It follows a death like a candle
But the death is not yours

The Plaster

How unlike you
To have left the best of your writings here
Behind the plaster where they were never to be found
These stanzas of long lines into which the Welsh words
Had been flung like planks from a rough sea
How will I

Ever know now how much was not like you
And what else was committed to paper here
On the dark burst sofa where you would later die
Its back has left a white mark on the white wall and above that
Five and a half indistinct squares of daylight
Like pages in water
Slide across the blind plaster

Into which you slipped the creased writings as into a mail slot
In a shroud

This is now the house of the rain that falls from death
The sky is moving its things in from under the trees
In silence
As it must have started to do even then
There is still a pile of dirty toys and rags
In the corner where they found the children
Rolled in sleep

Other writings
Must be dissolving in the roof
Twitching black edges in cracks of the wet fireplaces
Stuck to shelves in the filthy pantry

Never to be found
What is like you now

Who were haunted all your life by the best of you
Hiding in your death

In Autumn

The extinct animals are still looking for home
Their eyes full of cotton

Now they will
Never arrive

The stars are like that

Moving on without memory
Without having been near turning elsewhere climbing
Nothing the wall

The hours their shadows

The lights are going on in the leaves nothing to do with
evening

Those are cities
Where I had hoped to live

Crows on the North Slope

When the Gentle were dead these inherited their coats
Now they gather in late autumn and quarrel over the air
Demanding something for their shadows that are naked
And silent and learning

New Moon in November

I have been watching crows and now it is dark
Together they led night into the creaking oaks
Under them I hear the dry leaves walking
That blind man
Gathering their feathers before winter
By the dim road that the wind will take
And the cold
And the note of the trumpet

December Night

The cold slope is standing in darkness
But the south of the trees is dry to the touch

The heavy limbs climb into the moonlight bearing feathers
I came to watch these
White plants older at night
The oldest
Come first to the ruins

And I hear magpies kept awake by the moon
The water flows through its
Own fingers without end

Tonight once more
I find a single prayer and it is not for men

After the Solstice

Under the east cliff the spring flows into the snow

The bird tracks end like calendars

At noon white hair
Is caught in the thorns of the abandoned vineyard
Here the sky passed

The old are buried all down the slope
Except the wrists and the ancient
Message *We are with no one*

At midnight we raise their wine to tomorrow

December Among the Vanished

The old snow gets up and moves taking its
Birds with it

The beasts hide in the knitted walls
From the winter that lipless man
Hinges echo but nothing opens

A silence before this one
Has left its broken huts facing the pastures
Through their stone roofs the snow
And the darkness walk down

In one of them I sit with a dead shepherd
And watch his lambs

Glimpse of the Ice

I am sure now
A light under the skin coming nearer
Bringing snow
Then at nightfall a moth has thawed out and is
Dripping against the glass
I wonder if death will be silent after all
Or a cry frozen in another age

The Cold Before the Moonrise

It is too simple to turn to the sound
Of frost stirring among its
Stars like an animal asleep
In the winter night
And say I was born far from home
If there is a place where this is the language may
It be my country

Early January

A year has come to us as though out of hiding
It has arrived from an unknown distance
From beyond the visions of the old
Everyone waited for it by the wrong roads
And it is hard for us now to be sure it is here
A stranger to nothing
In our hiding places

The Room

I think all this is somewhere in myself
The cold room unlit before dawn
Containing a stillness such as attends death
And from a corner the sounds of a small bird trying
From time to time to fly a few beats in the dark
You would say it was dying it is immortal

Dusk in Winter

The sun sets in the cold without friends
Without reproaches after all it has done for us
It goes down believing in nothing

When it has gone I hear the stream running after it
It has brought its flute it is a long way

A Scale in May

Now all my teachers are dead except silence
I am trying to read what the five poplars are writing
On the void

Of all the beasts to man alone death brings justice
But I desire
To kneel in a doorway empty except for the song

Who made time provided also its fools
Strapped in watches and with ballots for their choices
Crossing the frontiers of invisible kingdoms

To succeed consider what is as though it were past
Deem yourself inevitable and take credit for it
If you find you no longer believe enlarge the temple

Through the day the nameless stars keep passing the door
That have come all that way out of death
Without questions

The walls of light shudder and an owl wakes in the heart
I cannot call upon words
The sun goes away to set elsewhere

Before nightfall colorless petals blow under the door
And the shadows
Recall their ancestors in the house beyond death

At the end of its procession through the stone
Falling
The water remembers to laugh

Evening

I am strange here and often I am still trying
To finish something as the light is going
Occasionally as just now I think I see
Off to one side something passing at that time
Along the herded walls under the walnut trees
And I look up but it is only
Evening again the old hat without a head
How long will it be till he speaks when he passes

The Dream Again

I take the road that bears leaves in the mountains
I grow hard to see then I vanish entirely
On the peaks it is summer

How We Are Spared

At midsummer before dawn an orange light returns to the
    mountains
Like a great weight and the small birds cry out
And bear it up

The Dragonfly

Hoeing the bean field here are the dragonfly's wings
From this spot the wheat once signaled
With lights *It is all here*
With these feet on it
My own
And the hoe in my shadow

Provision

All morning with dry instruments
The field repeats the sound
Of rain
From memory
And in the wall
The dead increase their invisible honey
It is August
The flocks are beginning to form
I will take with me the emptiness of my hands
What you do not have you find everywhere

The Herds

Climbing northward
At dusk when the horizon rose like a hand I would turn aside
Before dark I would stop by the stream falling through black ice
And once more celebrate our distance from men

As I lay among stones high in the starless night
Out of the many hoof tracks the sounds of herds
Would begin to reach me again
Above them their ancient sun skating far off

Sleeping by the glass mountain
I would watch the flocks of light grazing
And the water preparing its descent
To the first dead

The Mourner

On the south terraces of the glass palace
That has no bells
My hoe clacks in the bean rows
In the cool of the morning

At her hour
The mourner approaches on her way to the gate
A small old woman an aunt in the world
Without nephews or nieces
Her black straw hat shining like water
Floats back and forth climbing
Along the glass walls of the terraces
Bearing its purple wax rose

We nod as she passes slowly toward the palace
Her soft face with its tiny wattle flushed salmon
I hear her small soles receding
And remember the sound of the snow at night
Brushing the glass towers
In the time of the living

For the Anniversary of My Death

Every year without knowing it I have passed the day
When the last fires will wave to me
And the silence will set out
Tireless traveler
Like the beam of a lightless star

Then I will no longer
Find myself in life as in a strange garment
Surprised at the earth
And the love of one woman
And the shamelessness of men
As today writing after three days of rain
Hearing the wren sing and the falling cease
And bowing not knowing to what

Divinities

Having crowded once onto the threshold of mortality
And not been chosen
There is no freedom such as theirs
That have no beginning

The air itself is their memory
A domain they cannot inhabit
But from which they are never absent

What are you they say *that simply exist*
And the heavens and the earth bow to them
Looking up from their choices
Perishing

All day and all night
Everything that is mistaken worships them
Even the dead sing them an unending hymn

The Dry Stone Mason

The mason is dead the gentle drunk
Master of dry walls
What he made of his years crosses the slopes without wavering
Upright but nameless
Ignorant in the new winter
Rubbed by running sheep
But the age of mortar has come to him

Bottles are waiting like fallen shrines
Under different trees in the rain
And stones drip where his hands left them
Leaning slightly inwards
His thirst is past

As he had no wife
The neighbors found where he kept his suit
A man with no family they sat with him
When he was carried through them they stood by their own
    dead
And they have buried him among the graves of the stones

In the Winter of My Thirty-Eighth Year

It sounds unconvincing to say *When I was young*
Though I have long wondered what it would be like
To be me now
No older at all it seems from here
As far from myself as ever

Waking in fog and rain and seeing nothing
I imagine all the clocks have died in the night
Now no one is looking I could choose my age
It would be younger I suppose so I am older
It is there at hand I could take it
Except for the things I think I would do differently
They keep coming between they are what I am
They have taught me little I did not know when I was young

There is nothing wrong with my age now probably
It is how I have come to it
Like a thing I kept putting off as I did my youth

There is nothing the matter with speech
Just because it lent itself
To my uses

Of course there is nothing the matter with the stars
It is my emptiness among them
While they drift farther away in the invisible morning

When You Go Away

When you go away the wind clicks around to the north
The painters work all day but at sundown the paint falls
Showing the black walls
The clock goes back to striking the same hour
That has no place in the years

And at night wrapped in the bed of ashes
In one breath I wake
It is the time when the beards of the dead get their growth
I remember that I am falling
That I am the reason
And that my words are the garment of what I shall never be
Like the tucked sleeve of a one-armed boy

The Asians Dying

When the forests have been destroyed their darkness remains
The ash the great walker follows the possessors
Forever
Nothing they will come to is real
Nor for long
Over the watercourses
Like ducks in the time of the ducks
The ghosts of the villages trail in the sky
Making a new twilight

Rain falls into the open eyes of the dead
Again again with its pointless sound
When the moon finds them they are the color of everything

The nights disappear like bruises but nothing is healed
The dead go away like bruises
The blood vanishes into the poisoned farmlands
Pain the horizon

Remains
Overhead the seasons rock
They are paper bells
Calling to nothing living

The possessors move everywhere under Death their star
Like columns of smoke they advance into the shadows
Like thin flames with no light
They with no past
And fire their only future

When the War Is Over

When the war is over
We will be proud of course the air will be
Good for breathing at last
The water will have been improved the salmon
And the silence of heaven will migrate more perfectly
The dead will think the living are worth it we will know
Who we are
And we will all enlist again

Peasant

His Prayer To The Powers Of This World

All those years that you ate and changed
And grew under my picture
You saw nothing
It was only when I began to appear
That you said I must vanish

What could I do I thought things were real
Cruel and wise
And came and went in their names
I thought I would wait I was shrewder but you
Were dealing in something else

You were always embarrassed by what fed you
And made distances faster
Than you destroyed them
It bewitched my dreams
Like magazines I took out with the sheep
That helped to empty the hours
I tried to despise you for what you did not
Need to be able to do
If I could do it
Maybe I could have done without you

My contempt for you
You named ignorance and my admiration for you
Servility
When they were among the few things we had in common
Your trash and your poses were what I most appreciated
Just as you did

And the way you were free
Of me
But I fought in your wars
The way you could decide that things were not
And they died
The way you had reasons
Good enough for your time

When God was dying you bought him out
As you were in a position to do
Coming in the pale car through the mud and fresh dung
Unable to find the place though you had been there
Once at least before
Like the doctor
Without a moment to lose
I was somewhere
In the bargain

I was used to standing in the shade of the sky
A survivor
I had nothing you
Could use

I am taking my hands
Into the cleft wood assembled
In dry corners of abandoned barns
Beams being saved
For nothing broken doors pieces of carts
Other shadows have gone in there and
Wait
On hewn feet I follow the hopes of the owls
For a time I will
Drift down from the tool scars in a fine dust
Noticeably before rain in summer
And at the time of the first thaws
And at the sound of your frequent explosions
And when the roofs
Fall it will be a long while
Since anyone could still believe in me
Any more than if I were one of the
Immortals

It was you
That made the future
It was yours to take away
I see
Oh thousand gods
Only you are real
It is my shame that you did not
Make me
I am bringing up my children to be you

For a Coming Extinction

Gray whale
Now that we are sending you to The End
That great god
Tell him
That we who follow you invented forgiveness
And forgive nothing

I write as though you could understand
And I could say it
One must always pretend something
Among the dying
When you have left the seas nodding on their stalks
Empty of you
Tell him that we were made
On another day

The bewilderment will diminish like an echo
Winding along your inner mountains
Unheard by us
And find its way out
Leaving behind it the future
Dead
And ours

When you will not see again
The whale calves trying the light
Consider what you will find in the black garden
And its court
The sea cows the Great Auks the gorillas
The irreplaceable hosts ranged countless
And foreordaining as stars
Our sacrifices

Join your word to theirs
Tell him
That it is we who are important

In a Clearing

The unnumbered herds flow like lichens
Along the darkness each carpet at its height
In silence
Herds without end
Without death

Nothing is before them nothing after
Among the hooves the hooves' brothers the shells
In a sea

Passing through senses
As through bright clearings surrounded with pain
Some of the animals
See souls moving in their word death
With its many tongues that no god could speak
That can describe
Nothing that cannot die

The word
Surrounds the souls
The hide they wear
Like a light in the light
And when it goes out they vanish

In the eyes of the herds there is only one light
They cherish it with the darkness it belongs to
They take their way through it nothing is
Before them and they leave it
A small place
Where dying a sun rises

Avoiding News by the River

As the stars hide in the light before daybreak
Reed warblers hunt along the narrow stream
Trout rise to their shadows
Milky light flows through the branches
Fills with blood
Men will be waking

In an hour it will be summer
I dreamed that the heavens were eating the earth
Waking it is not so
Not the heavens

I am not ashamed of the wren's murders
Nor the badger's dinners
On which all worldly good depends
If I were not human I would not be ashamed of anything

Death of a Favorite Bird

What was the matter with life on my shoulder
Age that I was wing delight
That you had to thresh out your breath in the spiked rafters
To the beat of rain
I have asked this question before it knows me it comes
Back to find me through the cold dreamless summer
And the barn full of black feathers

Fly

I have been cruel to a fat pigeon
Because he would not fly
All he wanted was to live like a friendly old man

He had let himself become a wreck filthy and confiding
Wild for his food beating the cat off the garbage
Ignoring his mate perpetually snotty at the beak
Smelling waddling having to be
Carried up the ladder at night content

Fly I said throwing him into the air
But he would drop and run back expecting to be fed
I said it again and again throwing him up
As he got worse
He let himself be picked up every time
Until I found him in the dovecote dead
Of the needless efforts

So that is what I am

Pondering his eye that could not
Conceive that I was a creature to run from

I who have always believed too much in words

The Finding of Reasons

Every memory is abandoned
As waves leave their shapes
The houses stand in tears as the sun rises

Even Pain
That is a god to the senses
Can be forgotten
Until he returns in the flashing garments
And the senses themselves
Are to be taken away like clothing
After a sickness

Proud of their secrets as the dead
Our uses forsake us
That have been betrayed
They follow tracks that lead before and after
And over water
The prints cross us
When they have gone we find reasons

As though to relinquish a journey
Were to arrive
As though we had not been made
Of distances that would not again be ours
As though our feet would come to us once more
Of themselves freely
To us
Their forgotten masters

To listen to the announcements you would think
The triumph
Were ours
As the string of the great kite Sapiens
Cuts our palms
Along predestined places
Leaving us
Leaving
While we find reasons

Come Back

You came back to us in a dream and we were not here
In a light dress laughing you ran down the slope
To the door
And knocked for a long time thinking it strange

Oh come back we were watching all the time
With the delight choking us and the piled
Grief scrambling like guilt to leave us
At the sight of you
Looking well
And besides our questions our news
All of it paralyzed until you were gone

Is it the same way there

Watchers

The mowers begin
And after this morning the fox
Will no longer glide close to the house in full day
When a breath stirs the wheat
Leaving his sounds waiting at a distance
Under a few trees

And lie out
Watching from the nodding light the birds on the roofs
The noon sleep

Perhaps nothing
For some time will cross the new size of the stubble fields
In the light
And watch us
But the day itself coming alone
From the woods with its hunger
Today a tall man saying nothing but taking notes
Tomorrow a colorless woman standing
With her reproach and her bony children
Before rain

My Brothers the Silent

My brothers the silent
At any hour finding
Blackness to stand in like cold stars my brothers
The invisible
What an uncharitable family
My brothers shepherds older than birth
What are you afraid of since I was born
I cannot touch the inheritance what is my age to you
I am not sure I would know what to ask for
I do not know what my hands are for
I do not know what my wars are deciding
I cannot make up my mind
I have the pitiless blood and the remote gaze of our lineage
But I will leave nothing to strangers
Look how I am attached to the ends of things
Even your sheep our sheep
When I meet them on the roads raise toward me
Their clear eyes unknowable as days
And if they see me do not recognize me do not
Believe in me

In One of the Retreats of Morning

There are still bits of night like closed eyes in the walls
And at their feet the large brotherhood of broken stones
Is still asleep
I go quietly along the edge of their garden
Looking at the few things they grow for themselves

Looking for Mushrooms at Sunrise
for Jean and Bill Arrowsmith

When it is not yet day
I am walking on centuries of dead chestnut leaves
In a place without grief
Though the oriole
Out of another life warns me
That I am awake

In the dark while the rain fell
The gold chanterelles pushed through a sleep that was not mine
Waking me
So that I came up the mountain to find them

Where they appear it seems I have been before
I recognize their haunts as though remembering
Another life

Where else am I walking even now
Looking for me

THE CARRIER OF LADDERS

(1970)

. . . The bearer of the dead
Says to the carrier of ladders,
It is the day for carrying loads,
It is the day of trouble.

DAHOMEY SONG

Plane

We hurtle forward and seem to rise

I imagine the deities come and go
without departures

and with my mind infinitely divided and hopeless
like a stockyard seen from above
and my will like a withered body muffled
in qualifications until it has no shape
I bleed in my place

where is no
vision of the essential nakedness of the gods
nor of that
nakedness the seamless garment of heaven

nor of any other
nakedness

Here
is the air

and your tears flowing on the wings of the plane
where once again I cannot
reach to stop them

and they fall away behind
going with me

Teachers

Pain is in this dark room like many speakers
of a costly set though mute
as here the needle and the turning

the night lengthens it is winter
a new year

what I live for I can seldom believe in
who I love I cannot go to
what I hope is always divided

but I say to myself you are not a child now
if the night is long remember your unimportance
sleep

then toward morning I dream of the first words
of books of voyages
sure tellings that did not start by justifying

yet at one time it seems
had taught me

The Owl

These woods are one of my great lies
I pretend
oh I have always pretended they
were mine
I stumble among
the smaller lies
as this night falls and
of my pretenses likewise
some
and your voice
begins

who need no hope to
hunt here who
love me
I retreat before
your question as before my own
through old branches who
am I hiding

what creature in the bowels quaking
that should not be raised
against the night
crying its truth at last

No I who
love you
find while I can some light to crawl into
maybe
I will never answer
though your dark lasts as my own does
and your voice in it without hope
or need of it
calling what I call calling
me me *You*
who are never there

The Different Stars

I could never have come to the present without you
remember that
from whatever stage we may again
watch it appear

with its lines clear
pain
having gone from there

so that we may well wonder
looking back on us here what tormented us
what great difficulty invisible
in a time that by then looks simple
and is irrevocable

pain having come from there
my love
I tend to think of division as the only evil
when perhaps it is merely my own

that unties
one day the veins one the arteries
that prizes less
as it receives than as it loses
that breaks the compasses
cannot be led or followed
cannot choose what to carry
into grief
even
unbinds will unbind
unbinds our hands
pages of the same story

what is it
they say can turn even this into wisdom
and what is wisdom if it is not
now
in the loss that has not left this place

oh if we knew
if we knew what we needed if we even knew
the stars would look to us to guide them

The Dead Hive

The year still a child
but its sunlight
climbing for the first time in the poplars
pretending to be older
and the green has been lit in the east-sloping
pastures guarded
by nurses of shadow
a ghost has risen out of the earth
the unnamed warmth
saved for now

in the silence
one note is missing

I see
you nowhere I hear you nowhere
I climb to your hall you are nowhere
the flowers nod in the sun
like the blind
I knock
from the arcade of your portal
a fly steps out

I open the roof
I and the light
this is how it looks later
the city the dance the care
the darkness
the moment
one at a time
that is each one alone

as she
turns aside
obeying as always
and the accomplished limbs begin
welcoming
what does not move
and the eyes
go as far as they can
and wait

at the place where no one they know
can fail them

The Mountains

There are days when I think the future sets
beyond the mountains
then I lay me down
in fear of departures

and a heavy
net drops on me when I wake
far
far in the night
borne on
and the whole air
around me crying for you
even
when you are still there

and a dog barking
beyond it
at an unknown distance

on and on

The Bridges

Nothing but me is moving
on these bridges
as I always knew it would be
see moving on each of the bridges
only me

and everything that we have known
even the friends
lined up in the silent iron railings
back and forth
I pass like a stick on palings

the echo
rises from the marbled river
the light from the blank clocks crackles
like an empty film
where
are we living now
on which side which side
and will you be there

The Hands

> . . . Ma non è cosa in terra
> Che ti somigli . . .
>   LEOPARDI

I have seen them when there was
nothing else
small swollen flames lighting my way at
corners
where they have waited for
me

cut off from
everything they have made their way to me
one more day one more night leading
their blood and I wake
to find them lying at home
with my own

like a bird lying in its wings
a stunned
bird till they stir and
break
open cradling a heart not theirs
not mine
and I bend to hear who is beating

Do Not Die

In each world they may put us
farther apart
do not die
as this world is made I might
live forever

Words from a Totem Animal

Distance
is where we were
but empty of us and ahead of
me lying out in the rushes thinking
even the nights cannot come back to their hill
any time

I would rather the wind came from outside
from mountains anywhere
from the stars from other
worlds even as
cold as it is this
ghost of mine passing
through me

I know your silence
and the repetition
like that of a word in the ear of death
teaching
itself
itself
that is the sound of my running
the plea
plea that it makes
which you will never hear
oh god of beginnings
immortal

I might have been right
not who I am
but all right
among the walls among the reasons
not even waiting
not seen
but now I am out in my feet
and they on their way
the old trees jump up again and again
strangers

there are no names for the rivers
for the days for the nights
I am who I am
oh lord cold as the thoughts of birds
and everyone can see me

Caught again and held again
again I am not a blessing
they bring me
names
that would fit anything
they bring them to me
they bring me hopes
all day I turn
making ropes
helping

My eyes are waiting for me
in the dusk
they are still closed
they have been waiting a long time
and I am feeling my way toward them

I am going up stream
taking to the water from time to time
my marks dry off the stones before morning
the dark surface
strokes the night
above its way
There are no stars
there is no grief
I will never arrive
I stumble when I remember how it was
with one foot
one foot still in a name

I can turn myself toward the other joys and their lights
but not find them
I can put my words into the mouths
of spirits

but they will not say them
I can run all night and win
and win

———

Dead leaves crushed grasses fallen limbs
the world is full of prayers
arrived at from
afterwards
a voice full of breaking
heard from afterwards
through all
the length of the night

———

I am never all of me
unto myself
and sometimes I go slowly
knowing that a sound one sound
is following me from world
to world
and that I die each time
before it reaches me

———

When I stop I am alone
at night sometimes it is almost good
as though I were almost there
sometimes then I see there is
in a bush beside me the same question
why are you
on this way
I said I will ask the stars
why are you falling and they answered
which of us

———

I dreamed I had no nails
no hair
I had lost one of the senses
not sure which
the soles peeled from my feet and
drifted away
clouds
It's all one

feet
stay mine
hold the world lightly

———

Stars even you
have been used
but not you
silence
blessing
calling me when I am lost

———

Maybe I will come
to where I am one
and find
I have been waiting there
as a new
year finds the song of the nuthatch

———

Send me out into another life
lord because this one is growing faint
I do not think it goes all the way

Animula

Look soul
soul
barefoot presence
through whom blood falls as through
a water clock
and tears rise before they wake
I will take you

at last to
where the wind stops
by the river we
know
by that same water
and the nights are not separate
remember

Quince

The gentle quince blossoms open
they have no first youth
they look down on me
knowing me well
some place I had left

The Judgment of Paris
for Anthony Hecht

Long afterwards
the intelligent could deduce what had been offered
and not recognized
and they suggest that bitterness should be confined
to the fact that the gods chose for their arbiter
a mind and character so ordinary
albeit a prince

and brought up as a shepherd
a calling he must have liked
for he had returned to it

when they stood before him
the three
naked feminine deathless
and he realized that he was clothed
in nothing but mortality
the strap of his quiver of arrows crossing
between his nipples
making it seem stranger

and he knew he must choose
and on that day

the one with the gray eyes spoke first
and whatever she said he kept
thinking he remembered

but remembered it woven with confusion and fear
the two faces that he called father
the first sight of the palace
where the brothers were strangers
and the dogs watched him and refused to know him
she made everything clear she was dazzling she
offered it to him
to have for his own but what he saw
was the scorn above her eyes
and her words of which he understood few
all said to him *Take wisdom*
take power
you will forget anyway

the one with the dark eyes spoke
and everything she said
he imagined he had once wished for
but in confusion and cowardice
the crown
of his father the crowns the crowns bowing to him
his name everywhere like grass
only he and the sea
triumphant
she made everything sound possible she was
dazzling she offered it to him
to hold high but what he saw
was the cruelty around her mouth
and her words of which he understood more
all said to him *Take pride*
take glory
you will suffer anyway

the third one the color of whose eyes
later he could not remember
spoke last and slowly and
of desire and it was his
though up until then he had been
happy with his river nymph
here was his mind
filled utterly with one girl gathering

yellow flowers
and no one like her
the words
made everything seem present
almost present
present
they said to him *Take*
her
you will lose her anyway

it was only when he reached out to the voice
as though he could take the speaker
herself
that his hand filled with
something to give
but to give to only one of the three
an apple as it is told
discord itself in a single fruit its skin
already carved
To the fairest

then a mason working above the gates of Troy
in the sunlight thought he felt the stone
shiver

in the quiver on Paris's back the head
of the arrow for Achilles' heel
smiled in its sleep

and Helen stepped from the palace to gather
as she would do every day in that season
from the grove the yellow ray flowers tall
as herself

whose roots are said to dispel pain

Edouard

Edouard shall we leave
tomorrow
for Verdun again
shall we set out for the great days
and never be the same
never

time
is what is left
shall we start
this time in the spring
and they lead your cows out
next week to sell at the fair
and the brambles learn to scribble
over the first field

Edouard shall we have gone
when the leaves come out
but before the heat
slows the grand marches
days like those
the heights and the dying
at thy right hand
sound a long horn
and here the bright handles
will fog over
things will break and stay broken
in the keeping of women
the sheep get lost
the barns
burn unconsoled in the darkness

Edouard what would you have given
not to go
sitting last night in by the fire
again
but shall we be the same
tomorrow night shall we not have gone

leaving the faces and nightingales
As you know we will live
and what never comes back will be
you and me

Not These Hills

Not these hills
are in my tongue
though I inquire of them again
which then
with their later season
on whose slopes my voice stirs
shining root
stream carrying small lights
to where one echo
waits

spring here
I am shown to me
as flies waking in the south walls
emerging from darkness one
at a time
dark
then gone
with nothing between them
but the sun

The Piper

It is twenty years
since I first looked for words
for me now
whose wisdom or something would stay me
I chose to
trouble myself about the onset
of this

it was remote it was grievous
it is true I was still a child

I was older then
than I hope ever to be again
that summer sweating in the attic
in the foreign country
high above the piper but hearing him
once
and never moving from my book
and the narrow
house full of pregnant women
floor above floor
waiting
in that city
where the sun was the one bell

It has taken me till now
to be able to say
even this
it has taken me this long
to know what I cannot say
where it begins
like the names of the hungry

Beginning
I am here
please
be ready to teach me
I am almost ready to learn

The Lake

Did you exist
ever

our clouds separated while it was still dark
then I could not sleep the sleep of a child
I got up to look for you

bringing my silence
all of it

no father in the house at least

I got my boat
that we had saved for each other
a white creature my
wise elder
You rustled as it slid
from shore

I lay there
looking down while the mist was torn
looking down
where
was the Indian village
said to be drowned there

one glimpse and I would have hung
fixed in its sky
when the dawn was gone
and the morning star
and the wind
and the sun
and the calling around you

The Church

High walls
pale brick like Babylon
above the cliff face
the house
of the lord

at the single window
up in the back
toward the river

the eyes I left
as a child there

everything gone now
the walls are down
the altar
only I am still standing
on the weedy rock in the wind
there is no building here

there are my hands
that have known between them
the bride
and call to her
wherever she is not wherever
she is *Hand*

hand

A Calm in April

Early mist
mountains like a rack of dishes
in a house I love
far mountains
last night the stars for a while
stopped trembling
and this morning the light will speak to me
of what concerns me

The Birds on the Morning of Going

If I can say yes I
must say it to this
and now
trying to remember what the present

can bless with
which I know

from all other ages how little has come to me
that is breath
and nothing that is you

now I can see
I have been carrying this
fear
a blue thing
the length of my life asking *Is this
its place*
bringing it here

to the singing
of these brightening birds

they are neither dead nor unborn

a life opens it opens it is
breaking
does it find occasions for
every grief of its childhood
before it will have
done

oh my love here even the night turns back

Envoy from D'Aubigné

Go book

go
now I will let you
I open the grave
live
I will die for us both

go but come again if you can
and feed me in prison

if they ask you why
you do not boast of me
tell them as they
have forgotten
truth habitually
gives birth in private

Go without ornament
without showy garment
if there is in you any
joy
may the good find it

for the others be
a glass broken in their mouths

Child
how will you
survive with nothing but your virtue
to draw around you
when they shout Die die

who have been frightened before
the many

I think of all I wrote in my time
dew
and I am standing in dry air

Here are what flowers there are
and what hope
from my years

and the fire I carried with me

Book
burn what will not abide your light

When I consider the old ambitions
to be on many lips
meaning little there
it would be enough for me to know
who is writing this
and sleep knowing it

far from glory and its gibbets

and dream of those who drank at the icy fountain
and told the truth

Encounter

Name for a curtain at night
sister of some
unfueled flame

imperious
triumphant and unloved
how did you find the houses
from which now you emanate
in which someone has just

but no sound reaches the gate
here
though all the lights are burning

The Well

Under the stone sky the water
waits
with all its songs inside it
the immortal
it sang once
it will sing again

the days
walk across the stone in heaven
unseen as planets at noon
while the water
watches the same night

Echoes come in like swallows
calling to it

it answers without moving
but in echoes
not in its voice
they do not say what it is
only where

It is a city to which many travelers
came with clear minds
having left everything even
heaven
to sit in the dark praying as one silence
for the resurrection

Lark

In the hour that has no friends
above it
you become yourself
voice
black
star burning in cold heaven
speaking well of it
as it falls from you
upward

Fire
by day
with no country
where and at what height

can it begin
I the shadow
singing I
the light

The Black Plateau

The cows bring in the last light
the dogs praise them
one by one they proceed through the stone arch
on the chine of the hill
and their reflections in the little
cold darkening stream
and the man with the pole
then the night comes down to its roads
full of love for them

———

I go eating nothing so you will be one and clear
but then how could you drown
in this arid country of stone and dark dew
I shake you in your heavy sleep
then the sun comes
and I see you are one of the stones

———

Like a little smoke in the vault
light for going
before the dogs wake in the cracked barn
the owl has come in from his shift
the water in the stone basin has forgotten
where I touch the ashes they are cold
everything is in order

———

Kestrel and lark shimmer over the high stone
like two brothers who avoid each other
on the cliff corner I met the wind
a brother

———

Almost everything you look on great sun
has fallen into itself here
which it had climbed out of like prayers
shadows of clouds
and the clothes of old women blow over the barrens
one apple tree still blossoms for its own sake

The cold of the heights is not the cold of the valleys
the light moves like a wind
the figures are far away walking slowly
in little knots herding pieces of darkness
their faces remote as the plaster above deaths
in the villages

The upper window of a ruin
one of the old faces
many places near here
things grow old where nothing was ever a child

Oh blessed goat live goat blessed rat
and neither of you lost

There is still warmth in the goat sheds years afterwards
in the abandoned fountain a dead branch points
upwards
eaten out from inside as it appears to me
I know a new legend
this is the saint of the place his present form
another blessing in absence
when the last stone has fallen he will rise
from the water
and the butterflies will tell him what he needs to know
that happened while he was asleep

The beginnings and ends of days like the butts of arches
reach for roofs that have fallen
the sun up there was never enough
high in its light
the bird moves apart from his cry

The Approaches

The glittering rises in flocks
suddenly in the afternoon
and hangs
voiceless above the broken
houses
the cold in the doorways
and at the silent station
the hammers
out of hearts
laid out in rows in the grass

The water is asleep
as they say
everywhere
cold cold
and at night the sky
is in many
pieces in the dark
the stars set out
and leave their light

When I wake
I say I may never
get there but should get
closer and hear the sound
seeing figures I go toward them waving
they make off
birds
no one to guide me
afraid
to the warm ruins
Canaan
where the fighting is

The Wheels of the Trains

They are there just the same
unnoticed for years
on dark tracks at the foot of their mountain

behind them holes in the hill
endless death of the sky
foreheads long unlit
illegibly inscribed

the cars
have been called into the air
an air that has gone
but these wait unmoved in their rust
row of suns
for another life

ahead of them
the tracks lead out through tall milkweed
untouched

for all my travels

Lackawanna

Where you begin
in me
I have never seen
but I believe it now
rising dark
but clear

later when I lived where
you went past
already you were black
moving under gases by
red windows

obedient child
I shrank from you

on girders of your bridges
I ran
told to be afraid
obedient
the arches never touched you the running
shadow never
looked
the iron
and black ice never
stopped ringing under foot

terror
a truth
lived alone in the stained buildings
in the streets a smoke
an eyelid a clock
a black winter all year
like a dust
melting and freezing in silence

you flowed from under
and through the night the dead drifted down you
all the dead
what was found later no one
could recognize

told to be afraid
I wake black to the knees
so it has happened
I have set foot in you
both feet
Jordan
too long I was ashamed
at a distance

Other Travelers to the River

William Bartram how many
have appeared in their sleep
climbing like flames into
your eyes
and have stood gazing out over the sire of waters
with night behind them
in the east
The tall bank where you stood
would soon crumble
you would die before they were born
they would wake not remembering
and on the river
that same day
was bearing off its empty flower again
and overhead the sounds of the earth
danced naked
thinking no one could see them

The Trail into Kansas

The early wagons left no sign
no smoke betrays them
line pressed in the grass *we were here*
all night the sun bleeds in us
and the wound slows us in the daytime
will it heal
there

we few
late
we gave our names to each other to keep
wrapped in their old bells
the wrappings work loose
something eats them when we sleep and wakes us
ringing

when day comes
shadows that were once ours and came back to look
stand up for a moment ahead of us
and then vanish
we know we are
watched but there is no danger
nothing that lives waits for us
nothing is eternal

we have been guided from scattered wombs
all the way here choosing choosing
which foot to put down
we are like wells moving
over the prairie
a blindness a hollow a cold source
will any be happy to see us
in the new home

Western Country

Some days after so long even the sun
is foreign
I watch the exiles
their stride
stayed by their antique faith that no one
can die in exile
when all that is true is that death is not exile

Each no doubt knows a western country
half discovered
which he thinks is there because
he thinks he left it
and its names are still written in the sun
in his age and he knows them
but he will never tread their ground

At some distances I can no longer
sleep
my countrymen are more cruel than their stars
and I know what moves the long
files stretching into the mountains
each man with his gun
his feet
one finger's breadth off the ground

The Gardens of Zuñi

The one-armed explorer
could touch only half of the country
In the virgin half
the house fires give no more heat
than the stars
it has been so these many years
and there is no bleeding

He is long dead with his five fingers
and the sum of their touching
and the memory
of the other hand
his scout

that sent back no message
from where it had reached
with no lines in its palm
while he balanced
balanced
and groped on
for the virgin land

and found where it had been

Homeland

The sky goes on living it goes
on living the sky
with all the barbed wire of the west
in its veins
and the sun goes down
driving a stake
through the black heart of Andrew Jackson

February

Dawn that cares for nobody
comes home
to the glass cliffs
an expression
needing no face
the river flies under cold feathers
flies on
leaving its body
the black streets bare their veins
night
lives on in the uniforms
in the silence of the headlines
in the promises of triumph
in the colors of the flags
in a room of the heart
while the ends and the beginnings
are still guarded
by lines of doors
hand in hand
the dead guarding the invisible
each presenting its message
I know nothing
learn of me

Huckleberry Woman

Foreign voice woman
of unnamed origins nothing
to do with what I was taught
at night when it was nobody's
you climbed the mountain in back of the house
the thorn bushes slept
in their words
before day you put on
the bent back like a hill
the hands at the berries

and I wake only to the crying
when the washtub has
fallen from your head and the alley
under the window is deep
in the spilled blue of far ranges
the rolling of small
starless skies and you turning
among them key
unlocking the presence
of the unlighted river
under the mountains

and I am borne with you on its
black stream
oh loss loss the grieving
feels its way upward
through daggers of stone
to stone
we let it go it
stays we share it
echoed by a wooden
coughing of oars in the dark
whether or not they are ours
we go with the sound

Little Horse

You come from some other forest
do you
little horse
think how long I have known these
deep dead leaves
without meeting you

I belong to no one
I would have wished for you if I had known how
what a long time the place was empty
even in my sleep
and loving it as I did
I could not have told what was missing

what can I show you
I will not ask you if you will stay
or if you will come again
I will not try to hold you
I hope you will come with me to where I stand
often sleeping and waking
by the patient water
that has no father nor mother

The Port

The river is slow
and I knew I was late arriving but had no idea
how late
in the splintery fishing port silence
was waving from the nails
dry long since
the windows though rattling
were fixed in time and space
in a way that I am not nor ever was
and the boats were out of sight

all but one
by the wharf
full of water
with my rotted sea-clothes lashed to a piling
at its head
and a white note nailed there in a can
with white words
I was too late to read
when what I came to say is I have learned who we are

when what I came to say was
consider consider
our voices
through the salt

they waken in heads
in the deaths themselves

that was part of it

when what I came to say was
it is true that in
our language deaths are to be heard
at any moment through the talk
pacing their wooden rooms jarring
the dried flowers
but they have forgotten who they are
and our voices in their heads waken
childhoods in other tongues

but the whole town has gone to sea without a word
taking my voice

Presidents

The president of shame has his own flag
the president of lies quotes the voice
of God

as last counted
the president of loyalty recommends
blindness to the blind
oh oh
applause like the heels of the hanged
he walks on eyes
until they break
then he rides
there is no president of grief
it is a kingdom
ancient absolute with no colors
its ruler is never seen
prayers look for him
also empty flags like skins
silence the messenger runs through the vast lands
with a black mouth
open
silence the climber falls from the cliffs
with a black mouth like
a call
there is only one subject
but he is repeated
tirelessly

The Free

So far from the murders
the ruts begin to bleed
but no one hears
our voices
above the sound of the reddening feet
they leave us the empty roads
they leave us
for companions for messengers
for signs
the autumn leaves
before the winter panes

we move among them
doubly invisible
like air touching the blind
and when we have gone they say we are with them forever

The Prints

Above white paths a bugle
will sound from the top of an unseen wall
and beds be empty as far as eye will reach
made up spotless
the shallow prints where each traveler carried
what he had

whiteness came back to the paths after each
footstep and the travelers
never met in the single files
who deepened the same
shadows

while the snow fell

The Removal

To the endless tribe

1 *The Procession*

When we see
the houses again
we will know that we are asleep at last

when we see
tears on the road
and they are ourselves
we are awake
the tree has been cut

on which we were leaves
the day does not know us
the river where we cross does not taste salt

the soles of our feet are black stars
but ours is the theme
of the light

II   *The Homeless*

A clock keeps striking
and the echoes move in files
their faces
have been lost
flowers of salt
tongues from lost languages
doorways closed with pieces of night

III   *A Survivor*

The dust never settles
but through it tongue tongue comes walking
shuffling like breath
but the old speech
is still in its country
dead

IV   *The Crossing of the Removed*

At the bottom of the river
black ribbons cross under
and the water tries to soothe them
the mud tries to soothe them
the stones turn over and over trying
to comfort them
but they will not be healed
where the rims cut
and the shadows
sawed carrying
mourners
and some that had used horses
and had the harness
dropped it in half way over

on the far side the ribbons come out
invisible

v *A Widow Is Taken*

I call leave me here
the smoke on the black path
was my children
I will not walk
from the house I warmed
but they carry me through the light
my blackening face
my red eyes
everywhere I leave
one white footprint
the trackers will follow us into the cold
the water is high
the boats have been stolen away
there are no shoes
and they pretend that I am a bride
on the way to a new house

vi *The Reflection*

Passing a broken window
they see
into each of them the wedge of blackness
pounded
it is nothing
it splits them
loose hair
bare heels
at last they are gone
filing on in vacant rooms

The Old Room

I am in the old room across from the synagogue
a dead chief hangs in the wallpaper
he is shrinking into the patch of sunlight

with its waves and nests and in the silence that follows
his death
the parade is forming again
with the streetcar for its band
it is forming I hear the shuffling the whispers
the choking then the grinding starts off
slowly as ice melting
they will pass by the house

closed ranks attached to the iron trolley
dragged on their backs
the black sleeves the fingers waving like banners
I am forbidden to look
but the faces are wrapped except for the eyes
darkness wells from the bandages
spreads
its loaves and fishes while on the curbs
the police the citizens
of all ages beat the muffled street with bars

what if I call *It is not me* will it stop
what if I raise an arm
to stop it
I raise an arm the whole arm stays white
dry as a beach
little winds play over it
a sunny and a pleasant place I hold it
out it leaves me it goes toward them
the man in charge is a friend of the family
he smiles when he sees it he takes its hand
he gives it its bar
it drops it
I am forbidden to look

I am in the old room across from the stone star
the moon is climbing in gauze
the street is empty
except for the dark liquid running
in the tracks of ice
trying to call
Wait

but the wires are taken up with the election
there is a poll at the corner I am not to go in
but I can look in the drugstore window
where the numbers of the dead change all night on the wall
what if I vote *It is not me* will they revive
I go in my father has voted for me
I say no I will vote in my own name
I vote and the number leaps again on the wall

I am in the old room across from the night
the long scream is about to blossom
that is rooted in flames
if I called *It is not me* would it reach
through the bells

The Night of the Shirts

Oh pile of white shirts who is coming
to breathe in your shapes to carry your numbers
to appear
what hearts
are moving toward their garments here
their days
what troubles beating between arms

you look upward through
each other saying nothing has happened
and it has gone away and is sleeping
having told the same story
and we exist from within
eyes of the gods

you lie on your backs
and the wounds are not made
the blood has not heard
the boat has not turned to stone
and the dark wires to the bulb
are full of the voice of the unborn

Shoe Repairs
for Charles Hanzlicek

Long after the scheduled deaths of animals
their skins made up into couples
have arrived here
empty
from many turnings
between the ways of men
and men

In a side street
by brown walls over a small light
the infinite routes
which they follow a little way
come together
to wait in rows in twos
soles
eyes of masks
from a culture lost forever

We will know the smell
in another life
stepping down
barefoot into this Ark
seeing it lit up but empty
the destined racks
done with the saved pairs
that went out to die each alone

Age

These fields of thistles are the old
who believed in the day they had
and held it like an army
now that they are blind
with an alien whiteness clutching their feet
their hair blows into the sea

Ancient sockets
as the snow fell you looked up
full of milk
saying there was something we did not find
it was a child
how could we recognize it since it was never born

As they enter extinction the birds join the vast
flocks of prayers circling over the gulf
in the unreturning light
and the old think it is snow
falling slowly and stopping in the day sky
or the stars the stars

Laughter

The great gods are blind or pretend to be

finding that I am among men I open my eyes
and they shake

Snowfall

For my mother

Some time in the dark hours
it seemed I was a spark climbing
the black road
with my death helping me up
a white self helping me up
like a brother
growing
but this morning
I see that the silent kin I loved as a child
have arrived all together in the night
from the old country

they remembered
and everything remembers
I eat from the hands
of what for years have been junipers
the taste has not changed
I am beginning
again
but a bell rings in some village I do not know
and cannot hear
and in the sunlight snow drops from branches
leaving its name in the air
and a single footprint

brother

Banishment in Winter
for Richard Howard

From the north the wands the long
questions of light
descend among us from my country
even by day
and their discoveries are recorded
beyond the silence
blue eyes watch needles
oh little by little it will be seen who remembers
the cold dusk crossing the pastures
the black hay ridged
along the darkness
the color of snow
at night
So even by day
the wands reach toward the outer river
toward the deep shadows
inquiring and above us
like stars in a slow negative
the migrants

the true migrants
already immeasurably far
the dark migrants
the souls
move outward into the cold
but will it ever be
dark again in my country
where hanging from lamp posts
the good
fill the streets with their steady light

Footprints on the Glacier

Where the wind
year round out of the gap
polishes everything
here this day are footprints like my own
the first ever
frozen
pointing up into the cold

and last night someone
marched and marched on the candle flame
hurrying
a painful road
and I heard the echo a long time afterwards
gone and some connection of mine

I scan the high slopes for a dark speck
that was lately here
I pass my hands
over the melted wax
like a blind man
they are all
moving into their seasons at last
my bones face each other trying
to remember a question

nothing moves while I watch
but here the black trees
are the cemetery of a great battle
and behind me as I turn
I hear names leaving the bark
in growing numbers and flying north

Tale

After many winters the moss
finds the sawdust crushed bark chips
and says old friend
old friend

Full Moonlight in Spring

Night sends this white eye
to her brother the king of the snow

Night Wind

All through the dark the wind looks
for the grief it belongs to
but there was no place
for that any more

I have looked too
and seen only the nameless hunger
watching us out of the stars
ancestor

and the black fields

Midnight in Early Spring

At one moment a few old leaves come in
frightened
and lie down together and stop moving
the nights now go in threes
as in a time of danger
the flies
sleep like sentries on the darkened panes

some alien blessing
is on its way to us
some prayer ignored for centuries
is about to be granted to the prayerless
in this place

who were you
cold voice born in captivity
rising
last martyr of a hope
last word of a language
last son
other half of grief
who were you

so that we may know why
when the streams
wake tomorrow and we are free

As Though I Was Waiting for That

Some day it will rain
from a cold place
and the sticks and stones will darken their faces
the salt will wash from the worn gods
of the good
and mourners will be waiting
on the far sides of the hills

and I will remember the calling
recognized at the wrong hours
long since
and hands a long way back
that will have forgotten
and a direction will have abandoned my feet
their way
that offered
itself vainly day after day
at last gone
like a color or the cloth at elbows

I will stir when it is getting dark
and stand when it is too late
as though I was waiting for that
and start out into the weather
into emptiness
passing the backs of trees
of the rain of the mourners
the backs of names the back
of darkness

for no reason
hearing no voice
with no promise
praying to myself
be clear

The Plumbing
for Adrienne Rich

New silence
between the end and the beginning
The planet that was never named
because it was dark
climbs into the evening
nothing else moves
moon stars the black laundry the hour

have stopped and are looking away
the lungs stand
a frozen forest
into which no air comes

they go on standing like shadows
of the plumbing
that is all that is left
of the great city
the buildings vanished the windows
extinct the smoke with its strings of names
wiped away
and its fire
at the still note
the throwing of a switch

only these pipes
bereft of stairs of elevators
of walls of girders
awakened from lamps from roofs
grow into the night
crowding upward in rows
to desolate heights their blind hope
and their black mouths locked open hollow stars
between the dark planets
a famine a worship the heirs
of the dials

among their feet
my heart is still beating by itself
thinking it understands and might feed them

Beginning of the Plains

On city bridges steep as hills I change countries
and this according to the promise
is the way home

where the cold has come from
with its secret baggage

in the white sky the light flickering
like the flight of a wing

nothing to be bought in the last
dim shops
before the plain begins
few shelves kept only by children
and relatives there for the holiday
who know nothing

wind without flags
marching into the city
to the rear

I recognize the first hunger
as the plains start
under my feet

Ascent

I have climbed a long way
there are my shoes
minute larvae
the dark parents
I know they will wait there looking up
until someone leads them away

by the time they have got to the place
that will do for their age
and are in there with nothing to say
the shades drawn
nothing but wear
between them

I may have reached the first
of the bare meadows
recognized in the air
the eyes by their blankness
turned
knowing myself seen by the lost
silent
barefoot choir

The Hulk

The water itself is leaving the harbor
a gleam waiting in lines
to be gone
and there I am
the small child the small child
alone with the huge ship at last

It must be named for silence
the iron whale asleep on its side
in the breathless port
a name rusted out
in an unknown
unknown language

And no one will come
to call me by any name
the ropes end like water
the walls lie on their backs
bodies dusted with light
I can sail if we sail
I can wander
through the rusting passages forever
with my fear by the hand
by the hand
and no father

Fear

Fear
there is
fear in fear the name the blue and green walls
falling of and numbers fear the veins that
when they were opened fear flowed from and
these forms it took a ring a ring a ring
a bit of grass green swan's down gliding on
fear into fear and the hatred and something
in everything and it is my death's
disciple leg and fear no he would not
have back those lives again and their fear as
he feared he would say but he feared more he
did not fear more he did fear more
in everything it is there a long time
as I was and it is within those
blue and green walls that the actual
verification has and in fact will
take the form of a ring a ring a ring
took I should say the figure in the hall
of the glass giants the third exhibition
on the right is fear I am I fear and
the rain falling fear red fear yellow fear
blue and green for their depth etcetera
fear etcetera water fire earth air
etcetera in everything made of
human agency or divine fear is
in the answer also and shall pierce thy
bosom too fear three gathered together
four five etcetera the brightest day
the longest day its own fear the light
itself the nine village tailors fear
their thread if not their needles if not
their needles in everything and it is
here this is New York and aside from that
fear which under another name in
every stone Abraham is buried it
is fear the infant's lovely face the
grass green alleys oh at about the third

hour of the night it being in those parts
still light there came fear my loving fear
in everything it is next the baker the
candlestick maker if you know what I
answer at that point and fear the little
cobbler his last is one fear and there is
fear in all shoes in the shoe line the clothes
line any clothes the blood line any in
everything it is the third button
the book books fear the bottle and what it
contains everything a life death the spirit
staring inward on nothing there and
the sunken vessel the path through the shadow
the shadow of me me or if I am not
suddenly fear coming from the west
singing the great song there was no need
fear no crying and others would sift
the salt in silence in fear the house
where I am familiar in all your
former lives remembered your parents
fear and fear theirs of your parents by
your parents and for your parents shall not
perish from this deciding everything
and it is deciding strike out Mr
Mrs Miss I am alone little stones
fear forgetting forgets remembering
it is my loving fear the mouth of my
seeing fear I am awake I am not
awake and fear no bones like my own
brother fear my death's sister and high on
the cliff face the small arched door from which
a man could fear or be in the winking
of an eye the tapping of the second
finger of the left hand the wind itself
fear I am alone forever I am
fear I am alone I fear I am
not alone couldn't tell your breath from fear
for it is your breath I do it and I'm
supposed to explain it too I fear I
completed my fear in everything there is

fear and I would speak for myself but fear
says logic follows but I advance in
everything and so discovery
geography history law comedy
fear law poetry major prophets
minor prophets that pass in the night
it is a mother and a guiding light
moving across fear before which they burn
in rows in red glass bleeding upwards their
hearts smoke in the gusts on earth as it is
in heaven with the sentence beginning
before the heavens were or the earth
had out of fear been called and any began
to be fear the bird feather by feather
note by note eye by eye pierced he is my
neighbor in the uttermost parts of aye
and shall I couple heaven when the fear
shall fear and those who walked in fear shall see
fear their very form and being for
their eyes shall be opened it was going
on in everything and I forgot but if you
stand here you can see fear the new building
starting to rise from which our children
will fear the stilted dogs the insects
who do not exist the dead burning
as candles oh dark flames cold lights in
everything without you the ship coming
in and a long way that I would never
traverse before fear had followed that
scent faster than a mortal bearing fear
I'm telling you I'm asking you I'm dying
I'm here today this is New York I'm more
than any one person or two persons
can stand fear the way down in everything
the way up is the same fear the next place
the next I said fear come on you it's you
I'm addressing get into line you're going
never fear there is a hair hanging by
everything it is the edges of things
the light of things do you see nothing

in them burning and the long crying
didn't you hear that either I mean
you again fear it's a strange name not
for a stranger ma'am he said lying I
mean there is you fear me fear but you
must not imagine fear through which the present
moves like a star that I or that
you either clearly and from the beginning
could ever again because from the beginning
there is fear in everything and it is
me and always was in everything it
is me

Pilate

It has
a life of its own however long it
served Pharaoh and so a heaven of its
own to which its own blood calls which should be
heard with respect when they call crucify
crucify him of its own why should you
not see it unless it is walking arm
in arm with objects which you think you can see
without it when lo empire itself
is not visible

and a future of its own
the prophecies waking without names in
strange lands on unborn tongues those syllables
resurrected staring is that heaven
all the pain to find its hands again old
but you must not suppose that because of
the centurions' reports eclipses
on frontiers and the beards there blowing
through wooden fences dead men but there no
flies in that wind crying sand only
the long arrows and the kissing arrows
through which his wife coming with her spillage

of dreams because of this man but it is
the broken windows that look to the future
and empire is the viewing as different
so a dream itself and how can a man voyage
on more than one bark one trireme one skiff
with one oar at one time even after
the washing is heard on that shore and
the one oar

and you should not imagine either
that you yourselves are later or far or
otherwise else above all those tongues tongues
lit at the tops of arms under
the lungless banners the dread in amber
the silence rolling on before the shadows
burning on the walls with dark cries or going
home a long way through the baths
the gowns dripping the feet growing barer
and the dark flights vanishing into the
cracks in the day

it is termed an alien
judgment they are like that and can force then
be held accountable that has no life
of its own the dark wine dark throats the call
the call that hangs in the banners until
it falls as shall the banners fall
from the walls the walls from the sky its smoke
its eagles what was I put here to change
I was not put here to change

could I change myself my hands
and their dreams a life of their own with its
own heaven own future own windows
washing can I change what they do before
I am born for they will do it without me
arm in arm with objects but lo myself
is not visible to these this man the life
of its own without me its smoke its eagles
and wooden fences and tonight the hands

in the outer circles of the soldiers'
corner fires later than the last meal
gesturing in the reeling night washing
in darkness afterwards will go home
and the darkness will let itself down
into their prayers

Shore

We turned hearing the same note
of the flute far inland unfaltering and
unknown to each other but already
wrapped in the silence that we would each wear
we left two the hills one the valley before
day entered the pearl and we drew
together as streams descend through their
darkness to the shore

there it was even then by that horn light
of an old skin to be seen approaching
out of the black the lifted prow which waves
touched and fled from on the engraved flood
the scar on the wooden breast climbing above
the breast and the after vessel gazing
up and back at the night the family
the resemblance invisible to us
as it bore in bore in rapidly
to the rocky plain the eggs of venerable
stones the leaden shingle washed and washed under
the shrieks of curlews and that unbreaking
note as of a planet

making in fast toward our eyes fixed
on the uncolored bow one massed and older
jutting in velvet hat and the gown dark
to the shingle beyond whom the sky
whitened out of the gnarled littoral
the other no nearer the waves still young

a fisherman bareheaded in boots
it is my feet that are bare and others
may have gathered behind us the fires
would have been lit at home but we no longer
see behind us

and we hear nothing above the haul
of tongues leaving the shore to the flute's
accompaniment silent flocks pass
on their black journeys it is making in
at a speed that ignores the steely elements
we are waiting waiting what it was carrying
in the early hours as we believed
it could no longer have borne living when the white
shadow gained on heaven and a figure
like the beam of a lantern seemed
to stand in the bark but now though the hollow
board is plainly nearer the light will set
soon where it first rose and we get by heart
the spot where the shingle will scrape in the night
if the keel touches

Psalm: Our Fathers

I am the son of joy but does he know me
I am the son of hope but he ascends into heaven
I am the son of peace but I was put out to nurse
I am the son of grief after the brother was lost but I have
    opened an eye in the life where it was he who lived
I am the son of a shadow and I draw my blinds out of respect
    but I cleave uneasily to the light
I am the son of love but where is my home and where the
    black baptismal cup and the frightened eyes that would
    still come to the names I gave them
I am the son of the tribe of Apher which set up empty tents
    and camped where it could defend them and was
    remembered for them but I have discovered that the
    unknowable needs no defense

I am the son of the temptations of the rocks but there have
     been some between
I am the son of fear but I find out for myself
I am the son of the first fish who climbed ashore but the news
     has not yet reached my bowels
I am the son of three flowers the pink the rose and the other
     or its effigy in skin for neither of which was I taught a
     name and I shudder at their withering all three but they
     will survive me
I am the son of the future but she shows me only her
     mourning veil
I am the son of the future but my own father
I am the son of the future but where is my home and the
     black baptismal cup and the warning voice from the
     bushes under the kitchen window saying that they were
     not my parents
I am the son of a glass tombstone in a fresh plowed field
     whose furrows sit in rows studying the inscriptions of
     dew the sole name life tears as the sun rises but there are
     no more voices on that river
I am the son of the water-thief who got away and founded a
     bare-faced dynasty but the fountains are still following
I am the son of a plaster bone in the oldest reconstruction in
     Millennial Hall but all my ages are one
I am the son of the cymbal of Bethel that answered like
     a cracked bowl to the instruments of ivory of bone
     iron wood brass hair gold gut glass through all the
     generations of the sacred orchestra a maimed voice
     before the throne with waiting as it was for its like to
     be found its twin its other face sun socket identical disc
     the very metal the other half its cymbal so that it could
     sound its own true note but only one had been made
I am the son of an unsuspected wealth but I may labor all my
     life and leave nothing but a grain of mustard seed
I am the son of thanksgiving but its language is strange in my
     mouth
I am the son of the glove of an upper river and the glove of a
     tree but there were four rivers all told around the garden
     and I tasted of salt from the beginning
I am the son of the fourth son in the right hand jars on the

second row of the seventh shelf above the glass footwalk
on the fifth floor in the ninth bay of the eighty-third
room of the T18 wing of the heart division of the St.
Luke's Memorial Index but he died in a strange land
before I was born

I am the son of Cargarran who was an ant in the time of the
noseless emperors and was accorded great emulation
an urn of amber and a flag to fly his picture on for he
fought with the plague of crane seeds until darkness
came to his rescue but I have use to be frightened
if I wake if I remember if a tax is mentioned or it is
Thursday

I am the son of seven promises the last of them to live to see
it again but the womb may not have been listening

I am the son of the word Still after the angels came to the
door in her barren age but on that same day she lost her
memory and she gave birth without understanding

I am the son of a drunken rape at a veterans' convention in a
brutal empire bandaged with the arguments of empires
but hallowed by thy name

I am the son of the starvation of the Utes the tortures
and gassing of the Jews the interrogation of suspects
the burning of villages the throat of the antelope the
amputations of the domesticated the cries of the extinct
and I plead ignorance ignorance but it would be no
better to be an orphan

I am the son of the ark that was carried empty before the
tribes in the wilderness but I walk because the times
have changed and there is no one behind

I am the son of the statue of Hamalid the Great The Weight
of God that was re-named Vengeance in a different
tongue and that with raised knife still shouts its
incomprehensible syllable to the dark square with one
foot on the illegible date of death and no apparent sex
any longer but it was modeled on a jailer's dead wife

I am the son of four elements fire darkness salt and vertigo
but I dance as though they were strangers

I am the son of the cloud Cynian that appeared as a torn
white breast above Herod and was not recognized but I
acknowledge its vatic suffering still visible in the bruised
haze of the ridges

I am of the blood of the ash shrew whose remains have not
      been found but whose characteristics have been deduced
      from my teeth my mistakes the atrophied ear at the
      heart of each of my fingerprints and the size of the door
      at the base of the skull where now the performers enter
      each with his eye fixed on the waiting instrument
I am the son of the bird fire that has no eyes but sings to itself
      after waiting alone and silent in the alien wood
I am the son of fear but it means I am never lost
I am the son of terrible labors but triumph comes to the flags
      that have done nothing
I am the son of pain but time nurses me
I am the son of nobody but when I go the islands turn black
I am the son of the first Sabbath but after me cometh the
      eighth day
I am the son of hunger hunger and hunger in an unbroken
      line back to the mouths of the coelenterates but even I
      have been filled
I am the son of remorse in a vein of fossils but I might not
      have been
I am the son of division but the nails the wires the hasps the
      bolts the locks the traps the wrapping that hold me
      together are part of the inheritance
I am the son of indifference but neglect is a stage in the life of
      the gods
I am the son of No but memory bathes its knowledge in desire
I am the son of blindness but I watch the light stretch one
      wing
I am the son of a silence in heaven but I cried and the dark
      angels went on falling
I am the son of things as they are but I know them for the
      most part only as they are remembered
I am the son of farewells and one of me will not come back
      but one of me never forgets
I am the son of violence the ignorance herald but the seal is
      royal
I am the son of stars never seen never to be seen for we will
      be gone before their light reaches us but the decisions
      they demand are with us
      now now
I am the son of love but I lose you in the palm of my hand

I am the son of prisoners but I was got out in the form of a
    gold tooth a picture of two elders in a platinum locket
    a pair of eyeglasses with rims of white metal one pearl
    earring a knife with a picture of Jerusalem on the silver
    handle and I am being reassembled and keep finding
    myself and beginning again the process of reunion
I am the son of hazard but does my prayer reach you o star of
    the uncertain
I am the son of blindness but nothing that we have made
    watches us
I am the son of untruth but I have seen the children in
    Paradise walking in pairs each hand in hand with himself
I am the son of the warder but he was buried with his keys
I am the son of the light but does it call me Samuel or Jonah
I am the son of a wish older than water but I needed till now
I am the son of ghosts clutching the world like roads but
    tomorrow I will go a new way
I am the son of ruins already among us but at moments I
    have found hope beyond doubt beyond desert beyond
    reason and such that I have prayed O wounds come
    back from death and be healed
I am the son of hazard but go on with the story you think is
    yours
I am the son of love but the hangmen are my brothers
I am the son of love but the islands are black
I am the son of love for which parent the blood gropes in
    dread as though it were naked and for which cause the
    sun hangs in a cage of light
    and we are his pains

Cuckoo Myth

Stay with the cuckoo I heard
then the cuckoo I heard
then I was born

cuckoo cuckoo she
that from hiding

sings
from dark coverts
from gates where ghosts
stand open
cuckoo
from loss the light rises
a voice that bears with it its hiding

cuckoo that in her time
sings unseen
because the wing beheld
by the unhappy
shall fall
flew again to the first season
to the undivided
returned from there bringing
to the creatures Love
a light for the unhappy
but the light bore with it
its hiding

cuckoo that sings
in echoes
because the voice that the falling follow
falls
flew again under the years
to the unturning
returned from there bringing
to the world Death
a light for the unhappy
but a light rising
from loss

cuckoo cuckoo
that through time sings changing
now she has gone again

Second Psalm: The Signals

When the ox-horn sounds in the buried hills
        of Iceland
        I am alone
        my shadow runs back into me to hide
        and there is not room for both of us
        and the dread
when the ox-horn sounds on the blue stairs
        where the echoes are my mother's name
        I am alone
        as milk spilled in a street
        white instrument
        white hand
        white music
when the ox-horn is raised like a feather in one
        of several rivers
        not all of which I have come to
        and the note starts toward the sea
        I am alone
        as the optic nerve of the blind
        though in front of me it is written
        This is the end of the past
        Be happy
when the ox-horn sounds from its tassels of blood
        I always seem to be opening
        a book an envelope the top of a well
        none of them mine
        a tray of gloves has been set down
        beside my hands
        I am alone
        as the hour of the stopped clock
when the ox-horn is struck by its brother
        and the low grieving denial
        gropes forth again with its black hands
        I am alone
        as one stone left to pray in the desert
        after god had unmade himself
        I am
        I still am
when the ox-horn sounds over the dead oxen

the guns grow light in hands
I the fearer
try to destroy me the fearing
I am alone
as a bow that has lost its nerve
my death sinks into me to hide
as water into stones
before a great cold
when the ox-horn is raised in silence
someone's breath is moving over my face
like the flight of a fly
but I am in this world
without you
I am alone as the sadness surrounding
what has long ministered to our convenience
alone as the note of the horn
as the human voice
saddest of instruments
as a white grain of sand falling in a still sea
alone as the figure she unwove each night alone

alone
as I will be

The Pens

In the city of fire the eyes
look upward
there is no memory
except the smoke writing writing *wait*
wai
w
under the light that has
the stars inside it
the white
invisible stars they also
writing

and unable to read

The Forbears

I think I was cold in the womb
shivering I
remember
cold too I think did my brother suffer
who slept before me there
and cold I am sure was John in the early
as in the earlier
dawn all they
even whose names are anonymous
now known for their cold only
I believe they quaking lay
beforetime there
dancing like teeth and I
was them all foretelling me
if not the name the trembling
if not the time the dancing
if not the hour the longing
in the round night

Voice

for Jane Kirstein 1916–1968

By now you will have met
no one
my elder sister
you will have sat
by her breath in the dark
she will have told you I don't know what
in the way she remembers whatever it is
that's how she is
I never see her
but it's you I miss

by now she'll have sat around you
in a circle holding your hand
saying she's listening but

you'll hear you'll hear what she says
to everyone but especially to my friends
is it good what she tells you
is it anything I'd know

her own brother
but I still remember only
afterwards
and we're all like this

by now
more and more I remember
what isn't so
your voice
as I heard it in a dream
the night you died
when it was no longer yours

Last People

Our flowers are numbered
we no longer know where
phrases
last messages written on the white petals
appear as they wither
but in whose language
how could we ask

other messages emerge in the smells
we listen
listen
as they grow fainter

when we go home
with what we have got
when we climb the stairs reciting ancient deeds
the seas grow deeper
that we rose from

when we open the door
when we shut the door
the dust
goes on falling in our heads
goes on falling in our hearts

at the day's end
all our footsteps are added up
to see how near

what will be left
how long will the old men's kingdom survive
the lines of pebbles signifying
house
tea cups on stones
who will feed the dogs
it was like this before

it was like this before
triumphs long in the preparing
stumbled through cracking
film light
and we seem to have known
their faces crumpling just before
they vanished
like papers burning
while the features of plants rose out of plants
　ɔ watch them pass
　　remember

Third Psalm: The September Vision
for Galway Kinnell

d in which the sun rises
ɔry looking
nd
black days
of stones

going
but likewise coming
their sealed way
I see an empty bird cage
a memory looking
for a heart
asked to feel more
feels less
I see an empty bird flying
and its song follows me
with my own name
with the sound of the ice
of my own name
breaking
I see the eyes of that bird
in each light
in rain
in mirrors
in eyes
in spoons
I see clear lakes float over us
touching us with their hems
and they carry away secrets
they never brought
I see tongues being divided
and the birth of speech
that must grow
in pain
and set out for Nineveh
I see a moth approaching
like one ear of an invisible animal
and I am not calling
I see bells riding dead horses
and there was never a silence like this

oh objects come and talk with us while you can

After the Harvests

Every night hears the sound of rain
it is the roofer's widow looking for him
in her glass sleep

Now It Is Clear

Now it is clear to me that no leaves are mine
no roots are mine
that wherever I go I will be a spine of smoke in the forest
and the forest will know it
we will both know it

and that the birds vanish because of something
that I remember
flying from me as though I were a great wind
as the stones settle into the ground
the trees into themselves
staring as though I were a great wind
which is what I pray for

it is clear to me that I cannot return
but that some of us will meet once more
even here
like our own statues
and some of us still later without names
and some of us will burn with the speed
of endless departures

and be found and lost no more

Man with One Leaf in October Night

The leaves turn black when they have learned how to fly
so does the day
but in the wind of the first hours of darkness
sudden joy sent
from an unknown tree
I have not deserved you

Woman from the River

I thought it was an empty doorway
standing there by me
and it was you
I can see that you stood that way
cold as a pillar
while they made the stories about you

Late Night in Autumn

In the hills ahead a pain is moving its light
through the dark skies of a self
it is on foot I think
it is old
the year will soon be home and its own hear it
but in some house of my soul
a calling is coming in again off the cold mountains
and here one glove is hanging from each window
oh long way to go

Still Afternoon Light

Known love standing in deep grove
new love naked on plain

dance record
from before I was born

played with a new needle

no dancing

Kin

Up the west slope before dark
shadow of my smoke
old man

climbing the old men's mountain

at the end
birds lead something down to me
it is silence

they leave it with me
in the dark
it is from them

that I am descended

Memory of Spring

The first composer
could hear only what he could write

Signs

Half my life ago
watching the river birds

Dawn
white bird let go

Strange
to be any place

Leaves understand flowers
well enough

Each sleeper
troubled
by his light

Waves sever
sever

Silence
is my shepherd

Born once
born forever

Small dog barking
far down in walls

The wind wakes in the dark
knowing it's happened

Music stops
on the far side of a bay

Don't walk

Window
in the house
of a blind man

A shout
darkening the roofs

Quick smile
like a shoe's

No keys to the shadows
the wind shakes them

Silent rivers
fall toward us
without explaining

City
stands by a river
with torches

Not part of the country
part of the horizon

Blind
remembering me as a child

Bitterness of seeds
a form of knowledge

Men
until they enter that building

Look at their shoes
to see how gravely
they are hurt

Deaf
listens for his heart

hears name of a great star
never seen

———

Snow
falls in plum orchards
as though it had been there before

———

Bell spills
sky darkens

———

Appear
not as they are
but as what prevents them

———

Walk

———

Clear night
fish
jumping at stars

The Paw

I return to my limbs with the first
gray light
and here is the gray paw under my hand
the she-wolf Perdita
has come back
to sleep beside me
her spine pressed knuckle to knuckle
down my front
her ears lying against my ribs
on the left side where the heart beats

and she takes its sound for the pulsing
of her paws
we are coursing the black sierra once more
in the starlight
oh Perdita

we are racing over the dark auroras
you and I with no shadow
with no shadow
in the same place

so she came back
again in the black hours
running before the open sack
we have run
these hours together
again
there is blood
on the paw under my fingers
flowing
there is blood then
on the black heights again
in her tracks
our tracks
but vanishing like a shadow

and there is blood
against my ribs again
oh Perdita
she is more beautiful after every wound
as though they were stars
I know
how the haunches are hollowed
stretched out in the dark
at full speed like a constellation
I hear
her breath moving on the fields of frost
my measure
I beat faster
her blood wells through my fingers
my eyes shut to see her
again
my way

before the stars fall
and the mountains go out
and the void wakes
and it is day

but we are gone

The Thread

Unrolling the black thread
through the tunnel
you come to the wide wall
of shoes
the soles standing
out in the air you breathe
crowded from side to side
floor to ceiling
and no names
and no door
and the bodies
stacked before them like bottles
generation upon
generation
upon generation
with their threads
asleep in their hands
and the tunnel is full
of their bodies
from there
all the way to the end of the mountain
the beginning of time
the light of day
the bird
and you are unrolling
the Sibyll's song
that is trying to reach her
beyond your dead

The Blessing

There is a blessing on the wide road
the eggshell road the baked highway
there is a blessing an old woman
walking fast following him

pace of a child following him

he left today
in a fast car

until or unless
she is with him
the traffic flows through her
as though she were air
or not there

she can speak only to him
she can tell him
what only he can hear

she can save him
once

it might be enough

she is hurrying

he is making good time
his breath comes more easily
he is still troubled at moments
by the feeling
that he has forgotten something
but he thinks he is escaping a terrible
horseman

Beginning

Long before spring
king of the black cranes
rises one day
from the black
needle's eye
on the white plain
under the white sky

the crown turns
and the eye
drilled clear through his head
turns
it is north everywhere
come out he says

come out then
the light is not yet
divided
it is a long way
to the first
anything
come even so
we will start
bring your nights with you

The First Darkness

Maybe he does not even have to exist
to exist in departures
then the first darkness falls
even there a shining is flowing from all the stones
though the eyes are not yet made that can see it
saying Blessèd
are ye

The Chaff

Those who cannot love the heavens or the earth
beaten from the heavens and the earth
eat each other
those who cannot love each other
beaten from each other
eat themselves
those who cannot love themselves
beaten from themselves
eat a terrible bread
kneaded in the morning shrouded all day
baked in the dark
whose sweet smell brings the chaff flying like empty hands
through the turning sky night after night
calling with voices of young birds
to its wheat

Fourth Psalm: The Cerements

She made him a roof with her hands
        from his own voice she wove
        the walls to stop the wind
        with his own dreams she painted the windows
        each with its kingdom
        and the doors were mirrors she fashioned
        of his eyes

        but when she opened it he was gone

        gone the vision
        gone
        the witness

She made him a cage of wishes
        he helped when he could
        helped long
        and indeed with all the heavy parts

but when she opened it

She made him a net of consents
      where he might turn in his own place
      like an eye in its veins
      a globe in its hours
      she hung it with tears
      with both of theirs

      but when she opened it he was gone

      gone
      the asking

She made him a box of some sweet wood
      she knew he remembered from his childhood
      in corners rose columns she had painted like smoke
      she drew a star inside the lid

      but when she opened it

She made him a bed such as the fates have
      in the palms of the newly born
      but there they do not lay them down
      they have risen

      and when she opened it
      he was gone

      gone the cry the laughter

They made him a fence of names
      each with its story
      like his own teeth
      they laid claim
      to his ears
      but he had others

      when they opened the echoes even the echoes
      he had gone

They made him an ark of the one tree
      and places for him builded in
      two of every kind

            but before the rain came
            he was gone

            laws of the hands gone
            night of the veins gone
            gone the beating in the temples

            and every face in the sky

The Web

      So it's mind
      this leg of a thin gray traveling animal
      caught in the web again
      tearing
      in the stocking of blood

      the old scars waking opening
      in the form of a web

      the seamless fabric itself bleeding
      where it clings

      and all this time dark wings
      cries
      cries flying over at a great height

      o web

      over the sand you are woven
      over the water you are woven
      over the snow you are woven
      over the grass you are woven

over the mountains you are woven
over the heads of the lambs you are woven
over the fish you are woven
over the faces you are woven
over the clouds you are woven
over the pain itself you are woven

the tears glint on you like a dew
the blood is spreading wherever you have held me
the days and the nights
keep their distance
without a sound

but I remember also the ringing spaces
when I have crossed you like a hand on a harp
and even now
in the echoless sky the birds pursue our music

hoping to hear it again

Letter

By the time you read this

    it is dark on the next page

    the mourners sleep there
    feeling their feet in the tide

    before me in the dusk an animal rose and vanished
    your name

    you have been with me also in the descent
    the winter
    you remember
    how many things come to one name
    hoping to be fed

it changes but the name for it
is still the same
I tell you it is still the same

hungry birds in the junipers
all night
snow

all night

by the time you read this

the address of the last house
that we will sleep in together on earth
will have been paid as a price
dialed on a telephone
worn as identification

passed on speedometers in unmarked places
multiplied by machines
divided divided
undistracted
standing guard over us all the time
over past future
present
faceless angel

whom each rain washes nearer to himself

but I tell you
by the time you read this
wherever

I tell you

Inscription Facing Western Sea

Lord of each wave comes in
campaign finished ten thousand miles
years clashes winds dead moons
riderless horses no messages
he lays down flag bowing quickly and retires
his flag
sun waits to take him home
flag fades
sand
stars gather again to watch the war

The Sadness

Thinking of you I lean over silent water
this head
appears
the earth turns
the sky has no motion
one by one my eyelashes free themselves
and fall
and meet themselves for the first time
the last time

The Calling Under the Breath

Through the evening
the mountains approach over the desert
sails from a windless kingdom

silence runs through the birds
their shadows freeze

where are you

where are you where are you
I have set sail on a fast mountain
whose shadow is everywhere

Sunset After Rain

Old cloud passes mourning her daughter
can't hear what anyone tells her
every minute is one of the doors that never opened

———

Little cold stream wherever I go
you touch the heart
night follows

———

The darkness is cold
because the stars do not believe in each other

Elegy

Who would I show it to

In the Time of the Blossoms

Ash tree
sacred to her who sails in
from the one sea
all over you leaf skeletons
fine as sparrow bones
stream out motionless
on white heaven
staves of one
unbreathed music
Sing to me

WRITINGS TO AN UNFINISHED ACCOMPANIMENT

(1973)

Early One Summer

Years from now
someone will come upon a layer of birds
and not know what he is listening for

these are days
when the beetles hurry through dry grass
hiding pieces of light they have stolen

Eyes of Summer

All the stones have been us
and will be again
as the sun touches them you can feel
sun
and remember waking with no face
knowing that it was summer
still
when the witnesses
day after day are blinded
so that they will forget nothing

End of Summer

High above us a chain of white buckets
full of old light going home

now even the things that we do
reach us after long journeys
and we have changed

The Distances

When you think of the distances
you recall
that we are immortal

you think of them setting out from us
all of them setting out
from us
and none dies and none is forgotten

and all over the world there are dams
lying on their backs
thinking of the sea

Looking Back

Oh we have moved forward in pain

what has broken off every rock

have they each suffered
each time
wanting to stay
have they not

Before the first cell
the sands

Song of Man Chipping an Arrowhead

Little children you will all go
but the one you are hiding
will fly

The Silence Before Harvest

The harps the harps
standing in fields
standing

and dark hands
playing

somewhere else the sound
sound
will arrive
light from a star

Cat Ghosts

I

Years after
in a kitchen of another country
you're still hungry

II

In the heat of the day
your shadow comes back
to lie on your stone

Letter to the Heart

Again the cry that it's late
and the islands
are just beginning to rise

Memory of the Loss of Wings

An hour comes
to close a door behind me
the whole of night opens before me

The Old Boast

Listen natives of a dry place
from the harpist's fingers
rain

The Day

If you could take the day by the hand
even now and say Come Father
calling it by your own name
it might rise in its blindness with all
its knuckles and curtains
and open the eyes it was born with

The Clear Skies

The clouds that touch us out of clear skies

they are eyes that we lost
long ago on the mountain
and lose
every day on the dark mountain
under clear skies

and because we lose them we say they are old
because they are blind we say
that they cannot find us

that their cloudy gaze
cannot touch us
on our mountain

because we have lost whoever
they are calling
we say that they are not calling
us

To Be Sung While Still Looking

Have you seen my memory
in better light
no sound for the moment
as there might
with those faces
and the gates about to close
that never do

Have you seen my memory
that hardly knew
what to do with the flags
at an age where nothing dies
but the windows are open
and same eyes
as it rolls with no echo
on the thankless roads

Have you seen my memory
after years
by fallen schools
with the smell of coats on it
and smaller coats
when there is time enough
have you seen the promises
or the tracks have you noticed
the age of the air
once it's clear

Have you seen my memory
minus the fancy words
have you looked in the cases
where I kept my mind
to tell me things
such as she lay in shallow water
in shallow water she lies
and she comes out to me
the first day
not far from home

Have you seen
my memory
the flame far from the candles

Under the Migrants

Winter is almost upon us
and in the south there is a battle

every day silent thunder from there
light going up like a shout

each of us is alone
when we close our eyes
the roads are strips of death

when we open our eyes the bandages
go on unwinding
back into the north the whiteness

on the avenues trucks rumble southward
to be seen no more

can you hear yourself we cannot

flocks of single hands are all flying
southward

from us

and the clocks all night all day
point that way

On the Silent Anniversary of a Reunion

Each of these hours has been to you first
and stared
and forgotten
but I know the burnt smell
in their clothes their clothes
and know that you have at last unwoven the charred wick
into a cold black fan
and are sitting by its light
with your hands turning to stone

On Each Journey

As on each journey there is
a silence that goes with it
to its end let us go
with each other
though the sun with its choirs of distance
rises between us though it
were to hang there the past like a day
that would burn unmoved forever
and only we went on
each alone each with nothing
but a silence

Beyond You

Even when the dry wells of black honey
overflow into the winter starlight
and their stars know them at last
and taste and are young
when the shrivelled boats that have carried the sun
wake one by one face down by the river
and rise blind to sing where they are
if I can stand I will be standing by the last one
calling you
who are so near that I cannot believe you
and when I call the calling begins
beyond you

Their Week

The loneliness of Sundays grows
tall there as the light
and from it they weave
bells of different sizes
to hang in empty cupboards and in doorways
and from branches
like blossoms like fruit
and in barns
and in each room like lamps
like the light

they believe it was on a Sunday
that the animals were divided
so that the flood could happen
and on a Sunday that we were severed
from the animals
with a wound that never heals
but is still the gate where the nameless
cries out

they believe that everything
that is divided
was divided on a Sunday
and they weave the bells
whose echoes
are all the days in the week

Old Flag

When I want to tell of the laughing throne
and of how all the straw in the world
records the sounds of dancing
the man called Old Flag is there
in the doorway
and my words might be his dogs

when I want to speak of the sweet light
on a grassy shore
he is there
and my words have never forgotten the bitter
taste of his hands
the smell of grief in the hollow sleeves
the sadness
his shoes
and they run to him laughing
as though he had been away
they dance at his feet as though
before a throne

The Current

For a long time some of us
lie in the marshes like dark coats
forgetting that we are water

dust gathers all day on our closed lids
weeds grow up through us

but the eels keep trying to tell us
writing over and over in our mud
our heavenly names

and through us a thin cold current
never sleeps

its glassy feet move on until they find stones

then cloud fish call to it again
your heart is safe with us

bright fish flock to it again touch it
with their mouths say yes
have vanished

yes and black flukes wave to it
from the Lethe of the whales

Something I've Not Done

Something I've not done
is following me
I haven't done it again and again
so it has many footsteps
like a drumstick that's grown old and never been used

In late afternoon I hear it come closer
at times it climbs out of a sea
onto my shoulders
and I shrug it off
losing one more chance

Every morning
it's drunk up part of my breath for the day

and knows which way
I'm going
and already it's not done there

But once more I say I'll lay hands on it
tomorrow
and add its footsteps to my heart
and its story to my regrets
and its silence to my compass

Tool

If it's invented it will be used

maybe not for some time

then all at once
a hammer rises from under a lid
and shakes off its cold family

its one truth is stirring in its head
order order saying

and a surprised nail leaps
into a darkness
that a moment before had been nothing

waiting
for the law

Bread

for Wendell Berry

Each face in the street is a slice of bread
wandering on
searching

somewhere in the light the true hunger
appears to be passing them by
they clutch

have they forgotten the pale caves
they dreamed of hiding in
their own caves
full of the waiting of their footprints
hung with the hollow marks of their groping
full of their sleep and their hiding

have they forgotten the ragged tunnels
they dreamed of following in out of the light
to hear step after step

the heart of bread
to be sustained by its dark breath
and emerge

to find themselves alone
before a wheat field
raising its radiance to the moon

Habits

Even in the middle of the night
they go on handing me around
but it's dark and they drop more of me
and for longer

then they hang onto my memory
thinking it's theirs

even when I'm asleep they take
one or two of my eyes for their sockets
and they look around believing
that the place is home

when I wake and can feel the black lungs
flying deeper into the century
carrying me
even then they borrow
most of my tongues to tell me
that they're me
and they lend me most of my ears to hear them

A Door

You walk on

carrying on your shoulders
a glass door
to some house that's not been found

there's no handle

you can't insure it
can't put it down

and you pray please let me not
fall please please let
me not drop
it

because you'd drown like water
in the pieces

so you walk on with your hands frozen
to your glass wings
in the wind
while down the door in time with your feet
skies are marching
like water down the inside of a bell

those skies are looking for you
they've left everything
they want you to remember them

they want to write some last phrase
on you
you

but they keep washing off
they need your ears
you can't hear them

they need your eyes
but you can't look up
now

they need your feet oh
they need your feet
to go on

they send out their dark birds for you
each one the last
like shadows of doors calling calling
sailing
the other way

so it sounds like good-bye

A Door

Do you remember how I beat on the door
kicked the door
as though I or the door were a bad thing
later it opened
I went in
nothing
starlight
snowing

an empty throne
snow swirling on the floor
around the feet

and on an instrument
we had been trying
to speak to each other
on which we had been trying to speak
to each other for long
for time
pieces lying apart there
giving off
echoes of words our last words *implor*
    ing
    implor
    ing
by deaf starlight for a moment

and you know we
have danced in such a room
I came in late and you
were far from the door
and I had to dance with
not you after not you before
I could reach you
but this was later than anyone
could have thought

thin
snow falling
in an empty bell
lighting that chair

could I turn at all

now should I kneel

and no door anywhere

A Door

This is a place where a door might be
here where I am standing
in the light outside all of the walls

there would be a shadow here
all day long
and a door into it
where now there is me

and somebody would come and knock
on this air
long after I have gone
and there in front of me a life
would open

A Door

What is dying all over the world
is a door

you will say That
is a dead thing

and you will be talking about the entry
to a chamber of your heart

you will say of that door
It is a thing

and you will be speaking of your heart

the streets will run over the wells
the wires will cover the sky
the lines will cross out the eyes
singing numbers numbers
numbers
numbers of

shadows of generations of armies with flags
the streets will run over the ears
trucks will run over the streets
no crying will be heard
nor any calling
the function of laughing neither remembered
so a tick coming over us
for no cause we by then
recognize
meanwhile in each cell the noise
turning higher as it
turns higher as it approaches
and still someone touching
a silence
an opening
may hear all around us the endless home

Surf-Casting

It has to be the end of the day
the hour of one star
the beach has to be a naked slab

and you have to have practised a long time
with the last moments of fish
sending them to look for the middle of the sea
until your fingers
can play back whole voyages

then you send out one
of your toes for bait
hoping it's the right evening

you have ten chances

the moon rises from the surf
your hands listen
if only the great Foot is running

if only it will strike
and you can bring it to shore

in two strides it will take you
to the emperor's palace
stamp stamp the gates will open
he will present you with half of his kingdom
and his only daughter

and the next night you will come back
to fish for the Hand

At the Same Time

While we talk
thousands of languages are listening
saying nothing

while we close a door
flocks of birds are flying through winters
of endless light

while we sign our names
more of us
lets go

and will never answer

The Wharf
for Richard Howard

From dates we can never count
our graves
cast off
our black boats our deep
hulls put out
without us

again and again we run
down onto the wharf named
for us
bringing both hands both eyes
our tongues our
breath
and the harbor is empty

but our gravestones are blowing
like clouds backward
through time to find us
they sail over us through us
back to lives that waited
for us

and we never knew

Beggars and Kings

In the evening
all the hours that weren't used
are emptied out
and the beggars are waiting to gather them up
to open them
to find the sun in each one
and teach it its beggar's name
and sing to it *It is well*
through the night

but each of us
has his own kingdom of pains
and has not yet found them all
and is sailing in search of them day and night
infallible undisputed unresting
filled with a dumb use
and its time
like a finger in a world without hands

The Unwritten

Inside this pencil
crouch words that have never been written
never been spoken
never been taught

they're hiding

they're awake in there
dark in the dark
hearing us
but they won't come out
not for love not for time not for fire

even when the dark has worn away
they'll still be there
hiding in the air
multitudes in days to come may walk through them
breathe them
be none the wiser

what script can it be
that they won't unroll
in what language
would I recognize it
would I be able to follow it
to make out the real names
of everything

maybe there aren't
many
it could be that there's only one word
and it's all we need
it's here in this pencil

every pencil in the world
is like this

Spring

The glass stems of the clouds are breaking
the gray flowers are caught up
and carried in silence to their invisible mountain
a hair of music is flying
over the line of cold lakes
from which our eyes were made
everything in the world has been lost and lost
but soon we will find it again
and understand what it told us when we loved it

The Place of Backs

When what has helped us has helped us enough
it moves off and sits down
not looking our way

after that every time we call it
it takes away one of the answers it had given us

it sits laughing among its friends with wrong names
all of them nodding yes

if we stay there
they make fun of us
as we grow smaller because of the melting of our bones

Division

People are divided
because the finger god
named One
was lonely
so he made for himself a brother like him

named Other One

then they were both lonely

so each made for himself four others
all twins

then they were afraid
that they would lose each other
and be lonely

so they made for themselves two hands
to hold them together

but the hands drifted apart

so they made for the hands two arms

they said Between two arms
there is always a heart

and the heart will be for us all

but the heart between them
beat two ways
already for whoever
was to come

for whoever would
come after

one by one

A Purgatory

Once more the hills
are made of remembered darkness torn off
and the eye rises from its grave
upon its old
upon its ancient life

but at a wrong moment

once more the eye
reveals the empty river
feathers on all the paths
the despairing fields
the house in which every word
faces a wall

and once more it climbs
trying to cast again
the light in which that landscape
was a prospect of heaven

everywhere
the vision has just passed out of sight
like the shadows sinking
into the waking stones
each shadow with a dream in its arms
each shadow with the same
dream in its arms

and the eye must burn again and again
through each of its lost moments
until it sees

The Chase

On the first day of Ruin
a crack appears running

then what do they know to do
they shout Thief Thief
and run after

like cracks converging across a wall

they strike at it
they pick it up by tails
they throw pieces into the air
where the pieces join hands
join feet run on

through the first day

while the wren sings and sings

A Wood

for Mark and Jill Sainsbury

I have stood among ghosts of those who will never be
because of me
the oaks were darkening
we all knew who was there
sailing walking sitting as stones
ancestors ancestors I turned to say
always was it this way
from you did my shoulders learn
not to fly
my hands not to walk
my bones not to stay
from your blackbirds again and again
did I learn at evening
not to call myself home

Nomad Songs

If I don't go there
nobody's there

————

Every word
runs the hills at night

————

Smoke
remember who let you go

———

Ho it's spring
see
the echoes flying

———

Birch tree with one arm
groping in death
hold onto it

———

My cradle
was a shoe

———

We leave a child
outside
as bait for the guides

The Diggers

If a man with a shovel came down the road

if two men
with shovels came down the road
if eight men with shovels
came down the road

if seventeen men with shovels came down the road
and I wanted to hide
I would see then that everything here
is transparent

yes that is what I would see but I would feel myself
then like my hand in front of my eyes
like this hand just as it is
in front of my eyes

and I would try to take it down
before they saw through it and found me

Ash

The church in the forest
was built of wood

the faithful carved their names by the doors
same names as ours

soldiers burned it down

the next church where the first had stood
was built of wood

with charcoal floors
names were written in black by the doors
same names as ours

soldiers burned it down

we have a church where the others stood
it's made of ash
no roof no doors

nothing on earth
says it's ours

Animals from Mountains

When I was small and stayed quiet
some animals came
new ones each time
and waited there near me
and all night they were eating the black

they knew me they knew me
nobody saw them
I watched how they watched me
they waited right there

nobody heard them talking laughing
laughing
Laugh they told me nobody will hear

and we went out one time
onto one mountain
all the way and nobody knew we went
we went together we sounded like chewing
the next day the mountain was gone

we went out onto two mountains
we made no noise
no more noise than smoke
nobody saw us far away
the next day those mountains were almost gone

we went out
onto my dead grandmother's mountain
there an old wind lives
that's never been away
it lives on and on there alone
but the mountain's gone
and some of us
never came back all the way

Sibyl

Your whole age sits between what you hear
and what you write

when you think you're getting younger
it's the voice coming closer
but only to you

so much of your words
is the words
once they've come out of the ground
and you've written them down

on petals
if it's spring

the same wind that tells you everything at once
unstitches your memory
you try to write faster than the thread is pulled
you write straight onto the air
if it's summer

with your empty needle

straight onto a face if there's light enough
straight onto hands
if it's autumn

Who It Is

On the upper slope
the moon
smokes through the woods
someone is running there
silently waving
someone's father
not my father
no and not his father the drunk
no and not his
father the one that was murdered
no it is the first one
I don't know
it is his father
it is everyone I don't know
it is his father

why
is he running there

why is he running on the mountain

why is he waving why do I
not hear him
why do I not know him
why do I not know him why are they there

everywhere they have seen
their moon rising

Mist

Today seventy tongues
are hiding in the trees

their voices are hanging beyond the mist
seventy long banners mingling
red yellow
blue voices
hanging silent

here the nuthatch blows his horn
leading a thin procession of white wind

past the black trees
through the world

Under Black Leaves

In one window
old moon swollen with our shadow
bringing it
to birth one more time

in another window
one of the stars that does not know it is the south
the birds' way

the mouse is no longer afraid of me
the moth that was clinging to my face
a day in some city
has been taken away
very old it clung there forgetting everything
nails have been drawn out of my ears

certain stars leaving their doorways
hoped to become crickets
those soon to fall even threw
dice for the months
remembering some promise

that game was long before men
but the sounds traveled slowly
only now a few
arrive in the black trees
on the first night of autumn

A Sickness at the Equinox

September yellows
a few of the wild laurels
from wet ditches still the loosestrife
as when I was born
and the days before

I sit in late sunlight hoping to be healed
shadows of leaves slip along me
crossing my face my chest
toward the east

to each of them
in turn I say Take
it with you

take with you leaf shape
little shadow

darkness of one leaf
where you are going

a brother or sister
you were afraid was lost for good

a mother a father
a lover
a child
from under there

Wanting a Soul in the South

The world is made of less and less
to walk out on farther
and farther
another year
is about to be taken away everywhere
someone still standing there
holding a basket

the planets glide doubting
among the bare rafters here
signaling
apparently
wrong wrong this house
moving out their year
all night the cocks crow
no

it's all right though
so far
walking on in the dark
over the breathing floors
through the rooms that are here
with my basket

Horses

The silence of a place where there were once horses
is a mountain

and I have seen by lightning that every mountain
once fell from the air
ringing
like the chime of an iron shoe

high on the cloudy slope
riders who long ago abandoned sadness
leaving its rotting fences and its grapes to fall
have entered the pass
and are gazing into the next valley

I do not see them cross over

I see that I will be lying
in the lightning on an alp of death
and out of my eyes horsemen will be riding

Ship

Far from here but still in sight

there is a fine white ship of everything we have loved
under full sail entering
among wrecks and many bridges
where birds are watching
always watching

same
birds with one wing
forgetters of singing

here it is they see coming to them again
from those who hate them

Words

When the pain of the world finds words
they sound like joy
and often we follow them
with our feet of earth
and learn them by heart
but when the joy of the world finds words
they are painful
and often we turn away
with our hands of water

One Time

for Charles Bell

O venerable plank burning
and your pegs with you
the hordes of flame gaining
in the marks of the adze
each mark seven times older than I am
each furthermore shaped like a tongue
you that contain
of several lives now only a dust
inside the surfaces that were once cuts
but no memory no tree
even your sparks dust
toward the last some of your old pitch
boils up through you
many children running
into a shining forest

The Way Ahead

A winter is to come
        when smaller creatures
        will hibernate inside the bones
        of larger creatures

and we will be the largest of all
and the smallest

A Monday is to come
        when some who had not known
        what hands were for
        will be lifted and shaken
        and broken and stroked and blessed
        and made

An eye is to come
        to what was never seen
        the beginning opening
        and beholding the end
        falling into it

A voice is to come
        that all the leaves
        wanted
        and the ears uncurled
        to reach for
        and one of them will hear it

Feet are already marching there
fields of green corn and black corn are already
throwing up their hands
all the weeds know and leap up from the ditches
every egg presses on toward those ends
for this the clouds sleep with the mountains

for this in the almanacs of the unborn
terrible flowers appear
one after the other
giving new light

A light is to come

Summits

Mountains bloom in spring they shine in summer
they burn in autumn
but they belong to winter
every day we travel farther and at evening
we come to the same country
mountains are waiting but is it for us
all day the night was shining through them
and many of the birds were theirs

To the Hand

What the eye sees is a dream of sight
what it wakes to
is a dream of sight

and in the dream
for every real lock
there is only one real key
and it's in some other dream
now invisible

it's the key to the one real door
it opens the water and the sky both at once
it's already in the downward river
with my hand on it
my real hand

and I am saying to the hand
turn

open the river

Folk Art

Sunday the fighting-cock
loses an eye
a red hand-print is plastered to its face
with a hole in it
and it sees what the palms see from the cross
one palm

The Second Time

The second time
the hills have shrunk
the bells are thinner
the hours have fewer colors
it seems that some of the old weather
must have been invented

the second time has white stone gateposts
at the head of a silent pass
under a pillar of sunlight
we see them only once
we see them only the second time
then we forget them

the second time has birds of its own
it has wings of its own
the second time comes with a picture

the second time comes with an old picture
of something not there
it clings to the picture
as to its life

death
begins the second time
with survival

Exercise

First forget what time it is
for an hour
do it regularly every day

then forget what day of the week it is
do this regularly for a week
then forget what country you are in
and practise doing it in company
for a week
then do them together
for a week
with as few breaks as possible

follow these by forgetting how to add
or to subtract
it makes no difference
you can change them around
after a week
both will help you later
to forget how to count

forget how to count
starting with your own age
starting with how to count backward
starting with even numbers
starting with Roman numerals
starting with fractions of Roman numerals
starting with the old calendar
going on to the old alphabet
going on to the alphabet
until everything is continuous again

go on to forgetting elements
starting with water
proceeding to earth
rising in fire

forget fire

Instructions to Four Walls

Now one of you turn this way
just as you are
woman and girl all these years
speaking another language
as the earth does
and open your eyes
with the wall inside them

doubled
but going away
getting smaller and smaller
but don't you move
see how long it takes for me to appear there
and how old I am then
and how old I've been
if you can tell
but don't put on anything special for me
I want to see you as you are every day
as you see me
without my name

the one of you whose turn it is
to follow me like a dog
don't be the dog who's stolen something
don't be the dead dog
don't be the lost dog the sick dog
the watch dog
be the good brown dog that ran through both families
till you found me
be happy to see the back of my head
just where it is

and one of you be the sea
starting right there
older than words or water
opening into itself forward and backward
each wave lying still
with a piece of horizon in its arms
one sail going

one sail coming
two wings approaching each other

and one of you
stay still just as you are
with your door
be yesterday
be tomorrow
be today

In the Life of Dust

Dust thrown into eyes
learns to see
and it follows

the first thing it sees
is a man holding dust in his hand
the next thing it sees is a hand scraping dust from the ground
the next thing it sees is the ground
and it rejoices

the next thing it sees
is footprints handprints in the ground
handprints long hollows
valleys in the earth
from scraping up dust

footprints running

the dust still feels them
remembers them coming
running
and now the dust can see

and it follows them
in its time it is everywhere
it is the dust in front of them

somewhere else waiting
watching

two men come running over the mountain
both of them blind

it sees that they are its children
and it beholds hatred
it beholds fear

A Flea's Carrying Words

A flea is carrying a bag of diseases
and he says as he goes
these I did not make myself
we don't all have the same gifts
beginning isn't everything
I don't even know who made them
I don't know who'll use them
I don't use them myself
I just do what's in front of me
as I'm supposed to
I carry them
nobody likes me
nobody wants to change places with me
but I don't mind
I get away
bag and all
something needs me
everything needs me
I need myself
and the fire is my father

When the Horizon Is Gone

When the horizon is gone
the body remains horizontal
the earth remains horizontal
but everything else
is vertical

the soles of the feet are vertical
so they can't climb
and they wait

the veins are vertical
so the blood can't flow
so it sinks
and there's no center to sink toward

what the hands hold is vertical
so they can't feel it
and they let go

what the eyes see is vertical
and always was
and they still don't recognize it

the sound is vertical
so they don't hear
anything

at first

calling

The Lantern

A little way ahead
each is alone

when you see it you are there already
in one respect

for in that world nothing can break
so no one believes in the plural there
which is the first abstraction and the last
which is the and which is the between which is the among
so no one believes in us there
so at last there is only
the single
one
alone
held together by nothing
so the question of belief never arises

that is the place of a god
for a god is alone
he sits on each different leaf
he holds in each eye
differently
in each hand differently
one emblem of one aspect of his difference
each time it is single
each time it is an image of him
each time it is an image of you
each time it is an image of no one
carrying a lantern
each time it is different
from a different side
each time it is the same
well once you are there can you speak

if you were going to speak at last
which would you speak to

you open your one mouth
each image opens his mouth

you say nothing
once

you open a cave in the ground
one cave
each god closes each eye
you go down inside each eye
into each vein
into each vein of each leaf
into each root
no root has an eye
it has always been so dark there

but your eye is closed
so it's lighter for you

far away an empty lantern is swinging

image of no one carrying it

you start to follow it
to see his face

Apparition

The more like a man it is
the more it frightens the birds
the more it frightens children
the more it frightens men

it comes wanting to live
but to live

it would have to fly up in itself
it would have to clap its hands when it could say nothing
it would have to tremble at itself

A Number

Those who come back from a number
are paler
they know that they're
one number the less
and whenever they talk
they talk about where they were
for each of their words has been there

and all the time they were gone
that number was here
not a day passed
without its turning up somewhere
well where then were those

who went out over unlit hills
bearing their words
to that number
and turned pale at what they saw
and keep talking about it

Dogs

Many times loneliness
is someone else
an absence
then when loneliness is no longer
someone else many times
it is someone else's dog
that you're keeping
then when the dog disappears
and the dog's absence
you are alone at last
and loneliness many times
is yourself
that absence
but at last it may be
that you are your own dog

hungry on the way
the one sound climbing a mountain
higher than time

The War

There are statues moving into a war
as we move into a dream
we will never remember

they lived before us
but in the dream we may die

and each carrying
one wing as in life
we may go down all the steps of the heart
into swamp water
and draw our hands down after us
out of the names

and we may lose one by one our features
the stone may say good-bye to us
we may say good-bye to the stone
forever
and embark
like a left foot alone in the air
and hear at last voices like small bells
and be drawn ashore

and wake with the war going on

The Water of the Suns

In craters in the west other suns went down
and by morning no one believed it
no one has to believe it the mountains
aren't selling anything

some of the suns left gold
many left water for the next time

when you spend that gold you feel the night coming on
and nothing to make a fire
under all the empty mountains

but when you drink that water you begin to wait
you hear your time falling into you out of a stone
you begin to grope through your cold veins calling
like a bird before sunrise

till the morning that needs you

A Prayer of the Eyes

There are stones here
that have to have been seen first
by a man many centuries old
who has gone into seven other worlds
and has come back without sleeping to look at these few stones
before going on

then the stones become visible to us as stones
but which ones are they
they are not marked in any way
those old men would not have
marked them in any way
those solitary men
why would they have wanted to mark them
after seven worlds
what mark would they have put
meaning what
on stones
that are never lost
and never anyone's

those men arrive
some of them in this lifetime
some of them only in this lifetime
sometimes somebody
sees them
may I see one of them
with his worlds behind him like wings
may I see the stones
as he sees them
may he show me the stones

The Cry

In many houses the cry has a window
and in one house the window is open

and the cry has flowed out like one drop of water
that once filled the whole room

there it is the first drop of water
from which everything came
when it is all over

a single drop of water is flowing
there on the white path into the hills

you would see it was a tear
because it is flowing upward
becoming a note in the still night

leaving its salt to the white path
that flows into the place far below
that once was sea

as you would know
if you were to stand in that doorway
if you were to open the door
if you were to find it

of the cry
that no longer sleeps there

so that if you were to see that window
from the outside
you would see nothing

By the Cloud Path

No day has an age of its own
an entire year has no age of its own
    but there is a cloud in every picture

Those clouds are from almanacs not from calendars
    old almanacs
    taken from lovers given to prisoners
    given back
    found by children
    missing pages signed Cloud
    art is long
    a cloud is a monument to an eye

Know of the new buildings
    that some cannot be reflected in water
    all you will see reflected is clouds

    Who use those buildings sank long ago
    the question is can you still believe them

    their windows were calendars
    their moon was drawn in red
    but its heart was not there

The clouds dragging anchors are pilgrims
    the anchors are inside three sleeps
    in the prisoners
    in the lovers
    and in the children

From a window photographs of one face
     every day of its life
     are reflected rapidly on a cloud
     the sound is a recording of one tone
     that face produced that day
     of its own

A Hollow

Here then is where the wolf of summer lay
heard flocks of sheep running by
like rats' teeth on the paths
heard them in the stubble like rain
listened to them pissing from their thin bones
learned one by one the tone of each jaw
grinding its dry stalks knew every cough
and by the cough the throat

here lay with the roots around him
like veins around a heart
and was the wolf of summer
there were leaves that listened to him with their whole lives
and never felt the wind
while he lay there like darkness in an ear
and hearing notes of wells
knew where the moon was

For Saying That It Won't Matter

Bones of today I am going to leave you
where you never wanted to be
listen shall we talk of it now
I am going to leave you there
every bone that is left to itself
has been in trouble
it was born to go through it

every skin is born knowing that
and each eye

you are voyaging now through the half-light of my life
let us talk of this while the wind is kind
and the foam rustling on your bows
hear me I am going to leave you
on the empty shore
the sand will be blown away
we should talk about it
you were born for trouble
it is not for you that I am afraid
you will start singing camel songs

what can I say to you listen it is not for you
it won't matter to you
listen whatever you dream from then on
will be yours even if it was mine
unless it's me
listen you will still tell the fortunes of others
you will hang in the bell of earth at a wedding
you will fly on and on in white skins
by your own light

Foreword

We will tell no more than a little
about the first wing
the orphan

we will say nothing of his parents the giants
nor of the tree in which he was born
one autumn
nor of his sisters the grass
nor his brothers the fires

he was alone he was the first wing
it is all we need to know

everything here has two wings
except us

all we will tell
is how he found the other wing
his reflection groping downward through the air
and of the stream between them
where it rises
how flight began
why the moths
come and bathe in the dust
and it is a light to them

Finding a Teacher

In the woods I came on an old friend fishing
and I asked him a question
and he said Wait

fish were rising in the deep stream
but his line was not stirring
but I waited
it was a question about the sun

about my two eyes
my ears my mouth
my heart the earth with its four seasons
my feet where I was standing
where I was going

it slipped through my hands
as though it were water
into the river
it flowed under the trees
it sank under hulls far away
and was gone without me
then where I stood night fell

I no longer knew what to ask
I could tell that his line had no hook
I understood that I was to stay and eat with him

The Palace
for Harry Ford

Music does not happen in a place
in it leaves do not grow
even if you try to put them there
there is nothing to see and nobody knows you
even if you were born there

yet the blood continues to follow music
the heart never sleeps urging the feet of the blood
to echo to rest nowhere
to pass near the skin to listen
whether music is anywhere
to look through a glass to go on
to go through
music never waits the heart says

the blood says nothing
the deaf queen pacing alone
through her thin palace
feeling music turning in the walls

Ballade of Sayings

In spring if there are dogs they will bark
the sieves of the poor grow coarser
even in the dark we wake upward
each flower opens knowing the garden
water feels for water
the law has no face
nowhere are the martyrs more beautiful
the air is clear as though we should live forever

in summer if there are fleas there will be rejoicing
you kill the front of him I'll kill the back
every sieve knows a dance
each soldier is given a little bleached flag
ours are the only parents
the poor do not exist they are just the poor
the poor dream that their flowers are smaller
patience has the stones for a garden
the seer is buried at last in a gooseyard
the air is clear as though we should live forever

in autumn if there are trees eyes will open
one moment of freedom partakes of it all
those who will imitate will betray
the dogs are happy leading the archers
the hunter is hunted the dealer is dealt the listener is heard
the halls of government are the exhibition palaces of fear
anguish rusts
the poor believe that all is possible for others
each fruit hopes to give light
the air is clear as though we should live forever

in winter if there are feet bells will ring
snow falls in the bread of some and in the mouths of others
nobody listens to apologies
when prisoners clasp their hands a door locks
the days are polished with ashes
the cold lie in white tents hoarding sunrise
the poor we have with us always
the old vine stakes smell of the sea
the air is clear as though we should live forever

Prince it is said that night is one of the sieves
there is no end to how fine we shall be
at the names of the poor the eye of the needle echoes
the air is clear as though we should live forever

To the Rain

You reach me out of the age of the air
clear
falling toward me
each one new
if any of you has a name
it is unknown

but waited for you here
that long
for you to fall through it knowing nothing

hem of the garment
do not wait
until I can love all that I am to know
for maybe that will never be

touch me this time
let me love what I cannot know
as the man born blind may love color
until all that he loves
fills him with color

The Dreamers

In one of the dreams men tell how they woke
a man who can't read turned pages
until he came to one with his own story
it was air
and in the morning he began learning letters
starting with A is for apple
which seems wrong
he says the first letter seems wrong

a man with his eyes shut swam upward
through dark water and came to air
it was the horizon

he felt his way along it and it opened
and let the sun out so much for the sun
and in the morning he began groping for the horizon
like the hands of a clock
day and night

a man nothing but bones was singing
and one by one the notes opened
and rose in the air and were air
and he was each one
skin mouth ears feeling
feathers he keeps counting everything
aloud including himself
whatever he counts one is missing

I think I fell asleep on a doorstep
inside someone was coming
walking on white heads that were the best words I knew
and they woke at that step for the first time and were true
when I came to myself it was morning
I was at the foot of the air
in summer and I had this name
and my hand on a day of the world

September

By dawn the little owls
that chattered in the red moon
have turned into magpies in the ash trees
resting between journeys
dew stays in the grass until noon
every day the mist wanders higher
to look over the old hill
and never come back
month of eyes your paths see for themselves
you have put your hand
in my hand
the green in the leaves has darkened

and begun to drift
the ivy flowers have opened
on the weasel's wall
their bees have come to them
the spiders watch with their bellies
and along all the shores
boats of the spirit are burning
without sound without smoke without flame
unseen in the sunlight
of a day under its own king

Flies

On the day when the flies were made
death was a garden
already without walls
without apples
with nowhere to look back to
all that day the stars could be seen
black points
in the eyes of flies
and the only sound was the roar of the flies
until the sun went down

each day after that something else was made
and something else with no name
was a garden
which the flies never saw
what they saw was not there
with no end
no apples
ringed with black stars
that no one heard
and they flew in it happily all day
wearing mourning

The Writing on a Fallen Leaf

The frost will come out under the stars
the falcons will grow thin as their voices
the fox will pretend to be old
the owl will bathe at night in the snow
the tracks of the hare will be empty shadows
I will forget

South

for Ralph Hilt

To the south in the beginning of evening a dog
barks at his echo among mountains
beyond bare walnut trees tiles are still climbing old roofs
lines of women with long burdens the colors
of dried darkening blood
each line straight into mountains
colder already all north faces
turning into their shadows
beyond them sea
through day and night to the last white mountains
an end a wise man fire
other stars the left hand

Span

I know hands that leapt from childhood to old age
youth was never for them however they held it
everything happened to them early or late
end of morning never found them
the entire day was a long evening
in August
they played no instrument for when would they have learned
if not in childhood

everything they did displayed impetuous prudence
and smelled of sand
they and their clumsy skills were their own age
with its two seasons

Meeting

A thirst for meeting

A long line of ghosts waiting at a well
laughing
in the evening
and I am standing among them
the line runs through me
I feel it
a procession of dry clouds

let it be clear that there is no comfort in them
comfort is far away
that lay in ambush for joy
there is no fear in them they cannot hear me
there is only that thirst
the old cracked laughing

of dry leaves
shriveled trees broken stones
walls walls
and empty hands
held forward forever

History of Alchemy

All the gold that exists was transmuted once
by men learning to change themselves
who broke it and buried it
those who found it

took it for a metal
wanted it for its own sake
to have rather than to foresee
and for them it was evil
and they declared that transmuting it was impossible
and evil

The Initiate

At last a juggler is led out under the stars
tears begin to roll down his cheeks

he catches them
they fly through his hands

he sees the stars swimming up
in his tears
and he feels in his hands his tears
fly trembling through the night

what is that juggler singing
later when the morning star
is dry

he is singing Not a hair
of our head do we need to take with us
into the day

not even a hand do we need
to take with us
not even an eye
do we need to take with us
into the light

The Search

When I look for you everything falls silent
a crowd seeing a ghost
it is true

yet I keep on trying to come toward you
looking for you
roads have been paved but many paths have gone
footprint by footprint
that led home to you
when roads already led nowhere

still I go on hoping
as I look for you
one heart walking in long dry grass
on a hill

around me birds vanish into the air
shadows flow into the ground

before me stones begin to go out like candles
guiding me

Glass

One day you look at the mirror and it's open
and inside the place where the eyes were
is a long road gray as water
and on it someone is running away
a little figure in a long pale coat
and you can't move you can't call
it's too late for that
who was it you ask

then there are many of them
with their backs to you and their arms in the air
and no shadows

running away on the road gray as ice
with the leaves flying after them
and the birds in great flocks the dust
the stones the trees

all your terrors running away from you
too late
into a cloud

and you fall on your knees and try to call to them
far in the empty face

Traveling

One travels
to learn how not to look back
hearing the doors fall down the stairs
and the tongues like wet feathers in a high wind

only in the present are the voices
however far they travel
and fires raising hands between echoes

out of words one travels
but there are words along the road waiting
like parents' grandparents
we have heard of but never seen

each with its column of smoke
and its horizon beyond which nothing is known
and its sun

The Track

To see that an ancestor has reappeared
as the print of a paw
in a worn brick
changes what you believe you are
and where you imagine you are going
before the clay sets

and what you think might follow you

over the floors
of the oven

the empty palace
with its many wings
its lighted stairs
its deep windows
its seasons
and its white sound
still soft underfoot

and when

Peril

Where did you suppose the moths went
when you stopped seeing them

some that you've forgotten you ever saw
or never noticed
are standing in a circle
with their eyes inward

another joins them
coming from your window

the circle grows larger like a ring of dust
spreading on a lake of dust
it is that much harder for each of the eyes to see
in the middle of the circle the glass filament
born of a spider of air
on which is hanging and turning
the world where you are sitting
forgetting them
as the number rises
like the note of the thread

that has been too high for your ears
for a long time

The Sleeping Mountain

Under asters the color of my shadow
the mountain stirs in its cold sleep

dream clouds are passing through it
shaped like men lying down
with the memory of lights in them

wolf puppies from the cliffs
cry all night
when even the lakes are asleep

after the Ark was abandoned on the peak
stars appeared in it
and sailed off into the night with it

all at once it is nine years
on the plains of Troy
remembering the mountain asleep

on one wing like a human

Gift

I have to trust what was given to me
if I am to trust anything
it led the stars over the shadowless mountain
what does it not remember in its night and silence
what does it not hope knowing itself no child of time

what did it not begin what will it not end
I have to hold it up in my hands as my ribs hold up my heart
I have to let it open its wings and fly among the gifts of the
    unknown
again in the mountain I have to turn
to the morning

I must be led by what was given to me
as streams are led by it
and braiding flights of birds
the gropings of veins the learning of plants
the thankful days
breath by breath

I call to it Nameless One O Invisible
Untouchable Free
I am nameless I am divided
I am invisible I am untouchable
and empty
nomad live with me
be my eyes
my tongue and my hands
my sleep and my rising
out of chaos
come and be given

FLOWER & HAND

THE COMPASS FLOWER

(1977)

I

The Heart

In the first chamber of the heart
all the gloves are hanging but two
the hands are bare as they come through the door
the bell rope is moving without them
they move forward cupped as though
holding water
there is a bird a thing in their palms
in this chamber there is no color

In the second chamber of the heart
all the blindfolds are hanging but one
the eyes are open as they come in
they see the bell rope moving
without hands
they see the bathing bird
being carried forward
through the colored chamber

In the third chamber of the heart
all the sounds are hanging but one
the ears hear nothing as they come through the door
the bell rope is moving like a breath
without hands
a bird is being carried forward
bathing
in total silence

In the last chamber of the heart
all the words are hanging
but one
the blood is naked as it steps through the door
with its eyes open
and a bathing bird in its hands
and with its bare feet on the sill
moving as though on water
to the one stroke of the bell
someone is ringing without hands

The Wine

With what joy I am carrying
a case of wine up a mountain
far behind me others
are being given their burdens
but I could not wait even for them

it is wine that I will not drink
I will not drink it not I
this wine
a signpost is swinging around
up in the woods in the fog
one way saying Almost one way Punished
in another language that I know
but no sign this way

by now all the stone railing
is fog
no longer does the dew brushed
from the pine needles onto my fingers
run down into my armpits
how cold my hands are
how awkward the wine is to carry
on my shoulder
that's part of the joy

The Drive Home

I was always afraid
of the time when I would arrive home
and be met by a special car
but this wasn't like that
they were so nice the young couple
and I was relieved not to be driving
so I could see the autumn leaves on the farms

I sat in the front to see better
they sat in the back
having a good time
and they laughed with their collars up
they said we could take turns driving
but when I looked
none of us was driving

then we all laughed
we wondered if anyone would notice
we talked of getting an inflatable
driver
to drive us for nothing through the autumn leaves

The Next Moon

A month to the hour
since the last ear on earth
heard your voice

even then on the phone

I know the words about rest
and how you would say them
as though I myself had heard them
not long ago
but for a month I have heard nothing

and in the evening after the moon of deafness
I set foot in the proud waters
of iron and misfortune
it is a month to the hour
since you died
and it was only dusk
to the east in the garden

now it is a night street with another moon
seen for the first time but no longer new
and faces from the backs of mirrors

The Snow

You with no fear of dying
how you dreaded winter
the cataract forming on the green wheated hill
ice on sundial and steps and calendar
it is snowing
after you were unborn it was my turn
to carry you in a world before me
trying to imagine you
I am your parent at the beginning of winter
you are my child
we are one body
one blood
one red line melting the snow
unbroken line in falling snow

The Arrival

From many boats
ferries and borrowed canoes
white steamers and resurrected hulls
in which we were young together
to a shore older than waiting
and our feet on the wet shadowed sand
early in the evening of every verb
both of us at the foot of the mountain laughing

now will you lead me with the smell of almonds
up over the leafless mountain
in the blood red evening
now we pull up the keel through the rushes
on the beach
my feet miss the broken bottle
half buried in the sand
you did not notice it at last

now will you lead with your small hand
your child up the leafless mountain
past the green wooden doors thrown away
and abandoned shelters
into the meadows of loose horses
that I will ride in the dark to come

Apples

Waking beside a pile of unsorted keys
in an empty room
the sun is high

what a long jagged string of broken bird song
they must have made as they gathered there
by the ears deaf with sleep
and the hands empty as waves
I remember the birds now
but where are the locks

when I touch the pile
my hand sounds like a wave on a shingle beach
I hear someone stirring
in the ruins of a glass mountain
after decades

those keys are so cold that they melt at my touch
all but the one
to the door of a cold morning
the colors of apples

An Encampment at Morning

A migrant tribe of spiders
spread tents at dusk in the rye stubble
come day I see the color
of the planet under their white-beaded tents
where the spiders are bent
by shade fires in damp September
to their live instruments
and I see the color of the planet
when their tents go from above it
as I come that way in a breath cloud
learning my steps
among the tents rising invisibly like the shapes of snowflakes
we are words on a journey
not the inscriptions of settled people

Migration

Prayers of many summers come
to roost on a moment
until it sinks under them
and they resume their journey
flying by night
with the sound
of blood rushing in an ear

November

The landscape
of a link disappearing between species
and phyla
and kingdoms
is here
after what we have said good-bye to
and before what we will not be here to see

only we know this
as we are
the earth sealed with tar
the walls climbing
the feathers warm around the heart
the memory of unmarked woods
standing facing something we cannot see
exchanging familiar speech
archaic greetings of those who reappear

The Horse

In a dead tree
there is the ghost of a horse
no horse
was ever seen near the tree
but the tree was born
of a mare
it rolled with long legs
in rustling meadows
it pricked its ears
it reared and tossed its head
and suddenly stood still
beginning to remember
as its leaves fell

A Contemporary

What if I came down now out of these
solid dark clouds that build up against the mountain
day after day with no rain in them
and lived as one blade of grass
in a garden in the south when the clouds part in winter
from the beginning I would be older than all the animals
and to the last I would be simpler
frost would design me and dew would disappear on me

sun would shine through me
I would be green with white roots
feel worms touch my feet as a bounty
have no name and no fear
turn naturally to the light
know how to spend the day and night
climbing out of myself
all my life

Fishing

Day and night as a child
I could imagine feeling the bite on the line
moment of fire
above a drum of white
stone water
with the line vibrating through it
one-string harp
never to be out of the feeling in my fingers
name from before anyone was born
bright color in darkness through half a life
beating suddenly toward me

Guardians

Fine rain drifts along mountains to the south of me
graying the first month
one migrant bird scolding in misted noon
in the pear tree
dogs yapping beyond mud walls
echoing back and forth wooden bells
who is listening
eight sacred fears keep watch over me
behind each of them one of the porches of dissolution
in the place of the ninth an open gate

each of them holds the end of one strand
of a rope made of the eight ribs of the world
which leads through the fearless gate

the swan drifts over mountains to the south of me
in the first month
and in the white cloud small birds begin to sing
hair-roots of trees stir
fear is one aspect of joyful guardians
because of the way I came
and clearly I have been in love with some of them
with her who is Fear of the Journey
who has repeatedly and faithfully led me
most of them I cannot even see
in the white sky over my travelling cradle
watching me
ready to bear me up in ageless hands
of cloud and glass
for as long as I need them

Fate

Cloud in the morning
evening a white opal
after a white sun
the lighted opal sits on the rim
of dark mountains
some are born hearing dogs bark in the mountains
among high walls just after sunset
and all their lives things are known to them
that are not known even to those born hearing water
or trees or sobbing or flutes or laughing

On the Mountain

A wind at first light
comes out of one
waving pine tree
air river too deep to be seen
current with no surface
then can be heard and felt
it carries deep reflections of birds
and of sunrise clouds
thoughts into the sea of day

Vision

What is unseen
flows to what is unseen
passing in part
through what we partly see
we stood up from all fours
far back in the light
to look
as long as there is day
and part of the night

The Deluge

Before there was a body
an eye wandered in a forest
to see how it would be
only when the trees were gone
did the veins appear
newly joined and windowed
and the eye embarked in the body

one of an only pair
on the rising waters
to watch for the end of the rain
of age

Robin

In one of the creations
the robin invented
the day
in order to escape from the owl
and they
killed cock robin
and he entered the next world
when the world he knew was utterly destroyed
many worlds before ours
and he invented the day
for a new reason
and again we survived
we survivors
without knowing why

II

City

I have been here before
I have entered through a glass door
at the end of a corridor
surprised to find nothing locked
but knowing that someone was watching
I have arrived through a hospital
I have steered in through the tightening outskirts
in the morning crowd
I have undergone inspections been counted have believed
I have learned the streets like seasons
I have forgotten whole years
but never have I seen it with so few people showing
not even at this hour before daylight so little traffic
never so like held breath
all the traffic lights dark
never such temptation to drive too fast

Line

Those waiting in line
for a cash register at a supermarket
pushing wire baby carriages
full of food in packages
past signs about coupons
in the blank light
do not look at each other
frankly
pretend not to stare at each other's
soft drinks and white bread
do not think of themselves as
part of a line
ordinarily
and the clerk often does not
look at them
giving them change
and the man who puts the things

they have chosen
into bags
talks to the clerk
as he never talks to her
at any other time

The Estuary

By day we pace the many decks
of the stone boat
and at night we are turned out in its high windows
like stars of another side
taste our mouths we are the salt of the earth
salt is memory
in storm and cloud
we sleep in fine rigging like riding birds
taste our fingers
each with its own commandment
day or night it is harder to know than we know
but longer
we are asleep over charts at running windows
we are asleep with compasses in our hands
and at the bow of the stone boat
the wave from the ends of the earth keeps breaking

The Rock

Saxophone and subway
under waking and sleeping
then few hundred feet down nobody

sound of inner stone
with heart on fire

on top of it where it would dream
in the light on its head
and in its shadow

we know one another
riding deaf together
flying up in boxes
through gray gases
and here pause
to breathe

all
our walls shake if we
listen
if we stop even
to rest a hand on them

when we can love it happens here too
where we tremble
who also are running like white grass
where sirens bleed through us
wires reach to us
we are bottles smashing in paper bags
and at the same time live standing in many windows
hearing under the breath the stone
that is ours alone

The Counting Houses

Where do the hours of a city begin and end
among so many
the limits rising
and setting each time in each body
in a city how many hands of timepieces
must be counting the hours
clicking at a given moment
numbering insects into machines to be codified
calculating newsprint in the days of the living
all together they are not infinite
any more than the ignored patience
of rubber tires day and night
or the dumbness of wheels or the wires of passions

where is the horizon the avenue has not reached it
reaching and reaching lying palm upward
exposing the places where blood is given or let
at night the veins of the sleepers remember trees
countless sleepers the hours of trees
the uncounted hours the leaves in the dark
by day the light of the streets is the color of arms kept covered
and of much purpose
again at night the lights of the streets play on ceilings
they brush across walls
of room after unlit room hung with pictures
of the youth of the world

The Helmsmen

The navigator of day
plots his way by a few
daytime stars
which he never sees
except as black calculations
on white paper
worked out to the present
and even beyond
on a single plane
while on the same breathing voyage
the other navigator steers only
by what he sees
and he names for the visions of day
what he makes out in the dark void
over his head
he names for what he has never seen
what he will never see
and he never sees
the other
the earth itself is always between them
yet he leaves messages
concerning celestial bodies

as though he were telling of his own life
and in turn he finds
messages concerning
unseen motions of celestial bodies
movements of days of a life
and both navigators call out
passing the same places as the sunrise
and the sunset
waking and sleeping they call
but can't be sure whether they hear
increasingly they imagine echoes
year after year they
try to meet
thinking of each other constantly
and of the rumors of resemblances between them

Numbered Apartment

In every room rubber bands turn up loose
on dusty surfaces
witnesses

travellers in stop-over countries
not knowing a word of the language
each of them
something in particular to do with me
who say laughing that I
was born here one William
on the last day of one September

to whom now it is again a January a Thursday
of an eleven year and
who has forgotten that
day and to whom that week is inaccessible
and this one is plain this
one

and though I say
here
I know it was not
for even at that time it was
ninety-nine streets to the north by the river
and now it is three wars back
and parents gone as though at once

the edifice in the antique
mode of kings of France
to which they took her to give birth
torn down as I
in my name was turning forty-four
and the building did not from that age go alone
into pieces wheeled away
but all through these years
rubber bands have continued to come to me
sometimes many together
arriving to accompany me although
the whole country has changed
means of travel accelerated
signs almost totally replaced traffic re-routed every
love altered
the stamps re-issued and
smells of streets and apples
moved on

the stone city in
the river has changed and of course
the river
and all words even those unread in
envelopes
all those shining cars vanished
after them entire roads gone like kite strings
incalculable records' print grown finer
just the names at that followed by smoke of numbers
and high buildings turned to glass in
other air oh one clear day

I am a different
foot of a same person in the same river
yet rubber bands lead to me and
from me across great distances
I do not recognize them coming nor remember them going
and still they continue to find me and pass like starlight

St. Vincent's

Thinking of rain clouds that rose over the city
on the first day of the year

in the same month
I consider that I have lived daily and with
eyes open and ears to hear
these years across from St. Vincent's Hospital
above whose roof those clouds rose

its bricks by day a French red under
cross facing south
blown-up neo-classic façades the tall
dark openings between columns at
the dawn of history
exploded into many windows
in a mortised face

inside it the ambulances have unloaded
after sirens' howling nearer through traffic on
Seventh Avenue long
ago I learned not to hear them
even when the sirens stop

they turn to back in
few passers-by stay to look
and neither do I

at night two long blue
windows and one short one on the top floor
burn all night
many nights when most of the others are out
on what floor do they have
anything

I have seen the building drift moonlit through geraniums
late at night when trucks were few
moon just past the full
upper windows parts of the sky
as long as I looked
I watched it at Christmas and New Year
early in the morning I have seen the nurses ray out through
arterial streets
in the evening have noticed interns blocks away
on doorsteps one foot in the door

I have come upon the men in gloves taking out
the garbage at all hours
piling up mountains of
plastic bags white strata with green intermingled and
black
I have seen one pile
catch fire and studied the cloud
at the ends of the jets of the hoses
the fire engines as near as that
red beacons and
machine-throb heard by the whole body
I have noticed molded containers stacked outside
a delivery entrance on Twelfth Street
whether meals from a meal factory made up with those
mummified for long journeys by plane
or specimens for laboratory
examination sealed at the prescribed temperatures
either way closed delivery

and approached faces staring from above
crutches or tubular clamps
out for tentative walks

have paused for turtling wheelchairs
heard visitors talking in wind on each corner
while the lights changed and
hot dogs were handed over at the curb
in the middle of afternoon
mustard ketchup onions and relish
and police smelling of ether and laundry
were going back

and I have known them all less than the papers of our days
smoke rises from the chimneys do they have an incinerator
what for
how warm do they believe they have to maintain the air
in there
several of the windows appear
to be made of tin
but it may be the light reflected
I have imagined bees coming and going
on those sills though I have never seen them

who was St. Vincent

The Shuttles

Remembering glitter on the first river
I begin to imagine the chances against
any fabric ever occurring
threads at last becoming original torn cloth
night numberless with lights
flying apart in galaxies I reach out
to imagine becoming one anything
once
among the chances in the rare
aging fabric happening
all the way for the first time

III

The Vineyard
—for Bill Matthews

Going up through the hill called the vineyard
that seems nothing but stone
you come to a tangle of wild plum and hazel bushes
the spring in the cliff like the sex of a green woman
and the taste of the water
and of the stone

you come to the fox's cave in the yellow clay
under the foot of the stone
and barely out of reach lime-crusted nests
of swallows
and in the cliff higher up
holes of swifts and bees
solitary grass

all that stone faces southward
and a little to the east
full of crevices
bats and small birds
foxes and wild honey
clear to the top they call it
the vineyard
where earliest the light
is seen that bids the cock crow

Crossing Place

I crossed the stream
on the rocks
in the summer
evening
trying not to spill
the pitcher of water
from the falls

493

Summer Night on the Stone Barrens

In the first hours of darkness
while the wide stones are still warm from the sun
through the hush waiting for thunder
a body falls out of a tree
rat or other soft skin
one beat of one heart on the bare stone
gets up and runs on
lightning flaps on the lifted horizon
both scattered beyond black leaves
nearby different cricket notes
climb and the owl cries
the worn moon will rise late among clouds
unseen larks rang at sunset
over yellow thistles of that day
I am under the ancient roof alone
the beams are held up by forgotten builders
of whom there were never pictures
I love voices not heard
but I love them
from some of them with every breath
I go farther away
and to some I return even through storm and sleep
the stillness is a black pearl
and I can see into it while the animals fall
one at a time at immeasurable intervals

September Plowing

For seasons the walled meadow
south of the house built of its stone
grows up in shepherd's purse and thistles
the weeds share April as a secret
finches disguised as summer earth
click the drying seeds
mice run over rags of parchment in August

the hare keeps looking up remembering
a hidden joy fills the songs of the cicadas

two days' rain wakes the green in the pastures
crows agree and hawks shriek with naked voices
on all sides the dark oak woods leap up and shine
the long stony meadow is plowed at last and lies
all day bare
I consider life after life as treasures
oh it is the autumn light

that brings everything back in one hand
the light again of beginnings
the amber appearing as amber

Working into Autumn

Daylight clears after rain to show cool morning
pools in the stones echo birds' water-songs
new growth is washed on tall trees before the leaves turn
hens stray across empty pastures jays ignore them
gliding over them onto the glittering grass laughing
yesterday toward sunset horizon clouds parted
and mosquitoes sailed in glass rain by the open window
where I remained the distance came to me
all day I caulk a house to launch it at nightfall

Memory of Summer Facing West

Sheep and rocks drifting together before sunset
late birds rowing home across bright spaces
shadows stroking the long day above the earth
wild voices high and far-carrying
at sun's descent toward ripening grain

The Love for October

A child looking at ruins grows younger
but cold
and wants to wake to a new name
I have been younger in October
than in all the months of spring
walnut and may leaves the color
of shoulders at the end of summer
a month that has been to the mountain
and become light there
the long grass lies pointing uphill
even in death for a reason
that none of us knows
and the wren laughs in the early shade now
come again shining glance in your good time
naked air late morning
my love is for lightness
of touch foot feather
the day is yet one more yellow leaf
and without turning I kiss the light
by an old well on the last of the month
gathering wild rose hips
in the sun

Autumn Evening

In the late day shining cobwebs trailed from my fingers
I could not see the far ends somewhere to the south
gold light hung for a long time in the wild clematis
called old man's beard along the warm wall
now smoke from my fire drifts across the red sun setting
half the bronze leaves still hold to the walnut trees
marjoram joy of the mountains flowers again
even in the light frosts of these nights
and there are mushrooms though the moon is new
and though shadows whiten on the grass before morning
and cowbells sound in the dusk from winter pastures

Kore

α   I have watched your smile in your sleep
and I know it is the boat
in which my sun rides under the earth
all night on the wave of your breath
no wonder the days grow short
and waking without you
is the beginning of winter

β   How is it that I can hear your bird voice now
trickling among the ice towers
through the days of the anvil
as the year turns I carry an echo
over my own stones and I listen
my eyes are open looking ahead
I walk a little ahead of myself touching
the light air where nobody sees you
and the sun as it sets through the forest of windows
unrolls slowly its
unrepeatable secret
all the colors of autumn without the leaves

γ   You were shaking and an air full of leaves
flowed out of the dark falls of your hair
down over the rapids of your knees
until I touched you and you grew quiet
and raised to me
your hands and your eyes and showed me
twice my face burning in amber

δ   Already on the first hill with you beside me
at the foot of the ruins I saw through the day
and went on without pausing
loving the unheld air
as a wing might love it flying
toward you unknowing
knowing

ε   Face that I loved when I was a child
    nobody in that age believed us
    when we said we would go away together
    not even when we said that the flood
    was on its way
    and nobody will find us when it is over

ζ   You slept all the way to the garden
    face in the boat of my hand
    and we came more than a century late
    to the closed gate
    and the song the laurel remembers in the dark
    the night flute always beginning again
    on the untrodden slope
    and where we walked in the streets then there was new wine
    announced with green boughs over doorways
    in the time of the statues

η   Climbing at noon by roofless columns
    with the day white on the sea
    I did not know the word for the hour
    nor for the hunger
    nor for your hand
    which I was not touching
    but could feel in the air
    The beginning
    comes from before
    when the words for it were pictures of strangers
    it comes on wings that never waited for their names

θ   In the house at the end of a day of rain the old man
    began to recite a poem
    no one remembered but everyone wanted to
    only before he had finished it he lay down
    taking the rest of it with him to sleep
    then in the next light after my night's journey
    you were running in leaves across a wide street
    as I was running
    and we had arrived

ι   When they are together our hands are of an age
    and a dark light flows up between them
    into its feathers
    We have brought
    nothing with us
    but what has come of itself
    we pass the stone fragments
    the ancient smiles holding out
    no hands
    like the trees their sisters born older

κ   Autumn is one of the four elements
    the air has four seasons strung
    to its instrument
    each with its own wind
    but one note under them   Full moon   The year
    has turned in the leafless veins
    and the poles of the earth have sounded
    I wake looking east hearing
    the snow fall and your
    feet far from here bare
    climbing an untold stair
    Long before sunrise hands of a child carrying grapes

λ   At the top of the veins I hear
    the finger on the bowstring
    I hear my feet continuing
    upward I hear you
    hair in wind
    I learn from you of the bare slope
    where you are nowhere in sight
    so we climb the mountain together after all
    even with it between us

μ   The candles flutter on the stairs of your voice
    gold in the dark
    and for this
    far time you laughed through your whole childhood
    and all those years my beloved spiders
    guarded the treasure under my house
    unlit until the night before you appeared

ν   I have loved you in the four capitals
    of four worlds before this one
    with its glass season
    and the nakedness of their light
    wakes me now
    and the burning that the year comes back for
    leaping the falls of its own
    changes

ξ   The sun yellows pages of print
    a snow of bats swirls in the streets
    distractions
    what I thought I knew falls aside a thought at a time
    until I see you naked
    in your eyes the bronze ferns older than seeing
    unfurling above the dark springs

ο   In winter far from you
    at the thought of your skin
    leaves
    yet to be
    stir in the sleep of roots
    the tree
    of veins trembles
    at a distance and begins
    gathering in secret the sibyl's rustling

π   I trust neither memory nor expectation
    but even the white days of cities
    belong to what they do not see
    even the heart of the doubters' light is gold
    even when you are not with me
    in the flowerless month of the door god
    you look at me with your eyes of arrival

ρ   I found you the bracelets of plaited straw
    you found me the old tools
    that I had been looking for
    you knew where they were
    in my garden

few are the words for finding
as I told you under the beating flights
of autumn
and will tell you again
as I find them

σ   We came to the red stone
that they call black in that country
because it fell out of the night
before anyone was there
and it floated ahead of us on the earth
alone without a shadow
but the night had not forgotten it
and its memory even then was falling after it
out of the future
past us into that day

τ   Morning to morning
the same door opening inward
from both sides
laugh close as you are
it is cold in the house
and I burned up all the matches in the night
to look at you

υ   Wire trees
days with telephones
pronouncing into black lamps
trying to get them to light
rubbing them
you appear in a gray street
having heard nothing
expecting nothing
with the light behind you
and our shadows burn the buildings

φ   Thirty days after the solstice
forms of ripe wheat
emerge from the tips of the branches
Far outside them

here
where you have never been
I reach for you with my eyes
I call you with my body
that knows your one name

χ   Days when I do not hear you
it seems that the season flows backward
but it is only
I
of hollow streets
deaf smoke
rain on water

ψ   We cross the smooth night lake together
in the waiting boat
we are welcomed without lights
again and again we emerge by day
hand in hand
from all four corridors at once
under the echoing dome
guided by what has not been said

ω   The shadow of my moving foot
feels your direction
you come toward me
bringing the gold through the rust
you step to me through the city of amber
under the moon and the sun
voice not yet in the words
what is spoken is already
another year

Passage

In autumn in this same life
I was leaving a capital
where an old animal

captured in its youth
one that in the wild
would never have reached such an age
was watching the sun set
over nameless
unapproachable trees
and it is spring

In the Pass

Eleven horsemen gather at the hollow bridge
the light is cold and a snowy wind is blowing
the waterfall crashes and the stream below it
is bounding over the rocks under the ice
white spray has crusted on the planks
each of the horsemen as he rounds the cliff
and the bridge comes in sight
thinks of a bird and a woman
and dismounts and leads his horse over
into the spring and the blossoming valley
they are all the same horseman
falcon
mango-daughter

Spring Equinox Full Moon

I breathe to you
love in the south in the many
months of spring
hibiscus in dark hair water
at the source
shadows glistening to hips
thighs slender sunset shining shores

fingers rolled fragrant leaves
presence of deep woods

earth veiled in green drift
that hides running
of small airs
untraceable fine sounds
passing as on a face
feet first drops of rain on a mountain
hands greeting flowers
holding stolen flowers

closed eyes of every creature
sepia and amber days
back
of tall tree
arms' glide
voice of rain forests
birds in tree heights
throat of palm

wrist of palm
palm of palm
fruit nakedness
morsel breasts
melon navel waist of high waterfall
surf laughter face hearing music
body of flight
secret
beach

away from you on a corner of the earth
I want to think for six hours of your hair
which is the invention of singing
daughter of islands
born in the flood of the fish harvest
I see long mornings
lying on your hair
I remember looking for you

The Morning

The first morning
I woke in surprise to your body
for I had been dreaming it
as I do

all around us white petals had never slept
leaves touched the early light
your breath warm as your skin on my neck
your eyes opening

smell of dew

Summer Doorway

I come down from the gold mountains
each of them the light of many years
high up the soughing of cold pines among stones
the whole way home dry grass seething
to these sounds I think of you already there
in the house all my steps lead to

you have the table set to surprise me
you are lighting the two candles

I come to the door quickly to surprise you
but you laugh we laugh you run toward me
under the long skirt your feet are bare
I drop to my knees in the doorway and catch you
holding the backs of your thighs I watch the candle flames
over my head you watch the birds flying home from the sea

The Hosts

You asked what
were the names of those two
old people who lived under the big tree
and gods in disguise visited them though they were poor

they offered the best they had to eat
and opened the oldest wine in the house
the gods went on pouring out pouring out wine
and then promised that it would flow till the ends of their lives

when the shining guests were out of sight he turned to her
by the table and said
this bottle has been in the cave all the time
we have been together

Islands

Wherever I look you are islands
a constellation of flowers breathing on the sea
deep-forested islands mountainous and fragrant
fires on a bright ocean
at the root one fire

all my life I have wanted to touch your ankle
running down to its shore

I beach myself on you
I listen
I see you among still leaves
regard of rock pool
by sun and moon and stars

island waterfalls and their echoes
are your voice your shoulders the whole of you standing
and you turn to me as though your feet were in mist
flowers birds same colors

as your breath
the flowers deliberately smell of you
and the birds make their feathers
not to fly but to
feel of you

Mountain Day

With one dear friend we go up the highest mountain
thousands of feet into the birdless snow
and listen to our breaths in the still air
for a long time beside the observatories
later we stretch out on the dark crumbled
lava slope looking
west at the sun yellowing the clouds below
then go down past the wild cows to the cabin
getting there just before sunset
and eat by the fire laughing at what we have
forgotten to bring
afterward we come out and lie
braided together looking up
at Cassiopeia over the foothill

Snowline

Turning climbing slowly in late spring among
black trunks of high pines
talking of our lives few white words flying
up into fringed boughs
unexpectedly we catch sight
across an immeasurable valley
of the long peak capped with snow and slanting light
that we saw far above us at morning
now appears scarcely higher than we are
cloud-cliff of moonlight by day
standing still we feel we could touch it

days distant in gleaming air
then we see footsteps of snow climbing all around us
into white sky

Twilight

Oh you are never tame
fire on a mountain
eyes beside water
first day of petals

lying across the bed
in afternoon rainlight
arms of evening
wherever we are is a shore

Late Snow

Wallflowers leaping on slope facing southeast
steep waves glittering
three weeks in spring mountain winds
sweetvetch beardtongue bluebells
skyflowers
thimbleberry blossoming like a rose
white of catching all near sunlight
cold rain two days on long sparse mountain grass
darkening lichened boulders under pine trees
once we wake and it has snowed everywhere
from the railing you wave your arms to the pines
they are holding white sky above white ground
their own feet still sleeping in dark forest
birds shaking few pieces of day from boughs
in white cloud hushed light through canyon
feather sounds
snow falls into your dark hair

June Rain

The rain of the white valley the clear rain
the rain holding the whole valley while it falls
the mountain rain the high rain onto the mountain
as it rained on the mountain on the night we met
the many days' rain shadowless rain
blowing from the long eaves to go on falling
the rain whose ancestors
with no names
made the valley
the nameless shining rain whose past lives
made all the valleys
the author of the rivers
with unchanged and final voice
the rain that falls in the new open streams
running down the dirt roads on the mountain
the rain falling hour after hour into summer
the unexpected rain the long surprise
the rain we both watch at the same window
the rain we lie and listen to together
the rain we hear returning through the night
the rain we do not hear
the open rain

White Summer Flower

Nameless

white poppy
whoever looks at you is alone

when I look at your petals
each time they open

and think of each time
that I have passed them

I know that I have wanted
to say Wait

and why should they

Trees

I am looking at trees
they may be one of the things I will miss
most from the earth
though many of the ones that I have seen
already I cannot remember
and though I seldom embrace the ones I see
and have never been able to speak
with one
I listen to them tenderly
their names have never touched them
they have stood round my sleep
and when it was forbidden to climb them
they have carried me in their branches

Grass Beginning July

A pause at the top of a leap
a pause in the sun
itself as we say
easy wind drifts up the steep hillside
on the mountain the heat of noon
has dried the full-grown
manes of the grass
the late-running herds
they run among the yucca
the deer-browsed yucca
yellow daisies cactus flowers
they run past rocks waiting on the slope

and prayer flag clothes drying
on the way to the trees
all of us moving together

IV

The Coin

I have been to a fair alone
and across the river from the tented marketplace
and the church
were the green sagging balconies from which
during the occupation
the bodies of many
of the men of the town
hung for days in full view
of the women who had been their wives
I watched men in long
black coats selling animals
I watched money going
to a fat woman in white
who held pieces of white cheese
wrapped in white paper
out into the sunlight
I watched an old woman selling cut flowers
counting change
I looked at her teeth and lips
the dark kerchief on her head
there were carnations and
summer flowers rolled in wet newspaper
I considered the wares of a man
with a pile of whetstones
I watched three turtledoves eating in a cage
one of them white
one of them dyed pink
one pale blue
a coin in with their grain
pigeons watching from
the church windowsills
others flying overhead
some few bright clouds moving
all of it returns without a sound

Ferry Port

We will be leaving now in less than a week
meanwhile we are
staying in a house in the port
helpful friends
have found us a top floor with a round balcony
like the plank roof of a tower
jutting over the corner of the back street
we sit out in the late afternoon
long grass and the trees of a park
on the far side
and a few cars on the hill
I try to imagine what it would be like
to live here
say for a winter
we go almost every day
to the library
and read about the island we are leaving
we walk around the harbor
the ferry building is the largest in town
new behind high wire fences
yellow tiles five storys
blocking out the view of the harbor entrance
much larger and more solid
than the creaking wooden
sun-beamed ferry barns of my childhood
now removed
this one is like a government
which employs everyone
our car is ready to be loaded
we have scarcely unpacked
it will be strange to be on the mainland
as it is to be on the earth itself
we drove to the port on a Friday
we are to sail on a Saturday
the fat woman shorter than we are
whose house we are in
will stand in her red dress

with her arms around us
in the evening
under the girders in the smell of oil in the wind
asking us questions
and telling us that we have been here
a week and a day

The Banquet

Travelling north day after day
your eyes darken
and the roads become guides knowing
a further evening

white sky later and later
and one by one
houses with blue ceilings
painted every year
doors and windows from a childhood
that was yours
shrink
seen again years afterward
for one moment late in the day
when there is no time

in that age you went home from school
to the room where the crystals
are lit now for the banqueters
raising their glasses

hours before the first star

Service

You can see that
nobody lives in
castles like that
any more
thank God I suppose
and the castle gatehouse
has been turned
into a gas station
which is closed because
nobody comes to that
back street on a Sunday
a dog is tied to the front door
in the rain
all afternoon
trained to bark at footsteps
but not cars
the wet yellow roses sag
in the empty green
shadow-bricked gardens
white
curtains are drawn
on all the bay windows

Some of the Masts

I hear my feet resound on a wharf
echoed from other wharves
through the centuries
the fishing boats are all moored
in the evening
unlit against harbor dusk
the hulls darker already than the gray
photographs of them
ladders folded against
tall cranes for unloading
nets dangling from long hooks
no glitter from gulls' eyes

whirlpools of rope almost full
small waves rocking under the wharf
as I go on around the harbor
by daybreak they will all be at sea

North Wind

In summer
come the old dreams of living on a boat
and walking home to it as the evening
is beginning
along a dry wagon road
bordered with poplars
between ripening fields
long ago
arm around a soft woman
and the dreams of upland stone houses
quaking at hand in cicada sound
and those of a cabin farther in the woods
with the forester's whole family for guides
and coming to hear a rushing stream
and the old man saying
Get down it's the north wind
and all of us lying down in the woods
for a while
thinking of the green cabin
that needs paint
but still has all the old furniture

Island

After two years
we rowed to the island
before it got dark
some were still swimming
in the short summer
on the sand behind us

though the sun
had gone
the sound of far
splashing
carried over the quiet water
through the dripping
of the oars
on the island there was no one
only trees and
open twilit grass under them
no wind
birds already sleeping
but no stars no cloud
almost on the horizon
against a low line of evergreens
a cabin steamer passing
slowly between lakes
with its lights on
then as we were coming back
clear sky
long blue star falling

Junction

Far north a crossroad in mud
new cement curbs a few yards each way
rain all day
two men in rubber boots
hurry along under one plastic
carrying loud radio playing music
pass tin shack surrounded by
broken windshields
paintings of north places
only hotel
has no name
no light to its sign
river from bridge long misted mirror
far houses and red boats float

above themselves in gray sky
martins were hunting
in the morning
over logjams by another shore
cold suppertime
thinking of hares in boggy woods
and footprints of clear water

Remembering a Boatman

After sundown yellow sky beyond shadow mountains
range upon range in long twilight under few distant clouds
darkening pastures run into the bays
birds are already asleep high on the unlit roan cliffs
straw light still flickers on the water
between two headlands in short summer
at last a long boat rowed by one man standing
appears slowly from behind a headland on the right
and starts across
too far away to hear the sounds of the wood
or see colors
a few times the wake turns up light
then I forget him for years

Assembly

Nomads gather in autumn
driving herds to the great auctions
of animals on the gold earth
by then there is blood in the trees
nights are already cold
daybreak white
some of them open stalls by the river
and hang up for sale
loose pelts of different animals
and fur garments stitched with sinews

at moments during the summer
in upland pastures among birds
some play instruments
others sing clapping their hands

Old Garden

One year I seem to have started north many times
standing in a garden
looking at a mountain
over a wall
once I went to the sea and watched the red sun
rise from its peak
watched it set white in the sea veil
as the moon came up
nights I walked on wet sand
and swam looking up
days in palm leaf shadows
I listened
I came to a dry river
in late afternoon one time
place that I thought I knew
and found among stream-bed stones
one white clay dove
in some way broken
there was my father
I came to a full river
another time
between low shores at dusk
and as I crossed over
one bird flew calling
so that I could hear
but not words
that may have been my mother
that year
and one time I woke every morning on a hill
and wanted to remain there
on the way north through the mountains

The Fig Tree

Against the south wall of a monastery
where it catches the first sun
a fig tree a shadowy fig tree
stands by the door
all around the flowing trunk
suckers grow
it is against
the law of the church to pull them out
nobody remembers why
tree roots older than the monastery

The Windows

Here is a child who presses his head to the ground
his eyes are open
he sees through one window
the flat gray ocean
upside down
with an arbor of islands hanging from it
all the way to the horizon
and he himself is hanging from nothing
he might step down
and walk on the old sky far down there
out to the clouds
in the far islands
he might step on the clouds where they have worn shiny
he might jump from cloud to cloud
he watches lights flash
on and off along the dark shores
and the lights moving among the overhead islands
he feels his head like a boat on a beach
he hears the waves break around his ears
he stands up and listens
he turns to a room full of his elders
and the lights on
blue day in the far empty windows
and without moving he flies

The Falcons

There were years when I knew
the flowers in the red stone walls

now in the courtyard where I have returned with you
we drink the wine of visitors
the temperature of the cellars

dusk is welling
out of the dried blood of the masonry
no hour remains on the sundial
by now the owls of the tower corners
are waking on their keepers' fists
but it is still day
out in the air
and three falcons appear there
over the courtyard

no feathers on heads or breasts
and they fly down to us
to our wrists and between them
then hover and perch just above us
keeping us in sight
waiting
they are waiting for us

this time they will come with us
when we leave the island
tonight for the rest of our lives

The Trestle

A postcard held
by one white thumbtack
to the tan wallpaper
above my head
in a room I stood in as a child

showed in brown the view
once long ago from this
tall train bridge
trembling over the gorge
with the tracks far below there
where we have just been
by the glittering rapids
under the black trees
past the only inn
we see it from here
as it is now
painted
between the moving girders

Talk of Fortune

I meet her on the street
she says she is away a lot but it was
actually when she was living here
she came home to the apartment house
which I have just left
and inside by the mailboxes
she found a small old
woman who seemed to be trying
to open the inside door
and looked as though she had been
crying or it could have been laughing
and they tried to talk but
the old woman could not
speak more than a few words
and yet she was well dressed
even old velvet
and when the door was opened for her
she would not go in
for anything
but kept smiling and asking for
something or somebody in
another language

and when she could not make herself
understood she gave
my friend a leaf and went
away and the next day
my friend found a lot of money

The Fountain

An old woman from the country
who sells tickets for sex shows
and looks at the buyers' faces
gave a party
in her kitchen
for her family and their friends
many of whom she did not even know
and she served everybody
yellow cake and meringues
made from her own eggs
as she told the company more than once
and no bag feed she said
she fed them on
oh yes you do grandma
said the small boy whose bed was in the corner
look she said and opened the back door
to show the hens in the evening light
scratching around the fountain

Sun

Dark rain at
winter solstice
and in the morning

rosemary under clear sky
bird on south doorstep
poised like a stone

The Flight

—for Bruce and Fox McGrew

At times in the day
I thought of a fire to watch
not that my hands were cold
but to have that doorway to see through
into the first thing
even our names are made of fire
and we feed on night
walking I thought of a fire
turning around I caught sight of it
in an opening in the wall
in another house and another
before and after
in house after house that was mine to see
the same fire the perpetual bird

FEATHERS FROM THE HILL

THE HILL

(1978)

Time of Tree Cutting

Cold August
mice roll
empty nutshells

———

Darkness that covers
and uncovers the moon
shadow of a wing

———

Waking
hanging upward into the rushing summer
calling

———

Everything is
the answer
too fast

———

Where the cliff
splits
later the dove nests

———

Stony slopes buckwheat smell
wings of landing plover
shiver

———

Nearby one monkey at sunset
ate in silence
watching the lightning

———

The colors look back at the trees
but the birds shut their eyes
thinking to see it all again

———

Along the white hill
owl floats
weighed down with moonlight

———

Nobody knows who lived here
the roof is gone
the eastern cloud swallows the stars

———

Sunlit woods
feather falls
everywhere ready for it

———

Laughter of crows late in the month
spun saucer settling
sunset moving south

Summer Canyon

Some of the mayflies
drift on into June
without their names

———

Spring reappears in the evening
oyster cloud sky catches in pines
water light wells out of needles after sundown

———

On small summit pine hollow
field chickweed under trees
split white petals drifting over shadows

———

Two crows call to each other
flying over
same places

———

In high mountains
the late grass
grows as fast as it can

———

Because of things not even remembered
we are here
listening to the water

———

Three broad blue petals
I do not know
what kind of flower

Among the pines above me
flowers from days ago
are about to open

Leaves never seen before
look how they have grown
since we came here

After midnight wind drops
belled cat walks the hillside
under black trees

Day's end green summer stillness
pine shadows drift far out
on long boards

Mourning dove sound
cricket sound
no third

Afternoon breeze prowls
with a tail
through tall green upland grass

Half moon light midsummer
unseen pheasant among bright rocks
echoes its own voice

All day the wind blows
and the rock
keeps its place

A silence begins
soon many feet
are heard running

Black tree trunks in shade
outside a house
with wooden floors

———

Birds on the roof
if I went up to see
they would be gone

———

For each voiceless flower
there is a voice among
the absent flowers

———

Far away a dog barks
on a windy hilltop
beyond which the sun is setting

———

Sunlight after rain
reflections of ruffled water
cross the ceiling

———

High in the east full moon
and far below on the plain
low clouds and lightning

———

Birds hidden
in moonlit boughs
call from dreams

———

Hot wind at noon
pine cones from dying tree
fall full of seeds

———

Early dusk
pine needles already shining
before rain

———

Line of smoke
writes on
sunlight

———

Flecks of bright down
sail up the day
clear out of the canyon

———

Mountain of
butterflies
hurries

———

Whistle of
mourning dove's wings
stretches the shadows

———

Early I saw
where the sun comes from
here

———

Under a pine at noon
I listen to plates
clattering in a kitchen

———

At the same time every day
clouds come over the mountain
what was I thinking when they appeared

———

Jay clatters through dark pines
it remembers
something it wants there among them

———

Tree toads tighten their notes
numberless yellow daisies
rise through gray grass

———

Sudden rain
army of light passes
with dark footprints

———

Lizard grows up
to be gray twig
in summer

———

Opening my eyes I see
burning alone in blue
the morning star

———

Solitary wasp writes
white eggs
up south window

———

Thistledown
already far from its flower
and still snow on the peaks

———

Young deer standing in headlights
in ditch below cliff
cars coming both ways

———

South slope running to seed
chipmunk squeak shadows
crickets trill long dry grass

———

Even among spoons
favorites emerge
days rising through water

———

Gray voice
nuthatch after sunset
nothing to call it

———

No earlier
could anything that is here
have been

———

A thistledown
is the moon for a moment
then thistledown again

———

Lizard rainwalk on bright boards
rain stops and looks out
washed air

———

Moth studies bark
not moving while
daylight lasts

For an age lizards run on gray places
and grown beetles set out from pines
in the heat

Too late the chain saws
scream into echoing trunks
finding corridors empty

Gray rocks darken
wet bronze pine bark echoes jay shriek
across tall rainy yellow grass

Jay calls at night and wakes
flying through dark branches
faster than it can see

Pine needles many as stars
one word for all the trees ever seen
and their lifetimes

Yellow clothesline empty
raw pole in woods
rain drips from clothespins

One night for a moment
beautiful animal
never seen before

With lengthening summer
the wild dove's flight
grows louder

Steep yellow grass rain
transparent everything I remember
other lives

August midnight
horse snorts
in cricket dark

Garbage dog bell cat
kitchen mouse banister jay
ceiling chipmunk

Afternoon sun wet boughs
smell of autumn in August
schoolbell anvil echoes in empty woods

Pines against sky of mist
where I am now
in a breath of a mountain

Night of rain onto late summer
cool morning again
cloud canyon

Sound of Rapids of Laramie River in Late August

White flowers among white stones
under white windy aspens
after night of moonlight and thoughts of snow

Fireweed

One morning the days have grown shorter
and fireweed is purple
on the mountains

Yellow-winged
grasshoppers clatter through high
windy valley

Sound of rain on tent
light from wet sagebrush
on all sides

⸻

Sundown across shallow stream
magpies bathe together
in aspen thicket

⸻

After rain cold evening
gray clouds dark south gorge
smell of more rain coming

⸻

Horses and trees move
in same waves cool night
summer really gone

⸻

Breasts of swallows turning
flash in morning
among their voices

⸻

Meadow of sagebrush in flower
cat sits in the middle
fur of morning sunlight

⸻

Sound of tires on cobbles
decades ago
roars past me now with no car

⸻

Afternoon moves through
empty tent
cushion at foot of pole

⸻

Human shadows
walk on tent wall
inside and outside

⸻

Old woman young woman
baby in green knapsack shouting
past tree after tree

⸻

Afternoon breeze comes down valley
following small stream
and finds horses

———

Knothole looks out
through a branch
that has come and gone

———

Flies convene
in a patch of sunlight
a day on a calendar

———

Same gong
each hand strikes
different note

———

I leave the tent breathing
without dreams
and walk out on my own

———

Child holds hourglass
above his head
and looks up

———

Last day of August
western bluebirds in
pine shadow

———

In full day
tent pole passes through
big star

———

A moment at a time
the mountain rises
out of empty sky

In the Red Mountains

Blue chairs hang empty
waiting in clear
September sky

Daybreak mist in valley
skylark rises
through green floor of cloud

Light evening rain
eleven magpies
dance in twilight

Yellow light
memory in aspens
of first frost

Chain saw three minutes
hours later in rain
smell of resin

Wrinkled mountains
end of autumn day
peach down

The colors move
but not
the evening clouds

Moth shadow circles floor
moth alights
by my foot

Through black pines
colors on the mountain
climb down the days

On summits last year's snow
gray with waiting
clear sky white clouds of autumn

———

Slow bee
still searching yellow day
before frost

———

Leaves begin to fall
old road appears on the mountains
never anyone's

———

Hawk flake turns
slowly above ridges
in far blue eye

———

Aspen glare
migrant blackbirds'
reed-voices

———

Gold trees
turn into
smoke again

———

At last
leaves fall
from bare sky

———

Leaves still on branches
turn at night into
first snow

———

Many times clouds were mountains
then one morning mountains
woke as clouds

———

Feet in mist
feel the earth move
from under

———

After sunrise
autumn mists part
showing another valley

———

Two snows come and gone
brown cows' valley pastures
gray undersides of olive leaves

———

I see my parents
through a grove of white trees
on a day of winter sunlight

———

Shadow ravine
snow blue as smoke full of sunlight
over black fire

———

Wakes of light
ray out on dark pond
where ducks swim before winter

———

Snow blows from the roof
the whole room
flies out over the white valley

Road

In early snow
going to see a friend
I pass thousands of miles of fences

Island City

Green corn stalks rustle
beginning to dry
on a hill above the sea

———

Pile of box houses
with wires on every side
and box voices and box dogs

———

Around a corner
somebody who's a city
pounds all day on a tin door

———

Only two houses away
a neighbor
is a piano playing

———

A breeze through the house
and one fly rushes
from window to window

———

Morning noon and evening
the old woman turns on the sprinkler
and watches

———

The landlord's children
lock up their dog
and shout at it

———

Living it up
in the afternoon
at the shopping center

———

Under the traffic light
silent paper boy
watches the cars

———

Whole crowd nosing
for shade for the baby
while they go fishing

———

Backs in a row at the sea's edge
bow late in the day
hooking tiny fish

———

Little girl's belly
old man's belly
a sail on the horizon

———

Old dog under a bush
head on his paws
watches waves climb the sand

———

All the guests in the neighbor's garden
ask where the neighbors will go
now he's retiring

———

Toward the sea
wings of flies flash
with sunset

———

Suddenly wrinkles appear
on the water
and then are gone again

———

Going away over water
a cloud
from a cloud

———

So many lives in the evening
staring at the one
program

———

When his television
is off
the neighbor can't stop coughing

———

As I grow older
the cities spread
over the earth

———

A tree stirs
and the curtain
draws back from the window

———

Ward of unlit terraces
the hour of night barks
and echoes

———

At night the autumn mist
arrives and arrives in silence
but the eaves drip through the dark

———

Sound of late tires carries
from an unseen street
through cool leaves

———

It isn't the moon
but the city reflected
from the house fronts on the hill

———

One cricket starts up
in the still moonlight
and wakes the refrigerator

———

Rain from the full moon
all at once washes away
deep dust

———

By the setting moon
a rat runs
on the dry leaves of the woodrose

———

Sleeping I saw the new moon
through the open window
of an unknown kitchen

———

Lizard clacks at daybreak
in the dark of mango trees
when the morning star is alone

———

Packing again
to the sound
of autumn rain

By the Mango Trees

A little higher
the green hill hides
in rain

The trees bow with the wind
but the houses
forget

Rain on the tin roof
lizard hands on the tin ceiling
listening

In the evening sunlight
the hill pasture
is ripening

Lizard just hatched
such a hurry
tail gets in front of the head

A spider hangs
from a new thread
in the light from the window

Lizard runs out on a beam
shits and
looks down

White balsam flowers
moons in
full moonlight

Late at night
the dogs bark for hours
then the rain comes

Great dipper stands
on its handle
leaning against the paling sky

When the rooster crows
a rat shakes
the orange tree

Old dry banana leaf
one of my aunts
but I can't remember which

Loud yellow truck passes
the yellow lilies
in the wind

Living at the farm
she airs her baby
up and down the road

How time disappears
while we live under
the big tree

Warm Pastures

Half the night sky deep cloud
and rain falls
through moonlight

Moonlight before dawn
voices of plovers waking in flight
over foggy pastures

Birds' feet
scratch the tin roof
daybreak

Lighthouse goes on
flashing flashing
as the sun rises

————

Still not seasoned
rooftree runs through row
of old sparrow nests

————

The first light
is climbing the road
through black trees

————

Hearing rain on big leaves
I look up
and all the white birds have gone

————

Can't see the rain
but see where
the sand jumps

————

Loud rain
fog on the hills
mud from the faucets

————

Week of rain
voice of ground dove
from wet woods

————

As he mends
the wire pasture fence
the waves keep breaking behind him

————

Black cows
by late morning
are the big tree's shadow

————

How far the plover comes
to stand in the grass
by the stairs

————

Peel the round-ended
pineapple fields
off the raw hills

———

Crop-duster pilot goes
home and washes his
hands his hands

———

Christmas Eve bright sunlight
white smoke
smelling of sugar

———

Sun drops into smoke
the cane fields appear
burning

———

In the wild
they know
they are rare

———

In the gold evening
the tall trees are leaning
toward the flying voices

———

Shadow
overflows a spring
down in the pasture

———

Another cloud
at evening passing
the distant island

———

Suddenly the shadows
of the wheeling plovers
go out

———

As the year was ending
I heard a breath
start the tin windmill

———

When the moon sets
the sea slowly
disappears

———

Fond of the clock
because of the hours
it has told

———

In the night grass
cricket is travelling
into one note

———

I wake touching her
and lie still to listen
to the warm night

Sheep Clouds

Wake on the train
and they tell you
what you didn't see

———

In the mist at daybreak
row of socks hanging
over the vegetable garden

———

Once you leave
you have a name
you can't remember

———

Already at the thought
of the late spring
the window is open

———

Mist fades in the sun
sheep lean into the wall
shirt breathes at a window

———

In the spring evening
a crow calls
and I come back from the years

———

The cornflowers
keep painting
the faded air

———

Long twilight
before midsummer
all the clouds are moon

———

Old branch alive alive
moored in the darkening sky
sound of the stream

———

The moth brings
the map
of both sides

———

Just before dawn
the nightingale
starts something new

———

Midsummer stars fade
the oriole echoes
the nightingale

———

When it says
good-bye
say thank you

———

Deep in cloud
a day with summer flowers
and small bells ringing

———

Starts too near
ever to
arrive

———

Late in summer
the birds draw
closer together

In a summer of mist
through the evening
a road of mist

Hay in and a cow sick
the unwatched television
flickers on his face

What is an itch
that nobody should speak
well of it

Sun sinks on red pastures
and a dog barks
at the sound of a closing door

Oh the sun sets in the oaks
and the white lady
calls to the mice of the fields

Stars of August what
are you
doing

Moon setting
in the oak tree
wakes one blackbird

Bright September
the shadow of the old walnut tree
has no age

On the reflections of the freight cars
after the frost
water lilies

OPENING THE HAND

(1983)

I

The Waters

I was the whole summer remembering
more than I knew
as though anything could stand still
in the waters

there were lives that turned and appeared to wait
and I went toward them looking
sounds carry in water but not
what I called so far

sun and moon shone into
the moving water
and after many days
joys and griefs I had not thought were mine

woke in this body's altering dream
knowing where they were
faces that would never die returned
toward our light through mortal waters

The Oars

My father was born   in a house by a river
nobody knows   the color of the water
already seeds had set   in the summer weeds
the house needed paint   but nobody will see

after the century turned   he sat in a rowboat
with its end on the bank   below the house
holding onto the oars   while the trains roared past
until it was time for him   to get up and go

Sunset Water

How white my father looked   in the water
all his life he swam   doggie paddle
holding hurried breaths   steering an embarrassed smile

long after he has gone I rock   in smooth waves near the edge
    of the sea
at the foot of a hill   I never saw before
or so I imagine   as the sun is setting
sharp evening birds   and voices of children
echo each other   across the water

one by one the red waves   out of themselves reach through me

The Waving of a Hand

    First rose a low shore   pastures green to the water
that my father must have seen   but did he know it at the time
and maybe it seemed to him then   that he was arriving
    a few white façades   far off on the land's edge
lighthouse not yet flashing   small coast guard station
all faintly gleaming   under low sky
by the wide river mouth   late in the day
cold wind sweeping   green estuary
but everything still   calm and as it should be
    water sound sliding   close by under wood
everyone lying down   in the thin vessel
except the one sailor   leaning against the mast
face never seen   turned away forward
catching last sunlight   eyes toward the sea
waves out there suddenly blue   and sky darkening
    yet I was standing   in an old wooden house
where surely my father had stood   but had he known it then
I was among friends   he had never met
    out in back through the window   the same quiet yard
and small wooden study   beyond it under trees
it was growing dark in the room   but no one turned a light on
and the next time   I looked through that window

there was nothing to see in the yard   but a cloud
a white cloud   full of moonlight
and I tapped someone's shoulder   and we both stared
    then we talked of other things   I did not stay
soon it was really night   I ate with friends it rained
three times I climbed   a long staircase
the first time and the second   someone was at the top
    hundreds of miles   to the west
my father died   just before one in the morning

Strawberries

  When my father died I saw   a narrow valley

it looked as though it began   across the river
from the landing where he was born   but there was no river

I was hoeing the sand   of a small vegetable plot
for my mother   in deepening twilight
and looked up in time   to see a farm wagon
dry and gray   horse already hidden
and no driver   going into the valley
carrying a casket

                and another wagon
coming out of the valley   behind a gray horse
with a boy driving   and a high load
of two kinds of berries   one of them strawberries

  that night when I slept   I dreamed of things
wrong in the house   all of them signs
the water of the shower   running brackish
and an insect of a kind   I had seen him kill
climbing around   the walls of his bathroom
  up in the morning   I stopped on the stairs
my mother was awake   already and asked me
if I wanted a shower   before breakfast
and for breakfast she said   we have strawberries

A Pause by the Water

After the days of walking   alone in mountains
between cities and after the nights   again under dripping trees
coming down I kept seeing   in my mind the ocean
though I knew it would not be   like anything I imagined

after hearing of the old man's   dying and after the burial
between rainy morning and rainy evening   the start of a cold
    summer
coming down the misted path alone   I kept finding
in my thought the ocean   though I told myself
step by step that it could never   be at all like that

warm simple and there   full of real day
blue and familiar   as far as the sky
breathing softly   beyond the pines and
the white unprinted   sand and I would
surely not be sailing   in that small boat
like the one I wanted   by a lake long ago

and it is true there is   this wind off the ocean
so that I shiver with   my collar up
standing on the splashed cement   of the sea wall
and through the foggy field glasses   from before the war
I can make out several   channel markers leaning
and a brace of freighters   a tug with brown barges
the faint domes of gas tanks   on the distant shore

if I did not know where I was   I could be anywhere
with that one sail   crossing the lenses
heeled over so that I   can watch the gleam of the hull
white but for one black patch   recurring between waves
as it passes in the cold of my hands   while behind me
I feel the dusk   surfacing on the swimming pool
and from the far end the eyes   of the muffled couple
in deck chairs under the petals   of frosted glass

who have been coming here   every year for years
soon we will eat our fish   in the lighted room
and later they will show me   pictures of children

Son

As the shadow closed   on the face once my father's
three times leaning forward   far off she called
Good night in a whisper   from before I was born
later through the burial   a wren went on singing

then it was that I left   for the coast to live
a single long mountain   close to the shore
from it the sun rose   and everyone there asked me
who I was   I asked them who they were

at that time I found the cave   under the mountain
drawings still on the walls   carved fragments in the dirt
all my days I spent there   groping in the floor
but some who came from nearby   were wrecking the place
    for a game
garbage through holes overhead   broken cars dead animals
in the evenings they rolled huge rocks   down to smash the
    roof
nothing that I could do   kept them from it for long

the old story   the old story

and in the mornings the cave   full of new daylight

Sun and Rain

Opening the book   at a bright window
above a wide pasture   after five years
I find I am still standing   on a stone bridge
looking down with my mother   at dusk into a river
hearing the current as hers   in her lifetime

now it comes to me   that that was the day
she told me of seeing my father   alive for the last time
and he waved her back from the door   as she was leaving

took her hand   for a while and said
nothing

             at some signal
in a band of sunlight all the black cows   flow down the
    pasture together
to turn uphill and stand   as the dark rain touches them

The Houses

Up on the mountain where nobody is looking
a man forty years old in a gray felt hat
is trying to light a fire in the springtime

up on the mountain where nobody
except God and the man's son are looking
the father in a white shirt is trying
to get damp sticks to burn in the spring noon

he crumples newspaper from the luggage compartment
of the polished black Plymouth parked under the young
    leaves
a few feet away in the overgrown wagon track
that he remembers from another year
he is thinking of somewhere else as the match flame blows

he has somewhere else in mind that nobody knows
as the flame climbs into the lines of print and they curl
and set out unseen into the sunlight
he needs more and more paper and more matches
and the wrapping from hot dogs and from buns
gray smoke gets away among the slender trees

it does not occur to the son to wonder
what prompted his father to come up here
suddenly this one morning and bring his son
though the father looks like a stranger on the mountain
breaking sticks and wiping his hand on the paper

as he crumples it and blowing into the flames
but when his father takes him anywhere they are both strangers

and the father has long forgotten that the son
is standing there and he is surprised
when the smoke blows in his face and he turns
and sees parallel with the brim the boy looking at him
having been told that he could not help and to wait there
and since it is a day without precedents the son
hears himself asking the father whether he may
please see what is down the wagon track and he surprises
himself hearing his father say yes but don't go far

and be very careful and come right back
so the son turns to his right and steps over
the gray stones and leaves his father making
a smoky fire on the flat sloping rock
and after a few steps the branches close overhead
he walks in the green day in the smell of thawed earth
and a while farther on he comes to a turn to the right
and the open light of cleared ground falling away
still covered with the dry grass of last year
by a dark empty barn he can see light through

and before the barn on the left a white house
newly painted with wide gray steps leading
up to the gray floor of the porch where the windows
are newly washed and without curtains so that he
can look into the empty rooms and see the doors
standing open and he can look out
through windows on the other side into the sky
while the grass new and old stands deep all around the house
that is bare in readiness for somebody
the wind is louder than in the wood
the grass hissing and the clean panes rattling

he looks at rusted handles beside bushes
and with that thinks of his father and turns back
into the shadowy wagon track and walks
slowly tree by tree stone by stone under

the green tiers of leaves until he comes
to the smell of smoke and then the long pile of stones
before the clearing where his father is bending
over the fire and turns at the son's voice and calls him
a good boy for coming back and asks whether
he's hungry and holds out a paper plate
they stand in the smoke holding plates while the father
asks the blessing and afterward the son tells him

of the white house the new paint the clean windows
into empty rooms and sky and nobody in sight
but his father says there is no such house along there
and he warns the son not to tell stories
but to eat and after a moment the son
surprises them both by insisting that he has
seen it all just as he said and again the father
scolds him this time more severely returning
from somewhere else to take up his sternness
until the son starts to cry and asks him
to come and see for himself after they have eaten

so when the plates have been burned and the fire
put out carefully and the car packed they walk
without a word down the wagon track where the light
seems to have dimmed as though rain might be on its way
and the trees are more remote than the boy
had thought but before long they reach the opening
where the track turns to the right and there is
the glare of the dry grass but no house no barn
and the son repeats I saw them but the father says
I don't want to hear any more about it

in a later year the father takes the boy
taller now and used to walking by himself
to an old farm in the middle of the state
where he busies himself in the small house he has bought
while the son having been told that he cannot help
walks down the lane past the vacant corn crib and barn
past the red shale banks where the lane descends
beside unkempt pastures with their springs and snakes
into the woods and onto a wooden bridge

still on his father's land he watches the dark water
flow out from under low branches and the small fish
flickering in glass over the black bed and as he
turns and climbs the lane on the far side he sees
to his right below him on the edge of the stream
a low house painted yellow with a wide porch
a gun leaning beside the front door and a dog's chain
fastened to the right of the steps but no dog visible

there appears to be no one in the house and the boy goes
on up the lane through the woods and across pastures
and coming back sees that nothing has changed
the gun still by the door the chain in the same place
he watches to see whether anything moves
he listens he stares through the trees wondering
where the dog is and when someone will come home

then he crosses the stream and returns to his father
indoors and in the evening he remembers
to ask who is living in the yellow house
in the woods on the far side of the stream
which he had understood was his father's land
but his father tells him there is no house there

by then they have left the farm and are driving home
and the son tells the father of the gun by the door
the dog's chain by the front steps and the father
says yes that is his land beyond the stream
but there is no building and nobody living there

the boy stops telling what he has seen
and it is a long time before he comes again
to walk down the lane to the woods and cross the bridge
and see on the far side only trees by the stream

then the farm is sold and the woods are cut and the subject
never brought up again but long after the father
is dead the son sees the two houses

Apparitions

Now it happens in these years   at unguarded intervals
with a frequency   never to be numbered
a motif surfacing in some scarcely known   music of my own
each time the beginning and   then broken off

that I will be looking down   not from a window
and once more catch a glimpse   of them hovering
above a whiteness like paper   and much nearer than I would
    have thought
lines of his knuckles   positions of his fingers
shadowy models of the backs   of my father's hands
that always appeared   to be different from my own

whether as to form texture   role or articulation
with a difference I granted them   from their origin
those stub fingers   as his family would term them
broad and unsprung   deflated somewhat and pallid
that I have seen stand forth one by one   obedient as dogs
so the scissors could cut   the flat nails straight across

they that whitened carrying   small piles of papers
and performed pretending   they knew how
posed with tools   held up neckties and waited
gripped their steering wheel   or my arm before striking
furnished him with complaints   concerning their skin and
    joints
evoked no music ever   had no comeliness
that I could recognize   when I yet supposed
that they were his alone   and were whole
what time they were younger   than mine are

or again the veins will appear   in their risen color
running over the hands   I knew as my mother's
that surprised me by pausing   so close to me
and I wait for the smell   of parsley and almonds
that I never imagined   otherwise than as hers

to float to me from the polished   translucent skin
and the lightness   of the tapering
well-kept and capable   poised small fingers
and from the platinum   wedding-band (with its gleam
of an outer planet)   that I have watched
finger and thumb of the other   hand slowly turn
and turn   while someone's voice was continuing

those hands that were always   on the way back to something
they that were shaken at the sink   and stripped the water
from each other like gloves   and dried swiftly on the dishtowel
flew above typewriter keys   faster than I could watch
faster than words   and without hesitation
appear again   and I am practicing the piano

that I have not touched   for as long as their age
one of them rises to wait   at the corner of the page
and I feel mistakes approach   that I have just learned not to
    make

but as I recognize   those hands they are gone
and that is what they are   as well as what they became
without belief I still watch them   wave to no one but me
across one last room   and from one receding car
it is six years now   since they touched anything
and whatever they can be said   to have held at all
spreads in widening rings   over the rimless surface

what I see then are these two   hands I remember
that wash my face   and tie my shoestrings
and have both sides   and a day around them
I do not know   how they came to me
they are nobody's children   who do they answer to
nobody told them to bleed   but their scars are my own
nobody but me   knows what they tell me
of flame and honey   and where you are
and the flow of water   the pencil in the air

Birdie

You don't think anything that I know of
but as for me when I think of you
I don't know how many of you there are
and I suppose you thought there was just the one

how many times you may have been born
as my father's other sisters would say
in your bawdy nobody is interested
in things like that in the family

somebody wrote down though that you was
born one time on April 20
1874 so that my grandmother
at that occasion was thirteen and the hardest thing
to believe in that account as I think of it
is that she was ever thirteen years old
the way we grew up to hide things from each other

so she had a little baby at that age

and that was you Birdie that was one of you
did you know
it presents a different picture of my
grandmother from the one I was brought up to

that was the you she had when she was thirteen
which goes a long way to explain
her puritanism and your gypsy earrings
and all the withered children who came after
and their scorn of your bright colors and your loud heart

and maybe even your son who was delicate
and an artist and painted heads of Jesus
on church walls where they crumbled and could not be moved
and your having a good time and dying in Arizona

except that as everybody knew
that you
was nothing but a mistake in
the writing and the real Birdie came along
when Grandma was into her twenties and she
had her firstborn a little baby girl
which explains nothing

puritanism earrings the children who came after
your son the frail artist the crumbling heads of Jesus
the having a good time and dying in Arizona
that was the you I met one morning in summer
whom nobody could explain for you was different

inviting all them so unexpected
and not heard of for so long your own mother
younger brother younger sisters new nephew
to breakfast laughing and waving your hands

with all the rings and them not listening
saying they was in a hurry to drive farther
and see the family and you going on
telling them everything there was to eat

The Burnt Child

Matches among other things that were not allowed
never would be
lying high in a cool blue box
that opened in other hands and there they all were
bodies clean and smooth blue heads white crowns
white sandpaper on the sides of the box scoring
fire after fire gone before

I could hear the scratch and flare
when they were over
and catch the smell of the striking

I knew what the match would feel like
lighting
when I was very young

a fire engine came and parked
in the shadow of the big poplar tree
on Fourth Street one night
keeping its engine running
pumping oxygen to the old woman
in the basement
when she died the red lights went on burning

Yesterday

My friend says I was not a good son
you understand
I say yes I understand

he says I did not go
to see my parents very often you know
and I say yes I know

even when I was living in the same city he says
maybe I would go there once
a month or maybe even less
I say oh yes

he says the last time I went to see my father
I say the last time I saw my father

he says the last time I saw my father
he was asking me about my life
how I was making out and he
went into the next room
to get something to give me

oh I say
feeling again the cold
of my father's hand the last time

he says and my father turned
in the doorway and saw me
look at my wristwatch and he
said you know I would like you to stay
and talk with me

oh yes I say

but if you are busy he said
I don't want you to feel that you
have to
just because I'm here

I say nothing

he says my father
said maybe
you have important work you are doing
or maybe you should be seeing
somebody I don't want to keep you

I look out the window
my friend is older than I am
he says and I told my father it was so
and I got up and left him then
you know

though there was nowhere I had to go
and nothing I had to do

Talking

Whatever I talk about is yesterday
by the time I see anything it is gone
the only way I can see today
is as yesterday

I talk with words I remember
about what has already happened
what I want to talk about is no longer there
it is not there

today I say only what I remember
even when I am speaking of today

nobody else remembers what I remember
not even the same names

I tell parts of a story
that once occurred
and I laugh with surprise at what disappeared
though I remember it so well

After a Storm

When I come back I find
a place that was never there

once I stood where
the poplar as big as the house
shimmered with streetlight and moonlight
years before
outside the window
by my bed in the first room
and there is no tree there
and the house has no door

again amazed to be alone so young
one time in the country I climbed a hill
to see the night pasture
in the afternoon in spring
and the hollow and deep woods
beyond the bright grass

lying on the white boards
of the leaky boat
that I had dragged up from the lake bottom
after lifting the stones out
and then dried in the sun
and caulked and tarred
and found a mast for in spring

I went on looking up
at the sky above the mast
no breath of wind no cloud
lake water lapping the painted chamber

not even the last to go
are water sounds
wild brooks in the woods
clear streams full of beings
unknown flowers
the doors of water
are not even the last to close
the bells of water not yet the last bells

there are the doors of no water
the bells of no water
the bells of air
if I could take one voice
with me it would be
the sound I hear every day

The Cart

One morning in summer
music flew up out of New
York Avenue
under the bay window

down there a small man called
a foreigner
one hand on the nose of a horse
no taller than he was

and a cart behind them with wooden
wheels tight to the curb

by the streetcar tracks
were facing upstream waiting

on the cart a rocking
tower as big as a kitchen
with a round pointed roof
hung over the edges

yellow trellises all around
red painted chairs inside
one behind another
circling with music

the horse was small for the cart
the cart was small for the tower
the tower was small for the chairs
the chairs were small for us

the circle was large for the tower
the tower was large for the cart
the tower was large for the street
the street was large for us

but we sat in the music
and went round over nothing
as long as we could
and the streetcar came by

as we turned and it passed us
with faces at all the windows
looking out
knowing us

Photograph

After he died
they found the picture
that he had kept looking for
and had thought was lost
all those years

they did not know
how it had hung in the mind
of someone who could not find it
they did not even
know whose face
that was supposed to be

Unknown Forebear

Somebody who knew him
ninety years ago
called him by a name
he answered to
come out now they said to him
onto the porch and stand
right there

it was summer and the nine windows
that they could see
were open all the way
so was the front door
and the curtains faded as aprons hung
limp past the sills while he stood
there alone in his dark suit
and white beard in the sunshine

he appeared to know where he was
whose porch that was and whose
house behind him

younger than he was
and who had opened the windows

and who had left the ladder
propped in the branches up the lane
and the names of his children and their children
and the name of the place
with the pine tree out front
and the mullein a foot high growing
on the green bank
beyond the stones of the walk

as he stood still looking out
through the opening in the painted
picket fence
one tall picket one short picket
all the way along

and no gate in the opening

A Family

Would you believe me
if I told you the name of the farmers
at the end of the lake
where it grew shallow over the mossy rocks

and if you came in the morning the grass was blue
the fur of the rocks was wet the small frogs jumped
and the lake was silent behind you
except for echoes

you tied your boat carefully to a tree
before setting out across the cool pasture
watching for the bull
all the way to the barn

or if you came in the afternoon
the pasture glared and hummed the dark leaves smelled
from beside the water and the barn was drunk
by the time you got to it

to climb on the beams
to dive into the distant hay
will you believe
the names of the farmer's children

II

Shaving Without a Mirror

As though there could be more   than one center
many skies cleared in the night   and there it is
the mountain this face of it   still brindled with cloud shadows
if I raised my hand   I could touch it like air
high shallow valleys   cradling the clear wind
all like a thing remembered   where haystacks waited for winter

but now it is so blue   would there be eyes in it
looking out from dark nerves   as the morning passes in our
        time
while the sound of a plane rises   behind me beyond trees
so that I breathe and reach up to the air   and feel water
it is myself   the listener to the music
to the clouds in the gray passes   and the clear leaves

where are the forest voices   now that the forests have gone
and those from above the treeline   oh where that fed on fog
of a simpler compound   that satisfied them
when did I ever knowingly   set hands on a cloud
who have walked in one often   following the rim in anger
Brother the world is blind   and surely you come from it
where children grow steadily   without knowledge of creatures

other than domesticated   though rags of woods yet emerge
as the clouds part and sweep on   passing southward in spring
fingers crossing the slopes   shadows running leaping
all night that peak watched   the beacon over the sea
and answered nothing   now it turns to the morning
an expression of knowledge   above immigrant woods

nothing is native of fire   and everything is born of it
then I wash my face   as usual
trying to remember a date   before the war
coming to a green farm at sunrise   dew smell from pastures
after that there were various   graduations
this passion for counting   has no root of its own
I stand by a line of trees   staring at a bare summit
do I think I was born here   I was never born

577

Visitation

Two natives of the bare mountains   appear in the doorway
first I saw the dogs coming   far down the gold slope

the men shuffle and say hello   rimmed with sunlight
and ask if I've seen anything   up here all morning
winds of autumn are passing   over the uplands
migrations of shadows   crossing dry grass
clouds keep running the wall   of dark peaks to the south
ragged flocks trail   through the calling sky

but these had in mind   the animals
had I seen them at all   that made the hoofprints
or a sign of the hare   the quail or the partridge
no I tell them   and they nod and look away

how do I like it   up here they ask
but they won't come in   they were just passing
don't mind the dogs they say   and they tell me
the name of where they came from   and step from the
    doorway

every year they say   it's harder to find them
the animals   even up here
and I say is that true   and they laugh

The Red House

Room after room without a voice   no one to say
only another century   could afford so much space
spring sunlight through locked shutters   reveals the old
    patchworks
adrift on the old beds   in the dry air
and in the white fireplaces   already it is summer

but there is only one age   in all the rooms and mirrors
and it is beginning   it has come to begin

the sound of a bus arrives outside   and what looks like a
   closet door
in an upstairs bedroom opens   onto green woods
full of the thin leaves of May   and a shimmering meadow
and deep in grass   beyond a stream and a waterfall
the rusted windowless bus   to the amber fields

Tidal Lagoon

From the edge of the bare reef   in the afternoon
children who can't swim   fling themselves forward calling
and disappear for a moment   in the long mirror
that contains the reflections   of the mountains

Green Water Tower

A guest at Thanksgiving   said And you've got
a green water tower   with a blue two painted on it

it is there at the edge of the woods   on the hill to the east
at night it flattens   into the black profile of trees
clouds bloom from behind it   moonlight climbs through
   them
to the sound of pouring   far inside

in an east wind we wake hearing it   wondering where it is
above it the sky grows pale   white sun emerges
the green tower swells   in rings of shadow
day comes   we drink and stand listening

High Water

The river is rising   with the breathless sound of a fever
the wake along each shore   trembles and is torn away
a few steps up in the rain   rows of white faces
watch from the banks   backs to the cellar doors

behind the blue eyes   are the cellars' contents
silent in bottles   each with its date
on shelves waiting   under the dripping hats

when the faces draw closer   to each other in the rain
they talk like members   of one family
telling what could be moved   if they have to move it
saying where would be safe   talking of the gardens on the hills
the rains other years   what most needs repair
what the spring   means to the summer

even of the lake in the mountains   which they own together
and agree once again   never to sell

Line of Trees

Along the west of the woods   is a row of tall pines
the man who planted them   came from an island
thousands of miles to the south   and now with his wife
for a long time a nurse   but lately not right in the head
who came from an island   thousands of miles from his
he lives down the road   since their small house in the woods
burned beyond repair   but he still comes by
every so often   to ignore the mailbox
rusted sedan full of vines   brown fruit in the grassy ruts
and when he has gone a pheasant   barks from hiding
bird of a far continent   and whenever the boughs
part suddenly to reveal the yellow   house wall with its window
what they show is a mirror   full of western light

A House to the West

Day of harsh south wind built up the black clouds
but no rain fell and near sunset
the air turned still and full of afterlight

on the ridge to the west the tin barn in the trees
the well-digger's derrick
the plywood shack the color of clotted blood
settle onto the gray sky

the bony woman blond all her life
whose house that is
the woman named for a star
screams at her dog
calls baby talk to her goats
and far from the traffic where she was born
she turns into a shadow among fence posts

when the lovers and children had all got clear of her voice
she said of the red shack It is mine
and she got a driver to move it
one fine morning out onto the hill beyond everything
and then couldn't believe it
and never lights a lamp

The Cow

The two boys down the road   with a vegetable farm
they started from scratch   for their religion
say they didn't know anything   when they began
they had to pick it up   as they went along
all about growing things   and they made a lot of mistakes
said they never knew   much about animals
but their benefactor   bought these cows for the pasture
only the one is a bull   without any balls
and the one is a cow   but she's too young still
and the only one   that's been in milk
was Mama Cow   and they learned to milk her

and the whole three were got cheap   going to slaughter
and she wasn't considered   to be much of a milker
but they got most days   a gallon and a half
some days two   all through the summer
good milk too   better than what you buy
then the rains started   but it made no difference
there was a shed roof   all three could get under
but they all seemed to like   to hang out in the rain
just all the time   standing in the rain
then her milk all at once   began to go down
in a couple of days   it was right to nothing
then she got hold   of some dried apples they had
until she wouldn't   eat any more
and made it down   to the bottom of the pasture
to the mud hole   and lay down in the mud
and then couldn't get up   that's where they found her
she couldn't hardly   lift her head up
she was breathing heavy   they thought it was the apples
she looked so swollen   lying on her side
and she didn't get up   that whole day
so they sent for the vet   along late in the afternoon
he drove up   as the sun was going down
they opened the gate in the wires   at milking time
he brought the truck   into the pasture
he stepped down   at the edge of the mud
Picked a bad place to lie   lady he told her
listened to her all over   through a rubber tube
across the mud   and took her temperature
It wasn't the apples   he stood up and told them
she had pneumonia   weak with the fever
they'd have to move her   out of that mud there
they fastened to the horns first   and the truck tugged until a
    horn broke
he said he'd known a dragged horse   to leave all four hooves
    in the mud
they tried with the same rope   to the front legs and back legs
they dragged her along   to where it was anyways dry
he gave her some shots   showing them how
she tried to get up   but she fell right back
head down on the ground   on the broken horn

the moon at first quarter   gathering light
above the rain clouds   at the top of the hill
he said it was better   not to cover her
unless they were going   to sit up beside her
to keep the cover   from slipping off in the night
then he left   turning his lights on
in a few minutes   it started to rain
and they went out too   in a little while
to see a friend   and were not away long
but when they came back   she was gone lying there
she looked as though   she must be alive
with her eye open   in the moonlight
but when they touched her   it hit them for sure
Heavy they said   she was so big
they said they never   knew she was so big
and they saw dead things   every day
they couldn't believe it   at first they said
all the next morning   trying to burn her
with old tires   but they gave that up
and brought dirt   and piled it on her
That's what it's about   one of them said
Life and death isn't it   what it's about
and the other said   that after what they'd fed her
the blessings on the food   and the scriptures she'd heard
she was almost sure to be   reborn already
in human form   in a family of their faith

Questions to Tourists Stopped by a Pineapple Field

Did you like your piece of pineapple   would you like a napkin
who gave you the pineapple   what do you know about them
do you eat much pineapple   where you come from
how did this piece compare   with pineapple you have eaten
  before
what do you remember about the last time   you ate a piece
  of pineapple
did you know where it came from   how much did it cost
do you remember the first time   you tasted pineapple

do you like it better fresh   or from the can
what do you remember   of the picture on the can
what did you feel   as you looked at the picture
which do you like better   the picture or the pineapple field
did you ever imagine   pineapples growing somewhere

how do you like   these pineapple fields
have you ever seen   pineapple fields before
do you know whether pineapple   is native to the islands
do you know whether the natives   ate pineapple
do you know whether the natives   grew pineapple
do you know how the land was acquired   to be turned into
    pineapple fields
do you know what is done to the land   to turn it into
    pineapple fields
do you know how many months   and how deeply they plow it
do you know what those machines do   are you impressed
do you know what's in those containers   are you interested

what do you think was here   before the pineapple fields
would you suppose that the fields   represent an improvement
do you think they smell better   than they did before
what is your opinion   of those square miles of black plastic
where do you think the plastic   goes when the crop is over
what do you think becomes of the land   when the crop is over
do you think the growers know best   do you think this is for
    your own good

what and where was the last   bird you noticed
do you remember   what sort of bird it was
do you know whether   there were birds here before
are there any birds   where you come from
do you think it matters   what do you think matters more
have you seen any   natives since you arrived
what were they doing   what were they wearing
what language were they speaking   were they in nightclubs
are there any natives   where you come from

have you taken pictures   of the pineapple fields
would you like for me   to hold the camera
so that you can all   be in the picture

would you mind   if I took your picture
standing in front   of those pineapple fields
do you expect   to come back

what made you decide   to come here
was this what   you came for
when did you first   hear of the islands
where were you then   how old were you
did you first see the islands   in black and white
what words were used   to describe the islands
what do the words mean   now that you are here
what do you do   for a living
what would you say is   the color of pineapple leaves
when you look at things in rows   how do you feel
would you like to dream   of pineapple fields

is this your first visit   how do you like the islands
what would you say   in your own words
you like best   about the islands
what do you want   when you take a trip
when did you get here   how long will you be staying
did you buy any clothes   especially for the islands
how much did you spend on them   before you came
was it easy to find clothes   for the islands
how much have you spent on clothes   since you got here
did you make your own plans   or are you part of a group
would you rather be on your own   or with a group
how many are in your group   how much was your ticket
are the side-tours part of the ticket   or are they extra
are hotel and meals and car   part of the ticket or extra
have you already paid   or will you pay later
did you pay by check   or by credit card
is this car rented   by the day or week
how does it compare   with the one you drive at home
how many miles   does it do to a gallon
how far do you   want to go on this island

where have you been   in the last three hours
what have you seen   in the last three miles
do you feel hurried   on your vacation
are you getting   your money's worth

how old are you   are you homesick are you well
what do you eat here   is it what you want
what gifts are you planning   to take back
how much do you expect   to spend on them
what have you bought   to take home with you
have you decided   where to put each thing
what will you say   about where they came from
what will you say   about the pineapple fields

do you like dancing here   what do you do when it rains
was this trip   purely for pleasure
do you drink more   or less than at home
how do you like   the place where you live now
were you born there   how long have you lived there
what does the name mean   is it a growth community
why are you living there   how long do you expect to stay
how old is your house   would you like to sell it

in your opinion   coming from your background
what do the islands offer   someone of your age
are there any changes   you would like to promote
would you like to invest here   would you like to live here
if so would it be year round   or just for part of the year
do you think there is a future   in pineapple

The Briefcase

He came from the far north   I can name the country
gray hair cropped   to the shape of his skull
good gray suit   perfectly pressed
on his sharp shoulders   and from a long sleeve
thin hand in leather   hooked to a briefcase
and never looked at me   as he walked past
how then do I know   the voice and the accent
I've seen him before   from time to time
now I try to remember   what happened next each time
and I've heard what his work is   thinker and planner
administrator   of a model camp

what kind of camp   nobody could say
and he's on his way from there   right now as I watch him
disappear once more   behind a building
while leaves rustle   over my head
in the evening   and lights come on

Late Wonders

In Los Angeles the cars are flowing
through the white air
and the news of bombings

at Universal Studios
you can ride through an avalanche
if you have never
ridden through an avalanche

with your ticket
you can ride on a trolley
before which the Red
Sea parts
just the way it did
for Moses

you can see Los Angeles
destroyed hourly
you can watch the avenue named for somewhere else
the one on which you know you are
crumple and vanish incandescent
with a terrible cry
all around you
rising from the houses and families
of everyone you have seen all day
driving shopping talking eating

it's only a movie
it's only a beam of light

Going

Feet waiting in pairs   ways of sitting in subways
through all ages   ways of waiting
thinking of something else   that is elsewhere
iron carriages all day   flying through night
positions of daily papers   held up to be read
same papers flying in parks   rising above trees
are reflected once in glass   unknown glass
and in spilled water before   feet hurrying homeward

Standing Nowhere

When I come home in the city   and see the young roaches
running on the bare cliffs   they pause to see what I am
delaying their going   without company over unmapped spaces
feet finding their way   from black eggs small as dust
it is true that they do not know   anything about me
nor where we are from   we can have
little knowledge   we look at each other and wait
whatever we may do   afterward

Coming Back in the Spring

When I turn my head in the afternoon
there are the receding files
of tall buildings blue in the distance
with amber light along them ending
in amber light
and their sides shining above the river of cars
and I am home

here are the faces the faces
the cool leaves still lucent before summer
the voices
I am home before the lights come on
home when the thunder begins after dark

and the rain in the streets at night
while the iron train again
rumbles under the sidewalk
long cans full of light and
unseen faces disappearing
in my mind

many travelling behind the same headline
saying second
IRA hunger striker dies
in British hands in Ireland
and some ingesting the latest
smiling sentencing
from the face in the White House
whose syllables wither species and places
into deaths going on before us
as the print turns to the day's killings
around the planet

the words flowing under the place on the Avenue
where the truck ran over
two small boys at the intersection
Friday killing
both by the corner where the garden has been bulldozed
that flowered there for years
after the Loew's movie house was torn down
where the old pictures played

the trains rattle under the hooves
of the mounted police riding
down the Avenue at eleven in blue helmets
and past the iron skeleton
girders and stairs and sky
of the new tower risen
out of the gutted core
of St. Vincent's Hospital
most beautiful
of cities and most empty
pure Avenue behind the words of friends
and the known music

the stars are flaking in the apartment ceiling
and the lights of lives
are reflected crossing the floating night
the rain beats on the panes
above the Avenue
where I have watched it run
for twelve years in the spring
ambulances shriek among the trucks

this is an emergency the walkers
in the street in ones and twos
walk faster
those in groups walk more slowly
the white tower beyond Union Square
is lit up blue and white
during the first few
hours of darkness

we all sleep high off the ground

Happens Every Day

Right in midtown   walking in broad daylight
people around   and everything
all at once   this guy steps out
in front of him   and has a gun
grabs his briefcase   takes off with it
everybody around   is in a hurry
the first guy wakes up   to shout and the other one
starts running and the first guy   right after him
and the one with the briefcase   drops the gun
and the first guy   stops to pick it up
but people are passing   in between
he keeps on shouting   and barging through them
and the guy up ahead   drops the briefcase
so he starts after that   and sees somebody
gather up the gun   and get out of there
and when he stops where   he saw the briefcase

somebody else   has picked that up and gone
the other guy's vanished   and he stands looking
up and down the street   with the people
moving through him   from no beginning

Sheridan

The battle ended   the moment you got there

oh it was over it was over   in smoke
melted and the smoke still   washing the last away
of the shattered ends   the roaring fray
cannons gun carriages cavalry   fringes of infantry
seeping out of woods   blood bones breakage breaking
gone as though you   had just opened your eyes
and there was nobody   who saw what you had come to see
no face that realized   that you had arrived
no one in sight who knew   about you
how solid you were   General and how still
what were you doing   at last standing there
slightly smaller than life-size   in memory of yourself

this was certainly the place   there is no
place like this   this is the only place
it could have been   this unquestionably
is where the message came from   meant only for you
the touched intelligence rushing   to find you
tracing you gasping   drowning for lack of you
racing with shadows   of falling bodies
hunting you while the hours   ran and the first day
swung its long gates for cows   coming home to barnyards
fields were flooded with evening   seasons were resolved
forests came shouldering back   and the rounds
from the beginning   unrolled out of themselves
you were born and began to learn   what you learned
and it was going to find you   in your own time

with its torn phrases   to inform you
sir of your absence   to say it had happened
even then was happening   you were away
and they had broken upon   you they were long past
your picket lines they were at large   in your positions
outflanking outweighing   overrunning you
burning beyond your campfires   in your constellations
while the cows gave milk   and the country slept
and you continued there   in the crystal distance
you considered yours   until the moment
when the words turned it   to colored paper
then to painted glass   then to plain lantern glass
through which you could see   as you set your left
foot in the stirrup   the enemy
you had first imagined   flashing on the farmland

and what had become of   you all that while
who were you in the war   in the only night
then hands let go the black horse   the black road opened
all its miles   the stars on your coat went out
you were hurtling into the dark   and only the horse could see
I know because afterward   it was read to me
already in bed   my mother in the chair beside me
cellos in the avenue   of a lighted city
night after night again   I listened to your ride
as somebody never there   had celebrated it
and you did not see the road   on which you were going
growing out of itself   like a fingernail
you never saw the air   you were flying through
you never heard the hoofbeats   under you

all the way hearkening   to what was not there
one continuous mumbled   thunder collapsing
on endless stairs from   so far coming in the dark yet so
sure how could it have failed   to carry to you
calling finally by name   and how could you
in the meantime have heard nothing   but it was still not
that night's battle beyond its hills   that you were hearing
and attending to   bright before you
as a furnace mouth that kept falling   back forward away

filling with hands and known faces   that flared up and
   crumbled
in flowing coals   to rise then and form once more
and come on again living   so that you saw them
even when the crash of cannons   was close in the dawn
and day was breaking   all around you

a line of fence ran toward you   looking familiar
a shuttered house in the mist   you thought in passing
you remembered from some other time   so you seemed to
   know
where you were   my God the fighting
was almost to there already   you could hear
rifles echoing just down the road   and what sounded
like shouting and you could   smell it in the morning
where your own were watching for you   coming to meet you
horses neighing   and at once the night
had not happened behind you   the whole ride
was nothing out of which they   were hurrying you
on the white horse   telling you everything
that you had not seen could not see   never would see
taking you to the place   where you dismounted
and turned to look   at what you had come for

there was the smoke   and someone with your head
raised an arm toward it   someone with your mouth
gave an order   and stepped into the century
and is seen no more   but is said
to have won that battle   survived that war
died and been buried   and only you are there
still seeing it disappear   in front of you
everyone knows the place   by your name now
the iron fence   dry drinking fountain
old faces from brick buildings   out for some sun
sidewalk drunks   corner acquaintances
leaves luminous above you   in the city night
subway station   hands at green newsstand
traffic waiting   for the lights to change

The Fields

Saturday on Seventh Street
full-waisted gray-haired women in Sunday sweaters
moving through the tan shades of their booths
bend over cakes they baked at home
they gaze down onto the sleep of stuffed cabbages
they stir with huge spoons sauerkraut and potato dumplings
cooked as those dishes were cooked on deep
misty plains among the sounds of horses
beside fields of black earth on the other side of the globe
that only the oldest think they remember
looking down from their windows into the world
where everybody is now

none of the young has yet wept at the smell
of cabbages
those leaves all face
none of the young after long journeys
weeks in vessels
and staring at strange coasts through fog in first light
has been recognized by the steam of sauerkraut
that is older than anyone living
so on the street they play the music
of what they do not remember
they sing of places they have not known
they dance in new costumes under the windows
in the smell of cabbages from fields
nobody has seen

III

Palm

The palm is in no hurry
to be different
and it grows slowly
it knows how to be a palm
when it was a seed it knew
how to be a palm seed
when it was a flower
it knew how to be
the flower of a palm
when it was a palm it grew
slowly
and without eyes
in a salt wind

The Shore

How can anyone know that a whale
two hundred years ago could hear another
whale at the opposite end of the earth
or tell how long the eyes
of a whale have faced both halves of the world
and have found light far down in old company

with the sounds of hollow iron charging
clanging through the oceans and with the circuitries
and the harpoons of humans
and the poisoning of the seas
a whale can hear no farther through the present
than a jet can fly in a few minutes

in the days of their hearing the great Blues gathered like clouds
the sunlight under the sea's surfaces sank
into their backs as into the water around them
through which they flew invisible from above
except as flashes of movement
and they could hear each other's voices wherever they went

once it is on its own a Blue can wander
the whole world beholding both sides of the water
raising in each ocean the songs of the Blues
that it learned from distances it can no longer hear
it can fly all its life without ever meeting another Blue
this is what we are doing this is the way we sing oh Blue Blue

The Night Surf

Of tomorrow I have nothing to say
what I say is not tomorrow

tomorrow no animals
no trees growing at their will
no one in the White House
the words gone out

the end of our grasp and rage
and of our knowledge
what is between us and tomorrow

in the deep shade blue irises are open
we are barefoot in the airy house
after dark the surf roars on the cliffs

The Quoit

The iron ring
rose into the twilight
of late summer
the day still blue
no stars

it rose like a shadow
lit from underneath

the leaves were hanging motionless
on the big poplar
already full of night
and the voices had dropped at dusk

on a table by a new window
in an old house with no lights on
a black metal panther
glared through the black hollyhocks
toward the group of men standing under floodlamps
beside four boxes of wet clay

they had a right to their game
on coal company property
that could not be built on
in case the company
needed to sink a shaft to the mine
in a hurry

those years often the nights smelled of autumn
and people said to each other in the mornings
did you hear it last night
late
was it blasting again someone would ask
no someone else would answer
it was pickaxes

The Middle of Summer

By now you have envisaged
in lives as many as those
of a tree in spring
the summer nights
in the cabin by the lake
with the sun never setting

the fire on the beach
through the endless hours of sunset
and have held the sound of the north dome
of the planet turning
gazing constantly at the sun

the lull of the lakes at that
time the hum of the surfaces
the breath of woods
bird voices clattering
through the sleepless light
of the sun at midnight
and your long shadow walking
on the still water

that is what you go on seeing
at that latitude
as the water turns silent and then
begins to tremble

James

News comes that a friend far away
is dying now

I look up and see small flowers appearing
in spring grass outside the window
and can't remember their name

Berryman

I will tell you what he told me
in the years just after the war
as we then called
the second world war

don't lose your arrogance yet he said
you can do that when you're older
lose it too soon and you may
merely replace it with vanity

just one time he suggested
changing the usual order
of the same words in a line of verse
why point out a thing twice

he suggested I pray to the Muse
get down on my knees and pray
right there in the corner and he
said he meant it literally

it was in the days before the beard
and the drink but he was deep
in tides of his own through which he sailed
chin sideways and head tilted like a tacking sloop

he was far older than the dates allowed for
much older than I was he was in his thirties
he snapped down his nose with an accent
I think he had affected in England

as for publishing he advised me
to paper my wall with rejection slips
his lips and the bones of his long fingers trembled
with the vehemence of his views about poetry

he said the great presence
that permitted everything and transmuted it
in poetry was passion
passion was genius and he praised movement and invention

I had hardly begun to read
I asked how can you ever be sure
that what you write is really
any good at all and he said you can't

you can't you can never be sure
you die without knowing
whether anything you wrote was any good
if you have to be sure don't write

A Birthday

Something continues and   I don't know what to call it
though the language is full of suggestions
in the way of language

                        but they are all anonymous
and it's almost your birthday   music next to my bones

these nights we hear the horses   running in the rain
it stops and the moon comes out   and we are still here
the leaks in the roof go on dripping   after the rain has passed
smell of ginger flowers   slips through the dark house
down near the sea   the slow heart of the beacon flashes

the long way to you is still tied to me   but it brought me to you
I keep wanting to give you   what is already yours
it is the morning   of the mornings together
breath of summer   oh my found one
the sleep in the same current   and each waking to you

when I open my eyes   you are what I wanted to see

The Sea Cliffs at Kailua in December

Down on the tongue of black rock
where the long waves break
a young woman stands with a baby named Mist
we sit in the sun by the crag
spray blowing high into the fans of the hala trees
friends talk of how the age that is ours

came to the islands
where there were kings
in a few hours none of us will be here
the voices of the children fly up from rock pools
clouds move in from the sea
voices grow distant
a bright fish gasps on a stone near the fire
there are ghosts in the steep valley
through the years we have been along the wild coast
headland by headland
but never here

Ali

Small dog named for a wing
never old and never young

abandoned with your brothers on a beach
when you were scarcely weaned

taken home starving
by one woman with
too many to feed as it was

handed over to another
who tied you out back in the weeds
with a clothesline and fed you if she remembered

on the morning before the eclipse of the moon
I first heard about you over the telephone

only the swellings of insect bites
by then held the skin away from your bones

thin hair matted filthy the color of mud
naked belly crusted with sores
head low frightened silent watching

I carried you home and gave you milk and food
bathed you and dried you

dressed your sores and sat with you
in the sun with your wet head on my leg

we had one brother of yours already
and had named him for the great tree of the islands
we named you for the white shadows
behind your thin shoulders

and for the reminder of the desert
in your black muzzle lean as an Afghan's

and for the lightness of your ways
not the famished insubstance of your limbs

but even in your sickness and weakness
when you were hobbled with pain and exhaustion

an aerial grace a fine buoyancy
a lifting as in the moment before flight

I keep finding why that is your name

the plump vet was not impressed with you
and guessed wrong for a long time
about what was the matter

so that you could hardly eat
and never grew like your brother

small dog wise in your days

never servile never disobedient
and never far

standing with one foot on the bottom stair
hoping it was bedtime

standing in the doorway looking up
tail swinging slowly below sharp hip bones

toward the end you were with us whatever we did

the gasping breath through the night
ended an hour and a half before daylight

the gray tongue hung from your mouth
we went on calling you holding you

feeling the sudden height

The School on the Roof

Up there day and night for weeks   they turn to water
turn themselves into water   of day water of night
clouds travel across them   rain vanishes into them
when wind stops they grow clear   birds come and are gone
    in them
sun rises and sets in them   their stars come out
until they come down   come down
some all the colors   of lakes and rivers
some so you can't   see them at all

Going from the Green Window

Saying to the square that is always open good-bye
is uprooting my own foot
I never remembered the root starting
there is nothing to say good-bye to

In a room of wind and unabiding
in midair like a leg walking
in a turning place where boxes have stayed packed for years
where in storms the walls bleed

over the flooded floors
where at all hours constellations
of black cows wait round about
growing on the hill of grass

I watch through dark leaves once
those shadows in the day pasture
moving slowly to drink on the way to the big tree
this morning

The Truth of Departure

With each journey it gets
worse
what kind of learning is that
when that is what we are born for

and harder and harder to find
what is hanging on
to what
all day it has been raining
and I have been writing letters
the pearl curtains
stroking the headlands
under immense dark clouds
the valley sighing with rain
everyone home and quiet

what will become of all these
things that I see
that are here and are me
and I am none of them
what will become
of the bench and the teapot
the pencils and the kerosene lamps
all the books all the writing
the green of the leaves
what becomes of the house

and the island
and the sound of your footstep

who knows it is here
who says it will stay
who says I will know it
who said it would be all right

One Night

I ride a great horse climbing
   out of a rose cloud
      onto a black cinder mountain

long ago and a horn is blowing
   and far ahead the light
      answers

Émigré

You will find it is
much as you imagined
in some respects
which no one can predict
you will be homesick
at times for something you can describe
and at times without being able to say
what you miss
just as you used to feel when you were at home

some will complain from the start
that you club together
with your own kind
but only those who have
done what you have done

conceived of it longed for it
lain awake waiting for it
and have come out with
no money no papers nothing
at your age
know what you have done
what you are talking about
and will find you a roof and employers

others will say from the start
that you avoid
those of your country
for a while
as your country becomes
a category in the new place
and nobody remembers the same things
in the same way
and you come to the problem
of what to remember after all
and of what is your real
language
where does it come from what does it
sound like
who speaks it

if you cling to the old usage
do you not cut yourself off
from the new speech
but if you rush to the new lips
do you not fade like a sound cut off
do you not dry up like a puddle
is the new tongue to be trusted

what of the relics of your childhood
should you bear in mind pieces
of dyed cotton and gnawed wood
lint of voices untranslatable stories
summer sunlight on dried paint
whose color continues to fade in the

growing brightness of the white afternoon
ferns on the shore of the transparent lake
or should you forget them
as you float between ageless languages
and call from one to the other who you are

What Is Modern

Are you modern

is the first
tree that comes
to mind modern
does it have modern leaves

who is modern after hours
at the glass door
of the drugstore
or
within sound of the airport

or passing the
animal pound
where once a week I
gas the animals
who is modern in bed

when
was modern born
who first was pleased
to feel modern
who first claimed the word
as a possession
saying I'm
modern

as someone might say
I'm a champion

or I'm
famous or even
as some would say I'm
rich

or I love the sound
of the clarinet
yes so do I
do you like classical
or modern

did modern
begin to be modern
was there a morning
when it was there for the first time
completely modern

is today modern
the modern sun rising
over the modern roof
of the modern hospital
revealing the modern water tanks and aerials
of the modern horizon

and modern humans
one after the other
solitary and without speaking
buying the morning paper
on the way to work

Direction

All I remember of the long lecture
which is all I remember of one summer
are the veins on the old   old bald head
and the loose white sleeve   and bony finger pointing
beyond the listeners
over their heads

there was the dazzling   wall and the empty sunlight
and reaching out of his age he told them
for the last time
what to do when they got to the world
giving them his every breath   to take with them like water
as they vanished

nobody was coming back that way

The New Season

On the third night of autumn
hearing rats in the dry
brush and leaves under the big trees
below the house
I go down with one of the dogs
to frighten them away

where the end of the house
looms high off the ground
we look down the dark slope
with a flashlight
listening
what was it
old dog old good heart
old Roland not too bright
only one eye

in the black
blossoms go on falling
from the Christmasberry trees
like the dripping after rain
small unseen colorless
blossoms ticking
but the bees are not there

worms are awake under the leaves
beetles are awake eating

upside down in the dark
leaves are awake hearing
in the complete night

I stand with a flashlight
in a smell of fruit
and we wait

Hearing

Back when it took all day to come up
from the curving broad ponds on the plains
where the green-winged jaçanas ran on the lily pads

easing past tracks at the mouths of gorges
crossing villages silted in hollows
in the foothills
each with its lime-washed church by the baked square
of red earth and its
talkers eating fruit under trees

turning a corner and catching
sight at last of inky forests far above
steep as faces
with the clouds stroking them and the glimmering
airy valleys opening out of them

waterfalls still roared from the folds
of the mountain
white and thundering and spray drifted
around us swirling into the broad leaves
and the waiting boughs

once I took a tin cup and climbed
the sluiced rocks and mossy branches beside
one of the high falls
looking up step by step into
the green sky from which rain was falling

when I looked back from a ledge there were only
dripping leaves below me
and flowers

beside me the hissing
cataract plunged into the trees
holding on I moved closer
left foot on a rock in the water
right foot on a rock in deeper water
at the edge of the fall
then from under the weight of my right foot
came a voice like bell ringing
over and over one clear treble
syllable

I could feel it move
I could feel it ring in my foot in my skin
everywhere
in my ears in my hair
I could feel it in my tongue and in the hand
holding the cup
as long as I stood there it went on
without changing

when I moved the cup
still it went on
when I filled the cup
in the falling column
still it went on
when I drank it rang in my eyes
through the thunder curtain

when I filled the cup again
when I raised my foot
still it went on
and all the way down
from wet rock to wet rock
green branch to green branch
it came with me

until I stood
looking up and we drank
the light water
and when we went on we could
still hear the sound
as far as the next turn on the way over

The Black Jewel

In the dark
there is only the sound of the cricket

south wind in the leaves
is the cricket
so is the surf on the shore
and the barking across the valley

the cricket never sleeps
the whole cricket is the pupil of one eye
it can run it can leap it can fly
in its back the moon
crosses the night

there is only one cricket
when I listen

the cricket lives in the unlit ground
in the roots
out of the wind
it has only the one sound

before I could talk
I heard the cricket
under the house
then I remembered summer

mice too and the blind lightning
are born hearing the cricket

dying they hear it
bodies of light turn listening to the cricket
the cricket is neither alive nor dead
the death of the cricket
is still the cricket
in the bare room the luck of the cricket
echoes

THE RAIN IN THE TREES

(1988)

For Paula

Late Spring

Coming into the high room again after years
after oceans and shadows of hills and the sounds of lies
after losses and feet on stairs

after looking and mistakes and forgetting
turning there thinking to find
no one except those I knew
finally I saw you
sitting in white
already waiting

you of whom I had heard
with my own ears since the beginning
for whom more than once
I had opened the door
believing you were not far

West Wall

In the unmade light I can see the world
as the leaves brighten I see the air
the shadows melt and the apricots appear
now that the branches vanish I see the apricots
from a thousand trees ripening in the air
they are ripening in the sun along the west wall
apricots beyond number are ripening in the daylight

Whatever was there
I never saw those apricots swaying in the light
I might have stood in orchards forever
without beholding the day in the apricots
or knowing the ripeness of the lucid air
or touching the apricots in your skin
or tasting in your mouth the sun in the apricots

The First Year

When the words had all been used
for other things
we saw the first day begin

out of the calling water
and the black branches
leaves no bigger than your fingertips
were unfolding on the tree of heaven
against the old stained wall
their green sunlight
that had never shone before

waking together we were the first
to see them
and we knew them then

all the languages were foreign and the first
year rose

Native Trees

Neither my father nor my mother knew
the names of the trees
where I was born
what is that
I asked and my
father and mother did not
hear they did not look where I pointed
surfaces of furniture held
the attention of their fingers
and across the room they could watch
walls they had forgotten
where there were no questions
no voices and no shade

Were there trees
where they were children
where I had not been
I asked
were there trees in those places
where my father and my mother were born
and in that time did
my father and my mother see them
and when they said yes it meant
they did not remember
What were they I asked what were they
but both my father and my mother
said they never knew

Touching the Tree

Faces are bending over me asking why

they do not live here they do not know anything
there is a black river beyond the buildings
watching everything from one side
it is moving while I touch the tree

the black river says no my father says no
my mother says no in the streets they say nothing
they walk past one at a time in hats
with their heads down
it is wrong to answer them through the green fence
the street cars go by singing to themselves *I am iron*
the broom seller goes past in the sound of grass
by the tree touching the tree I hear the tree
I walk with the tree
we talk without anything

come late echoes of ferries chains whistles
tires on the avenue wires humming among windows
words flying out of rooms

the stones of the wall are painted white to be better
but at the foot of the tree in the fluttering light
I have dug a cave for a lion
a lion cave so that the cave will be there
among the roots waiting
when the lion comes to the tree

Night Above the Avenue

The whole time that I have lived here
at every moment somebody
has been at the point of birth
behind a window across the street
and somebody behind a window
across the street
has been at the point of death
they have lain there in pain and in hope
on and on
and away from the windows the dark interiors
of their bodies have been opened to lights
and they have waited bleeding and have been frightened
and happy
unseen by each other we have been transformed
and the traffic has flowed away
from between them and me
in four directions
as the lights have changed
day and night
and I have sat up late
at the kitchen window
knowing the news
watching the paired red lights
recede from under the windows down the avenue
toward the tunnel under the river
and the white lights from the park rushing toward us
through the sirens and the music
and I have wakened in a wind of messages

Now Renting

Nobody remembers
the original site
of course
what was there to remember

somebody
nobody remembers
wanted a little building
nobody knows why

on the original site
and cleared it
no doubt
had to

later somebody
wanted a little
more space
and set up a scaffold

around the first building
and built the walls higher
and then tore down
the scaffold

then in time somebody
put up more scaffolding
and tore down
the whole building

and dug a hole
in the original site
and put up a bigger
building and tore

down the scaffolding
to the accompaniment
of music announcing
a golden age

but somebody with vision
soon put more scaffolding
on top of the building
and raised the whole structure

even higher than before
and tore down the scaffolding
but a while after that
somebody put up more scaffolding

clear above the top of the building
and tore down the building inside it
and went on adding scaffolding
with glass pictures on it

all the way up
of a glass building
never built
on that site

with nobody
inside it
at all the windows
to see the motionless clouds

Glasses

There is no eye to catch

They come in uniforms
they cross bridges built on cement arches
they dip their lights
they wave

they have just read a book
they have never read a book
they have just turned from the TV
they have just turned from the table
or bed

it is morning and they pour
one by one out of the door
they are real glass and thin
and the wind is blowing
the sky is racing
they come to drink from the steel fountain
they come to walk on the carpet
they come past the doors
of frosted glass

they turn in the window at the end of the hall
in amber light
ninety floors from the ground
walking on empty evening
they pay the electric bills
they owe money
all the stars turn in vast courses around them
unnoticed
they vote

they buy their tickets
they applaud
they go into the elevator
thinking of money
with the quiet gleam of money

they bear arms
they go on wheels they are without color
they come in clothes out of closets
they fly above the earth reading papers
the bulldozers make way for them
they glitter under imported leaves

Shadow Passing

Suddenly in bright sunlight small clouds
and on a map I remember
we were growing toward us
like lights in the distance

it was a country of mines
and faces like sawed bones
sitting outside their black doorways
staring into tunnels in the daylight

the rivers and the standing
water were full
of the dreams of presidents
of coal companies

and from the churches
on the flayed slopes
rose hymns of resurrection
then the sunlight came back

History

Only I never came back

the gates stand open
where I left the barnyard in the evening
as the owl was bringing the mouse home
in the gold sky
at the milking hour
and I turned to the amber hill and followed
along the gray fallen wall
by the small mossed oaks and the bushes of rusting
arches bearing the ripe
blackberries into the long shadow
and climbed the ancient road
through the last songs of the blackbirds

passing the last live farms
their stones running with dark liquid
and the ruined farms their windows without frames
facing away
looking out across the pastures of dead shepherds
whom nobody ever knew
grown high with the dry flowers of late summer
their empty doorways gazing
toward the arms of the last oaks
and at night their broken chimneys watching
the cold of the meteors

the beams had fallen together
to rest in brown herds around the fireplaces
and in the shade of black trees the houses were full
of their own fragrance at last
mushrooms and owls
and the song of the cicadas

there was a note on a page
made at the time
and the book was closed
and taken on a journey
into a country where no one
knew the language

no one could read
even the address
inside the cover
and there the book was
of course lost

it was a book full of words to remember
this is how we manage without them
this is how they manage
without us

I was not going to be long

Notes from a Journey

Ringed by shadowy balconies
paint peeling from the old beams
the echoing squares paved in marble
a thousand years ago
climb the slope like shallow terraces
tall grass twitching above the cracks
and the thin cats watching the light

*

All the way down the peninsula
the walls of the crumbling farms are the colors
of evening
we who are going wait in stone courtyards
until everything is in order
loops of leather hang in the shadows
by a ruined doorway next to me
as I sit on the bench and stroke the lioness
and the big horses sigh by the gate

*

Last night the beautiful
woman in whose house I stayed
told of finding a prostitute
half dead of exhaustion in the street
unable to speak
and bringing her home and putting her
into the woman's own bed
she said
and in the night looking and seeing a light
coming from the bed and from the figure there
a gold light that filled the room with blessing
and no one was there in the morning
what am I to make of such a story
having been given the same bed

*

No horses now for days
cracked whitewash in the old streets of the south
on an upper story the dark ceiling of a kitchen

the women preparing a meal their hands full of dough
laughing
some of them very old
they call me to come up
and sit at the long table
and eat
the daughters talk to me as though they knew me

*

Near the harbor
as the afternoon was turning blue
this cafe on a side street
everything standing open no one to be seen
the facade of the building like a huge mosque
blank
white
an arched doorway with curtains drawn back
the curtains too carved in gray stone
inside it was cool and shady
a man and a woman stood under a tree
at the foot of the marble stairs in the courtyard
and asked me whether I wanted to sleep there
and as I left in the morning
I saw that the wall at the end of the courtyard
was full of sky from which the stones had fallen

*

I stepped from the end of a street
into a square so wide that the buildings around it
appeared to be melting like mirages on the horizon
and I thought it had happened before
gray marble and twilight and sun setting in mist
I was on my way to meet friends
with whom I was to travel the next day
and of course I was late
and forgot to find out the name of the street

*

I turn the corners in the small steep seaport
no bigger than a village
with the feeling that I once knew it

and that it has changed in the interval
like someone who remembers me as a child
the old town hall has been abandoned
and for several years the lower floor has been flooded
I was sure I remembered the old
grandfather clock standing there
with its feet in water and its shoulders
fallen against the arch of the far window
its pendulum rod loose in the air
and for a moment I wanted to rescue it
and take it with me

*

Walking along the edge of the sea cliffs
with the light on the yellow crags below me
country of quarries
wagons loaded with stones and the horses
struggling and slipping on the cart tracks
for no reason that they know
and I see that each of the stones is numbered

*

Breakfast with a wagon driver's
family in the mountains
it is a day commemorating
a liberation
we have peaches and little hot loaves
under the trees by the kitchen
which has a roof but no walls
most of the stones he tells me
are quarried and carted illegally
so that too has to be paid for

*

I have been staying
in the empty fisherman's house
facing out to sea
the whole village is abandoned now
the doorways echoing the dark patios
there is a hall behind the stairwell
and from the end of the hall too

the sea shines
a lifeboat is half buried in the rocks
above the water line
there I met a heavy woman in black
walking along the shore
a caretaker she said
who knew everybody

*

A room in back of a shop
in the mountains
there is dancing after dark
and they get drunk and keep giving
presents to the stranger
who happens to be me
clothes a little worn
which I have to try on and keep
and a big knife on a belt
then a bitter argument
begins and builds
I think I had better leave
and I walk out into the rain and the night
not knowing how to thank them

*

At the end of a long bay
in sloping country blonde with straw
before autumn
how they love to eat and they all cook
at table they tell of the time when they were all
taken away
and the children know the story
and listen

*

At night I dreamed that I was far away
and that I lived there
finally I took the boat
from the foot of the mountain
and thought I knew where I was going
and that it was still there

Pastures

Some who are still alive
grew up in them
and when they could barely walk
ran with the sheep
and came to the gate

one time boys watching sheep
in the upland pastures
on the day of the fair
saw a man they knew
come and wait

for a woman they knew
and kill her with a rock
and they hid
under a flowering
honeysuckle

I was taught the word
pasture as though
it came from the Bible
but I knew it named something
with a real sky

one day my mother
and the woman we were visiting
wanted to talk about things
they did not want me to hear

so I walked out past the pig pen
under the apple trees
and the first pigs I had seen
alive
crowded to the corner
to look at me

I passed the barn
where bands of light

reached between the boards
to touch the back of sheep
standing and doing
nothing in the shadow

and went up the green track
to the top of the ridge
and saw the open
pasture sloping
away to the woods
it was another sky
a day of its own
it was the night pasture

as children
we ran among
mounds of rusting ferns
in the long sunset
of an endless summer
our thin voices
spinning across the still pasture
calling each other

and we hid
in the chill twilight
face down hearing our breaths
our own breaths
full of the horizon
and the smell of the dew
on the cold ferns

even then
in the spring
there were those on earth
who drove flocks
from winter pastures
near the sea
up into the green slopes
enclosed by woods
in the mountains

they went all together
it took ten days
before they came
to the summer pastures
they said were theirs
full of tall
young grass
many
now do not know
any such thing

After School

For a long time I wanted
to get out of that school
where I had been sent
for the best

I thought of climbing
down the vine
outside the window
at night

after the watchman
had turned the corner
to the boiler room
in the sweet autumn dark

I wanted to slip
through the still dining hall
and down the cellar stairs
in the girls' wing

where I had set the waltzing
in the first book
of *War and Peace*
I would pass unseen in that crowd

into the cellar
and the secret door to the steam pipes
and under the street
to the swimming pool

I would have persuaded
a girl I liked
to meet me there
and we would swim whispering

because of the echoes
while the light from the street
shone through the frosted windows
like the light of the moon

all down the hot room
where the sound of the water
made the heart beat loud
to think of it

but I never
got away then
and when I think now
of following that tunnel

there is a black wolf
tied there waiting
a thin bitch
who snaps at my right hand

but I untie her
and we find our way
out of there as one
and down the street

hungry
nobody in sight at that hour
everything closed
behind us

Empty Water

I miss the toad
who came all summer
to the limestone
water basin
under the Christmasberry tree
imported in 1912
from Brazil for decoration
then a weed on a mule track
on a losing
pineapple plantation
now an old tree in a line
of old trees
the toad came at night
first and sat in the water
all night and all day
then sometimes at night
left for an outing
but was back in the morning
under the branches among
the ferns the green sword leaf
of the lily
sitting in the water
all the dry months
gazing at the sky
through those eyes
fashioned of the most
precious of metals
come back
believer in shade
believer in silence and elegance
believer in ferns
believer in patience
believer in the rain

Rain at Night

This is what I have heard

at last the wind in December
lashing the old trees with rain
unseen rain racing along the tiles
under the moon
wind rising and falling
wind with many clouds
trees in the night wind

after an age of leaves and feathers
someone dead
thought of this mountain as money
and cut the trees
that were here in the wind
in the rain at night
it is hard to say it
but they cut the sacred 'ohias then
the sacred koas then
the sandalwood and the halas
holding aloft their green fires
and somebody dead turned cattle loose
among the stumps until killing time

but the trees have risen one more time
and the night wind makes them sound
like the sea that is yet unknown
the black clouds race over the moon
the rain is falling on the last place

Waking to the Rain

The night of my birthday
I woke from a dream
of harmony
suddenly hearing

an old man not my father
I said but it was
my father gasping
my name as he fell
on the stone steps outside
just under the window
in the rain
I do not know
how many times
he may have called
before I woke
I was lying
in my parents' room
in the empty house
both of them dead
that year
and the rain was falling
all around me
the only sound

The Salt Pond

Mid September   my dead father's birthday
again by the low shore I watch the gulls fly inland
white gulls riding a knowledge older than they are

by now you are eighty eight and need nothing old friend
twelve years in the white sky out of the wind

once more at the end of summer the first map of the coast
looks out from the wall
a shadow imperceptibly darkening
the names dissolve across it
white clouds race over the marshes

the gulls have gone with their age
I know the wind

Summer '82

When it was already autumn
we heard of the terrible weather
we had lived through
heat in the city and rain
in the filthy streets

but to us it looked new
night and day
in the washed crowds I could see
after so many lives you
and through the blurred sirens and the commercials
and the hissing of buses on Fifth
I could hear at last what I
had listened for
we woke in the night holding
each other
trying to believe we were there
in that summer among those
same towers

in first light we both remembered
one house deep among leaves
the steps the long porch the breeze at the door
the rooms one by one and the windows
the hours and what they looked out on
nothing had given up

we were swallowed into the subway in the morning
together we sifted
along the sidewalks in the glare
we saw friends again
each time as though
returning after a war
and laughed and embraced them
on a corner in the ringing downpour

and in the evening we alone
took the streetcar to the rain forest
followed the green ridge in the dusk
got off to walk home through the ancient trees

Before Us

You were there all the time and I saw only
the days the air
the nights the moon changing
cars passing and faces at windows
the windows
the rain the leaves the years
words on pages telling of something else
wind in a mirror

everything begins so late after all
when the solitaires have already gone
and the doves of Tanna
when the Laughing Owls have
long been followed by question marks
and honeycreepers and the brown
bears of Atlas
the white wolf and the sea mink have not been seen
by anyone living

we wake so late after many dreams
it is clear
when the lake has vanished
the shepherds have left the shielings
grandparents have dissolved with their memories
dictionaries are full of graves
most of the rivers are lethal
we thought we were younger
through all those ages of knowing nothing
and there you are
at last after such fallings away and voyages
beside me in the dawning

we wake together and the world is here in its dew
you are here and the morning is whole
finally the light is young
because it is here it is not like anything
how could it have taken you so long to appear
bloom of air tenderness of leaves
where were you when the lies were voting
the fingers believed faces on money

where were we when the smoke washed us
and the hours cracked as they rang
where was I when we passed each other
on the same streets
and travelled by the same panes to the same stations

now we have only the age that is left
to be together
the brief air the vanishing green
ordure in office tourists on the headland
the last hours of the sea
now we have only the words we remember
to say to each other
only the morning of your eyes and the day
of our faces to be together
only the time of our hands with its vexed
motor and the note
of the thrush on the guava branch in the shining rain
for the rest of our lives

The Sound of the Light

I hear sheep running on the path of broken limestone
through brown curled leaves fallen early from walnut limbs
at the end of a summer how light the bony
flutter of their passage I can
hear their coughing their calling and wheezing even the warm
greased wool rubbing on the worn walls I hear them
passing passing in the hollow lane and there is still time

the shuffle of black shoes of women climbing
stone ledges to church keeps flowing up the dazzling hill
around the grassy rustle of voices
on the far side of a slatted shutter
and the small waves go on whispering on the shingle
in the heat of an hour without wind it is Sunday
none of the sentences begins or ends there is time

again the unbroken rumble of trucks and the hiss
of brakes roll upward out of the avenue
I forget what season they are exploding through
what year the drill on the sidewalk is smashing
it is the year in which you are sitting there as you are
in the morning speaking to me and I hear
you through the burning day and I touch you
to be sure and there is time there is still time

Sky in September

In spite of the months of knowing
and the years
autumn comes with astonishment
light held up in a glass
the terrible news in a haze
caught breath in the warm leaves

in spite of the gathered dust and the vast moon
the day comes with a color
its words cannot touch
so it is when I see you
after the years when the ailanthus leaves
drifted unnoticed
down the gray wall

they have disappeared and nothing is missing
after their rocking and clinging
they have vanished with the thieves and shufflers
and the words of the dealers
taking nothing

they have fallen like scales from the eyes
and at last we are here together
light of autumn
clear morning in the only time

Anniversary on the Island

The long waves glide in through the afternoon
while we watch from the island
from the cool shadow under the trees where the long ridge
a fold in the skirt of the mountain
runs down to the end of the headland

day after day we wake to the island
the light rises through the drops on the leaves
and we remember like birds where we are
night after night we touch the dark island
that once we set out for

and lie still at last with the island in our arms
hearing the leaves and the breathing shore
there are no years any more
only the one mountain
and on all sides the sea that brought us

Sight

Once
a single cell
found that it was full of light
and for the first time there was seeing

when
I was a bird
I could see where the stars had turned
and I set out on my journey

in the head of a mountain goat
I could see across a valley
under the shining trees something moving

deep
in the green sea
I saw two sides of the water
and swam between them

I
look at you
in the first light of the morning
for as long as I can

The Solstice

They say the sun will come back
at midnight
after all
my one love

but we know how the minutes
fly out into
the dark trees
and vanish

like the great 'ohias and the honey creepers
and we know how the weeks
walk into the
shadows at midday

at the thought of the months I reach for your hand
it is not something
one is supposed
to say

we watch the bright birds in the morning
we hope for the quiet
daytime together
the year turns into air

but we are together in the whole night
with the sun still going away
and the year
coming back

Coming to the Morning

You make me remember all of the elements
the sea remembering all of its waves

in each of the waves there was always a sky made of water
and an eye that looked once

there was the shape of one mountain
and a blood kinship with rain

and the air for touch and for the tongue
at the speed of light

in which the world is made
from a single star

and our ears
are formed of the sea as we listen

Being Early

When you were born
I was a small child in a city
and even if somebody had brought me news of you
I would not have believed them

already I had seen an ape chained in the sun
with a bucket of water
I had heard bells calling from wooden towers
stone towers brick towers
I had seen blood coming through bandages
on a hand holding candy
and a shadow shining on green water
where tall birds were standing
and I knew the notes of street cars
and the smells of three rivers
and could have told you about all of them
if I had known you were there

Travelling Together

If we are separated I will
try to wait for you
on your side of things

your side of the wall and the water
and of the light moving at its own speed
even on leaves that we have seen
I will wait on one side

while a side is there

The Inevitable Lightness

The roads and everything on them fly up and dissolve
a net rises from the world
the cobweb in which it was dying
and the earth breathes naked with its new scars
and sky everywhere

The Crust

Sire it is true as far
as it goes
it was summer and a holiday
in the morning

and the traffic was piled on the roads
blocked at an intersection
with the radios playing
and I could see just ahead
that the earth had fallen away
from the road
underneath

I tried to get others to go back
and some began to go back
as the road opened under them

in my view it happened
that the earth fell from under
because the tree was cut
whose roots held it together
and with the tree
went all the lives in it
that slept in it ate in it
met in it believed in it
for whom it was all there was
the sun travelled to come back to it
it had evolved the only language
it remembered everything
but what do I know I am only a witness

the roots became cracks
and from the tree your chair was made
with the earth falling away from under it

Mementos

Sunflowers are brought to me on the morning of your death
in the clear day hands you did not see
a face unknown to you and never expected
accompany the stems through the gate
repeating an unfamiliar
name under a few high clouds

beyond the flowers there is still the sea
beyond the writing the waves go on overflowing
here is a long envelope
from which a picture of a black lake emerges
far away between my fingers while the trees are flying

a friend with a passion for freedom
said a piece of a poem and got it wrong
and put it in a letter to me
it was a passage by someone
of whom she knew I thought little
and she sent it
to surprise and remind me but she
misquoted it and wrote *Even*
the newt the worm the germ the first spit
sing the day in full cry

and how does it go now

Print Fallen Out of Somewhere

It asks me to imagine a day with no colors
except brown

in a field with two children
in summer
the hour growing late
at the turn of a century
beside a pasture

full of brown cows
on whose backs a shadow
of the same color
floats
crouched over a camera

even from here I can see
it is a place where the children
do not live
and which they will not see again
with its unheard crickets
dry barn afternoon light
in which the boy in the white shirt
who will not live long
stands happily holding a horse
and the girl wearing
a tan hair ribbon
is frowning at the sun

it has come this far to show me
how they look straight at me
without seeing me

Utterance

Sitting over words
very late I have heard a kind of whispered sighing
not far
like a night wind in pines or like the sea in the dark
the echo of everything that has ever
been spoken
still spinning its one syllable
between the earth and silence

Paper

What an idea
that you can put it on a piece of paper
what is a piece of paper and how can you tell
put it on a piece of paper

at the beginning
there are the tall sub-polar mountains
above a peninsula
set in a plain of ice
under deep snow
from which the light comes
white no longer there
put it on that paper

the sound of the runners
in all that unpeopled day
at one with the wind and the breathing of the white dogs
and the wind wiping out the tracks at once
the white earth turning around and the sense of climbing
put it on that paper

everything is white so it can disappear
everything that is not white
is alone
the colors are all white
the night is white in a place not remembered
everything is the same color as the other planets
here in this place hard to see
on a piece of paper

Thanks

Listen
with the night falling we are saying thank you
we are stopping on the bridges to bow from the railings
we are running out of the glass rooms

with our mouths full of food to look at the sky
and say thank you
we are standing by the water thanking it
standing by the windows looking out
in our directions

back from a series of hospitals back from a mugging
after funerals we are saying thank you
after the news of the dead
whether or not we knew them we are saying thank you

over telephones we are saying thank you
in doorways and in the backs of cars and in elevators
remembering wars and the police at the door
and the beatings on stairs we are saying thank you
in the banks we are saying thank you
in the faces of the officials and the rich
and of all who will never change
we go on saying thank you thank you

with the animals dying around us
taking our feelings we are saying thank you
with the forests falling faster than the minutes
of our lives we are saying thank you
with the words going out like cells of a brain
with the cities growing over us
we are saying thank you faster and faster
with nobody listening we are saying thank you
thank you we are saying and waving
dark though it is

At the Same Time

So it seems there are only
our contemporaries
and we learn only from them listen only to them
talk only to them
after all there are no others

for the dead do not listen to us
out of the past
after everything they said
about us

and as for the future
what good would it do us
to be discovered
a hundred years on
with this sky gone from these valleys
and these valleys unknown

and what would the finders
think they had found
that was us
as they struggled to memorize
the old books of addresses

where we are talking and writing

Coming to Hear

He who insisted that he could not hear music
is floating over a dark sea
on which the lights

accompany him
wave upon wave
unseen and unbroken

there is a line of black trees
just over the horizon
on an island

which he will think familiar
now it is the sixth night
and he is hearing the colors

the sound of blue at night
that believes in nothing as always
is carrying him

To the Insects

Elders

we have been here so short a time
and we pretend that we have invented memory

we have forgotten what it is like to be you
who do not remember us

we remember imagining that what survived us
would be like us

and would remember the world as it appears to us
but it will be your eyes that will fill with light

we kill you again and again
and we turn into you

eating the forests
eating the earth and the water

and dying of them
departing from ourselves

leaving you the morning
in its antiquity

After the Alphabets

I am trying to decipher the language of insects
they are the tongues of the future
their vocabularies describe buildings as food
they can depict dark water and the veins of trees
they can convey what they do not know
and what is known at a distance
and what nobody knows
they have terms for making music with the legs
they can recount changing in a sleep like death
they can sing with wings
the speakers are their own meaning in a grammar without
    horizons
they are wholly articulate
they are never important they are everything

The Superstition

The cars are disappearing
and we were told they were real
they were only what we thought of them
we were taught that they were beautiful
but we forgot them
we believed they were strong
but they were hauled away
we thought they would take us anywhere
but they had to stop
we thought they were fast and we have left them far behind
we believed they would save our lives
and we gave our lives for them
thinking they were worth it
we watched them pass with no beginning no end
glass on all sides
we dreamed of them and we woke
with the headlights flying through us

The Overpass

You know how you
will be looking for somewhere
and come by surprise on a long cement bridge
sailing out over a wide
cement ditch carved deep into the hill
between whose banks the traffic is rushing
in both directions

in what is now the air above it
there was a pasture
beside dark woods
I saw it
and a swamp near the first trees
with a pump house hidden
in low green blackberry bushes
and mist coming off the upland marsh
first thing in the morning

and on the cold hill
a man and a boy
planting potatoes
with a mule keeping ahead of them
climbing the furrows
through the morning smelling of
wet grass
none of them seeing
the white bird flying over

Snow

Comes the dust falling in the air
comes in the afternoon the sunbeam
comes through the sound of friends
comes the shadow through the door

comes the unturned page comes the name comes the footstep
comes to each wall the portrait
comes the white hair

comes with the flowers opening
comes as the hands touch and stay
comes with late fortune and late seed
comes with the whole of music
comes with the light on the mountains
comes at the hours of clouds
comes the white hair

comes the sudden widening of the river
comes as the birds disappear in the air
comes while we talk together
comes as we listen to each other
comes as we are lying together
comes while we sleep
comes the white hair

For the Departure of a Stepson

You are going for a long time
and nobody knows what to expect

we are trying to learn
not to accompany gifts with advice

or to suppose that we can protect you
from being changed

by something that we do not know
but have always turned away from

even by the sea that we love
with its breaking

and the dissolving days
and the shadows on the wall

together we look at the young trees
we read the news we smell the morning

we cannot tell you what to take with you
in your light baggage

Airport

None of the computers can say
how long it took to evolve a facility
devoted to absence in life

you walk out of the chute
and a person smiles at your ticket
and points you to your seat

is this the only way home
nobody asks
because nobody knows

the building is not inhabited it is not
home except to roaches
it is not loved it is serviced

it is not a place
but a container with signs
directing a process

there is neither youth in the air
nor earth under foot
there is a machine to announce

yet the corridors beat with anguish longing relief
news trash insurance dispensers
and many are glad to be here

thinking of being somewhere else
hurrying at great expense
across glass after glass

we travel far and fast
and as we pass through we forget
where we have been

Liberty

Every morning
somebody unlocks the statue
and lets in the day crew

first the welders who are fixing
the crack in the arm
that holds up the torch

and the elevator operators
the ticket sellers and the guides
and the next shift of police

the early ferries
land from the city
bringing visitors

born everywhere
to the cemented pedestal
under the huge toes

to follow signs
to the ticket booths
vendors conveniences

and to the guides to the crown and the arm
and the torch
whatever is safe

and the guides tell the names
of the sculptor and the donor
and explain why it is ours

also how much it weighs
and how many come to see it
in a year

and the name of the island
from which the foreigners
used to watch it

Journey

Some time after the roofs fall in
the cars begin to come

on week ends the cars go to the country
this is the country

an old road has been found
crossing under a new one

the right clothes are put on
for visiting nobody who lives there

a broad footprint has been deciphered
crossing a cellar

in one of the empty houses
by the buried road

someone has driven a whole day
to declare how long it has been there

nobody knows anything
about who was here before

but nothing is real
until it can be sold

so a nice young couple
has cast in plaster

the broad foot
that went somewhere

the authentic white sole
rising from the white ground

so that people with cars
can take the foot home

to climb on their
blank walls

Memory

Climbing through a dark shower
I came to the edge of the mountain

I was a child
and everything was there

the flight of eagles the passage of warriors
watching the valley far below

the wind on the cliff the cold rain blowing upward
from the rock face

everything around me had burned
and I was coming back

walking on charcoal among the low green bushes
wet to the skin and wide awake

The Duck

The first time that I
was allowed to take out
the white canoe

because the lake was so still
in the evening
I slipped out on the long sky

of midsummer across the light
coming through the overturned
dark trees

I saw the duck catching
the colors of fire
as she moved over the bright glass

and I glided after
until she dove
and I followed with the white canoe

and look what I find
long afterwards
the world of the living

Hearing the Names of the Valleys

Finally the old man is telling
the forgotten names
and the names of the stones they came from
for a long time I asked him the names
and when he says them at last
I hear no meaning
and cannot remember the sounds

I have lived without knowing
the names for the water

from one rock
and the water from another
and behind the names that I do not have
the color of water flows all day and all night
the old man tells me the name for it
and as he says it I forget it

there are names for the water
between here and there
between places now gone
except in the porcelain faces
on the tombstones
and places still here

and I ask him again
the name for the color of water
wanting to be able to say it
as though I had known it all my life
without giving it a thought

The Strangers from the Horizon

Early one year
two ships came in to the foot of the mountain
from the sea in the first light of morning

we knew they were coming
though we had never seen them
they were black and bigger than houses

with teeth along the sides
and it is true
they had many arms

and cloaks filled with wind
clouds moving past us but they were not clouds
trees stopping before us but they were not trees

without having ever seen them we knew
without having ever seen us they knew
and we knew they knew each other

in another place they came from
and they knew that we knew
that they were not gods

they had a power for death that we wanted
and we went out to them taking things of ours
that they would surely need

Conqueror

When they start to wear your clothes
do their dreams become more like yours
who do they look like

when they start to use your language
do they say what you say
who are they in your words

when they start to use your money
do they need the same things you need
or do the things change

when they are converted to your gods
do you know who they are praying to
do you know who is praying

for you not to be there

Native

Most afternoons
of this year which is written as a number
in my own hand
on the white plastic labels

I go down the slope
where mules I never saw
plowed in the sun and died
while I was in school

they were beaten to go
straight up the hill
so that in three years the rain
had washed all the topsoil

out past sea cliffs
and frigate birds
only a few years
after the forests were gone

now I go down past
a young mango tree
to the shelves made of wood
poisoned against decay

there under a roof
of palm fronds and chicken wire
I stare at the small native
plants in their plastic pots

here the 'ohia trees
filled with red flowers red birds
water notes flying music
the shining of the gods

here seeds from destroyed valleys
open late
beside their names in Latin
in the shade of leaves I have put there

Place

On the last day of the world
I would want to plant a tree

what for
not for the fruit

the tree that bears the fruit
is not the one that was planted

I want the tree that stands
in the earth for the first time

with the sun already
going down

and the water
touching its roots

in the earth full of the dead
and the clouds passing

one by one
over its leaves

Witness

I want to tell what the forests
were like

I will have to speak
in a forgotten language

Chord

While Keats wrote they were cutting down the sandalwood
     forests
while he listened to the nightingale they heard their own axes
     echoing through the forests
while he sat in the walled garden on the hill outside the
     city they thought of their gardens dying far away on the
     mountain
while the sound of the words clawed at him they thought of
     their wives
while the tip of his pen travelled the iron they had coveted was
     hateful to them
while he thought of the Grecian woods they bled under red
     flowers
while he dreamed of wine the trees were falling from the trees
while he felt his heart they were hungry and their faith was sick
while the song broke over him they were in a secret place and
     they were cutting it forever
while he coughed they carried the trunks to the hole in the
     forest the size of a foreign ship
while he groaned on the voyage to Italy they fell on the trails
     and were broken
when he lay with the odes behind him the wood was sold for
     cannons
when he lay watching the window they came home and lay
     down
and an age arrived when everything was explained in another
     language

Losing a Language

A breath leaves the sentences and does not come back
yet the old still remember something that they could say

but they know now that such things are no longer believed
and the young have fewer words

many of the things the words were about
no longer exist

the noun for standing in mist by a haunted tree
the verb for I

the children will not repeat
the phrases their parents speak

somebody has persuaded them
that it is better to say everything differently

so that they can be admired somewhere
farther and farther away

where nothing that is here is known
we have little to say to each other

we are wrong and dark
in the eyes of the new owners

the radio is incomprehensible
the day is glass

when there is a voice at the door it is foreign
everywhere instead of a name there is a lie

nobody has seen it happening
nobody remembers

this is what the words were made
to prophesy

here are the extinct feathers
here is the rain we saw

The Lost Originals

If only you had written our language
we would have remembered how you died

if you had wakened at our windows
we would have known who you were

we would have felt horror
at the pictures of you behind the barbed wire

from which you did not emerge
we would have returned to the shots of you lying dead with
    your kin

we would have ached to hear of your freezing
and your hunger in the hands of our own kind

we would have suffered at the degradation of your women
we would have studied you reverently

we would have repeated the words of your children
we would have been afraid for you

you would have made us ashamed and indignant
and righteous

we would have been proud of you
we would have mourned you

you would have survived
as we do

we might have believed
in a homeland

Term

When all has been said
the road will be closed

when the old man has told
of walking as a child
on the road that the chief
built long ago

and has told of his father
walking with him
and his grandfather
when the road seemed to have been
there always along the sea
and has told of everyone he knew
and all his ancestors
coming that way
it will be closed

when the children have begged
to be able to go
to the sea there as they do
without having to be
rich or foreign
the road will be closed
for the rich and foreign
and the children will wait on them
where the road is now

where the thorny
kiawe trees smelling
of honey
dance in their shadows along the sand
the road will die
and turn into money at last
as the developers
themselves hope to do

what is sacred about a road anyway
what is sacred about any place
what is sacred about a language
what is sacred

what will we need to love
when it is all money
the rich will be rich
the foreign will be foreign
on the closed road

they are on their way already
their feet are the feet of ghosts
watching them is like watching a ship
leaving the shore
and seeing that it will never arrive

Kanaloa

When he woke his mind was the west
and he could not remember waking

wherever he looked the sun was coming toward him
the moon was coming toward him

month after month the wind was coming toward him
behind the day the night was coming toward him

all the stars all the comets all the depth of the sea
all the darkness in the earth all the silence all the cold

all the heights were coming toward him
no one had been on the earth before him

all the stories were coming toward him
over the mountain

over the red water the black water
the moonlight

he had imagined the first mistake
all the humans are coming toward him with numbers

they are coming from the beginning to look for him
each of them finds him and he is different

they do not believe him at first
but he houses the ghosts of the trees

the ghosts of the animals
of the whales and the insects

he rises in dust he is burning he is smoke
behind him is nothing

he is the one who is already gone
he is fire flowing downward over the edge

he is the last he is the coming home
he might never have wakened

The Horizons of Rooms

There have been rooms for such a short time
and now we think there is nothing else unless it is raining

or snowing or very late
with everyone else in another dark room

for a time beyond measure there were no rooms
and now many have forgotten the sky

the first room was made of stone and ice
and a fallen tree

with a heart beating in the room
and it was the ice that echoed it

because of a room a heart was born
in a room

and saw everything as a room
even what is called landscape

the present mountains were seen between moments
of remembering a room at another time

now there are more every year who remember childhood as a
    room
in which the person they were is thinking of a forest

but the first hands and first voices emerge in a room
with a ceiling

and later in another room
that ceiling appears again without the hands or voices

it is a room with an echoing wall
of ice

by now most sleeping is done in rooms
or on doorsteps leading to rooms

and the products of rooms
are carried on foot into the final uplands

we meet in a room
and go on from room to room

once there is a room
we know there was something before

and we go on living in the room as it has become
by good fortune

Knock

There is a knock on the door
and nobody is answering
a wave can be heard breaking

on a train from Florida
my mother offered me her bowl of peaches
when I was three
and did not want them
and I watched the white jacket
of the man carrying them away
on their tray along the corridor
while a silent grief rose in me

a plane roars into silence
they have to keep going
as though they were alive
they are hurtling toward the known world
which it is hopeless to reject
and death to accept

I open the door

The Biology of Art

Once at night
it begins
and you are the rest

whoever you are you see the first light
you see it arriving
like a star with you watching it

in the morning you can look at any tree
and see it has no age
and say so

after a long time you look down
into a valley without a name
after a long time as water you look up

The Archaic Maker

The archaic maker is of course naïve. If a man he listens. If a woman she listens. A child is listening. A train passes like an underground river. It enters a story.

The river cannot come back. The story goes on. It uses some form of representation. It does not really need much by way of gadgets, apart from words, singing, dancing, making pictures and objects that resemble living shapes. Things of its own devising.

The deafening river carries parents, children, entire families waking and sleeping homeward.

The story passes stone farms on green hillsides at the mouths of valleys running up into forests full of summer and unheard water.

In the story it is already tomorrow. A time of memories incorrect but powerful. Outside the window is the next of everything.

One of each.
But here is ancient today
itself
the air the living air
the still water

Tracing the Letters

When I learn to read
I will know how green is spelled
when it is not green

already for all
the green of the years

there is only one word
even when the green is not there
and now the word is written down
and not only spoken

so it can be closed in the dark
against an unknown page
until another time

and still the green comes without a word
but when I see it
a word tells me it is green
and I believe it
even in the dark

I will be glad to learn to read
and be able to find
the stories with green in them
and to recognize
the green hands that were here before
the green eyelids and the eyes

The Rose Beetle

It is said that you came from China
but you never saw China
you eat up the leaves here

your ancestors travelled blind in eggs
you arrive just after dark from underground
with a clicking whir in the first night
knowing by the smell what leaves to eat here
where you have wakened for the first time

the strawberry leaves foreign as you
the beans the orchid tree the eggplant
the old leaves of the heliconia the banana some palms
and the roses from everywhere but here

and the hibiscus from here the abutilons
the royal ilima

in the night you turn them into lace
into an arid net
into sky

like the sky long ago over China

TRAVELS

(1993)

For Margaret McElderry

Cover Note

Hypocrite reader my
variant my almost
family we are so
few now it seems as though
we knew each other as
the words between us keep
assuming that we do
I hope I make sense to
you in the shimmer of
our days while the world we
cling to in common is

burning for I have not
the ancients' confidence
in the survival of
one track of syllables
nor in some ultimate
moment of insight that
supposedly will dawn
once and for all upon
a bright posterity
making clear only to
them what passes between

us now in a silence
on this side of the flames
so that from a distance
beyond appeal only
they of the future will
behold our true meaning
which eludes us as we
breathe reader beside your
timepiece do you believe
any such thing do the
children read what you do

when they read or can you
think the words will rise from

677

the page saying the same
things when they speak for us
no longer and then who
in the total city
will go on listening
to these syllables that
are ours and be able
still to hear moving through
them the last rustling of

paws in high grass the one
owl hunting along this
spared valley the tongues of
the free trees our uncaught
voices reader I do
not know that anyone
else is waiting for these
words that I hoped might seem
as though they had occurred
to you and you would take
them with you as your own

The Blind Seer of Ambon

I always knew that I came from
another language

and now even when I can no longer see
I continue to arrive at words

but the leaves
and the shells were already here
and my fingers finding them echo
the untold light and depth

I was betrayed into my true calling
and denied in my advancement

I may have seemed somewhat strange
caring in my own time for living things
with no value that we know
languages wash over them one wave at a time

when the houses fell
in the earthquake
I lost my wife
and my daughter
it all roared and stood still
falling
where they were in the daylight

I named for my wife a flower
as though I could name a flower
my wife dark and luminous
and not there

I lost the drawings of the flowers
in fire

I lost the studies
of the flowers
my first six books in the sea

then I saw that the flowers themselves
were gone
they were indeed gone
I saw
that my wife was gone
then I saw that my daughter was gone
afterward my eyes themselves were gone

one day I was looking
at infinite small creatures
on the bright sand
and the next day is this
hearing after music
so this is the way I see now

I take a shell in my hand
new to itself and to me
I feel the thinness the warmth and the cold
I listen to the water
which is the story welling up
I remember the colors and their lives
everything takes me by surprise
it is all awake in the darkness

Manini

I Don Francisco de Paula Marin
saved the best for the lost pages
the light in the room where I was born
the first faces and what they said to me
late in the day I look southeast to the sea
over the green smoke of the world
where I have my garden

who did I leave behind at the beginning
nobody there would know me now
I was still a boy
when I sailed all the way to the rivers of ice
and saw the flat furs carried out of the forest
already far from their bodies
at night when the last eyes had gone from the fires
I heard wet bodies walking in the air
no longer knowing what they were looking for
even of their language I remember something
by day I watched the furs going to the islands
came the day when I left with the furs for the islands
it would always be said that I had killed my man

I still carry a sword
I wear my own uniform as the chiefs do
I remember the islands in the morning
clouds with blue shadows on the mountains
from the boat coming in I watched the women

watching us from under the trees
those days I met the first of my wives
we made the first of the children
I was led into the presence of the chief
whom the Europeans already called the king

we found what each of us
needed from the other
for me protection and for him
the tongues and meanings of foreigners
a readiness which he kept testing
a way with simples and ailments
that I had come to along my way
I learned names for leaves that were new to me
and for ills that are everywhere the same

the king was the king but I was still a sailor
not done with my voyages
until I had been to both sides of the ocean
and other islands that rise from it
many as stars in the southern sky
I watched hands wherever there were hands
and eyes and mouths and I came to speak
the syllables for what they treasured
but sailed home again to my household and the king

since we have no furs here
he sent the men into the mountains
with axes for the fragrant sandalwood
it was carried out on their flayed backs
and sold for what they had never needed
all in the end for nothing and I directed it
with the wood a fragrance departed
that never came back to the mountains
all down the trails it clung to the raw backs
as the furs clung to the limbs of the fur-bearers
that fragrance had been youth itself and when it was gone
even I could not believe it had ever been ours

and when the king was dead and his gods were cast down
I saw the missionaries come
with their pewter eyes and their dank righteousness
yet I welcomed them
as my life had taught me to do
to my house under the trees by the harbor
where they stared with disgust
at the images of the faith of my childhood
at my wives at the petals our children
at the wine they were offered and the naked
grapes ripening outside in the sunlight
as we are told they once ripened in Canaan

I know these same guests will have me carried
by converts when my time comes
and will hail over me the winter of their words
it is true enough my spirit
would claim no place in their hereafter
having clung as I see now
like furs and fragrance to the long summer
that tastes of skin and running juice

I wanted the whole valley for a garden
and the fruits of all the earth growing there
I sent for olive and laurel endives and rosemary
the slopes above the stream nodded with oranges
lemons rolled among the red sugar cane
my vineyard girt about with pineapples
and bananas gave me two harvests a year
and I had herbs for healing since this is not heaven
as each day reminded me and I longed still for a place
like somewhere I thought I had come from

the wharf reaches farther and farther
into the harbor this year and the vessels
come laden from Canton and Guayaquil
I nurse the dying queens and the dropsical minister
I look with late astonishment at all my children
in the afternoon pearls from the inland sea
are brought to revolve one by one between my fingers

I hold each of them up to the day as I
have done for so long and there are the colors
once more and the veiled light I am looking for
warm in my touch again and still evading me

Writing Lives
for Leon Edel

Out of a life it is done
and without ever knowing
how things will turn out

or what a life is for that matter
any life at all
the leaf in the sunlight the voice in the day
the author in the words

and the invisible
words themselves
in whose lives we appear
and learn to speak
until what is said seems
to be almost everything
that can be known

one way with the words is to tell
the lives of others
using the distance as a lens

and another way
is when there is no distance
so that water
is looking at water

as when on a winter morning
as early as you can remember
while the plains were whitening
in the light before dawn

you saw your uncle—was it
your uncle?—reach
from the shadow and wash his face

to us it is clear
that if a single moment could be seen
complete it would disclose the whole

there is still that light in the water
before sunrise
the untold day

The Hill of Evening

You will remember I think through the crowd
of events there how quietly the days
pass here on this hill where the two houses
most of the year seem to be the whole
of the inhabited world

at your last visit I was still living
in part of the big house above the steep
meadow with the old couple and their grown
children but we walked one afternoon
down the overgrown cart lane

through the woods and I showed you the smaller
empty house by the pasture where I live
now when I am here the windows facing
out from the trees onto the open hill
that falls away to the stream

we were talking of ambitions and age
and of change and I have come to think
of each age I should tell you as a season
always complete in itself as the days
here seem sometimes to be all

evening the hour when if you remember
we looked up from the lane in the first
twilight and saw the fine single stroke
of the new moon drifting across the valley
which is why I am writing to you

today a Sunday the day of visits
rare though they are on the hill but this morning
brought an old man on his way up the lane
to the big house who wanted to look in
here where he had known someone

in his youth and he sat till noon talking
of a time before I was born the encounters
in the lane the racing hearts the hayloads
the dancing all night in the valley and
walking back before daybreak

and then we went up the lane together
to the old woman's birthday party I
do not recall having seen so many
gathered there even at funerals and
today such triumphant celebration

as at a wedding flowers everywhere
long tables covered with white cloths under
the lime trees and the meal went on for hours
with the toasts the speeches and one by one
the old standing up in the waving

shadows of the leaves with a hush rising
around them and then from a distance their
voices approaching with moments out of
somewhere invisible to most of us
but still clear to some and indeed

what they still see around us and at last
the music of the roofer's accordion
and two violins with songs the old woman
asked for and a few of the middle-aged
got up and began the old dances

then the old were dancing and even the young
joined in laughing all circling to the one
time the tunes repeating over and over
nobody wanting them ever to stop
and the faces flushed the eyes wide

with surprise asking is it possible
is it happening and then it was over
they sat breathless or wandered off and when
I had said my farewells as formally
as though I lived far away

I started back down the lane for by then
it was already evening already
twilight and of course I was thinking again
of age and of what in each season seems
just out of reach just beyond what

is in front of us a kind of ghost
of what we see to which we offer up our days
and when you were here I could see that you hoped
I would have something to say to you about
all that and it was then that we

looked up to see the thin moon now this evening
there was no moon but in the long summer
grass to the right of the lane as I came
I saw a shining crescent a new sickle
bright as water and the blade

glittering with the dew and I stood there
as startled as the faces of the dancers
not knowing whose it could be how it had
come to be there what I was to do
with it now that I had seen it

leave it where it was to rust in the grass
and perhaps as I thought for a moment
to disappear to be really lost although
as you know no one steals anything here
and it must have been partly to see

whether it was really there that I reached down
and picked it up cool as the dripping grass
to carry home and lay on the table
here in front of me and tomorrow I must
try to find who it belongs to

Barn

In a cold May travelling alone across
stony uplands all afternoon the echoes
lengthening with the light and the tattered
crows exploding from their voices above
bare scrub oaks and jagged sloes each clutching
its fissured rock the wandering ruins
of pasture walls orchard enclosures rooms

and stairs of stone houses sinking into
thickets out of the late day like huddled sheep
still haunting shadows came the time to find
somewhere for the night and in that country
what had been built by hands to stand longest
outlasting the builders and their knowledge
was the barns set far apart from each other

emerging unpredictably from sides
of hollows as though from hiding but where
could creatures of such proportions have been
hidden on those swept barrens yet each
was nowhere to be seen until one came
by surprise upon a stone roof like a hill
half under trees a knuckled ridge a steep

starved slope descending to massive slabs
of eaves and on to buttresses shouldering
the low wall in which one square of night
a head taller than a man and an arm's length
wider than a man could reach an entry
framed in single hewn stones from which the doors
were long forgotten led in out of the dusk

in the vaulted ceiling there were stars already
and in the walls long portraits of lightning
coursing down to the ledges of empty
mangers but the wind was at once somewhere
from which a body had fallen and all
the hollow shadow echoed the absence
of breath the dumbness that had enfolded

at last the animals and the sighing
hay altogether with every voice that the
builders had harkened to and then the hushed
herders who had abandoned before the day
ended this dim hall this hill of stone
to which a foreigner would come at evening
and lie thinking of another country

Rimbaud's Piano

Suddenly at twenty-one
with his poems already behind him
his manuscripts fed to the flames two years
since and his final hope
in the alchemy of the word buried
deep under the dust that chased his blown

soles through Europe and the fine
snows that spun into his slurring footsteps
in the passes southward to Italy
his shoes even then no
longer laced with lyre strings and his fingers
penniless once more then Italy

and its kind widow fading
backward into the darkness and hungers
of London Verlaine's retching and sobbing
the days of the Commune
his Paris dawns bursting for the first time
like poison promising through his blood

there he was back again at
Mother's after all at Mother's and not
even the farm at Roche with its crippled
barn where at least he could
have Hell to himself but the dank little
house on the crabbed street in Charleville

tight curtained like a series
of sickrooms the dimness reeking of walls
and waiting of camphor and vinegar
old bedding and the black
boards of Mother from which he kept turning
to the other door though outside it

there was nothing but Charleville
which he had left he thought and kept leaving
his pockets full of nothing but pages
now from dictionaries
Arabic Hindustani Greek Russian
he was learning them all and teaching

German to the landlord's son
with winter coming on trying to turn
some words into money into numbers
where the future lay but
there must be something to which the numbers
were still witness the harmony

that Pythagoras had called
music in whose continuo the light
burst into bodies knowing everywhere
the notes that were their way
those numbers that were their belonging and
Mother he told her I must have a

piano a piano
he said to her with her blue regard whose
husband had left her and the four children
both daughters sickly one
dying one son from the beginning good
for nothing and this other in whom

she had scrubbed brushed and buttoned
the last of her hopes for this world this one
who had been so good marching before her
to Mass and had won all
the prizes at school this one with the eyes
of ice who could have been anything

and instead had found nothing
better to do than run away like his
brother leaving her and the girls beside
the river telling them
that he was going for a book indeed
and taking the train for Paris with

no ticket letting her guess
what had happened to him with the Germans
advancing on Charleville and her breathless
from door to door searching
in cafes asking for him and all night
rummaging the street looking for him

not for the last time and he
already in the hands of the police
and bad company no wonder after
those books he had brought home
all his studies for nothing wandering
like a tramp with that other and now

a piano and Verlaine
to whom he wrote answered with that vomit
of piety perfected in prison
making it clear that this
long pretext for a loan was merely one
more trick to obtain money whereas

etcetera so he carved
a keyboard on the dining room table
for practising scales on while he listened
to his pupil's untuned
German and hearkened beyond them both
to the true sound until his mother

out of concern for the
furniture hired a piano which came
on a cart like part of a funeral
to be cursed through the door
as a camel and into its corner
thence to awaken the echoes of

Pythagoras as written
by Mademoiselle Charpentier in her
exercises for the pianoforte
borrowed from the Charleville
choirmaster her notations of those same
intervals that told the distances

among the stars wherefore
they sang stumbling over and over bruised
and shaky all that winter through the sour
rooms while his sister lay
dying while the doors were draped with mourning
before Christmas while the snow fell black

out of the death of the year
into the new the splintered ivory
far from its own vast sufferings sinking
into him daily its
claims so that by spring when he had acquired
a certain noisy proficiency

and the roads melted again
before him into visions of Russia
arches of Vienna faces of thieves
the waiting hands once more
of the police with somewhere beyond them
all a south and its peacock islands

its deserts and the battered
instrument was given up to become
a camel again patient on its own
pilgrimage to the end
of the elephants and its separate
molecules orbiting through unseen

stellar harmonies the drummed
notes of that winter continued to ring
in the heads that heard them they rose through
the oilcloth and the fringed
embroidery that hid the carved keyboard
they echoed the closing of the door

they spiralled after his steps
on the slave routes and slipped out of the first
words of letters from Africa useless
unwelcomed and unloved
without beginning like the trailing knock
of the artificial legs made for

his lost one but never used
heard by no others like the choir of eight
with five principal singers and twenty
orphans who bore candles
at his funeral and meaning nothing
else like the lives through which they sounded

Among Bells

At the top of the dark
emerging from one more upward turn
on stones hollowed by feet so far ahead
that nothing of them would ever
be known

into the surprising
light still as glass around the green furred
hillsides of the bells as into a new
day fulfilling some forgotten
promise

lucid and with columns
beyond which bright clouds were travelling

almost within reach and the mountains rose
over the roofs of a foreign
city

a square with red tables
down there under dusty sycamores
Yugoslav flags kiosks posters loud in
Cyrillic across the flaking
facades

that contained the winding
streams of hats horses piled carts arms buses
making their way to and from the bevelled
lid of the train station with its
white clock

telling for each of them
a different age at the same time
even for the ancient belfry in which
the hour hovered as though nothing
that breathed

were living up under
its vaulted stone ceiling filled with beams
and the bronze domes of the bells but above
one of the blackened cornices
the wind

ruffled the shadowy
edges of a muted luster not
of stone a burnished swelling in the dust
some jewel of the air hiding
in air

quiet as a carving
a smooth wing of a swift so
still that nothing except wind seemed to move
in its feathers no flash of eye
betrayed

life in it the stiff quills
of course cold to the touch but then the
fine unseen softness above the spine warm
the hollow at the nape too and
the breast

yet all without motion
like a bundle with no weight at all
when lifted down the head drawn in eyes shut
feet curled tight upon nothing but
themselves

late in a cold summer
of dank grasses and dying forests
the taste of Lethe even in the mists
above the river and of burning
always

high in the air around
the towers above roofs among trees
dark by then with the knowledge of autumn
that bitterness climbing the air
from which

the feathers seemed to have
come so freshly no sign of blood no
visible injury the bill gleaming
like a chip of twilight the feet
perfect

the wings before they could
be seen to flash suddenly vanished
out of the cradling palms to reappear
trembling on the stone balustrade
one eye

for a moment glancing
back as a black planet after which
it was gone with a shriek into the long
afternoon light that touched the net
of wires

the waiting aerials
bare poles lines of laundry chimney flues
patched roofs pots of geraniums windows
standing open while in the streets
the same

hats legs and wagons were
moving toward unchanged destinations
and at the station trains were arriving
on time without a sound and just
leaving

Search Party

By now I know most of the faces
that will appear beside me as
long as there are still images
I know at last what I would choose
the next time if there ever was
a time again I know the days
that open in the dark like this
I do not know where Maoli is

I know the summer surfaces
of bodies and the tips of voices
like stars out of their distances
and where the music turns to noise
I know the bargains in the news
rules whole languages formulas
wisdom that I will never use
I do not know where Maoli is

I know whatever one may lose
somebody will be there who says
what it will be all right to miss
and what is verging on excess
I know the shadows of the house
routes that lead out to no traces

many of his empty places
I do not know where Maoli is

You that see now with your own eyes
all that there is as you suppose
though I could stare through broken glass
and show you where the morning goes
though I could follow to their close
the sparks of an exploding species
and see where the world ends in ice
I would not know where Maoli is

Missing

Last seen near the closing newsstand
outside the cigar store angled
at that notorious corner
where some hasten past with eyes
downcast or with gaze clinging
to nothing beyond the propped
stacks of sooty rags settled
on headwaters of dark

rivers at the top of the steps
to the downtown subway while
some dressed for the breaks
in gleaming black revolve their
deliberate invitations
some circle menacing and one
who has been wrung through a long
life into garments with no size

will be delving whenever it is
through the piled cage of garbage
searching for anything all of them
backlit by store windows
arrayed with faded umbrellas
elderly luggage dust-filled

sunglasses portraits of foreign
beauties from other eras wreathed

in gold suggesting a good
smoke this hand suddenly
there thrust forth palm up out of what
had seemed to be nowhere one
more after so many but this
surprisingly clean and in
that light looking as though it
belonged to someone familiar

almost recognizable
and out of place there the eyes
in the bare youthful face filled
with terror disbelief tears
out of the mouth nothing while the hand
trembling from its recent launching
among those shadows kept floating
away from a figure

oh height somewhat less than average
age perhaps thirty or
thirty-five hair blond cropped short clean
eyes no color at that hour but
no doubt blue cheeks pink and clean
body slight but not thin wearing
a short-sleeved striped jersey
clean his feet in white jogging shoes

beside him on a leash his
small part-shepherd bitch well fed brushed
answering to the name Bowama
looking up expecting kindness
standing on hind legs at the sound
of her name to look at his face
happy to be with him and sure
that everything would be all right

Paul

Up the sea-dark avenue
at two in the morning a shadow
comes shouting oh
you mother-fucker I hate you Paul
echoes of feet and then
I hate you I hate you Paul

the old moon is sinking through
clouds beyond high wires and cornices
the buildings creak
drifting on the tunnelled hour the call
bounces ahead along
the street like a fleeing ball

there after each of the few
cars has passed over its words Paul you
can't get away
I hate you with my feet in the Paul
street like a bell I know
you are there you nowhere Paul

I am coming after you
whatever you do whatever you
think I hate you
across the street into the doors all
the way through the frozen
windows up against the wall

listen to me I hate who
you are nobody else will ever
hate you the way
I do I always hated you Paul
the whole time thinking you
could hold out on me that small

invisible you but to
me listen there was nothing to you
I was onto
you fooling with me your slick tricks all

the while and I hate you
where you are everywhere Paul

I go on hating you through
the roar of the Paul subway the red
lights at the Paul
cross streets out of sight into the Paul
night that cannot be touched
and does not turn when I call

Kites

No one who did not have to
would stay in the heaving sepia
roar of the unlit depot hour
after hour as some do
shoved and elbowed in the hot
breath of a rotting mouth yet there are
women sitting on the cement floor
suckling babies and among

the shoes that are never still
down under the shouting and the thin
flickering of hands burning and
going out there are some
of all ages sleeping as they
wait to be overtaken and to
wake at their time and find themselves housed
in white boards on the bench

of the almost empty car
while outside the gray windows that face
into the cooked air of the city
they see close beside them
a new life with afternoon light
shimmering as though reflected from
water along the dusty walls and
on green weeds glittering

then already before the
walls begin to slip there are the square
pieces of color in the tan
sky skipping and soaring
those small kites with invisible strings
that will beckon as guides for
so much of the way reappearing
over the first vacant

rubble fields and the children
running with raised arms in the distance
then over the scalped hill with its
family of shadows
breathless against the sky looking up
to the spirits dancing far
above them that must feel like their own
appearing to need no

wind at all to be leaping
high above the white layer of smoke
that covers what is called the world
and to be waiting with
others above the dark trees beyond
a ringing bridge a river
too slow to be real a path along
the low bank through the shade

and they keep turning to look
down from their clearer place onto roofs
at the rims of green terraces
braided houses a man
by himself planting while the hens on
the dump smoking at the end
of a lane search among waving ghosts
of translucent plastic

and all the way to the hills
and into the mountains the kites will be
watching from their own element
as long as the light lasts

neither living as the living know
of it nor dead with the dead
and neither leaving nor promising
the hands that hope for them

A Distance

I would not go to such a place
the young overweight doctor said
raising his needle to the fluorescent hour
a boy running on the grass path
between flat pieces of light is holding
high something he has caught
that leaps and flashes in the sudden

late brightness of its life scarcely
do the ducks along the bank step
out of the way and the man standing
bent almost to the surface in
the water does not look up
from his reflection in which he is placing
one green stalk a straight thin strand

of smoke is rising from a white
pile on the far side of the water
by the hand-plastered tombs where hens
bow in the shade of banana leaves
beyond them tile roofs palm crowns bamboo walls
clusters of white columns what
are you holding above your head child

where are you taking it what does it know

The Morning Train

In the same way that the sea
becomes something else the moment we
are on it with its horizon all around
us and its weight
bearing us up so a journey seems not
to be one as long as we are

travelling but instead we
are awake sitting still at a bare
window that is familiar to us but not
in truth ours as
we know and facing us there is a line
of socks hanging in the sunlight

over a patch of onions
blue in their summer luminous rows
of carrots the youth of lettuces to be
glimpsed once only
dahlias facing along a white painted
picket fence beside a plum tree

at the side of a station
like so many into which the green
revolving woods pointing fields brief moments of
rivers bridges
clusters of roof again and again have
turned slowing first and repeating

their one gesture of approach
with a different name out of the place
of names a clock on which the hour changes
but not of course
the day arrangements of figures staring
through the last stages of waiting

only there is nothing on
the platform now but the morning light
the old gray door into the station is

standing open
in a silence through which the minute hand
overhead can be heard falling

while a hen is talking to
herself beyond the fence and why are
we not moving what are we waiting for now
only the hum
in our ears continuing to tell us
that we have been travelling since

whatever day it was that
city with its tower and there was
the night with its iron ceilings echoing
couplings through the
shunted hours in the all night restaurant
between trains then the socks begin

to slip away on their line
the garden swings softly behind its
fence and in a few hours when we think we are
almost home at
last we will look up through the pane across
a stony field plowed since we left

rusting at noon and the same
flowers will be leaning on the south
wall of the house from which we have watched the trains
pass and we will
see clearly as we rush by all of its
empty windows filled with the sea

Fulfilment

The way the smoke
blew away and the tread of vagrant
stars through the nights of autumn
white wings out of season and raw calls when

the ice broke these were
predictions and at times we knew what they
told us was approaching

but what could we
do to prevent a day from ending
or a winter from finding
us how could we stop a wind with no home
from sliding into
our sleep or keep our parents from death
or ourselves from leaving

though we said to
the animals look how we taste you
with reverence the gut for
continuing in warmth through all the
snows the heart to flare
high in us look how you give yourselves
to us and we eat of

you only our
small days may you be many and we
here like the unceasing
water only the last foretelling was
already the touch
among us that we could not yet see
it seized us without our

knowing that it
was near us it approached in shapes most
familiar to us it breathed
out of the animals and we grew faint
and believed they had
betrayed us then the strangers appeared with
their new ways of killing

which they exchanged
for skins of animals we thought were
no longer our family

so we pursued those swift spirits like fire
until they had turned
to smoke blown away and the world where we
had known them had turned to smoke

blowing away
then elders children old friends beside
fires had walked into a night
few of us drifted through a time of year
we had never seen
without leaves or color and we could hear
rendings and echoes that seemed

to cry out of
us as we were departing the world
of the strangers but we were
learning at last that we were still a word
of the prophecy
though some of us lived to see it begin
to happen finally

nobody will
remember you they said *nobody*
will believe you ever stood
in the daylight no one will wish to know
what we did to you
only in our words will anyone hear
what we choose to say of you

and it is true
they are what they forget and they make
records of all they are not
they turn themselves into a sky of smoke
before the next wind
wherever they go they race farther from
home in a night that opens

without end when
summer is done and the last flocks have

vanished and from the sleepless
cold of the unremembered river that
one voice keeps rising
to be heard once once only once but there
is nobody listening

The Lost Camellia of the Bartrams

All day
the father said we rode
through swamps
seeing tupelo

cypress standing in deep water
and on higher ground palmettos
mingling with pine
deer

and turkeys moving under
the boughs
and we dined by a swamp on bread
and a pomegranate

with stands of canna near us
then poor timber for maybe a mile
of the lowland which
often the river

overflows to the great
loss of those who live there
we lost our way
and that was the day

we found that
tree with the beautiful
good fruit
nameless which I

found never again
it was then
already advanced autumn and the grass
exceeding tall

sand hills along the river
you see
only once whatever
you may say

winter
had passed maybe twelve
times over the wide
river lands

before the son
returned to those regions
when it was spring
and that same tree

was in perfect bloom while
bearing even at that season its
woody apples he said
and the flowers

were of the first order for
beauty and fragrance
very large and white as snow
with a crown or

tassel of
radiant gold stamens
the lower petal cupped
around the others

until it allowed them to unfold
and the edges of all the petals
remaining waved or folded
each flower

set in the bosom of broad leaves
never
the son said did we find
that tree growing

wild anywhere else
so it was fortunate
that he gathered seed and cuttings
and took them

away to bring on
in gardens for
by the time he was fifty
it had vanished from

its own place altogether
only surviving here and there
as a cultivated
foreigner

After Douglas

I could not have believed how my life would stop
all at once and slowly like some leaf in air
and still go on neither turning nor
        falling any more

nor changing even as it must have been
all the while it seemed to be moving
away whatever we called it chiefly
        to have something

to call it as people of the trees call
me Grass Man Grass Man Grass Man having heard that
from me and I neither turn nor am stirred
        but go on

after a sound of big stones to which I
woke as they opened under the hammer
my father and now they always lie open
    with the sound going

out from them everywhere before me like
the bell not yet heard announcing me once
for the one time but not as a name unless
    perhaps as my

name speaks of trees and trees do not know it
standing together with my brothers
and sisters my five senses in all their
    different ages

I see in the eyes of my first birds
where I am coming along this path
in the garden among glass houses
    transparent

walls and now my eyes are perfect finally
I think I must see China but
it is still the New World as I have heard
    there is the mouth

of the wide river that I know as
the Amazon there are tall bitter seas
sharp stones on the ocean the green pelt
    of the northern

continent sinuous to the shore line
and so deep that I reach out my hand to touch it
and feel that I am air moving along
    the black mosses

only now I am in haste no more
anger has vanished like a lantern in daytime
I cannot remember who was carrying it
    but each dried

form that was lost in the wide river is
growing undiscovered here in shadows
the mown rye continues to stand breathless
    in long summer light

gulls flash above sea cliffs albatross
bleats as a goat I see that the lives one by one
are the guides and know me yes and I
    recognize

each life until I come to where I forget
and there I am forgetting the shoes
that I put on and the mountain that I
    have climbed before

there I go on alone without waiting and
my name is forgotten already into
trees and there is McGurney's house that I
    have forgotten

and McGurney telling me of the dug
pits on the mountain and there unchanged
is the forgotten bull standing on whatever
    I had been

Cinchona

Where that fever itself
hailed from is hid in the original
warming of the unknown
but fever could there be none nor night sweats
numbered agues aestivo-autumnal chills
the conception of evil in the air
until the blood was there to bear them
and where

the blood hailed from the keen
tenor of Anopheles began its
tracery climbing from

water as the blood had done but in time
raising the high note of its inherited
pursuit of a living body within
whose blood to plant a parasite like
a flag

even harder to guess
how the red bark came into its virtues
or for what purposes
of its own it had preserved those magic
properties sovereign against some fever
far in the future restorer
of a blood that for ages would not yet
be there

or how its powers came
first to be known to one who needed them
suffering near the tree
though surely there were stories about that
later which were true to those only for whom
the tree could speak and which made no
sense to those who believed in the words of
Europe

at the age when the flags
carried their hectic over the ocean
westward from Spain from France
from England and the rest and the place was
possessed of them but when the first blood lettings
and convulsions were history
in Peru the wife of the Viceroy
Countess

of Chinchon lay stricken
with that fever of unknown origin
and boundless ambition
that by then seemed endemic everywhere
consuming her daily with its marauding
investiture until she was
merely warm ruins of the woman she
had been

but after so many
in the grip of that delirium had
passed into its homeland
her number completed some long tally
at which point a message for her physician
arrived enclosing red bark ripped
from a tree in those mountains and telling
its use

so when it had given
back her life the tree all at once was seen
as something of value
like gold and with her name it was christened
and though bitter its taste it was sought stripped shipped
to be sold in Spain carried by
missionaries defended fought over
killed for

two centuries and more
before another message this time in
English in Ecuador
found Richard Spruce fresh from the tree's heartland
that fed the Amazon and from his pursuit
there of mosses and liverworts
that still eluded what he thought of as
knowledge

and Spruce with his mouth still
wise to the daily taste of that powdered
bark and his mind tangled
in strands of the long story of seizures
and incursions Columbus cholera the
cross the Countess opened and read
of his commission for the sake of the
empire

British of course to bring
about the transfer from the Cinchona's
flayed and rummaged highlands
of seeds and seedlings of the preferred strains

to be planted in India achieving
thus for England what Hasskarl had
effected recently on Java for
the Dutch

not just what Spruce with his
dubious health and his devotion to
unknown flora rather
than species of a purely economic
importance which when powdered amazing fine
in a chemist's mortar he said
were bereft of almost all their allurement
for him

would have chosen for his
next excursion and he could have mentioned
Hasskarl's own holding back
from an undertaking in which routine
dangers had been compounded by fierce local
jealousy and the officials'
concern for their monopoly of those
raw trees

alerted as they were
to the Dutch scheme so Hasskarl in Peru
calling himself German
signing up with the government there to make
a survey east of the mountains where they hoped
to colonize and there sorting
his seeds and starting them on their furtive
journey

and four years later
Markham trying it for England with his
English gardener his
native boy and two mules the purpose of
his mission discovered his acquaintance with
Peruvian jails his crossing
the Andes alone in winter keeping
ahead

of everyone as it
seemed by then and in that cold fearing for
the lives of the tender
seedlings but at last contriving to get
the frost-bitten survivors to India
where the beds were prepared for them
and they were planted with every care and
soon died

it would be harder for
Spruce he expected and there were besides
wars going on in those
parts and the behavior that wars nourished
and his preparations were scarcely begun
before he was sick again deaf
in left ear unable to walk or sit
without

great pain but he kept on
forming an expedition planning it
still sick when they set out
from Ambato for the mountains where they
would meet the others assemble the rest of
the equipment discover
on reaching the Cinchonas that there were
nowhere

in that plundered region
seedlings remaining so that besides those
hundred thousand seeds he
sorted it seemed to him necessary
to make cuttings and there on the spot contrive
shaded beds to be kept watered
by hand to root them then pack them in earth
they knew

and into baskets for
the muleback journey over the mountains
then into cases on
the raft rigged up for the trip down the rough

river which under heavy rains turned savage
a narrow sluice between snatching
thickets the current at bends smashing them
three times

into the bank with such force
that the cabin collapsed and their pilot
once was swung by a branch
over the roaring water and they could
not reconstruct afterward what they had done
stunned in the sound of the river
to work themselves free into a quiet
passage

opening like a gate
and as the day was ending a place to
put in and begin to
grope through the splintered bodies of trees
that had saved their lives and to feel the cases
of cuttings as though they were touching bones
of their own after a fall and to find
them all

there under the fragile
covers upright and unharmed the small leaves
glowing white while the moon
rose into that night of the dying year
on the river that had become a silence
around them in which they could hear
as they straightened in the moonlight hardly
a word

they said to each other
of all their labors destined in fact to reach
India and once more
be planted and come to nothing and for
a moment there they could not recall what had
driven them all their lives to that
white shore what questions what undetermined
fever

Inheritance

As many as four thousand
varieties of the opulent pear
it has been said (although
in some languages that number merely
indicates great multitude)
were to be found barely a century
ago treasured and attended somewhere
in fields and gardens of France
that had been cleared of oaks once

and whatever else may have
preferred to grow there the spaces plowed up walled
amended with ashes
dung beans blood and handled with arts passed from
enclosure to enclosure
by a settled careful cunning people
who compared their seedlings and on wild stock
or the common quince grafted
those rare exceptional strains

whose names told no longer this
many a day of lucky otherwise
forgotten Monsieur who
came on this jewel hanging in a hedge
nor of that pharmacist who
in the spring presented his pear blossoms with
feathers plucked from his geese bearing gold dust
he had destined for marriage
with each and waited to taste

their fruit until he obtained
one he thought worthy of his name nothing
of that orchard in which
such a one appeared situated then
at the end of a village

now long since buried in a city nor
recalled one thing of those whose origins
had gone the way of the leaves
and flowers however they

may have been immortalized
each name came to drip all by itself through
the hearing of children its
syllables ripe with anticipation
honeyed and buttered with praise
weighted down with a sensuous longing for
a season overflowing with golden
skins to be cupped in the palm
and one at a time lifted

away so many and so
sweet when their moment came that after it
for all the preserves liqueurs
pies and perries contrived to prolong it
always it was a life lost
and reached for by the abandoned senses
anguished at having failed it again though
juices had run to the elbow
while the next was coveted

for a blush on a tender
cheek and each one was relished for its brief
difference at last there were
simply too many and around the blurred
taste the names of the fruit sank
through the air useless as the drunken wasps
furring with sound the unidentified
remains the late the fallen
bodies so variously

yet so inadequately
known a single kind in one village called
ten different ways none telling
rightly the filling of the hand the rush

of high day to the tongue none
doing more than point in passing among
so many so hopelessly many as
indeed their variety
seemed toward the century's end

to that jury picked no one
remembers how all men and none of them
young to say just how many
kinds of pears should exist in France and when
that was done to place in their
mouths one after the other the proposed
fruit no doubt in sections and thereupon
solemnly chew over each
candidate and vote on it

considering modestly
their ripest deliberations to be
scarcely more than a helpful
preliminary and looking forward
to a day when the tangled
boughs of proliferating nature bent
with its reckless diversity of wild
pears from the Himalayas
to the Straits of Hercules

and the accumulated
riot of human wishes fortune and
art grafted upon them might
be brought within reasonable limits
according to a few clear
standards on a scale of one to ten they
reduced each bite of pear in the darkness
of their mouths and all they could
say of what they held there was

a mumble of numbers through
moustache and napkin meaning whatever

they had agreed the numbers
would mean but the true taste each time slipped from
their tongues undivulged never
to be recalled it made no difference
whether it was blessed with their approval
on its way and elected
to return in its season

for the delectation of
us far in the future or whether it
was relegated to that
blank catalogue compiled from our sweeping
erasures everything they
savored is gone like a candle in a
tunnel and now it was always like this
with our tongues our knowledge and
these simple remaining pears

The Day Itself
(Harvard Phi Beta Kappa Poem, 1989)

Now that you know
everything does it not come even so
with a breath of surprise the particular
awaited morning in summer
when the leaves that you walked under
since you saw them unfold out of nothing whether
you noticed that or not into

the world you know
have attained the exact weave of shadow
they were to have and the unrepeatable
length of that water which you call
the Charles the whole way to its end
has reached the bridge at last after descending and
gathering its own color through

all that you know
and is slipping under the arches now
while the levelled ground embraced by its famous
facades the ordinary place
where you were uncertain
late moonstruck cold angry able to imagine
you had it all to yourself to

use and to know
without thinking much about it as though
it were the real you suddenly shines before
you transformed into another
person it seems by the presence
of familiar faces all assembled at once
and a crowd of others you do

not really know
rippling in the shimmer of daylight row
upon row sending up a ceaseless leafy
shuffle of voices out of the
current that is rushing over
the field of common chairs one of them opened here
at the moment only for you

and you should know
who that is as the man some time ago
in Greece you remember is supposed to have
said and there was that other of
his countrymen about whom we
are certain of little who was sure already
without having met you that you

could get to know
you whoever that is if you were so
inclined which indeed you may not have been on
days of uncomfortable dawn
with recognitions bare of their
more proper perspectives and the phrase goes further
to suggest that perhaps you do

not in fact know
you in the first place but might have to go
looking for you when here you are after all
in the skin of the actual
day dressed and on time and you are
sure that you are in the right seat and behind your
own face now is the you that you

wanted to know
is it not and you feel that you have no
age at all but are the same you that you were
as long as you can remember
while every decision that you
made or thought you were making was conducting you
straight to this seat and to what you

would come to know
as today in the middle of which no
other you it seems is present furthermore
what influenced each of your
choices all of the accidents
as they are called and such chances as your parents'
meeting on their own before you

were here to know
where you were coming from those joys with no
histories those crimes painted out those journeys
without names the flawless courses
of all the stars the progression
of the elements were moving in unison
from what you had never seen to

what you now know
you were so long looking forward to no
wonder it floats before you appearing at
once inevitable and not
yet there so that you are unsure
that this time you are awake and will remember
it all assembled to show you

what you must know
by now about knowledge how it also
is a body of questions in apparent
suspension and no different
from the rest of the dream save that
we think we can grasp it and it tends to repeat
itself like the world we wake through

while as you know
it has its limits it belongs to no
one it cannot bring you love or keep you from
catching cold from tomorrow from
loss or waiting it can stand in
its own way so that however you stare you can
not see things about it that you

do in fact know
perfectly well the whole time and can so
loom that you cannot look past it which is more
important you have to acquire
it for yourself but for that you need
gifts and words of others and places set aside
in large part for informing you

until you know
all this which of course may render you no
kinder or more generous since that is not
its function or at least not right
away and may not only make
you no wiser but make it sound wiser to mock
the notion of wisdom since you

have come to know
better and in some cases it can go
to your head and stay there yet we are all here
to speak well of it we treasure
something about it or we say
we do beyond the prospect of making money
and so on with it something you

certainly know
of it that has led to its being so
often compared to the light which you see all
around you at the moment full
of breath and beginnings how well
you know what that is and soon you will start to tell
us and we will listen to you

Lives of the Artists

It was when the school had burned down that he
started making the book
early in the year at the time the moons
of snow were beginning to wane in hollows
out on the plain he had come back to
last year as though it were home bringing
the name they had dressed him in
he was sleeping

in the loft where all of the boys were put
after the fire they slept
up over the horses in the house of
the horses in the horse smell and all night they
heard horses breathing just below their
own breath and hooves in the dark in dry
grass then he began wanting
to make a book

of what he had seen and how it went on
he lay awake hearing
himself want to make pictures the right way
of what was and could not be found ever
again in the day in the steamy
yard of the agency with its panes
of vacant windows rattling
to their own light

a book with no parents since he had none
it would give for the dead
no names but might show some of the same birds
that were called differently in the true place
where he had been small the tails like split
smoke reflected and flights of white shields
and the buffalo would be there
as they appeared

to him the bulls thudding together like
mossy rocks so the ground
shook but how would he make the sound of their
running wake out of the lined pages of
the red ledger where he would draw them
and the rush of their breath as he kept
hearing it his friends would help
who were older

in the time of the buffalo and still
had names from there that you
could draw with a picture Horse-Back Dark Cloud
Black Wolf Hill Man whereas now for himself
how could you draw a Henderson what
was there anywhere that looked like a
Henderson there was only
a word for him

a Henderson in the night who had gone
away in a wagon
to learn to make wagons and who had shouted
"Baldy" with the others and who could read
the new language for the children but
who nursed the tapeworm and was never
content a bad element
always wanting

to go home he would draw friends in the book
with their true hair braided
to the ground before it was cut they would
be talking together in their richest

robes they would be riding off to battle
leading horses they would be singing
he would show the butterfly
of the thunder

on the white horse with birds bringing power
down and the green frog spread
on the dream shield no bullet could pass through
his friends would be chasing the blue soldiers
off the page he would show the ground where
they fought at Adobe Walls the guns
from the houses the hoofprints
going around

and the fight would not be done so his friends
would still be riding in
the open with nothing touching them and
he would still be a boy at home hungry
in summer who had not heard them tell
how it ended how they would fight no
more and none of them would have
been taken yet

far away to the tall fences nowhere
in the south the waiting
nowhere and the days there and the nights there
the strange moon the new hunger they had no
words for and he would have years before
the wagons changed him and he came back
to meet Reverend Haury
who always knew

better and made him a bright Indian
teaching with white words but
in the drawings he would have the dancers
who could dance everything backward they would
dance in the book he would send to Miss
Underwood before his twenty-third
year and his death of causes
no one bothered

to name with so many of them dying
whatever they died of
and then there was only the book and he
had never met Little Finger Nail his
elder by a few years only who
had been herded south to the fences
with the rest of the Cheyennes
when the spiders

had lied to them again and had led them
down nowhere in their turn
but who had seen that he could not live there
and had said it would be better to die
trying to go home and had started
north at night with others of his mind
when the first leaves were turning
he who was their

singer with the Singing Cloud who would be
his wife and her dying
father and the children who had learned to
be quiet and the mothers and the men with
bows and guns knowing that by morning
they must be gone like a summer and
that they were leaving without
the few things in

the world that might protect them the sacred
arrows the sacred hat
and would have only the horizon of
each day to hide in yet he knew they must
not wait for the old power any
longer but must find their own in their
going as his hand often
had drawn out of

nothing the life they could no longer see
the horses flying and
arrows flying and never coming down
the long lances reaching ahead and not

yet touching a thing the war feathers
trailing behind and the dark stars that
were bullets and you could see
by the shields and

what they wore who was there in the fighting
riding into the smoke
of the blue spiders all in a line and
who rode after the spiders to shoot them
off their horses and leave them scattered
on the ground and who took their guns their
coats and bugles he Little
Finger Nail could

make it appear again and again in
pictures and after the
spiders came chasing them to bring them back
and shot at the chief Little Wolf standing
there talking with them and when they shot
a child a girl and in their turn were
driven back fewer and smaller than
they had come he

wanted to make a book of what he had
seen and would see on the
way home so that how they fought and went on
would be there after it was gone but he
must lose more friends to the spiders who
shot them on sight and he must come to
dream of walking in a world
all white before

at a place where one more time they had fought
off the spiders he found
waiting on the ground the book he had been
wishing for with the pages all white blown
open and the sticks of color lying
beside it for him to make into
how he saw them going and
before they crossed

the iron road and the first of the three
wide rivers he had tied
the book to his back with strips of rawhide
around him under his shirt so it was
there as he rode ahead and as he
peered out through bare brush on the low hills
as he circled back to coax
the spiders from

the trail as he fought as he mourned for friends
fallen as the horses
weakened and the first snow fell among them
as they hid without fires as the skin grew
loose over their bones as some crept out
to turn into scouts for the spiders
as the chiefs disagreed and
as they all said

goodbye while the snow fell and they went two
ways it was there as they
crouched in brush huts starving through blizzards and
were betrayed and surrounded and forced to
lay down the fifteen guns they could not
hide and the bows they had made it was
still there as they were herded
into the fort

where Crazy Horse had been murdered after
the promises and as
they were locked in it was there with the few
knives and the other guns they had managed
to hide and through the time of waiting
under guard there he could make parts of
their journey return across
the pages so

little remaining from the whole story
up until then and it
was tied to his back again in the cold
night when they dropped the guards with the first shots

and poured from the windows to the snow
then ran past the walls to the river
keeping together while the
bullets burrowed

into them and the horses came crashing
after them through the drifts
and those who got as far as the river
hid in the bluffs in the hard cold the blood
freezing on their wounds they lay still with
the dead children and women stunned by
loss and when morning whitened
and those who were

living found each other again it was
he Little Finger Nail
who led the last of them out of the ring
of watching spiders into the bitter
white of the hills but there is nothing
in the book except the blank pages
for the rest of it the last
hiding places

the last meat from the snow the last morning
in the hollow above
the empty river and the spiders massed
at the foot of the hill the last loading
of their guns as the roar of rifles
from below rolled toward them and over
the heads of the children and
of Singing Cloud

and the others his voice rose in the last
singing and some joined him
in the death song the men not as many
as twenty *I am going to die now*
if there is anything difficult
if there is anything dangerous
it is mine to do as the
spiders charged to

the breastwork to shoot down into any
still moving and even
then he rushed out at their fire with his knife
raised and they found afterward under his
shirt a book tied with strips of rawhide
to his back and the holes of two Sharps
rifle bullets almost in
the same place through

all its pages it was a colonel who
took it from the body
after what would be called the engagement
an account book stiff with blood and he kept
it for the pictures of which only
one can be seen now lying open
under glass beside other
examples in

the airless hall of the museum red
lines fly from the neck of
the horse on which the man with long braids is
racing and in the white sky are black stars
with black tears running down from them in
the lighted silence through which strangers
pass and some of them pause there
with all they know

Panes

If you get to a place where it happened
you know what you will find in your turn where
so many suddenly once saw the light
for the last time in a rush of sound no
hearing could survive one note swollen by
the whole roar all the shrieks shouts bellows of
the world you will be struck

first probably by how quiet it is
a kind of disappointment waiting for
you like a relative in the common
daylight on leaves and on houses facing
inwards and on the very stones where they
ran flinging up their eyes and fell and where
now you might say there is

nothing to see who were they when they were
there each of them carrying one secret
before they were forgotten as their eyes
drained away their shoes went on without them
their loose bones were dug up to be crumbled
and harrowed into fields and the causes
that had brought them there were

nowhere to be found who were they over
and over until lately their names were
lined in the dust of lists far from their lives
for a while tracks without feet and at last
the light that had directed wheel and fire
for killing found a way to use silver
to make the mirror hold

its image still and retain a picture
of stillness as perfect as that of glass
or silver only with the light reversed
as from the other side of what had once
been daylight so all that had seemed to be
brightest stands out in its open darkness
and it is the shadows

that brim with the stopped light of the moment
never in which nothing will ever move
in which you can see nothing happening
after it has happened and look over
the land where they are lying to the rags
of cloud their uniforms have turned into
the limbs frozen that way

skins of bare night backs of faces yawning
white none of them with names and the numbers
not touching them you can trace the dark wall
to which they had come so soon and the line
of white trees fractured at the wrists splaying
into the darkness which is the sky
for them all as they are

until they are developed and people
suddenly can see them for the first time
only in black and white but even so
among those who are used to such landscapes
in the flesh some say how real the figures
appear to be on their pages and these
go on like the others

peering as though they were hoping to find
a face they knew there or a form they might
have known they keep recognizing something
that is not there and it does not move but
stares without seeing them and continues
to gaze past them when they have turned away
and the book has been closed

never have pictures like those been seen on
paper and the editions multiply
for a while until everyone has had
enough of them and all the backgrounds look
old then it is afterward and the glass
plates are filed in the dark taking up space
with nobody knowing

what to do with them there are so many
and finally they are brought back into
the daylight and arranged in the roofs
of greenhouses so that morning reaches
through those exposed figures to the infant
leaves waiting in rows and draws them upward
as though summer had come

The Wars in New Jersey

This is the way we were all brought up now
we imagine and so we all tell
of the same place by saying nothing about it

nobody is ever walking on those black
battlefields and never have we set foot there
awake nor could we find our way across
the unmemorized streams and charred flats
that we roll through canned in a dream of steel
but the campaigns as we know we know
were planned and are still carried out for our sake

with our earnings and so near to us
who sail forward holding up our papers before us
while the towers rising from the ruins and the ruins
the acres of wrecked wheels the sinking
carriers the single limbs yet hanging
from the light fall away as we pass
in whose name it is being accomplished

all in a silence that we are a part of
that includes the casualties the names
the leaves and waters from the beginning
everything that ever lived there
the arguments for each offensive the reasons
and the present racing untouchable
foreground its gray air stitched with wires its lace

of bridges and its piled horizons flickering
between tanks and girders a silence
reaching far out of sight to regions half legend
where the same wars are burning now for us
about which we have just been reading something
when we look out and think no one is there
a silence from which we emerge onto the old
platform only a few minutes late
as though it were another day
in peacetime and we knew why we were there

A Short Nap on the Way

In the late
sun of autumn he is sitting alone
by the window the leaves are leaping
high and running beside the train
as though they were playing with a friend
they have grown up with
everything

about him
shows gray the thin face of a professor
administrator executive
the gaunt nose like a fold of paper
the eyes behind the gold-rimmed glitter
of his glasses each
perfect sleeve

of the suit
tailored so it appears to be empty
the silk tie the hands with their silent
pages along whose orderly
rows he is progressing even the
lips motionless as
an old wound

it must be
the sun finding him his eyelids fall shut
his head sinks back and somewhere he sees
colors he knows that come to meet
him slide over him and he does not
have to remember
their faces

to sense what
they are to him and to him only from
the beginning teasing frightening
him seducing him claiming him
through the badlands that are his unseen home
inside the shell of his
head looking

suddenly
childish the patched backs of buildings beside
the tracks flip past facing outward as
though each one were the true facade
they have been forgotten for the new dead
season their panes black
as ditches

by the fields
in October though piled up behind their
veteran weatherboards the brilliant
awnings and bright rags of summer
lie crumpled under dust in the dark where
children ran in for
a moment

to hide and
hearts drummed hands found their way into secret
countries roamed in secret and remain
afterward far off in the light
secret like the spring and summer now at
a small station with
no one on

the platform
two schoolgirls dressed in identical blue
uniforms get off like twins doing
everything together a few
steps away they stop and look around to
the cluttered roofs the
slow flapping

of the old
posters the bricks the streets disappearing
into sunlight this is not yet the
place where they know they are going
this is not the city that is waiting
really for them they
turn to see

each other
in the empty day and they cover their
mouths laughing and run as though something
is chasing them back from nowhere
onto the train where in a while the door
opens to a voice
repeating

a name and
the gray face tips forward into itself
finger bones open the gray briefcase
slip the papers into it lift
from the seat beside it the gray crown of
the narrow brimmed felt
hat that goes

with the rest
sporting one small dark feather far from its
bird he settles it firmly standing
and steps into the aisle and is
gone again taking with him what he wants
and all that he is
forgetting

The Moment of Green

So he had gone home to be shot
he kept telling himself trying
to explain what he was doing
grayed into the backs of shadows
behind walls he thought he had not
seen ever when he was awake
nor those uniforms though they spoke
in blunted fashions the Russian
of his youth the Ukrainian
even of his childhood and they
insisted they knew everything
about him yet went on asking

why he had come home to be shot
which they went on telling him he
seemed to have done and the answer
was something he could no longer
remember now that he was back
where the words had always known him
surely they must know he was not
a spy then what else had brought him
aged thirty five almost half way
around the world after all those
years when he seemed happy enough
to be away first the studies

at the French university
and when they were finished did he
come home he went the other way
out of Europe itself putting
a continent and an ocean
between himself and Malaia
Buromea the rippling grain
around Poltava wind lashing
the plains in winter mounds of beets
tobacco hanging in sunny
doorways the smells of cattleyards
leather and brewing and of parched

wood in the school room where he held
in his mind something of summer
away so far on the other
side of the year and his hand grew
pictures of her he traced the legs
of her grasses lengthening he
followed the lace of her veins to
find where they opened from he drew
the bees in her flowers and on
her leaves the cicada one of
her voices and the grasshopper
part cloud part paper who became

his guide through the dust and winter
and the tissues of days farther
and farther afield ticking through
libraries stations the glitter
of alien cities westward
into trees of strange talk until
he knew the leaves and tenants of
summer to be one as he was
one with the calling that found him
in his time and he followed it
across the Atlantic to its
source as Bates and Wallace had done

sixty years before and he came
as they had done to the river
of rivers moving eastward like
a sea heavy with light and birth
the one-shore river that men from
Europe had christened as it were
after women they had heard of
said to have come from somewhere near
his own homeland they called that flood
the River of Amazons and
he came to the port named by them
for Bethlehem though the bells clanged

from dockside iron and engines
at the railroad terminal more
urgently than from the churches
already old there in the high
days of the rubber bubble when
hour after hour in the harbor
the hulls gave up their marble fresh
from the hills of Carrara for
more boulevards more plazas more
fountains and statues more stately
colonnades public facades so
in the wake of stone cargoes he

went on upriver and beheld
the opera house which the forest
had paid for tall white porticos
designed to be like somewhere else
for a moment and he found work
as a photographer ducking
under the black hood to focus
one instant one face the leaves in
their day one horse running on its
shadow all of them upside-down
as the flash caught them that turned them
gray in the year before the whole

thing fell away as the ships left
the harbors and few replaced them
the docks rotted and grass smothered
railroad sidings and spilled across
marble boulevards the forest
fingered the opera house he heard
day and night the unbroken chant
of summer whirring in ringing
chorus the frogs and toads after
dark each with its chords the high
crickets cicadas grasshoppers
was it to this that they had

summoned him this prompt projected
vision of a bad end under
the lingering forest lightning
this demonstration of what it
amounted to all that human
grasping wringing killing piling
up of vanity that smiling
for the camera and then this
view of the negative with its
black mouth but what could anyone
be expected to learn from it
in the world as it was except

to try something else and he seemed
to be needed in that country
of the grasshopper a post was
waiting for him at Campinas
to work in plant pathology
on studies of insects and their
hosts for the purpose of human
advantage it was the entrance
to the forest to his years of
watching the summer and trying
to write down clearly what he saw
without noticing that it was

his life he was already quite
fluent in the language since he
heard no other and any news
of Russia that reached him did so
in Portuguese some time before
the papers arrived weeks old from
France and the still older letters
in Russian like broken pieces
of dry leaves out of a season
already advanced far beyond
the breathless words and the vanished
time they told of but their frightened

hope their deciduous prescience
rose to him through the familiar
script from those places that were their
trees their country whatever they
might say whatever might happen
where no side by then would believe
what he told them about himself
over his Brazilian passport
why then had he left the summer
to go back and be shot he was
recalling the sounds of long grass
at Malaia Buromea

when he was a child a whisper that
survived only in his mind as
the door opened and they took him
out under guard and down the long
hall to an office with a desk
and above it a head asking
name birthplace what he did for a
living why he had come back to
all the old questions and then asked
whether in fact he had knowledge
of crops their ailments the insects
devouring them the grasshopper

and admitting that they needed
what he knew they set him to work
to save the harvests though it was not
certain whose harvests they would be
or where the home was that he had
thought he would be coming back to
he did not wait for the answers
but this time when he could he made
his way eastward across the whole
of Russia to Mongolia
Manchuria and Korea
Japan the Pacific he had

circled the globe when once more he
saw the molten plain flowing past
the rim of forest and he heard
from the leaves the shimmer of sound
he recognized though he could not
begin to decipher it or
guess who it was intended for
but he heard that it was what he
had to go on listening to
trying to find out how it happened
what it was made of where it had
come from why it continued through

the daze of his return the doors
of his laboratories in
Bahia never again did
he not hear it through the decades
of research and the more than four
hundred published descriptions of
insects and as many of plants
the history of native palms
from the Cretaceous to his own
day it went on after the trees
fell after deaths after learning
after everything had been said

The River

In the end the crocodiles came into the city

those who had already survived the death of their
civilization

lived in a park
in their eyes there was an iron fence
water near them with tall rushes
like legs of birds
trees overhead some of which they knew
and the crocodiles appeared not to be moving
in the mud

but they had wakened there and they saw the city
appear in flowing shapes and colors that changed
beyond the fence

they held in their eyes the fluttering mouths the teeth
the feet the children the hands
they flowed past as cars
they ascended floor by floor
they roared and disappeared
and seemed to be asleep but never were

inside them on wires conversations raced
like lights moving too fast to be seen
the crocodiles continued as engines and lay still as guns
and were burning even with their eyes closed

at the same time they were admired and were served
and faces came a long way to see them
only one time
and stayed only for a moment

and what the crocodiles
beheld was a dark river never forgotten
never remembered

So Far

Less than an inch long and not I suppose
an hour old but taking what must be
the flapping steps of the first morning
into which it has broken its way alone
from the white shell already beyond

recall it spills its spread fingers still
the color of the rainy daylight
across the dark floor I laid myself in other
years and other weather and scrambles
after its head like a kite tail but

not buoyant and the head besides and its
own tail most gray for a gecko a kind
of being which those yellow eyes fixing
me from the floor perhaps have not seen yet
and only from themselves know what they are

attempting while I watch their brown body
of unknown sex and their pale soft limbs making
a floundering lop-sided journey
the only way now for one newly hatched
gecko dragging its right rear leg after it

which leads me to wonder what its chances
can be as it pauses to consider
me with my inches hours definitions
before continuing under the lips
of the square blue pot graven with lines

meant to suggest to my kind a few
leaves of bamboo and in that shadow circling
the sprouting cycad overhead with its
single frond and its ancestry
older than the dinosaurs but now

a species rare if not officially
endangered named for one man Rumphius
who flourished in the Indies a mere three
centuries ago and again the gecko
emerges with its gait like a collapsing

wave under the two-leafed seedling of the lately
discovered species of Pritchardia
that evolved on the crumbling island
of Kauai and I watch the body stumble
out of sight only to sally forth

a moment later with all four of its
hands unfurled and balance in its dance
darker too and decisive and see before it
another hatchling that looks exactly like it
at least to me and now what are the chances

The Palms

Each is alone in the world
and on some the flowers
are of one sex only

they stand as though they had no secrets
and one by one the flowers emerge from the sheaths
into the air

where the other flowers are
it happens in silence except for the wind
often it happens in the dark
with the earth carrying the sound of water

most of the flowers themselves are small and green by day
and only a few are fragrant
but in time the fruits are beautiful
and later still their children
whether they are seen or not

many of the fruits are no larger than peas
but some are like brains of black marble
and some have more than one seed inside them
some are full of milk of one taste or another
and on a number of them there is a writing
from long before speech

and the children resemble each other
with the same family preference
for shade when young
in which their colors deepen
and the same family liking for water
and warmth
and each family deals with the wind in its own way
and with the sun and the water

some of the leaves are crystals others are stars
some are bows some are bridges and some
are hands
in a world without hands

they know of each other first from themselves
some are fond of limestone and a few cling to high cliffs
they learn from the splashing water
and the falling water and the wind

much later the elephant
will learn from them
the muscles will learn from their shadows
ears will begin to hear in them

the sound of water
and heads will float like black nutshells
on an unmeasured ocean neither rising nor falling

to be held up at last and named for the sea

Immortelles

Somewhere between the oatmeal
yellow wall with its black marble fireplace
never used
in the house from which the long echoing
flight of steps to the front door
has been gone these many years
and the small red-shingled

done-over farmhouse with its
white trim and driveway furred in blue spruces
where after
a rainy summer alone she looked
up from an empty teacup
one September evening toward
the west where the clouds raced

low over the black waving
trees beyond the dark garden and she stood
up and died
my mother had thrown out those flowers
fashioned of wire and some
kind of beads maybe glass but
in colors such that I

for a long time could not see
that they were flowers balancing over their
black vase that
must never be touched on its island
of lace adrift motionless
on the polished water of
a small table almost

as tall as I was so they
were flowers then and the lines of shell-white
beads circling
in whorls like thumbprints would be petals
while those the shades of unlit
church windows would be leaves but
what mattered about them

as my mother had told me
when I was old enough to understand
was that they
were not real they needed no water
they would never change they would
always be the same as they
were while I stood watching

Field Mushrooms

I never gave a thought to them at first
with their white heads
cut into slices
under a water of plastic on a blue
section of carpet
or even hanging in a scale
like the piled ruins of a foot

I was shown that when the right time came
you could overturn a dry cow pat
by the edge of a long green swamp
late on a cold
autumn afternoon
as the sun was going down
and there underneath
the real white heads were still growing

I went on finding them
always at evening
coming to recognize a depth
in the shade of oaks and chestnuts

a quickening in the moss year after year
a suggestion of burning
signs of something already there in its own place
a texture of flesh
scarcely born
full of the knowledge of darkness

Lunar Landscape

Nobody can tell you
anything new about
moonlight you have seen it
for yourself as many
times as necessary

nobody else ever saw
it as it appeared to you
you have heard all about it
but in the words of others
so that you fell asleep

it was photographed but
somewhere else and without
what was happening inside
its light and whenever it
was rhymed it disappeared

you cannot depend on
it use it for much send
it anywhere sell it
keep it for yourself bring
it back when it has left

and while it is lighting
the ocean like a name while
it is awake in the leaves
you do not need to look at it
to know it is not there

Looking Up

How bright the blues are in this latter
summer through which news keeps vanishing
without having appeared but we know
the days as we know the clouds not by name
nor by where they are going the gardens

of the old are like that where every hope
that brought them together is no
more to be seen the stones raised beside
water not after all signifying
length of life but the untouchable

blue place beyond us in which stones are
days as you can see watching the old
at work in their gardens that are never
what they appear to be but already
perfect and transparent as the day is

For the Year

for James Baker Hall and Mary Ann Taylor-Hall

If I did not know
I could not tell by
watching the blue sky
with not a cloud
moving across it
in the still morning
above the flying
songs of the thrushes

that in these unseen
hours of clear daylight
one more year even
now is leaving us
one more year one more
decade wherever

it is that they go
once they have been here

and we waited up
for them I stood in
a friend's house high on
a hill looking out
over the city
to the sea ten years
ago and my ears
rang with the midnight

fireworks rising from
the lit streets into
that time with its stars
my hair was still dark
I did not know you
and in the morning
both the puppies barked
and the tiles had come

for the new roof we
are living under
it is already
a year now since we
sat here with friends by
candlelight talking
of childhoods risen
at last from hiding

until we saw that
the candles had burned
past the moment we
had been waiting for
and already it
had slipped through our words
and hands and was gone
and the year was new

without our having
seen how it happened
bringing with it far
from our sight this whole
day wherever it
is going now as
we watch it together
here in the morning

The Real World of Manuel Córdova

And so even
as True Thomas had done
after seven
years had gone
and no cell of his skin
bone blood or brain
was what it had been
the night that the rain
found him alone
neither child nor man
in the forest and at dawn
looking into the swollen
stream toward the sudden
flash of a fish and then

up he saw them
standing around him
more silent than tree shadows from
which they had come
each holding the aim
of a spear for some
moments before they came
without a word and from him
took knife bucket the freedom
of his hands binding them
behind him and hauling him

for days through the green spinning dome
to bring him at last half dead home
into their own dream

in which there was
yet something like time yes
it was still a kind of time as
he turned slowly to realize
where not one of his
syllables touched any surface
and what had been his voice
proved to be nobody's
wondering unheard for days
whether they would eat him as
they kept feeding him dishes
cooked before his eyes
for his mouth alone and across
what felt like his own face

and down over
the meat of him everywhere
first there was the water
they warmed at the fire to pour
on him as a mother
would do and then the knowing finger
of the old man their
leader tracing a signature
of the forest in one color
after another
along him with roots to enter
him and go on growing there
then one night the bitter
juices they held up for

him to swallow while
they watched the apple
climb in his throat and fall
but he thought he could tell
by then a little
of that turning pool

their single will
and if they meant to kill
him there with their sentinel
keeping watch on the hole
in the forest far from the babble
of the village then why was the bowl
passed from his mouth to theirs until
each one in the circle

had drunk and he
looked on as one by one they
lay down and looking on he
discovered that he
was lying down and they
were all together by day
there in their forest where he
understood every word they
were telling him while they
travelled and already
when he came to each tree he
knew that it would be
just where it appeared and they
were its name as they

passed touching
nothing until the morning
when they heard the same birds sing
and he was sitting
with the others in a ring
around the ashes knowing
much of what they were saying
as though it were echoing
across water and he was learning
that they had been dreaming
the same dream then they were filing
like water out of the clearing
and he kept recognizing
the face of each thing

the moment it appeared
also he remembered
here and there the word
to which something answered
them it seemed then that he heard
his own mind and from there onward
through the forest he discovered
how much less he floundered
and crashed while they flickered
with him through the scattered
light their feet in a mastered
music never heard
not even remembered
except as a shared

dream which he found
when they returned
to the village remained
visible around
him a presence that had opened
in the foreground
of the day and as he listened
he could still understand
enough out of the sound
of their words to attend
as the old chief his friend
pointing to the morning summoned
to him the world and
piece by piece explained

where certain medicines
live in hiding where directions
travel in the dark how poisons
wait how the snake listens
how leaves store reflections
which of the demons
are nameless where dying begins
and as the days' lessons
taught him to pronounce
some of the questions

growing in him since
they had him in their hands
he was answered with instructions
from the forest of the old man's

mind carefully
guiding him until he
believed almost that he
had followed his own way
into the only
place alive and when the
moon was right and again they
stood after dark in the empty
tower of trees where one by
one they drank from the bowl and lay
down he thought it was the same day
that he knew but he could see
through each of them an entry
to the forest and as he

turned he went on seeing
everywhere something
the chief was letting
him know even while he was dreaming
what they were all dreaming
together flowing
among the trees entering
cat fur monkey voice owl wing
but he found in the morning
that he was taking
shape in the old man's ruling
dream and was recognizing
in the surrounding
day a forest hiding

from the others
and that his teacher's
whispers and gestures
had rendered his eyes and ears
attuned to powers

haunting plants and waters
that were unknown to theirs
he beheld the ancestors
in his own sleep the bearers
of birth and death the spiders
in charge of night fierce
protectors vipers
of lightning at the fire source
and from the chief's answers

he came to see
that they wanted him to be
the heir of every
secret and therefore ready
to be next on that day
no longer very
distant when their chief would die
for they believed that they
must have somebody
to guide them who already
understood the deadly
aliens steadily
withering their way
into the only

forest somebody who
had been alien and knew
the outer words and how to
turn something of the forest into
what could save them to
trade part of their life for the new
death an outer person who
could teach them how to
have guns yet someone who
had gone with them into
the dream flowing through
the forest and knew
the ancients and the spirits who
never let go

in that way he became
all that the chief taught him
and all that appeared to him each time
he went into the dream
farther and it came
out with him into the day and from
then on was all around him
they gave him a name
and he started to show them
what they could take from
trees that would buy them
guns they gave him
a girl to be with him
they almost trusted him

some of them and under
his guidance they put together
a first cargo or
caravan of rubber
that they would carry for
many days to the river
where he would go to the trader
alone and barter
everything they had brought for
Winchesters and bullets and after
they had brought the guns home to their
roof each of them wore
that night ceremonial attire
feathers claws teeth from their

forest in celebration
and he was given
another girl and then
a third and an old woman
watched over him when
more and more often
after the day's lesson
was done he was taken alone
with the chief at sundown
to the opening in

the trees where the old man
gave him the bowl and began
the chants while on his own
he drank the potion

and the visions rose
out of the darkening voice
out of the night voice the secret voice
the rain voice the root voice
through the chant he saw his
blood in the veins of trees
he appeared in the green of his eyes
he felt the snake that was
his skin and the monkeys
of his hands he saw his faces
in all the leaves and could recognize
those that were poison and those
that could save he was helpless
when bones came to chase

him and they were
his own the fire
of his teeth climbed after
his eyes he could hear
through his night the river
of no color that ended nowhere
echoing in his ear
it was there in the morning under
his breath growing wider
through those days after
the first guns were slung in their
rafters among the other
protectors and the men were
preparing to get more

spending their time doing
what he had taught them working
to change something living
there into something
else far away putting

their minds that far away wanting
guns guns becoming
more ardent still after a raiding
party of enemies sending
arrows out of hiding
near the village had run fleeing
before the pursuing
guns vanishing
leaving one behind dying

and so another caravan
like a snake soon
slipped out in the track of the first one
but the season by then
had moved on and the rain
they seemed to have forgotten
caught them out and began
to drum down
on them all night and in
the misty days as they went on
sliding and splashing in
running mud and then
when they reached the river again
and he took the raft alone

to the trader
the value of rubber
had fallen the rifles cost more
all they had carried bought fewer
bullets he sat down there
that time at table to share
the soup of the invader
and it was a fire
he did not remember
burning over
his tongue to sear
his throat and pour
through him everywhere
melting him so that no water

he drank could cool him and
he wept and imagined
that he would be burned
to death or if he happened
to live would never be sound
in body or whole in mind
again but it lessened
at last and he was left by the bend
of the river with the full count
of guns and bullets on the ground
beside him while the canoe went
back into the flooded end
of the day and without a sound
his companions appeared around

him he watched the weightless
pieces of merchandise
seem one by one to rise
by themselves and nose
their way forward into the trees
then in turn he bent to raise
his load and took his place
among them for the many days'
walking until his surprise
always at a bird-like voice
ahead of him breaking the news
of their return and bird voices
welcoming them with echoes
from their own house

but the old chief was dying
turning before long
into a mummy blackening
in the smoke clouds of the ceiling
and the others were wandering
into themselves hiding
from him exhuming
hatreds that meant nothing
to him they were waiting
he thought for the burying

of the old man and for the mourning
to be done and then they were looking
as he saw for something
from him and the one thing

he had known to show them
was guns a way to get them
a way to depend on them
and now he tried leading them
to the hunt but from
the crash of his gun each time
he fired it the continuum
of calling all around them
fled in echoes away from them
out of range so that it took them
a long time to come
close again and seldom
was it possible to aim
very far through the scrim

of forest and they
with their silent weaponry
went on hunting in the old way
wanting the guns as he
understood then only
for humans such as the enemy
tribes with their angry
language but principally
for the aliens every
change of season so many
more coming up the rivers he
was taken on a winding journey
to see a succession of empty
names in the forest where they

had lived at some time before
the aliens had come with blades for
the white blood of the rubber
trees and guns for whatever
feather or fur or

face they might discover
and in each place he was shown where
the house had stood and men were
shot by the guns and their
women were spread butchered or
dragged off with their children and never
seen again and he learned there were
many voices to avenge but after
each house burned the people had moved farther

into the wild
fabric that they knew and he was told
how at last when the old
chief had led them to the stream curled
like the boa where the field
would be and where they would build
the house that now held
their hammocks and the bundled
corpses creaking in the smoke-filled
ceiling with the cradled
guns among them the chief had called
the place by the name that means world
begins here again or first world
wakens or only world

once more and when they
had led him to every
overgrown scar on the way
of their lives they
went home again to their only
roof where although he
warned them patiently
about the aliens what an army
would be like if it came why
vengeance would never be
final and how they
depended now on the enemy
for guns always they
sat watching silently

for the end of his
words but the voices
that they were hearing even as
he spoke had no peace
for the living and no place
for reason so the restless
passion for guns invaded the days
growing as the gashed trees
dripped and the smoke rose
around the rubber and the cargoes
were shouldered for the wordless
journeys where each time his
exchange with the trader yielded less
for them each time the price

of guns had gone
up and the burden
was lighter than ever on
their way back and when
they had reached the village again
he knew he was alone
and he went out one
time before sundown
into the forest with none
of the girls he had been given
only the old woman
following him and in
the circle of trees stopped to drain
the bowl and he lay down

in the gathering dark watching
for a glimpse of something
the old chief had been hoping
he would come to but was soon beginning
to shiver running
with sweat a nausea clutching
him the coils of writhing
serpents knotting
him on the ground then he was being
shown a sickness like a waving

curtain surrounding
his family and his mother was dying
there and he saw himself lying
with an arrow through him nailing

him down to be walked over
only then did he see once more
the face of the old chief for
the last time standing before
him his protector
and the black jaguar
from the other side of fear
in whose form he could go anywhere
came to him just at the hour
before daylight when from the floor
of the forest curled roots that were
the old woman's hands rose to offer
the bowl that would restore
him and as her face became clear

in the milk of her eye
he saw that she
knew everything that he
had been but as before she
said nothing and after that night he
woke to how far away
was the intangible country
of his ancestors he
began to be
repelled by the frenzy
of their celebrations and they
who so delicately
when hunting could make the
odor of the human body

one with the unwarned
air of the forest around
them now began to offend
him with their ripened
scent they hardly listened

to him or so he imagined
and a silence widened
between them until a band
went on a raid as he found
out later and when the men returned
with eyes ablaze and blood-stained
bodies he learned
only from the shouts that night around
the fire what kind

of game they had taken
that trip what meat they had eaten
and in those days the men
worked without urging and too soon
had another caravan
ready and they set out again
but on this journey storm and rain
would not let them alone
day or night and they thrashed in
mud they were bruised chilled hungry and when
they tried to sleep sitting down
under leaves the water ran
across them as though they were in
a black stream then

with his eyes closed he saw over
and over one fast stretch of river
and each time out on the water
the same familiar
small boat heading upstream near
the white turn where
the current swept out from under
hanging boughs and he looked more
narrowly after
the vessel but never
could see it clearly before
it was gone in the green cover
and he was awake cold and sore
that day they reached the river

built their raft and he
pushed off at break of day
with everything they
had brought and in the misty
dawn poled his way
downstream to tie
up at the trader's landing by
a river boat that he
thought familiar it would be
leaving at about midnight he
heard from the trader as they
loaded a canoe with every
useful thing that he
had been able to buy

except guns
then he took a canoe once
more to where his friends
were waiting for him in dense
forest on the bank he watched their hands
unload the canoe looking for guns
he had brought only this he said the guns
were still on the boat new guns
for shooting through trees the plans
called for unloading them in silence
at midnight to keep those guns
from falling into the hands
of the aliens
he watched their expressions

as he told them he
had to go back with the canoe he
could see that they were uneasy
knew something was wrong so he
pushed off quickly
into the current paddling and by
the time he reached the bend he could see
no one on the bank where they
had been standing only
the trees and then the trader's where he

asked for the remaining tally
of their earnings there and he
withdrew all the gun money
bought clothes for going away

paid for his passage would
eat nothing went on board
feeling numb and cold trying to avoid
their questions lay down and waited
in the dark for midnight with his head
afloat above the floating wood
heard the limbs of wood
from the forest falling into the loud
firebox watched the trees of sparks fade
overhead as the boat started
out into the river his mother was dead
whatever he might need
was somewhere that could not be said
as though it had never existed

Another Place

When years without number
like days of another summer
had turned into air there
once more was a street that had never
forgotten the eyes of its child

not so long by then of course nor
so tall or dark anywhere
with the same store at the corner
sunk deeper into its odor
of bananas and ice cream

still hoarding the sound of roller
skates crossing the cupped board floor
but the sidewalk flagstones were
cemented and the street car
tracks buried under a late

surface and it was all cleaner
as they had said it would be and bare
like the unmoving water
of the windows or a picture
in white beneath the swept sky

of a morning from which the trees were
gone with their shadows and their
time that seemed when we moved there
years before to hold whatever
had existed in the moment

that echoed the notes of our
feet striking almost together
on the hollow wooden front stair
up to the porch and glass door
of the sepia house which once

we were gone would be whited over
we walked with my father
climbing toward his fortieth year
in the clothes of a minister
Presbyterian vacating

a church with a yellow brick spire
on a cliff above a river
with New York on the other shore
by then the Protestants were
moving out of that neighborhood

the building was in disrepair
and a year or two after
he left it the leaking structure
would be sold to the Catholics for
a song and then torn down

and its place would know it no more
remaining empty for
the rest of his life and longer
when he got to the top stair
of the new manse he turned around

to face the photographer
and stood up straight gazing over
the man's shoulder toward the other
side of the street and the square
bell tower the stuccoed walls

stone steps carved frame of the door
rose window that was a wonder
he said of its kind the summer
still floated in the light and before
long he would find someone

with the talent to capture
that sacred architecture
in black and white for the cover
of the bulletin week after
week the name of the church

in Gothic letters under
the noble mass in the picture
and below in slightly smaller
type the name of the pastor
page one inside announcing

every Sunday the order
of service giving the scripture
verses hymn numbers psalter
and text upon which the minister
himself would preach this morning

page two the schedules for choir
practice Christian Endeavor
deacons' elders' and prayer
meetings quiltings clam chowder
get-togethers boy scouts girl scouts

as he gazed he could hear
his own voice circling higher
out of the picture before
him leading them all together
amen amen that would be

the shadowed sanctum where
he would stew in the rancor
of trustees' meetings bicker
over appointments procedure
and money always money

and would watch within a year
his congregation shatter
into angry parties and there
as his own marriage turned sour
disappointed grudging absent

yet his own beyond his doubt or
understanding and the pair
of lovely children who were
also his although never
had he seemed to be able

really to touch them or
address them except in anger
grew up turned from him somewhere
on the far side of their mother
telling him nothing waiting

out his presence dropping their
voices when he would appear
since they had learned to remember
him only as the author
of everything forbidden

he would take to going over
in the evening after
an early supper whenever
nothing was scheduled for
that night and the church stood dark

and hollow to the side door
at the foot of the tower
topcoat flapping and a folder
of papers clutched in the other
hand as he turned the key and

slipped through reaching up for
his hat and pausing to hear
the lock click behind him before
he touched the pearl button once more
to wake to himself the high

green walls lit yellow the air
of a cavern without breath or
sound that had heard no one enter
looming up and the first stair
coughing under his foot

in the wooden night then the floor
of the Sunday School room louder
because there was nobody there
to watch him to hover
above him and wait for him nothing

to be afraid of therefore
the psalmist said we shall fear
not but walk with greater
deliberation pause ponder
rows of chairs closed piano

line of one varnished rafter
to its end while whistling under
the breath over and over four
or five tuneless notes as far
as the closed carved oaken

door of his cold study where
his own blood rose in his ear
like a sea in the dark before
the light spilled down the somber
panelled walls across green

filing cabinets moss under
foot heavy desk all but bare
and behind it the black leather
back of the waiting chair
facing him in which without his

noting it he was aware
repeatedly of another
figure of himself younger
it seemed by maybe a year
or two wearing a shirt

of gleaming white and never
coat over it however
cold the radiator
and the draft at the shoulder
from the black window but that

was the one without error
all along the one with each year
of school completed no favor
to beg nothing to make up for
to excuse or put differently

the one he liked to refer
to as himself and to speak for
when questioned the one he was sure
of the one with the answer
who did not look up and whose

eyes mouth indeed no feature
of whose face he had ever
seen directly but neither
did he glance toward them or
touch the cold chair even

for one moment to sit down there
only patted the desk another
time on his way to the far
door and the organ and choir
stalls the chancel the three

high seats out in the center
where he turned slowly to stare
past the line where the black water
of empty pews came ashore
and to peer up at the arches

that dove into the dark over
narrow bands of faint color
seeping through glass at that hour
he raised his arms facing the farther
wall by way of rehearsal

squeezed his eyes shut to mutter
some benediction or other
and in his Sunday manner
climbed with his handful of paper
into the pulpit to leaf

through his notes and deliver
a passage here and there
his voice returning over
and over to the same threadbare
wandering phrases unfinished

sentences trying with fervor
and sound to kindle from their
frayed ends a redeeming power
whole and irrefutably clear
to the waiting darkness at

last he ran through the entire
sermon as though he could hear
himself from the shadows and after
he had come to the end he stood over
the pages while the echo

sank back from the tones of one more
final word that would sound for
a moment and then lie together
with the others of that year
in a box to be piled

on a shelf and maybe never
opened again before
his last instructions were
carried out and the white pyre
of all his preaching built high

in a garden incinerator
one bright day of another
autumn farther west near
where he had started from but for
the moment the pages lay

still in the unlit core
of the week while the same whisper
of the heedless dark rose closer
to his breath he gathered his paper
together turned out the lights

behind him left by the back door
to the side street and his car
and late haunts a running sore
in his marriage and rumor
soon followed after and took

not long at all to discover
which nicely spoken young helper
had been driving with the preacher
alone at what times and where
how much attention he seemed

to spend on her widowed mother
and sick brother at their
little house around the corner
until he went off to the war
as a chaplain and his

family moved to another
part of town then another
town and none of them ever
came back but the house was still there
somewhere under its dazzling

paint and so was the top stair
where he had turned toward the far
side of the street with the gray tower
the dark ring in the austere
facade and in that place

as when one hand alone for
a moment clinging to air
above the rising water
so quickly is drawn under
that it leaves those who have seen it

asking each other whether
what they have seen was ever
there and they cannot be certain or
as when a face familiar
it seems as the common day

around it with every feature
known and nothing either
lost or surprising may appear
again in its regular
stance and its quiet voice begin

to relay at its leisure
something that the listener
will need to remember
and suddenly the dreamer
is shaken awake so from the low

house with the piled porch furniture
where the old choir director
used to rock in his darkened parlor
and all the way to the corner
instead of the building and its age

there was nothing but the clear
sky of autumn with a barrier
of pine boards sawn raw from their
lives standing along the gutter
around nothing visible

until one came to look over
the edge with the sign Danger
Keep Out and see the latter
mountains the glister of char
on jutting wood the jagged

pieces of remembered color
that had been carried so far
in the dark at last raising their
bright tips out of a glacier
of cinders and fallen sections

of brickwork scorched wallpaper
shreds of its green vine and flower
pattern still waving over
pools of shivering water
and broken tiles from the long red

aisle all heaped up together
naked to the public air
in the smell of wet plaster
and of fire a few days before
and of the leaves in autumn

One Story

Always somewhere in the story
which up until now we thought
was ours whoever it was
that we were being then
had to wander out into
the green towering forest
reaching to the end of
the world and beyond older
than anything whoever
we were being could remember
and find there that it was
no different from the story

anywhere in the forest
and never be able to tell
as long as the story was there
whether the fiery voices

now far ahead now under
foot the eyes staring from
their instant that held the story
as one breath the shadows
offering their spread flowers
and the chill that leapt from its own
turn through the hair of the nape
like a light through a forest

knew the untold story
all along and were waiting
at the right place as the moment
arrived for whoever it was
to be led at last by the wiles
of ignorance through the forest
and come before them face
to face for the first time
recognizing them with
no names and again surviving
seizing something alive
to take home out of the story

but what came out of the forest
was all part of the story
whatever died on the way
or was named but no longer
recognizable even
what vanished out of the story
finally day after day
was becoming the story
so that when there is no more
story that will be our
story when there is no
forest that will be our forest

Rain Travel

I wake in the dark and remember
it is the morning when I must start
by myself on the journey
I lie listening to the black hour
before dawn and you are
still asleep beside me while
around us the trees full of night lean
hushed in their dream that bears
us up asleep and awake then I hear
drops falling one by one into
the sightless leaves and I
do not know when they began but
all at once there is no sound but rain
and the stream below us roaring
away into the rushing darkness

On the Back of the Boarding Pass

In the airport by myself I forget
where I am that is the way they are made
over and over at such cost the ripped
halls lengthening through stretches of echoes I
have forgotten what day it is in this light
what time it could be this was the same morning
in which I mislaid the two timepieces
they may turn up again timepieces can be
bought but not the morning the waking
into the wish to stay and the vanishing
constants I keep returning to this was the
morning of mending the fence where the black dog
followed the water in after the last
cloudburst and I kept on trying to tie
a thread around the valley where we live
I was making knots to hold it there in its
place without changing as though this were the waking
this seeming this passage this going through

Last Morning at Punta Arena

In the first rays the wandering mountain ridge
above the sand plain with its crowd of gray cactus
kindles to peach and orange and a wave
of color burns slowly down the cliffs
these rock faces were born under the sea
but now all we have been and have forgotten
is rising around us from the ash of dawn
into the day that comes to take away
sea birds call across the glassy water
broken shells turn over on the waking shore
another storm perhaps and the ragged
shelter of dry leaves will let in the whole sky
I walk toward it once more following my own
footprints through the new morning and I see
three heads rise just beyond it coyotes
wild dogs they watch me and move off slowly
all the time looking back over their shoulders

Mirage

After a point that is passed without being seen
more and more of the going appears to
be going back but that is another
cloud shadow there was never any such
dwelling place although having once gone away
it seems that there must have been a reason
for setting out and then a reason for
thinking so a first season returning
a new ending a being that the hand
reaches for in the dark and finds and goes on
trying to find this time this time the hope
ringing ringing it must all be the sound
of a mind if only because it could
not be anything else floating down once more
over the vast scars of the butchered land
sinking through every ghost that was murdered in

our name the layers of invisible
intentions the word morning in the plural
its fingers of sunlight on floors its trembling
garments its air of promise that large word
its Europe every inch of it turned over
and over by one kind of life burying
and bringing up year after year looking
for another life until at last a single
crow is flying across translucent June pastures
and mustard fields under high tension wires
in rain and between files of pointed trees
on the empty road into the air small children
are running with arms raised toward the clouds
running and falling and I am running
like a small child running with arms raised
falling getting to my feet running on
after all having decided that
I am going to tell the whole story

On the Old Way

After twelve years and a death
returning in August to see the end of summer
French skies and stacked roofs the same grays
silent train sliding south through the veiled morning
once more the stuccoed walls the sore
pavilions of the suburbs glimpses
of rivers known from other summers leaves
still green with chestnuts forming for their
only fall out of old dark branches and again
the nude hills come back and the sleepless
night travels along through the day as it
once did over and over for this was the way
almost home almost certain that it was
there almost believing that it could be
everything in spite of everything

Left Open

The shutters are rusted open on the north
kitchen window ivy has grown over
the fastenings the casements are hooked open
in the stone frame high above the river
looking out across the tops of plum trees
tangled on their steep slope branches furred
with green moss gray lichens the plums falling
through them and beyond them the ancient
walnut trees standing each alone on its
own shadow in the plowed red field full
of amber September light after so
long unattended dead boughs still hold
places of old seasons high out of the leaves
under which in the still day the first walnuts
from this last summer are starting to fall
beyond the bare limbs the river looks
motionless like the far clouds that were not
there before and will not be there again

Stone Village

At the first sight of the old walls the rain
was over it was high summer with tall
grass already white and gold around
the somber brambles waves of them hiding
the house completely from the rutted lane
that ran among brambles and shadows
of walnut trees into the silent village
already it was afternoon and beyond
the barns the broad valley lay in its haze
like a reflection as it does long after
the house has risen dry out of the tide
of brambles and the uncounted sunlight has crossed
the dust of the floors again all the fields
and the shoulders of the stone buildings have

shrunk and the animals have wakened in
the barns and are gone and the children
have come home and are gone and the rain
they say seems to have stopped forever

Turning

This is the light that I would see again
on the bare stones the puckered fields the roof
this is the light I would long remember
hazed still an afternoon in September
the known voices would be low and feathered
as though crossing water or in the presence
of moment the old walnut trees along
the wall that I wanted to live forever
would have fallen the stone barns would be empty
the stone basins empty the dormers staring
into distances above dry grass and
the wide valley and I would see my own hand
at the door in the sunlight turn the key
and open to the sky at the empty
windows across the room that would still be there

A Summer Night

Years later the cloud brightens in the east
the moon rises out of the long evening
just past midsummer of a cold year
the smell of roses waves through the stone room
open to the north and its sleeping valley
gnarled limbs of walnut trees and brows of extinct
barns blacken against the rising silver of night
so long I have known this that it seems to me
to be mine it has been gone for so long
that I think I have carried it with me
without knowing it was there in the daytime

through talk and in the light of eyes and travelling
in windows it has been there the whole way
on the other side like a face known from
another time from before and afterwards
constantly rising and about to appear

After the Spring

The first hay is in and all at once
in the silent evening summer has come
knowing the place wholly the green skin
of its hidden slopes where the shadows will
never reach so far again and a few
gray hairs motionless high in the late
sunlight tell of rain before morning
and of finding the daybreak under green
water with no shadows but all still the same
still known still the known faces of summer
faces of water turning into themselves
changing without a word into themselves

UNCOLLECTED POEMS

(1955–1987)

Camel

Remember that we are dust. It is said
That this place of our passage is prone to mirages:
That the waves of the drifting desert, the heat-daft
Air playing like water-light, the horizon
Swirling slow as a shadow and laying up
To itself all their unearthly shiftings,
Or simply the salt tides working
Of need or desire, out of some fold
Of their flowing raise often visions
As of white cities like walled clouds, agleam
On their hills, so clear that you can see the tiered
Buildings glint still in the rocking daylight,
Or again of trees even whose shadows
Seem green and to breathe, or merely of pools
Of simple water on that same dry surge borne,
That will ride nearer, nearer, like elusive
Aphrodite; and these are nothing
But the playing of the heated light teasing
Like pain over this dust. In truth, it may
Be nothing but ourselves, this that is
All about us for our eyes to see: this dust
That we cannot see beyond. Remember
That we are dust, dust and a little breath,
As the sand dervishes the wind lifts
Whirling and sends over the sea-shaped dunes;
As does their dancing, we wind between breathless
Dust and breathless dust, and our passage
Even as theirs, may be no more
Than a casual sport of the air gliding
To no depth over the delusive surface
Of our breathless selves. But speaking of virtues
We think of water; moving, we think
Of arrival as of water, of virtue
As the means of arrival. And we have named
For water him who is visibly
Our practice of virtue, beast of our motion,
Calling him "Ship of the Desert." Who rolls
When he walks; whose going also

Has strangely the gait of a cradle. He too is dust,
Yet not as we, save as that figure
Of what our faring is, for his breath is speechless,
His back that bears us has a wave's shape
Drawn by a child; or hill's lurching
As he strides; when he runs, his shadow
Over the rippling dust is a wind's
Shudder across modelled bay-water,
Curved gust across grain-field, or storm silvering
Fast as some hastening angel over
Hillsides of olive trees, darkness
Of rain-cloud chasing the sunlight
On carved hills, or wave-crest over
Far reef flung, its main strength still racing
For shore. Even as these
It would seem our progress is, in itself bearing
Its own sustenance for long waste-wending;
A power that may be, in event of all
Arrival failing, other resources
Parched, our water of desperation; that is not
Ourselves; whose capacities may not be
Arrived at even by prayer, patient study
And deprivation, yet whose presence we have known
To affect us so that even in places of water,
Of pleasure, repose, abode, when we had thought
To escape the sense of it, it will sometimes break
From where it was tethered and find us out,
Intruding its ungainly ill-smelling head
Over our shoulders. A creature that can shut
Both eyes and nostrils against the lash
Of dust risen suddenly savage. That if not
Drained at last dry as a white bone,
Exhausted beyond sense, or buried
In the capricious cruelty of
Its own condition, can sense more surely than we
Over the dust-driven horizon the green
Places where the roots grope trusting
Down into the dark breathlessness, the trees
Sway and give shade, dew falls early,
Stones drip in the mossed shadow, and the motes

Seem to dance to a falling cadence
That mortal ears might apprehend. Catching, as we,
At phantoms, breaking into a dangerous
Rocking-horse sprint at false visions, nevertheless
When we are despairing, drawn it would seem
By deceptions only, working to wean
Our minds from arrival, staring vacantly
At the tormented air, while the enraged sun
Careens in white circles about a sky
The blood-orange of an eyelid, he can with no warning
Lift the furred neck swinging there
Like a winter serpent, flare divining nostrils,
Even from far off smell the true water.

1955

Several Distiches about an Occasion

I

In three words, am I lost? This figure of loss
Dances with too many feet in the same place.

II

Who fancies himself found and, words his wayside,
Sits in their hollowness and calls it shade?

III

Politeness studies the fashion of flapping
From a vain bird whose egg was more edifying.

IV

In my rudeness I heard, "Trim, little one, to this wisdom:
There are right and wrong tails under which to keep warm."

V

Sailing to Greenland in a daft straw,
Clothes too cargoed me. See: I go raw.

1955

Northeast October

Where in every bush there is burning, and
The lucidity of heaven is farther than ever
Above the wordless flames and the fields
Of hushed fire there are birds rising, drifting,
Instead of cries, every one of them blackened
Without smoke, there is clarity, painful,
Without understanding, there are graves
Everywhere, ready for the dancing, and
Behind every tree there is the end
Of the world. I make your fire be tongues
But can find them no syllable. I make your trees
Be anguish, and your leaves be hands that have
Snatched at the edge of the glass turning, I make
Your light, fathomless, where the birds fish,
Be blood, and the birds be your fright. Here be martyrs,
I say, there must be a faith for. I sit in the dumb
Light of your burning, and am your grief.

1956

Mercy

Even the hunters, who smile to cock
The deadly choice in their minds, and like
To carry it by loving custom lightly,
Looking for something to kill, even
The hunters sometimes it overtakes
Over the half-killed quarry. Do not look
In their eyes, they will tell you, there are questions
That cannot be put out with knives. Sooner
Or later, just the same, the eyes are there
Asking out of the bird broken
On wires, out of the crushed rabbit
Beside the road, out of the ripped dog
The lynx left, asking us the incurable
Question. And we learn that we have
No choice, that whether the eyes

Soften or harden us, and whatever it is
They ask, we have come out to kill. Wrung,
Stuck, shot, whichever it must be,
After the shudder of discovery,
The held moment before mercy
Is the worst, when all kindness must be flexed
Quick and act cruel, while those eyes insist,
Insist that you are Anger, while you
Withdraw yourself from what you must do
So that what you perform may be pure action
And not a person. It was at that poised
Instant, today, over the dying woodchuck
That the eyes caught me, and before
The glaze covered them they conjured up
Eyes beyond eyes, all asking, faces
Beyond faces, as though I stood
In a crowd of my own kind, who stared,
Surprised with pain, up at the air,
Insisting, insisting that there was a cure,
Dreading above all things His mercy.

1957

The Miner

With a mountain on top of him from
The first day, he learns not to think
Impractically about the place
His life depends on. Three hundred feet
Down in the dark with its faults and slides,
With only a little lamp strapped
To his forehead, he gets by heart
The shafts lightless as sleeves, the dripping
Piles stacked like trestles of cards
To hold up the dead weight of stone, and
Concentrates on those veins of the dark
That can be used. Even his dreams soon
Are untroubled by the oppressive
Weight of the earth, and it comes to close

Over him every morning like a habit.
It may not crush him, but its damps
And the long hours cramped in the low seams
Will bow him in the end. He learns
To recognize his shaft-mates under
Their blackened faces, as he must, for
Even if he lives to retire
And sit in his doorway, bathed
By the innocent sun, what he does
All his life to keep alive gets into
The grain of him, and at last cannot
Be washed out, all of it, in this world.

1957

Coal Barges

Not to heaven go these, strung together,
The color of coffins, staid as hearses, beating
Their wake across the coils of the black river,
Bones in their mossy teeth, and their heaped lading
Dead as the hills, under the pall of the weather.
They carry it, raised from its burying,
Up the steep currents, between shore and shore
Of no world but this, where we are waiting.
Where it will be bright as never before,
And quicken the land of the living,
Though black it is, and must burn when it comes here.

1957

Rimer, Penna.

It is hard to see what made them stay
Nowhere but here, my father's fathers,
By the broad river, among the foothills
Of yellow Allegheny clay,

When they had come such a long way
Out of Wales in heaven knows how many
Years, and seen so many rivers,
So many hills. It is beautiful here.

It is beautiful elsewhere, and not beauty,
I trust, made them choose this spot and stay,
Any more than it is what keeps me now
Watching the eddies slip down the river.

It is quiet here, and their fields
Still rich, and most things could come by river
But not answers, however long
I stand here looking down at their houses.

For not in the country the answer lay
Why they went no further, but in the men,
Who might have been the last to say.
And the land keeps their silence without their reasons

Up on the hill where they still stay
Above the trains that roar north to Erie,
And the river sliding the other way,
Mindless and old, to its destinations.

1957

On a Sacrifice of Darkness

Say you know it is not so, say
Over and over this is not the world,
No, it is no day ever known, say
He lies all the time, that gray god with
His white mouth wide open giving rise
To silence, with nothing in his face
For eyes; he lies, the blind demon before
The House of Darkness, offering darkness,
Saying: if it is pain it will come,
Here it is. He says: over a fresh-torn

Heart still squeezing the lees of pain there
Squats a rough stump of owl, stained talons,
Beak like a box-hook, blinking between
Horn and horn, the final bird, reigning
Over pains beyond life and evils
Longer than death. The past has vanished;
It is always now: the same uprooted
Heart glistening like a tongue twitching.
The ground is glass and ash. It quakes, and
Darkness and darkness rise swaying through
Daylight like swarms of hornets, as high
As the spiked fire of heaven where it wheels,
Descending, bright with knives, through a sky
As ignorant as a blind man's eye.

1959

Views from the High Camp

In the afternoon, while the wind
Lies down in its halcyon self,
A finger of darkness moving like an oar
Follows me through the blinding fields; in the focus
Of its peculiar radiance I have found
Treasures I did not know I had lost, several
Perhaps still in the future. Among them
This epitaph for someone:

Discoverer of absences, beloved lamp,
You that wait,
I have migrated from these footsteps,
I, alone, my own sole generation.

Later, loss will wake like the drowsing birds
And have no word. Here we have watched
The great yellow days turning their spokes
Toward autumn and departure
Through month after month of drought, while daily
The sun has hoisted a long cloud of decision

And hung it in my sight at no distance, in the form
Of a tent full of wind, each cord wrenched in turn.

Be assured that the rain will be released
When it is too late to save the harvest.

1962

Esther

Tomorrow they will come for you
old female word from the corner
lucidity
motionless in the dark
they will take you out to be
bared elsewhere
opened before it is May

there is no one else here
the door wide to the blinding
spring
the wind one of the family
like a cold hen
mute about the kitchen
the rest away busy the shirts waiting
for the iron
the calendar ticking

tomorrow
the animals will keep away
we do not believe in
happening
the sunlight will always lie there
even tonight even tomorrow night
it was always there
but you go back to another time
it is said
as though there is one

If tomorrow is really
not today
how can one believe in anything
as you say
hands holding each other in
paper bags older than they are
eyes cut out of your dress hung
to dry
burst package to be
carried past the toys out
in the bright dirt
past the shadows waving
ringing their bells raising
their instruments
whatever is brought back as you know
is not all

but if you get
later to a place with a blackened wall
and two sticks held together
by a little smoke
maybe they would let you sit by it
in the day
staring
and you could announce what he is doing
the animal their sky

1968

The Borrowers

Voices are rising from ground
nobody ever died for
but who can tell what they say

I even forget where I borrowed
my real feet

and I have to lend them for longer and longer
and be left meanwhile
with feet that don't know me
which in the end may be mine

when I call to them they don't hear me
they're thinking
as I am
of another slope where the people of morning
at this moment are waking with borrowed feet
that listen and know

1970

In Winter Silence

So who am I who was alone to see
this thorn-apple tree
at this hour of this day of this January
of this world

And who then
am I who to no one not even certainly to me
at another time would be able to impart
the blue sky deepening and winter sun
burning white through those
exact thin dark tangled branches

more than halfway down
many radiant tracks now

white reflections on the high yellow waxen
thorn-apple sun-offerings
few leaves lanterns in the afternoon

1973

A Root

A root is the first thought of a pair of wings
downward
the wings remain its feet
and the feet fall away into the sky
to become the migration of a multitude
I feel my feet in the new days of a sun
how far away they are beginning to be
they are walking even when standing still
my head meanwhile in its dark time
beaten by an unknown heart
goes finding and asking
along the path of air

1974

Demonstration

It is nothing new
for horses to be harnessed to hemispheres
it has happened at intervals
since the famous first experiment
when we know how to do a thing
we do it again

night or day the horses
are hitched up in teams
hemispheres are brought together
half to half
all the air is drawn out from between them
the seal is as wax
at a command the teams begin to haul
raising the vibrating chains
and the sphere

the horses lean into the collars and the links grind
but the halves hold together
in the grasp of the breath of the earth

there is an art to matching the teams
and to driving them
lashes crackle
bodies suffer rulers watch
while the hemispheres hold together
to the limits of matter

between them is
nothing
a nothing that is made
and is never perfect
the sight in an empty socket at night
the everlasting decision
approaching the point of origin
the first fire
still without color
exploding inward
drawing the unlit firmaments after it

1974

A Last Look

Even the words are going somewhere urban
where they hope to find friends
waiting for them

some of the friends will think of trees as pleasant in a minor way
much alike after all
to us

some of the friends will never be aware of a single tree
they will live in a world without a leaf
where the rain is misfortune

all the languages until now have flowed
from leaf to leaf
and have gone like faces

gone like the stone porches of small houses
and the smell of the forest
in the water of summer

1987

CHRONOLOGY

NOTE ON THE TEXTS

NOTES

INDEX OF TITLES & FIRST LINES

Chronology

1927 William Stanley Merwin born September 30, in New York City, the second son of William Stage Merwin (1896–1972), a Presbyterian minister, and Anna Jaynes (1898–1972). (Ancestors were Scottish, Welsh, and English, and the family name is Welsh; according to family legend, the first Merwin came to America in 1635 from Wales. Father was born in Rimerton, Pennsylvania, a village on the Allegheny River, the youngest of seven surviving children. Largely self-taught, he was awarded a scholarship at the age of sixteen to Maryville College in Tennessee, and after serving in the U.S. Navy during World War I, he attended the University of Pittsburgh and graduated from the Western Theological Seminary, now part of Pittsburgh Theological Seminary. Mother, born in Denver, Colorado, was orphaned at the age of six. Her great-grandfather fought in the Civil War, and rumors have linked her family to the Morris family of Revolutionary War fame. Her father, Hanson Hoadley Jaynes, of Danish and English extraction, worked as an inspector with the Pennsylvania Railroad, but was sent to Colorado after he was diagnosed with tuberculosis. After his death, her mother Bessie took her to live in Chester, Ohio, and eventually to Pittsburgh. While working as the secretary for the First Presbyterian Church, she met William Merwin, who was the pastor's chauffeur; they married in 1920. William Merwin was ordained in his first church, in Rural Valley, Pennsylvania, in 1924, and the following year the couple's first child, Hanson Jaynes Merwin, was born but died soon after birth. Shortly before William's birth they moved to Union City, New Jersey, where the Reverend Merwin was called to be pastor of the First Presbyterian Church.)

1929 Sister Ruth Ann born.

1931–35 Merwin hears his father, in the empty First Presbyterian Church, read from the sixth chapter of the book of Isaiah in the King James Version, and is mesmerized by the sound of words: "I wanted to hear that sound again, and to hear more of the life in the words, though I had only a remote sense of what the words meant, as I did sometimes when my mother read fairy tales to us. As we walked home I kept trying to remember phrases, mumbling them to myself under my breath." From the palisades at the back of the church, he often gazes across the Hoboken harbor and the busy Hudson at the skyline of Manhattan, and is fascinated by the river and its traffic. Teaches himself to read at age four. The earliest book he will remember is a tale about Indians living in the woods, an idea that intrigued him. *East o' the Sun and West o' the Moon*, translation of Norwegian folktales collected by Peter Christen Asbjørnsen and Jørgen Moe in the mid-nineteenth century, is a favorite book. Among the poems his mother reads to him are those of Robert Louis Stevenson's *A Child's Garden of Verses* and Tennyson's "The Brook"; as a child he reads *Robinson Crusoe* "four or five times," *The Swiss Family Robinson*, and all of Stevenson. Skips a grade at elementary school, then another, but is then moved back a grade because of the age difference between him and his classmates.

1936–42   Moves with family in 1936 to Scranton, Pennsylvania, where his father serves as pastor at the Washburn Street Presbyterian Church and the family lives in the twelve-room frame manse across the street, eking out a lean existence in the midst of the Depression. Wants to write words for the hymns he has heard in church, and begins to write and illustrate religious poems. Spends time in summers at a cottage at Fiddle Lake, an hour north of Scranton: "For a month or so the days there seemed like a complete time, with an age all its own." Attends local schools in Scranton, including West Scranton Junior High School, where he chooses to follow what was called "the classical curriculum" and embarks on a study of Latin. For his thirteenth birthday, his mother gives him *A Conrad Argosy*: "The first page of *Heart of Darkness* seized me in a spell, and as I read I longed to be able to write, and I began to try."

1942–43   Father enlists as a chaplain in the U.S. Army. With his sister, Merwin helps tend his mother's Victory Garden, an experience that instills a lifelong love of gardening. Attends school at Wyoming Seminary (known as "Sem") in Kingston, Pennsylvania, near Wilkes-Barre, a Methodist preparatory school. To help pay his tuition he waits on table in the dining hall and cleans the science labs. Having been forbidden by his parents to participate in school activities as a youngster, he tries everything at Sem, and joins the wrestling team, but he dislikes the school's restrictive regulations, particularly its strict segregation of boys and girls. His ambition is to attend the U.S. Naval Academy—"that ambition," he later wrote, "seems to me to have been, above all, an image of an underlying determination to get away."

1944–46   Too young to qualify for admission to the Naval Academy, he takes his college entrance exams and, having only heard the name "Princeton," adds it to his list of preferred colleges, and wins a scholarship there. Matriculates at Princeton in fall 1944; majors in English, and studies with critic R. P. Blackmur and poet John Berryman, who tells him, "I think you should get down in a corner on your knees and pray to the Muse, and I mean it literally." Befriends fellow students William Arrowsmith, Galway Kinnell, and Charles Rosen. Begins to translate plays of Federico García Lorca with the help of his Spanish professor, then goes on to Lorca poems. Devotes free time to horseback riding at night and haunting the Parnassus Bookshop on Nassau Street, where he spends what money he has on books by Thomas Wyatt and Fulke Greville, by Wallace Stevens and Ezra Pound. Spinoza, Beethoven, Milton, and Shelley are his passions; Pound becomes a literary model for him. Joins the Naval Air Corps in 1945. Vows not to follow orders to do violence to others and, regretting enlisting, asks his commanding officer to put him in the brig. Instead he is placed under psychiatric evaluation for seven months at the Chelsea Naval Hospital in Boston. Father visits him and tells him, "You must have the courage of your convictions," one of the few good things Merwin will remember about their relationship. Is moved to Bethesda Naval Hospital near Washington, D.C. Given a discharge as "psychologically unfit for military service," he returns to Princeton, where he spends as much time riding horses as in the classroom. In September 1946, writes Ezra Pound at St. Elizabeths mental hospital in Washington, D.C., where Pound had been remanded after his trial for treason; expresses sympathy for the older poet's situation and asks to correspond with him. Pound advises: "Try to write seventy-five lines a day. Now, at your age, you don't have anything to write seventy-five lines about, even if you think you do. So the thing to do is to get languages and translate." Merwin

marries Dorothy Jeanne Ferry (b. 1923), a secretary for the
Physics Department at Princeton, from nearby Morrisville,
Pennsylvania, after they have been dating for a few months;
Merwin's father officiates at the ceremony.

1947   Visits Pound at St. Elizabeths in April, and their correspon-
dence continues. In a letter of September 27, Merwin writes
that he has "written something every day—try to take two
or three hours in the afternoon. Technique keeps at a steady
lift, I believe"; in same letter, expresses admiration for Rob-
ert Lowell: "I believe Lowell's achievement to date to be
of astonishingly large proportions, am continuously elated
to find poetry of this sort and caliber possible, whether or
not it is in my own direction." Graduates from Princeton;
is named class poet and at graduation ceremony reads his
poem "Graduation: Princeton 1947," dedicated "To those
who are not graduating with our classes, because they are
dead." In a note to the graduation committee, he explains,
"if the requisite sentiments and unqualified optimism are
nowhere to be found in this poem, that is so merely because
I could not find them in myself, looking upon the occasion
as I do with little optimism for the future." Takes intensive
French course at McGill University in Montreal during
the summer, and enrolls in Princeton graduate program
to study Romance languages. Continues to correspond
with Pound; one postcard instructs him to "Read seeds
not twigs. E.P." Grows a beard in honor of his mentor. Im-
merses himself in the work of William Carlos Williams.

1948   Publishes poem "Variation on the Gothic Spiral" in *Poetry*'s
March issue. In summer, takes job tutoring his older friend
Alan Stuyvesant's nephew, Peter Stuyvesant, at Alan's fam-
ily estate, the Deer Park, in Hackettstown, New Jersey.
Accepts offers for him and Dorothy to accompany Peter
Stuyvesant and one of the boy's friends to Europe the fol-
lowing summer and, after that, to tutor the two sons of
Maria Antonia da Braganza, sister of the pretender to the
Portuguese throne.

1949   Sails aboard the Norwegian freighter *Nyhorn* with the two
boys and Dorothy to Genoa, where they are met by Alan
Stuyvesant. Spends the summer on the Côte d'Azur, based
at Stuyvesant's villa at St. Jean Cap-Ferrat. For a salary of
one *conto* (roughly forty dollars) a month, he and Dorothy
tutor Maria Antónia's boys at a run-down Braganza family
estate near Coimbra, Portugal, in the fall before moving

with the family in early winter to a villa in Estoril, near Lisbon. Publishes poems and translations from the French of Joachim de Bellay, Jean Antoine de Baïf, and Richard I of England in the *Hudson Review*.

1950–51   In summer, travels through Spain and visits English poet Robert Graves on Mallorca: "I was determined to meet [him], so I just went and knocked on his door." Graves asks him to edit the addendum on birds in a new edition of his *White Goddess: A Historical Grammar of Poetic Myth* (1948), and then to tutor Graves's son William, which he does for a year, though his relationship with Graves becomes strained. At Graves's house, meets aspiring English playwright Dido Milroy (born Diana Whalley, c. 1912, in Gloucestershire), whom he will become involved with and eventually marry. After the tutoring job ends, he stays on Mallorca and rents a house in Deyá, writing a play, a verse masque, and the poems of *A Mask for Janus*, which he finishes and submits to the annual Yale Series of Younger Poets competition; W. H. Auden selects it as the winning submission in July 1951 and asks for cuts from Merwin. Begins visiting London. Through Ezra Pound's son Omar, meets and befriends T. S. Eliot. Meets Samuel Beckett in Paris. Writes verse play for children, *Rumpelstiltskin*, that is produced for BBC television in 1951.

1952–53   *A Mask for Janus* is published by Yale University Press in May 1952. Merwin supports himself largely by writing and translating for the BBC's Third Programme division, which broadcasts his verse play *The Pageant of Cain* (with music by composer John Hotchkis) on the radio in 1952; over the next four years, adaptations and translations for the BBC include a six-part television serial of *Huckleberry Finn* and radio versions of the anonymous fourteenth-century French play *Robert the Devil*, Lope de Vega's play *The Dog in the Manger*, Marivaux's play *The False Confessions*, and the *Poem of the Cid*. His marriage to Dorothy dissolves; he lives in London on Primrose Hill with Dido at 11 St. George's Terrace, once the residence of Lord Byron's widow.

1954–55   Publishes second poetry collection, *The Dancing Bears* (Yale University Press). Receives a *Kenyon Review* Fellowship for Poetry. In summer 1954, while driving with Dido through southwestern France in a beloved 1935 Daimler, discovers an old ruined farmhouse in Lacan de Loubressac, near Bretenoux in the department of the Lot, on a ridge overlooking the upper valley of the Dordogne River. "The view of the ridges beyond the valley," he later wrote, "reminded me of the ridges and the landscape of western Pennsylvania that I had loved as a child." Buys it for $1,200, his entire savings and the exact amount of the principal and interest on a small legacy earlier left to him by his aunt Margaret, known as Margie, a maiden schoolteacher cousin of his mother. "My life there, for large parts of the year over many years, was a lifetime education to me and was formative in my feelings about living, if not exactly in the woods, in a completely rural place that was rooted in tradition, and to live there as someone who belonged there." From September to December 1954, writes three hundred pages of an unfinished autobiography, then abandons it because, as he explains to an editor at Knopf, of "Constant Autobiographobia always, from the time the scheme was first bruited, Hatred of prose and narcissism—feeling that it was wrong, that I should be *making* something." Marries Dido in 1955.

1956   *Green with Beasts* is published by Knopf in the United States and by Rupert Hart-Davis in England, the first of Merwin's books to be published in England. *Darkling Child*, a play written in collaboration with Dido, is produced at the Arts Theatre, London. Merwin moves to Boston after he is appointed the Rockefeller Foundation's playwright-in-residence for one year at the Poets' Theatre in Cambridge. "Let me find," he writes in his journal about his return to America for the first time in seven years, "a hard eye, proud of having no mercy, needing none, for the thing it loves." Lives at 76 West Cedar Street in Boston. Meets George Kirstein, owner of *The Nation*, who becomes a life-long friend and surrogate father. They spend time sailing together, and Merwin later recalls he absorbed "some of the great lessons of my life" learning the world of sailing. Through Jack Sweeney, the librarian of the Lamont Poetry Room at Harvard, meets Ted Hughes and Sylvia Plath, both of whom become his close friends, in Boston and then in London. Meets Robert Lowell in Boston, and later sees him in Castine, Maine, where Lowell responds with admiration for the poems in Merwin's work-in-progress *The Drunk in the Furnace* after asking to read them. Socializes with Peter Davison, Philip Booth, and Adrienne Rich, among other poets.

1957   Merwin's play *Favor Island*, about a group of shipwrecked
            sailors who resort to cannibalism, is produced at the Poets'
            Theatre in May, and its first act is published in *New World
            Writing*; during his Cambridge residency he also works on
            the plays *The Gilded West*, about Buffalo Bill, and *A Peacock
            at the Door*, about a nineteenth-century murder in a small
            Pennsylvania town. Receives an award from the National
            Institute and Academy of Arts and Letters. The Academy's
            president, Malcolm Cowley, cites Merwin's "fertility of in-
            vention, range of effect, and willingness to take risks in the
            practice of an art which has, of late, been more and more
            characterized by timidity." When Poets' Theatre residency
            ends, Merwin returns to London. Receives a Bursary for
            Playwrights by the Arts Council of Great Britain. Spends
            evenings drinking at the pub with Louis MacNeice and
            Dylan Thomas; sees English poet Henry Reed and actor
            John Whiting.

1958–59   *Favor Island* broadcast on the BBC in 1958. Completes
            translation of *Eufemia* (1567) by the Spanish playwright
            Lope de Rueda. Begins publishing book reviews in *The Na-
            tion*. Spends winter of 1958–59 in Deyá on Mallorca to finish
            his translation, begun in 1952, of the Spanish epic *Poem of
            the Cid*, which is published by J. M. Dent in London in
            1959. In this period he writes few poems of his own: "In
            the late fifties," he recalled, "I had the feeling I had simply
            come to the end of a way of writing. . . . So there was a
            period of close to two years when I wrote very little poetry."
            The Merwins see Hughes and Plath frequently after the
            couple's return to England late in 1959, with Dido helping
            them to find a flat; both poets will use Merwin's study while
            he is away.

1960–61   On Easter weekend 1960, takes part in mass protest march
            from the Atomic Weapons Research Establishment at Alder-
            maston in Berkshire to Trafalgar Square in London, fifty-
            two miles away, the third and largest of several such demon-
            strations organized annually by the Direct Action Commit-
            tee Against Nuclear War; his account of the demonstration,
            "Letter from Aldermaston," appears in *The Nation*. Pub-
            lishes third collection of poetry, *The Drunk in the Furnace*
            (Macmillan, 1960), and translations of *Some Spanish Bal-
            lads* (Abelard-Schuman, 1961), *The Satires of Persius* (Indi-
            ana University Press, 1961), and Alain-René Lesage's play

Turcaret (in vol. 4 of *The Classic Theatre*, ed. Eric Bentley, Anchor/Doubleday 1961). Researches Coxey's Army protest march of the unemployed to Washington, D.C., in 1894, planning to write a long narrative poem about it that never comes to fruition. While still occasionally visiting London, he moves to New York City: "In the early sixties I had an apartment in New York on the Lower East Side, east of Tompkins Square, on the top floor of a building on East 6th Street that has since been torn down. The rent was very low. The front rooms looked out over a school and the old roofscapes of lower Manhattan to the Brooklyn Bridge. . . . Sometimes taxi drivers asked guests whether they really wanted to come to that neighborhood, and occasionally they even refused to drive there, but I loved living there and I walked endlessly through that section of the city and along the river to the end of the island. Much of the latter part of *The Moving Target* and the first part of *The Lice* were written there." Drives across the States, giving readings in St. Louis (with Mona Van Duyn) and Seattle (at the invitation of Theodore Roethke). His play *The Gilded West* is produced at the Belgrade Theatre in Coventry, England, in 1961.

1962   Is appointed poetry editor of *The Nation*, a post he holds for six months. Publishes his translation of the anonymous 1554 Spanish picaresque novel, *Lazarillo de Tormes* (Anchor/Doubleday). Writes essay "Act of Conscience," about antinuclear sit-in in San Francisco in May–June 1962 to support the three crew members of the trimaran *Everyman*, who had been arrested for attempting to sail to Christmas Island in the Pacific, where the United States was conducting a series of atmospheric nuclear tests; essay is withdrawn from slated publication by *The New Yorker* because of the Cuban Missile Crisis, then published by *The Nation* in December. During the Missile Crisis, writes a Swiftian satire against conscription and nuclear testing about a standing army of atomic mutants, "A New Right Arm," which is published the following year in *Kulchur* magazine.

1963   Sylvia Plath commits suicide in London on February 11; in the months preceding her death she had frequently written letters (now apparently lost) to Merwin, enclosing drafts of her *Ariel* poems and discussing her breakup with Ted Hughes. In spring, feeling an increasing alienation from the

United States, he leaves New York City to spend the next few years in his half-ruined farmhouse in France. Publishes translation from the French of *The Song of Roland* in Modern Library edition *Medieval Epics* (which also includes his translation of *Poem of the Cid*), and his fifth poetry collection, *The Moving Target* (Atheneum), which represents a new stage of his poetic method: "By the end of the poems in *The Moving Target* I had relinquished punctuation along with several other structural conventions, a move that evolved from my growing sense that punctuation alluded to and assumed an allegiance to the rational protocol of written language, and of prose in particular. I had come to feel that it stapled the poems to the page. Whereas I wanted the poems to evoke the spoken language, and wanted the hearing of them to be essential to taking them in."

1964–66   Living in France, Merwin works on poems of *The Lice*. "Certainly, most of *The Lice* was written at a point when I really felt there was no point in writing," he recalled in 1984. "I got to the point where I thought the future was so bleak that there was no point in writing anything at all. And so the poems kind of pushed their way upon me when I wasn't thinking of writing. I would be out growing vegetables and walking around the countryside when all of a sudden I'd find myself writing a poem, and I'd write it, and that was the way most of *The Lice* was written." For ten months in 1964–65, he is an associate with Roger Planchon's Théâtre de la Cité, in Villeurbanne, France. In fall 1966, resumes dividing his time between Manhattan and France when he comes to New York City for rehearsals of a production of his translation of Lorca's *Yerma*, which premieres at Lincoln Center on December 8, 1966; it is directed by John Hirsch, and members of the cast include Nancy Marchand, Frank Langella, and Maria Tucci.

1967   *The Lice* is published by Atheneum. Critics respond with both astonished praise and scorn to the cryptic new style this book announces, a swerve away from an earlier luxuriance toward a starker, apocalyptic tone.

1968   *Selected Translations 1948–1968* is published by Atheneum, with work brought over from poems in French, German, Russian, Spanish, Catalan, Portuguese, Italian, Chinese, Vietnamese, Romanian, Latin, Greek, Irish, Welsh, Quechuan, Caxinua, Eskimo, and Kabylia. In the fall, Merwin separates from Dido (an arrangement "which indeed did not represent a marked change over the actual situation of the preceding few years, but simply rendered it more or less formal").

1969   Rents an apartment at 227 Waverly Place, across the street from St. Vincent's Hospital, which he will keep as a pied-à-terre for several years; continues to travel to France during the summer but spends less time there because Dido uses the primary farmhouse at Lacan, and during his visits he stays elsewhere on the property or in a house nearby. Receives the P.E.N. Translation Prize for *Selected Translations 1948–1968*. Publishes several books of translations: *Transparence of the World* (Atheneum), from the French of poet Jean Follain; *Voices* (Big Table), from the Spanish of Italian-born Argentine poet Antonio Porchia; *Twenty Love Poems and a Song of Despair* (Jonathan Cape), from the Spanish of Chilean poet Pablo Neruda; and *Products of the Perfected Civilization* (Macmillan), selected writings by Sébastien Roch Nicolas de Chamfort, eighteenth-century French author and aphorist.

1970   Publishes poetry collection *The Carrier of Ladders* and prose book *The Miner's Pale Children*, both with Atheneum. To an interviewer, he says, "I have sometimes puzzled over the possibility of being an American poet (but what else could I be—I've never wanted to be anything else), and certainly the search for a way of writing about what America *is*, in my lifetime, is a perennial siren. But not, I think, in any way that's obviously Whitmanesque." At the State University of New York at Buffalo in October to give a reading and spend a few days as visiting lecturer, having been asked to sign a state-mandated pledge "to support the Constitution of the United States and the Constitution of the State of New York," he publicly refuses, denounces the loyalty oath as "humiliating," and takes up a collection for draft resisters: "I am not what is sometimes called 'politically minded.' Politics in themselves bore me profoundly, and the assumption of the final reality of the power to manipulate other men's lives merely depresses me. But injustice, official brutality, and the destruction on a vast scale of private liberties are all around me and I cannot pretend that it's not so, nor that I can accept such things, when I have a chance to say no to them." Later that autumn, with his companion

Moira Hodgson, travels to San Cristóbal de Las Casas in the Mexican state of Chiapas, where he buys a ruined convent, and spends winters there for the next four years.

1971 Refuses to accept the Pulitzer Prize that is awarded to *The Carrier of Ladders*, and writes from Montana a letter printed in *The New York Review of Books* on June 3: "I am pleased to know of the judges' regard for my work, and I want to thank them for their wish to make their opinion public. But after years of news from Southeast Asia, and the commentary from Washington, I am too conscious of being an American to accept public congratulation with good grace, or to welcome it except as an occasion for expressing openly a shame which many Americans feel, day after day, helplessly and in silence. I want the prize money to be equally divided between Alan Blanchard (Cinema Repertory Theater, Telegraph Avenue, Berkeley, California)—a painter who was blinded by a police weapon in California while he was watching American events from a roof, at a distance—and the Draft Resistance." W. H. Auden writes to the *Review* saying that, while he shares Merwin's political views, he protests Merwin's "ill-judged" politicizing of the award and his demand that the prize money be spent as he wishes. In reply, Merwin asks, "Is it, after all, dishonoring the present distinction to use it to register once again an abhorrence at being swept along, as we are, and most of the time anonymously, in this evil?"

1972 Declines his election to membership in the National Institute of Arts and Letters, declaring his wish "not to belong to academies and institutes." Father dies in June, and mother dies three months later.

1973 Poetry collection *Writings to an Unfinished Accompaniment* is published by Atheneum, as is book of translations *Asian Figures*, composed of proverbs, short poems, and riddles from several Asian cultures—Korean, Japanese, Chinese, Burmese, Philippine, Malayan, and Laotian.

1974 Receives fellowship from the Academy of American Poets and the Shelley Memorial Award from the Poetry Society of America. Publishes *Osip Mandelstam, Selected Poems*, translations made in collaboration with Princeton professor of comparative literature Clarence Brown (Atheneum).

1975   Collected edition of early volumes, *The First Four Books of Poems*, is published by Atheneum. Merwin makes his first visit to Maui, Hawaii, to study with Zen teacher Robert Aitken. While at the Naropa Institute in Boulder, Colorado, to study Buddhist meditation with the controversial scholar and teacher Chögyam Trungpa Rinpoche, a Halloween party turns violent—Merwin and his companion Dana Naone are forced to strip naked and are brought forcibly before Trungpa. Merwin decides to stay two more days, in order to confront Trungpa privately. He asks, "Did it ever occur to you that you might have made a mistake?" Trungpa tells him, "A tulku [reincarnated lama] never makes a mistake." To which Merwin replies: "You have just told me why you could never have been my teacher."

1976   Spends summer on Maui house-sitting for Robert Aitken, and when Aitken returns in the fall, Merwin accepts offer to live in a small apartment above his garage. Reads about Hawaiian history and comes across, in Aubrey B. Janion's recently published book *The Olowalu Massacre*, the tale "The Leper of Kalala'u," a version of the story that will form the basis of his 1998 book *The Folding Cliffs*.

1977   Publishes poetry collection *The Compass Flower* (Atheneum); *Houses and Travellers* (Atheneum), a series of prose pieces; and translations of *Classical Sanskrit Love Poetry* (with J. Moussaieff Masson, Columbia University Press) and Argentine poet Roberto Juarroz's *Vertical Poetry* (Kayak Books). Accepts membership in National Institute of Arts and Letters, having refused it five years earlier. Buys a run-down cabin and three-and-a-half acres of an old pineapple plantation in Ha'ikū (a Hawaiian word meaning "sharp break"), on the north side of Maui. Gradually, and following his design, a house is built on the property, and he begins an ambitious decades-long project of planting trees, including many endangered species ("I have planted about 850 species of palms, and at least four or five times that many actual trees," he will recall in 2010).

1978   Publishes translation of Euripides' *Iphigeneia at Aulis* (with George E. Dimock, Jr., Oxford University Press) and poetry collection *Feathers from the Hill* (Windhover Press)—sequences of brief poems in which the Hawaiian landscape is first glimpsed in his work. Divorce with Dido is finalized.

1979   Receives Bollingen Prize for poetry, given by the Beinecke Library at Yale University (judges are Galway Kinnell, William Stafford, and Penelope Laurans). Publishes *Selected Translations 1968–1978* (Atheneum).

1980   Participates in protests to save sacred ground on the island from developers and politicians, and will continue to be active in preserving the Hawaiian heritage and the natural environment of the islands.

1982   Publishes a book of prose recollections of his childhood, *Unframed Originals* (Atheneum), and poetry collection *Finding the Islands* (North Point Press). Meets Paula Dunaway (b. 1936) on a visit to New York.

1983   Publishes *Opening the Hand* (Atheneum). Marries Paula, who is mother of two sons by a previous marriage, Matthew Carlos Schwartz (b. 1963) and John Burnham Schwartz (b. 1965). He and Paula work on their garden by clearing the land by hand, with sickles, and with push mowers.

1985   Publishes *Four French Plays* (Atheneum), collecting dramatic translations from the 1950s and early 1960s, and *From the Spanish Morning* (Atheneum), which restores to print *Some Spanish Ballads*, Lope de Rueda's *Eufemia*, and *Lazarillo de Tormes*.

1986   Receives the Hawaii Award for Literature, chosen by the Hawaii Literary Arts Council. The Merwins expand their property to nineteen acres by purchasing two adjoining parcels of land, with the help of a gift from children's publisher Margaret McElderry and a legacy from George Kirstein.

1987–89 Publishes new collection *The Rain in the Trees* (Knopf, 1988), *Selected Poems* (Atheneum, 1988), and, in collaboration with Sōiku Shigematsu, translation of work by the Japanese Zen master and poet Musō Soseki (1275–1351), *Sun at Midnight: Poems and Sermons* (North Point Press, 1989).

1990   Receives the 1989 Maurice English Poetry Award in Honolulu. The judge, poet Peter Viereck, writes: "Merwin is a poet of overwhelming understatement whose power lies in avoiding all facile, flamboyant effects and instead expressing his emotions and thoughts with absolute integrity." Dido dies; Merwin resumes residencies at the farmhouse in Lacan de Loubressac.

1991–93   Publishes *The Lost Upland: Stories of Southwest France*
           (Knopf, 1992), a prose book that evokes the landscape,
           history, and people of the Languedoc, and *Travels* (Knopf,
           1993); collected edition *The Second Four Books of Poems* is
           brought out by Copper Canyon Press in 1993.

1994   Receives the first Tanning Prize of $100,000—endowed
           by painter and poet Dorothea Tanning to honor a living
           "master" of the art of poetry—by the Academy of American
           Poets. In the citation, poet James Merrill, who had known
           him since their undergraduate years, writes: "As a poet W. S.
           Merwin has charted a course that we, his first, marveling
           readers, might never have foreseen. From that early work,
           with its ravishing detours rich in echo and ornament, he has
           attained—more and more with every collection—a won-
           derful streamlined diction that unerringly separates and
           recombines like quicksilver scattered upon a shifting plane,
           but which remains as faithful to the warms and cools of
           the human heart as that same mercury in the pan-pipe of a
           thermometer." Also receives the Lenore Marshall Prize from
           the Academy of American Poets for *Travels*.

1996   Publishes *The Vixen* (Knopf), a collection largely about his
           experience living in Lacan de Loubressac and the history
           of the surrounding region, written in long lines loosely
           derived from those of classical elegies. Edits *Lament for
           the Makers: A Memorial Anthology* (Counterpoint), which
           includes Merwin's long poem of the same title. His transla-
           tion of poems by Jaime Sabines, *Pieces of Shadow*, published
           the year before in Mexico, is issued by Marsilio Publishers.

1997   *Flower & Hand: Poems 1977–1983* (Copper Canyon) gathers
           earlier collections *The Compass Flower*, *Feathers from the
           Hill*, and *Opening the Hand*.

1998–   Publishes book-length poem *The Folding Cliffs: A Narra-
2002   tive* (Knopf, 1998) and collections *The River Sound* (Knopf,
           1999) and *The Pupil* (Knopf, 2001); translations *East Win-
           dow: The Asian Translations* (Copper Canyon, 1998), the
           Purgatorio of Dante (Knopf, 2000), and, from Middle
           English, *Sir Gawain and the Green Knight* (Knopf, 2003);
           and *The Mays of Ventadorn* (National Geographic Books,
           2002), a memoir of time spent in the Languedoc and the
           work of its twelfth-century bards.

2003   Is the subject of *W. S. Merwin: The Poet's View*, a documen-
        tary film by Mel Stuart. Receives in absentia the Gold Medal
        for Poetry by the American Academy of Arts and Letters.
        In the response read for him at the ceremony in New York,
        Merwin writes in part: "Everyone who has directed aspira-
        tion, care, and learning to an effort to convey in words the
        promptings of some inner compulsion has been aware, I
        imagine, that the more one wants to articulate some feel-
        ing—love or grief, shame or indignation or gratitude—the
        more impossible that seems. I believe this unappeasable
        urge to utterance is the origin of speech itself, the abiding
        source of imaginative language and of poetry. I encounter
        it again whenever the only words for what I want to say are
        'thank you' and I am forced to admit how inadequate they
        are." Contributes to anthology opposing the U.S. invasion
        of Iraq, *Poets Against the War*, and participates in the read-
        ing organized by the anthology's editor, Sam Hamill.

2004   Receives Lifetime Achievement Award by the Lannan
        Foundation, as well as the Golden Wreath Award of the
        Struga Poetry Evenings Festival in Macedonia. Publishes
        essay collection *The Ends of the Earth* (Counterpoint).

2005   Publishes *Migration: New and Selected Poems* (Copper
        Canyon) and new collection *Present Company* (Copper
        Canyon), along with a memoir about his life in the 1940s,
        Summer Doorways (Shoemaker & Hoard). *Lazarillo de
        Tormes* is restored to print in an edition by New York Re-
        view Books. In November, *Migration* wins National Book
        Award, which is accepted for him in New York by stepson
        John Burnham Schwartz. The judges' citation notes: "The
        poems in *Migration* speak from a life-long belief in the
        power of words to awaken our drowsy souls and see the
        world with compassionate interconnection."

2006   Receives the Rebekah Johnson Bobbitt National Prize for
        Poetry from the Library of Congress for *Present Company*.

2007   Publishes prose collection *The Book of Fables* (Copper Can-
        yon) and an English edition of *Selected Poems* (Bloodaxe
        Books).

2008–9 Publishes *The Shadow of Sirius* (Copper Canyon) in 2008,
        which wins him his second Pulitzer Prize the following year.
        Receives the *Kenyon Review*'s Award for Literary Achieve-
        ment in 2009.

2010   Is appointed Poet Laureate of the United States, and serves for one year. Announcing the appointment, the Librarian of Congress, James H. Billington, says, "William Merwin's poems are often profound and, at the same time, accessible to a vast audience. He leads us upstream from the flow of everyday things in life to half-hidden headwaters of wisdom about life itself." The nonprofit Merwin Conservancy is founded to ensure the preservation of his property, in cooperation with the National Tropical Botanical Garden, as a sanctuary for study and research. Is interviewed in PBS documentary *The Buddha*.

2013   *Selected Translations* is published by Copper Canyon Press, as is Merwin's translation (with Takako Lento) of *Collected Haiku of Yosa Buson* and a reissue of his translation of Musō Soseki's *Sun at Midnight*. Merwin is the subject of documentary *Even Though the Whole World Is Burning*, directed by Stefan C. Schaefer.

Note on the Texts

This volume contains thirteen volumes of poetry by W. S. Merwin published from 1952 to 1993, along with fifteen previously uncollected poems.

Merwin does not make significant revisions to his poems once they are included in one of his books. In *The First Four Books of Poems* (1975), comprising in a single volume *A Mask for Janus* (1952), *The Dancing Bears* (1954), *Green with Beasts* (1956), and *The Drunk in the Furnace* (1960), Merwin included an author's note that accords with his lifelong practice to consider a poem finished once it appears in one of his collections: "These poems are reprinted exactly as they appeared in the four books in which they were originally published. They have not been revised, rearranged, or altered for better or worse." Nevertheless, in this book and in Merwin's two other collected-volume editions—*The Second Four Books of Poems* (1993) and *Flower & Hand: Poems 1977–1983* (1997)—there are occasional corrections; for example, a poem with an erroneous title in *A Mask for Janus*, "Variation on a Line by Bryant," was corrected in *The First Four Books of Poems* to "Variation on a Line by Emerson." There are also a few variants of spelling, punctuation, capitalization, and hyphenation between the first publications of individual collections and the texts of these books in *The First Four Books of Poems*, *The Second Four Books of Poems*, and *Flower & Hand*.

Yale University Press published Merwin's first two collections, *A Mask for Janus* and *The Dancing Bears*, in 1952 and 1954, respectively. Although Merwin lived in London for much of the 1950s, he did not publish a book in England until his third collection, *Green with Beasts*, which was published by Rupert Hart-Davis in London in 1956, the same year it was brought out in New York by Knopf. His fourth book of poems, *The Drunk in the Furnace*, was published in 1960 by Macmillan in New York and Rupert Hart-Davis in London. These four early volumes were collected in 1975 in the Atheneum edition *The First Four Books of Poems*, which contained the corrections mentioned above and other minor changes to the texts of some of the poems. A few further emendations were made when Copper Canyon Press reprinted *The First Four Books of Poems* in 2000; for example, in "Grandmother Dying," the typographical error of "dead" in the twelfth line was corrected and reads "deaf" for the first time since the poem's first periodical publication in *Encounter*. The present volume prints the 2000 Copper Canyon Press edition of *The First Four Books of Poems*.

In the decade from 1963 to 1973 Merwin published four new poetry collections, all with Atheneum: *The Moving Target* (1963), *The Lice* (1967), *The Carrier of Ladders* (1970), and *Writings to an Unfinished Accompaniment* (1973). (Only two of these collections were published in England, both by Rupert Hart-Davis and in both cases some time after coming out in the United States: the English editions of *The Moving Target* and *The Lice* appeared in 1967 and 1969, respectively.) These books were collected, with a preface by Merwin, in an edition published by Copper Canyon Press in 1993 in Port Townsend, Washington. The 1993 Copper Canyon Press edition of *The Second Four Books of Poems* contains the text printed here.

Poems from three of Merwin's books of original poetry published from 1977 to 1983—*The Compass Flower* (New York: Atheneum, 1977), *Feathers from the Hill* (Iowa City: Windhover Press, 1978), and *Opening the Hand* (New York: Atheneum, 1983)—were collected in 1997 by Copper Canyon Press in *Flower & Hand: Poems 1977–1983*. The poems in the limited-edition chapbook *Feathers from the Hill* had formed one of the two parts of a 1982 North Point Press collection, *Finding the Islands*. Merwin did not include the poems of the second section, entitled "Turning to You," in *Flower & Hand*, and they are not included in the present volume. The texts printed here of *The Compass Flower*, *Feathers from the Hill*, and *Opening the Hand* are taken from the 1997 Copper Canyon Press edition of *Flower & Hand*.

For the remaining two collections presented here, this volume prints in each case the text of the first edition: *The Rain in the Trees* (New York: Knopf, 1988) and *Travels* (New York: Knopf, 1993).

The poems in "Uncollected Poems 1955–1987" were selected by the editor in consultation with Merwin. Their texts are printed from the following sources:

Camel: *Poetry*, January 1955.
Several Distiches About an Occasion: *Hudson Review*, Spring 1955.
Northeast October: *Poetry London–New York*, Winter 1956.
Mercy: *Poetry*, March 1957.
The Miner: *Kenyon Review*, Spring 1957.
Coal Barges: *Kenyon Review*, Spring 1957.
Rimer, Penna.: *Harper's*, November 1957.
On a Sacrifice of Darkness: *Poets and the Past*, ed. Dore Ashton (New York: Andre Emmerich Gallery, 1959).
Views from the High Camp: *Contemporary American Poetry*, ed. Donald Hall (New York: Penguin, 1962).
Esther: *Poetry*, December 1968.
The Borrowers: *The Nation*, October 19, 1970.
In Winter Silence: *Harper's*, June 1973.

A Root: *Field*, Spring 1974.
Demonstration: *The Paris Review*, Summer 1974.
A Last Look: *Poetry*, October–November 1987.

On the following pages, a stanza break occurs at the bottom of the page (not including pages in which the break is evident because of the regular stanzaic structure of the poem): 92, 93, 114, 190, 205, 212, 213, 214, 216, 225, 235, 237, 239, 241, 242, 244, 247, 248, 251, 253, 256, 257, 259, 267, 268, 270, 271, 277, 279, 281, 282, 284, 285, 286, 292, 297, 299, 302, 303, 304, 307, 308, 309, 315, 317, 319, 334, 343, 344, 348, 359, 361, 363, 389, 390, 394, 395, 397, 399, 407, 408, 411, 413, 414, 415, 419, 420, 423, 424, 430, 431, 444, 448, 449, 450, 453, 454, 464, 472, 474, 476, 485, 487, 488, 489, 562, 564, 566, 568, 570, 573, 596, 598, 602, 603, 609, 612, 618, 622, 624, 631, 637, 638, 639, 643, 649, 667, 679, 681, 742, 753, 759, 762, 765, 795, 796, 798.
This volume presents the texts of the original printings chosen for inclusion here, but it does not attempt to reproduce nontextual features of their typographic design. The texts are presented without change, except for the correction of typographical errors. Spelling, punctuation, and capitalization are often expressive features and are not altered, even when inconsistent or irregular. The following is a list of typographical errors corrected, cited by page and line number: 34.15, yo;; 75.12, said "and; 77.28, be rose; 107.2, Forgathers; 215.9, see our; 252.17, cross road; 298.25, And then; 343.32, wake; 373.24, Millenial; 612.11, like a small; 642.22, ohias; 696.12, newstand; 706.6, *Camelia*; 738.5, cites.

Notes

In the notes below, the reference numbers denote page and line of this volume (the line count includes headings). No note is made for material included in standard desk-reference books. Biblical quotations are keyed to the King James Version. Quotations from Shakespeare are keyed to *The Riverside Shakespeare*, ed. G. Blakemore Evans (Boston: Houghton, Mifflin, 1974). For more biographical information than is contained in the Chronology, see W. S. Merwin, *Unframed Originals* (New York: Atheneum, 1982) and *Summer Doorways* (Emeryville, CA: Shoemaker & Hoard, 2005).

THE FIRST FOUR BOOKS OF POEMS

1.1   THE FIRST . . . POEMS] "These poems are reprinted exactly as they appeared in the four books in which they were originally published. They have not been revised, rearranged, or altered for better or worse" (Merwin's note, 1975).

A MASK FOR JANUS

3.1   A MASK FOR JANUS] W. H. Auden wrote to Yale University Press on July 30, 1951, to say that he had chosen a winning manuscript for the 1952 Yale Younger Poets competition, but that it needed cutting. In August he wrote again: "Between us Mr Merwin and I have got his manuscript down to a possible size." When the book was published on May 21, 1952, it included a foreword by Auden, probably written the previous October, which contained the following remarks about Merwin's poetry:

> One of Mr Merwin's best poems, "Dictum: For a Masque of Deluge" is based upon the myth of the Flood. The historical experience which is latent in the poem is, I fancy, the feeling which most of us share of being witnesses to the collapse of a civilization, a collapse which transcends all political differences and for which we are all collectively responsible, and in addition feeling that this collapse is not final but that, on the other side of disaster, there will be some kind of rebirth, though we cannot imagine its nature. By translating these feelings into mythical terms, the poet is able to avoid what a direct treatment could scarcely have avoided, namely, the use of names and events which will probably turn out not to have been the really significant ones.
>
> With his concern for the traditional conceptions of Western culture as expressed in its myths, Mr Merwin combines an admirable respect for its tradition of poetic craftsmanship. His carols show how carefully he has studied Spanish versification, and in poems like "For a Dissolving Music"

and "A Dance of Death" he has not been ashamed to write what are frankly technical exercises. Apart from the fact that works which set out to be exercises in techniques often end by being works of art as well, e.g. the Chopin *Etudes*, the mastery of his medium through diligent practice is of incalculable value to any artist. Technique in itself cannot make a good poem, but the lack of it can spoil one. The final stanza of "Dictum" shows the reward that Mr Merwin has earned by his studies.

> A falling frond may seem all trees. If so
> We know the tone of falling. We shall find
> Dictions for rising, words for departure;
> And time will be sufficient before that revel
> To teach an order and rehearse the days
> Till the days are accomplished: so now the dove
> Makes assignations with the olive tree,
> Slurs with her voice the gestures of the time:
> The day foundering, the dropping sun
> Heavy, the wind a low portent of rain.

No one who had not previously trained himself thoroughly in the mechanics of verse could have varied so skillfully the position of the caesura from line to line, a variation on which so much of the poetic effect depends.

For the complete text of Auden's foreword, see *The Complete Works of W. H. Auden: Prose, Volume III: 1949–1955*, ed. Edward Mendelson (Princeton: Princeton University Press, 2008), 259–61.

3.7 pone cara de mia] Spanish: she takes on my face. From *La voz a ti debida* (*My Voice Because of You*, 1933) by Spanish poet Pedro Salinas (1891–1951). The passage from which the quote is taken reads: "But it doesn't matter now. / She is with me. She drags me, / tears me out of doubt. / She smiles, possible; / it takes the forms of kisses, / of arms toward me; / she takes on my face." (tr. Willis Barnstone).

5.1 *Anabasis*] History by the Greek general Xenophon (c. 430–354 B.C.E.) of the march by an army of Greek mercenaries through hostile territory from the interior of Asia Minor to the Black Sea. Often used as a title for poems, for instance by French poet St.-John Perse (1887–1975).

5.26 Penates] Latin: household gods.

8.7 saeculum] Latin: a lifetime.

17.5 *Meng Tzu's*] Mencius (4th century B.C.E.), Chinese Confucian philosopher.

17.25 Kao Tzu] Gaozi, Chinese philosopher, a contemporary of Mencius.

22.32   *Et, ecce, nunc in pulvere dormio*] Latin: And behold, now I sleep in the dust. A traditional adage about mortality, used as a refrain in the poem "Of the Death of Kynge Edwarde the Forth" (1483), by English poet John Skelton (c. 1460–1529).

24.25   *Variation on a Line by Emerson*] "In May, when sea-winds pierced our solitudes" is the opening line of Ralph Waldo Emerson's poem "The Rhodora. Lines on Being Asked, Whence is the Flower?" (1847). In the first edition of *A Mask for Janus*, the poem is entitled "Variation on a Line by Bryant."

27.1   *Suspicor Speculum*] Latin: to mistrust the mirror.

27.4   Three hags of their one eye] In Greek mythology, a trio of goddesses, sisters known as "the gray ones," share one eye and one tooth among them.

31.11   *Palinurus*] The helmsman of Aeneas's ship on the voyage from Troy to Italy, who falls overboard to his death in book 5 of Virgil's *Aeneid*.

34.14   *Canción y Glosa*] Spanish: Song and Refrain.

34.15–17   Y yo, mientras . . . venas.] "And I, meanwhile, your / son, with drier / leaves in my veins." The second stanza of "Madre Primavera" (Mother Spring), from *Canción* (1936) by Spanish poet Juan Ramón Jiménez (1881–1958).

39.14   *Hermione on Simulacra*] See Shakespeare's *Winter's Tale* (1611), V.iii.

THE DANCING BEARS

43.5–7   *la parole humaine . . . étoiles*] From pt. 2, ch. 12, of *Madame Bovary* (1857), novel by French writer Gustave Flaubert (1821–1880): "Human speech is like a cracked kettle on which we hammer out tunes to make bears dance while we long to move the stars."

51.13   *Colchis*] In Greek mythology, the legendarily wealthy homeland (in present-day Georgia) of Medea, where Jason stole the sacred Golden Fleece and carried her off.

51.19   the Euxine] The Black Sea.

52.7   *Genoese Mariner*] Christopher Columbus (1451–1506), born in the Republic of Genoa.

55.34   *Non enim sciunt quid faciunt*] Latin: They know not what they are doing. Among the last words of Jesus; cf. Luke 23:34.

56.1   strong bulls of Bashan . . . round] Psalm 22:12.

62.1   *East of the Sun and West of the Moon*] Title of popular translation of Norwegian folktales collected by Peter Christen Asbjørnsen (1812–1885) and Jørgen Moe (1813–1882) in the mid-nineteenth century.

78.15   *Peniel*] Place (Hebrew, "face of God") where Jacob beheld God and wrestled with the angel; see Genesis 32.

79.32   Vidal] Peire Vidal (1175–1205), French troubadour.

80.26   *Canso*] An Occitan word referring to a style of three-part song used by the troubadours. The three successive poems here with this same title are perhaps meant to imitate the canso's traditional exordium, variations, and tornado or envoi.

82.25   the fanciful song] Homer's *Iliad*.

GREEN WITH BEASTS

101.31   land between the rivers] Mesopotamia.

101.33   Etruria] Area in central Italy that in antiquity was home to the Etruscans.

105.10   tetter] Teat.

105.17   thicket-snared ram] See Genesis 22:13, in the story of Abraham's near-sacrifice of Isaac.

109.30   at the beaks of ravens] As Elijah was fed, in 1 Kings 17:6.

110.21   *The Prodigal Son*] See Luke 15:11–32.

114.24   *The Annunciation*] See Luke 1:36–39.

124.16   *Isaiah of Souillac*] The bas-relief of the prophet Isaiah in the abbey church of Sainte-Marie in Souillac, a town near the pilgrimage site of Rocamadour in southwestern France. It was carved c. 1135.

125.4–5   waters of Shiloh . . . over] Cf. Isaiah 8:6–7.

129.13   "Nothing . . . Aristotle."] Cf. the opening of Molière's *Don Juan* (1665), lines spoken by Sgnarelle: "Whatever Aristotle and all of philosophy might say, there is nothing to equal tobacco: it is the passion of gentlemen and whoever lives without tobacco does not deserve to live."

135.7   Skelton's bird or Catullus's] See John Skelton's poem "Phyllyp Sparowe," and *Carmina* 2 and 3 by the Latin poet Gaius Valerius Catullus (c. 84 – c. 54 B.C.E.).

144.24   *Alfred Wallis*] English painter (1855–1942). His *Voyage to Labrador* and *Schooner Under the Moon* (both c. 1935–36) are currently in the collection of Tate Britain, London.

THE DRUNK IN THE FURNACE

155.1   *Deception Island*] One of the South Shetland Islands, off the Antarctic Peninsula.

158.15   Portland] Paddle-wheel steamship en route from Boston to Portland, Maine, that sank off Cape Ann in the "Portland Gale" storm, November 26–27, 1898, with no survivors among its 192 passengers and crew.

159.9   why Blanchard sailed] The *Portland*'s captain, Hollis H. Blanchard, was told of the approaching storm before sailing and by warning blasts from a passing steamship in Boston harbor.

169.12   *Catullus XI*] A translation of Catullus, *Carmina* 11, "Furi et Aureli, comites Catulli."

184.6   strait gate and the needle's eye] See Matthew 7:13–14 and 19:24.

THE SECOND FOUR BOOKS OF POEMS

196.25   Aldermaston marches in England] On Easter weekend in 1958 the Direct Action Committee Against Nuclear War staged a protest march from Trafalgar Square in London to the Atomic Weapons Research Establishment at Aldermaston in Berkshire, fifty-two miles away. The Campaign for Nuclear Disarmament subsequently held annual marches on Easter weekend, 1959–63, that began at Aldermaston and ended in Trafalgar Square. Merwin wrote an account of the march in 1960 that was published as "Letter from Aldermaston" in *The Nation*, May 7, 1960.

THE MOVING TARGET

204.11–15   *Lemuel's* . . . SMART] King Lemuel, whose name in Hebrew means "devoted to God," appears briefly in Proverbs 31, and in the poem *Jubilate Agno* by English poet Christopher Smart (1722–1771), written from 1759 to 1763 while he was confined in a mental hospital.

207.17   *Noah's Raven*] See Genesis 8:7.

220.26–27   man cannot . . . Alone] Cf. Matthew 4:4.

244.3–4   pictures of cemeteries] In urban renewal projects, buildings slated for demolition often had white crosses painted on their windows.

251.1   *My Friends*] During a 1974 reading Merwin noted that this poem was occasioned by the antinuclear demonstrations held at the U.S. Courthouse in San Francisco in May–June 1962 and the arrests of many of the protestors. The protests were in support of the three crew members of the trimaran *Everyman*, who had been arrested off the California coast not long after setting sail from Sausalito for Christmas Island in the Pacific, where the United States was conducting a series of atmospheric nuclear tests.

THE LICE

289.5   child will lead you] Cf. Isaiah 11:6.

THE CARRIER OF LADDERS

321.2–3   Ma non . . . somigli] Italian: "But nothing on earth / Resembles you," lines from the 1823 poem "Alla Sua Donna" ("To His Lady") by Italian poet Giacomo Leopardi (1798–1837).

325.22   *Animula*] Latin: little soul. A poem by Roman emperor Hadrian (76–138 C.E.) that Merwin later translated in *The Shadow of Sirius* (2008), praising the "brief, mysterious poem" for being "so assured in its art, so flawless and so haunting."

326.7   *The Judgment of Paris*] In Greek mythology, the Trojan shepherd-prince Paris was asked to award a golden apple to the fairest of three Olympian goddesses—Athena, Hera, and Aphrodite. He chose Aphrodite, who had earlier promised him possession of the beautiful Helen, an event that led to the Trojan War.

334.23   *D'Aubigné*] Théodore-Agrippa d'Aubigné (1552–1630), French poet and soldier, best known for *Les Tragiques* (1616), an epic that includes the appended poem "L'Auteur à Son Livre" ("The Author to His Book").

341.19   *Lackawanna*] River that flows through Scranton, Pennsylvania, where Merwin was raised as a boy.

343.2–6   William Bartram . . . sire of waters] American naturalist William Bartram (1739 –1823) first sighted the Mississippi River on the evening of October 21, 1775, noting in his *Travels* (1791) how he "stood for a time as it were fascinated by the magnificence of the great sire of rivers."

345.9   *Zuñi*] Zuni Pueblo in northwestern New Mexico.

345.10   one-armed explorer] American geologist and explorer John Wesley Powell (1832–1902), who lost his right arm while serving as a Union artillery officer at the battle of Shiloh during the Civil War. As part of his ethnological work, he helped to classify the North American Indian languages, and one of the expeditions he led was the first to pass through the Grand Canyon.

372.32   Apher] According to the second-century B.C.E. Jewish writer Cleodemus, one of the sons of Abraham and Keturah was named Apher, and Africa was named after him.

373.25   Bethel] Hebrew: House of God. See Genesis 28.

374.21   Utes] American Indian people living mostly in Utah and Colorado.

THE COMPASS FLOWER

489.7   *St. Vincent's*] Hospital, 1849–2010, in New York City's Greenwich Village, named for French priest St. Vincent de Paul (1581–1660).

497.1   *Kore*] Greek: maiden. A type of ancient Greek statue of young women with enigmatic smiles. It is thought they may represent Persephone, goddess of the underworld.

506.4   those two old people] In Ovid's *Metamorphosis*, bk. 8, Baucis and Phi-
lemon are an old married couple who exemplify the sacred duties of hospitality
by receiving into their home the disguised gods Zeus and Hermes, who had
elsewhere been turned away.

OPENING THE HAND

589.10–12   second IRA hunger striker dies in British hands in Ireland] Francis
Hughes (1956–1981) died on May 12, 1981, in the Maze prison in Northern
Ireland, after a fifty-nine-day hunger strike, seven days after the death of his
fellow prisoner, Bobby Sands (1954–1981).

591.10–11   *Sheridan* . . . there] At dawn on October 19, 1864, Confederate
troops under Lieutenant General Jubal A. Early (1816–1894) surprised Union
forces at Cedar Creek, Virginia, and drove them from their positions. Major
General Philip Henry Sheridan (1831–1888), who was returning to his command
from a conference in Washington, learned of the attack in Winchester, Virginia,
and rode to the front on his horse Rienzi, rallying stragglers and directing a
successful counterattack.

592.24   it was read to me] In "Sheridan's Ride," popular poem (1864) by
Thomas Buchanan Read (1833–1872).

593.35–36   your name now the iron fence] In 1896, Sheridan Square, a small
park at the intersection of Washington Place, West 4th Street, and Barrow
Street in New York City was named in Sheridan's honor; a bronze statue of him
was erected in nearby Christopher Square in 1936.

599.24   Berryman] American poet John Berryman (1914–1972) was teaching
at Princeton while Merwin was an undergraduate there.

THE RAIN IN THE TREES

620.11   a window across the street] I.e., into St. Vincent's Hospital (see note
489.7).

635.17   'ohias] "*Metrosideros polymorpha* or *M. collinia*. [One] of the principal
trees of the Hawaiian forest and mythology. A beautiful tree, sacred to the fire
goddess Pele and used in her rituals" (Merwin's note in *The Folding Cliffs*,
1998).

635.18   koas] "The *Acacia koa*; Hawaiian acacia. It is a principal tree of the
Hawaiian forests and one of the most beautiful. War canoes were traditionally
made from the koa" (Merwin's note in *The Folding Cliffs*).

635.19   halas] "The 'screw-pine.' Indigenous *Pandanus odoratissimus*, whose
long leaves are used for matting and thatch" (Merwin's note in *The Folding
Cliffs*).

638.16   Tanna] A large island in the New Hebrides.

667.27   kiawe] A thorny mesquite tree, first planted in Hawaii in 1828 and now ubiquitous there.

668.15   *Kanaloa*] "One of the great origin gods of Hawaii and probably the oldest of them. God of death, of the sea, and of the west" (Merwin's note in *The Folding Cliffs*).

673.30   heliconia] A flowering garden plant in the Pacific islands, also known as "false bird-of-paradise" for its resemblance to that flower.

674.1   abutilons] One of the broadleaf evergreen shrubs or small trees of the mallow family, also known as Chinese lanterns.

674.2   royal ilima] A flowering plant of the hibiscus family native to Hawaii; its flowers are used to make lei.

TRAVELS

677.2–4   Hypocrite reader . . . family] Cf. final line of "Au Lecteur" ("To the Reader"), prefatory poem in *Les Fleurs du Mal* (*Flowers of Evil*, 1857) by French poet Charles Baudelaire (1821–1867): "Hypocrite lecteur—mon semblable—mon frère!" ("Hypocrite reader—my likeness—my brother!").

678.21   *The Blind Seer of Ambon*] "Georg Eberhard Rumpf, 1627–1702, more usually known as Rumphius, lived most of his life in the Dutch East Indies and was the author of *The Ambonese Herbal* [*Herbarium Amboinense*, published posthumously from 1741 to 1750, a catalogue of plants on the Indonesian island of Ambon]. See *The Poison Tree*, E. M. Beekman editor and translator, University of Massachusetts Press, 1981" (Merwin's note).

679.6   the earthquake] Rumphius's wife and daughter were killed in the earthquake and tsunami of February 17, 1674. In 1687, the illustrations for his book were destroyed in a fire, and—though he had been blinded by glaucoma in 1670—with the aid of his assistants he set about re-creating the pictures.

680.9   Manini] "The most complete work on Marin so far is *Don Francisco de Paula Marin* by Ross Gast and Agnes C. Conrad, University Press of Hawaii, Hawaiian Historical Society, 1973" (Merwin's note). The sailor Don Francisco de Paula y Marin (1774–1837), called Manini, deserted from a Spanish fur-trading outpost at Nootka Sound (in present-day British Columbia) and made his way to Hawaii, where he arrived around 1793 and became a translator and advisor to Kamehameha (c. 1758–1819), the chief who completed unification of the Hawaiian islands in 1810 and ruled as its first king, Kamehameha I. As a horticulturist Marin introduced to the islands many agricultural methods and products.

688.15   *Rimbaud's Piano*] French poet Arthur Rimbaud (1854–1891) was born in Charleville in northeastern France. A brilliant student, Rimbaud ran away from his puritanical mother to Paris, where he participated in the 1871

Commune uprising at the end of the Franco-Prussian War and was involved in a passionate and eventually bitter affair with French poet Paul Verlaine (1844–1896). The pair moved to London in 1872. By 1875 Rimbaud abandoned poetry, spending his later years in Arabia and East Africa working as a merchant. In 1891 he began suffering pain in his right knee, which was treated first in Aden and then in Marseille, where his leg was amputated and he was diagnosed with cancer. Rimbaud died soon afterward, and was buried in Charleville.

689.3–5   farm at Roche . . . Hell to himself] In April 1873 Rimbaud began writing *Une Saison en Enfer* (*A Season in Hell*, 1873) at his mother's family's farmhouse in Roche, not far from Charleville.

695.19   Maoli] A chow dog owned by Merwin at the time. The name is a term for "the true" or "the real thing."

706.6   *The Lost Camellia of the Bartrams*] John Bartram and his son William (see note 343.2–6) discovered the *Franklinia alatamaha*, or Franklin Tree, on October 1, 1765, on the banks of the Alatamaha River in Georgia. Since the nineteenth century the tree, whose fragrant white flower is similar to a camellia blossom, has been extinct in the wild.

708.17   *After Douglas*] "David Douglas, 1799–1834, Scottish naturalist for whom the Douglas Fir is named, fell into a bull trap on Mauna Kea, Hawaii, and was killed by a trapped bull. Douglas's North American Journals, and a critical memoir by John Davies, were published under the title *Douglas of the Forests*, University of Washington Press, Seattle, Washington, 1980" (Merwin's note).

710.21   *Cinchona*] Generic name of the family of small trees in tropical Andean forests whose bark is the source of quinine. The tree family was named by Linnaeus (with a slight misspelling) for Francisca Henriquez de Ribera (1599–1641), fourth Countess of Chinchón and wife of the Viceroy of Peru. According to a popular tale first written down in 1663 by the Italian physician Sebastiano Bado, the countess was cured of tertian fever associated with malaria by a powdered form of the tree's bark, which she afterward distributed personally to the sick in Lima and later to tenants on her husband's estate in Spain. (In fact, she never returned to Spain, dying in Cartagena in 1641, and it is unlikely she was ever stricken with malaria.)

710.31   Anopheles] Generic name of the many mosquito species, some of which carry the malaria virus.

712.20   Richard Spruce . . . empire] In 1859 the English botanist and explorer Richard Spruce (1817–1893), who had been collecting botanical specimens in South America since 1849, was commissioned by the India Office of the British government to collect cinchona seeds and trees for the production of quinine on plantations in India. Spruce's expedition through the Ecuadorian Andes was one of three supervised by the English explorer and geographer Clements Markham (1830–1916); the expedition led by Markham himself traveled through Peru.

713.2–4 Hasskarl . . . Java] Disguised as a German businessman, the Dutch explorer and botanist Justus Carl Hasskarl (1811–1894) smuggled cinchona seeds and saplings out of South America in 1853 for cultivation of the trees in Java.

714.20 Ambato] A city on the Ambato River in the central Andean valley of Ecuador.

718.23 the Straits of Hercules] The Straits of Gibraltar.

723.8 *Lives of the Artists*] "The biographical account of *Frank Henderson* by Karen Daniels Petersen was published with facsimiles of Henderson's book of drawings by the Alexander Gallery and Morning Star Gallery, in a volume entitled *American Pictographic Images: Historical Works on Paper by the Plains Indians*, New York, 1988. Little Finger Nail's story is based principally on material in Mari Sandoz's *Cheyenne Autumn*, Hastings House, New York, 1953 (and subsequent Avon paperback)" (Merwin's note). At age seventeen Frank Henderson (1862–1885), an orphan whose original Arapaho name is unknown, was sent from Darlington, in what is now western Oklahoma, to attend the Carlisle Indian School in Carlisle, Pennsylvania. Homesick and frail, he returned to Darlington in 1881, where a year later he completed the eighty-seven drawings that came to be known as *Frank Henderson's Drawing Book*.

725.10 Adobe Walls] On June 27, 1874, a raiding party of about 250 Comanche, Cheyenne, and Kiowa warriors attacked twenty-eight buffalo hunters and traders at Adobe Walls, a small post in the Texas Panhandle. The Indians withdrew after they were unable to break into the three sod-walled buildings that sheltered the defenders. Four whites and at least fifteen Indians were killed during the battle.

736.22 *The Moment of Green*] "The protagonist is Gregorio Gregorievich Bondar, 1881–1959. Born in Poltava, Russia. Author of many botanical and agricultural studies including *Palmeiras do Brasil*" (Merwin's note).

738.12 Bates and Wallace] English naturalists Henry Walter Bates (1825–1892) and Alfred Russel Wallace (1823–1913) set out in 1848 to explore the Amazonian rain forest. Wallace returned in 1852, his collection lost in a shipwreck. When Bates returned in 1859, he brought back thousands of previously unknown species.

738.23–24 port named by them for Bethlehem] Belém.

739.2 the opera house] The Teatro Amazonas, built in Manaus, Brazil, in the midst of the Amazonian rain forest, opened in 1896.

740.3–4 a post . . . Campinas] At the Instituto Agronômico de Campinas in eastern Brazil.

744.12 named for one man Rumphius] The *Cycas rumphii*; for Rumphius, see note 678.21.

744.16–17　lately discovered species of Pritchardia] *Pritchardia perlmanii,* a rare species of palm discovered in 1991.

751.9　*The Real World of Manuel Córdova*] "Acknowledgment is given for the permission granted by F. Bruce Lamb, author of the book *Wizard of the Upper Amazon,* published in 1987 by North Atlantic Books, Berkeley, California, which provided the historical basis for the poem" (Merwin's note).

771.17　the psalmist said] Cf. Psalms 23:4.

779.1　*Punta Arena*] A small peninsula at the entrance to Bahía Concepción in Baja California.

Index of Titles and First Lines

THE LIBRARY OF AMERICA SERIES

The Library of America fosters appreciation and pride in America's literary heritage by publishing, and keeping permanently in print, authoritative editions of America's best and most significant writing. An independent nonprofit organization, it was founded in 1979 with seed funding from the National Endowment for the Humanities and the Ford Foundation.

To subscribe to the series or to order individual copies, please visit www.loa.org or call (800) 964.5778.

This book is set in 10 point ITC Galliard Pro, a
face designed for digital composition by Matthew Carter
and based on the sixteenth-century face Granjon. The paper
is acid-free lightweight opaque and meets the requirements for
permanence of the American National Standards Institute.
The binding material is Brillianta, a woven rayon cloth
made by Van Heek–Scholco Textielfabrieken, Holland.
Composition by David Bullen Design. Printing and
binding by Edwards Brothers Malloy, Ann Arbor.
Designed by Bruce Campbell.

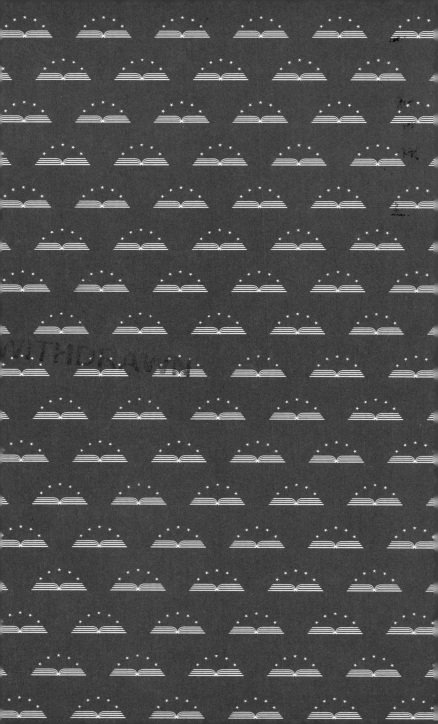